ENEMY OF THE STATE

OLIVER PRICE

Enemy of the State

*Political Surveillance in
Twentieth-Century Britain*

HURST & COMPANY, LONDON

First published in the United Kingdom in 2026 by
C. Hurst & Co. (Publishers) Ltd.,
New Wing, Somerset House, Strand, London WC2R 1LA
Copyright © Oliver Price, 2026
All rights reserved.

The right of Oliver Price to be identified as the author of this publication is asserted by him in accordance with the Copyright, Designs and Patents Act, 1988.

A Cataloguing-in-Publication data record for this book is available from the British Library.

ISBN: 9781805265290

EU GPSR Authorised Representative
Easy Access System Europe Oü, 16879218
Address: Mustamäe tee 50, 10621, Tallinn, Estonia
Contact Details: gpsr.requests@easproject.com, +358 40 500 3575

www.hurstpublishers.com

For my parents

JOHNNIE ... said that the secret police were here too. The visitor said "....... They don't interfere with me." JOHNNIE said —"of course they don't interfere with you, because you haven't the slightest intention of .... — but they interfere with me. That bloody telephone over there — the fact you phoned me, they know — what I said to you, they know — they open our letters — they go to our meetings. We are spending more on the bloody Secret Service now than we ever spent in years of British history. The spies are everywhere."

JOHNNIE talked of the police here knowing about all Parties, the visitor then asked what made him so certain that they were keeping track on all parties. ... He said that nothing of this had ever been published and would never be heard of "until we've cracked the archives one day, then you'll really know what was going on"

Extract from transcript of senior CPGB member John (Johnnie) Gollan, talking to a visitor at the CPGB HQ, King Street, picked up by a secret MI5 microphone. (KV 2/1777, serial 474bc, 'North Extract from Table re GOLLAN.', 28.1.48)

CONTENTS

Acknowledgements	xi
Abbreviations and Glossary	xiii
Introduction	1
1. Communism: The Insidious Disease	9
2. Friend or Foe?: Fascists in Interwar Britain	49
3. A 'Religious Dogma': Communism in Post-War Britain	89
4. Subversion and the Labour Party	127
5. Enemies of the State or Enemies of the Government?	163
Conclusion	207
Appendices	225
Notes	229
Bibliography	281
Index	301

ACKNOWLEDGEMENTS

Several years ago, I came across the story of the file MI5 had held on Eric Hobsbawm. It had just been declassified and the documents revealed the extent of the British state's surveillance of one of the twentieth century's most esteemed historians. It piqued my interest and made me wonder how many others had been watched by the intelligence community. Nothing more came of it until, several months later, I met Professor George Kassimeris at the University of Wolverhampton. I told him about Hobsbawm's file, and he thought it could be an interesting topic for a PhD thesis. George told me that day that it had the potential to not only become a PhD thesis but perhaps, in the future, a book. Well, here it is! I would like to thank George for his continual advice and support during my time as a PhD student. I had never contemplated undertaking a PhD until he encouraged me to do so. At times he has believed in me more than I have myself. What started off as a student-supervisor relationship has grown and he is now not just a great purveyor of wisdom but also a friend.

This book would not have been published without Michael Dwyer and his team at Hurst. I am incredibly grateful to Michael for deciding to take an interest in my manuscript and for seeing its potential as a book. My editor, Alice Clarke, has guided me through the publication process incredibly smoothly. Thanks also Georgina Isaacson and Heather Magee for copyediting and proofreading, as

ACKNOWLEDGEMENTS

well and Letty Allen and Daisy Leitch for seeing the book through production.

Throughout this whole project, the comments and advice of many people have been of great benefit and have helped me to improve the text. Thanks in particular to Mike Cunningham, Eamonn O'Kane, Keith Gildart, Andrew Defty, and Ben Halligan. Their suggestions and comments on previous drafts have been very helpful. Thanks are due to the staff at the National Archives, BBC Archives, British Library, Labour History Archive & Study Centre and the Bodleian Library, who were always helpful during my research for this project.

Finally, I would like to thank my parents, Helen and Derek for their love, unfailing support, and encouragement. I am eternally grateful and simply would not have been able to successfully complete this project without them. I would like to dedicate this book to them.

ABBREVIATIONS AND GLOSSARY

AAM	Anti-Apartheid Movement
ARCOS	All Russian Co-operative Society
AUEW	Amalgamated Union of Engineering Workers
BEU	British Empire Union
BF	British Fascisti or British Fascists
	The British Fascisti was renamed the British Fascists in 1924 to avoid the charge that it owed its allegiance to a foreign power —Italy— and that it was receiving funds from abroad. It was still known as the Fascisti after 1924 and was most commonly referred to as the BF.
BL	British Leyland
BUF	British Union of Fascists
Cambridge Five	The 'Cambridge Five' were five communist students—Guy Burgess, Donald Maclean, Kim Philby, Anthony Blunt and John Cairncross—who were recruited by Soviet intelligence whilst at Cambridge University in the 1930s. Between them they subsequently gained positions in various

ABBREVIATIONS AND GLOSSARY

	governmental departments including the Foreign Office, MI5 and MI6, and passed documents from their departments to the Soviets.
CBE	Commander of the British Empire
CIA	Central Intelligence Agency (US foreign intelligence agency)
CLP	Constituency Labour Party
CND	Campaign for Nuclear Disarmament
Cominform	Founded in 1947 to coordinate Communist Party activities in Europe. Dissolved in 1956.
Comintern	An organisation founded by Lenin in 1919 to promote world revolution. It was dissolved in 1943. Also known as the Communist International or the Third International.
CPGB	Communist Party of Great Britain
DG	Director General
DNI	Director of Naval Intelligence
DS19	Defence Secretariat 19
EEC	European Economic Community
EL	Economic League
FBI	Federal Bureau of Investigation
GC&CS	Government Code and Cypher School. Britain's signals intelligence agency. Renamed as **GCHQ** in 1946.
GCHQ	Government Communications Headquarters
GPO	General Post Office
HOW	Home Office Warrant
IIB	Industrial Intelligence Bureau
IPI	Indian Political Intelligence

ABBREVIATIONS AND GLOSSARY

IRD	Information Research Department
JIC	Joint Intelligence Committee
KGB	Committee for State Security (Soviet foreign intelligence agency)
King Street	16 King Street, Covent Garden, London, was the headquarters of the **CPGB**
MI5	Britain's domestic intelligence service. Also known as **Security Service**
MI6	Britain's foreign intelligence service. Also known as **SIS**
MT	Militant Tendency. Also initially known as the Revolutionary Socialist League (RSL)
NATO	North Atlantic Treaty Organisation
NCCL	National Council of Civil Liberties
NEC	National Executive Committee of the Labour Party
NV	Negative Vetting. Sometimes referred to as the 'purge procedure'
NUM	National Union of Mineworkers
NUWM	National Unemployed Workers' Movement
OBE	Order of the British Empire
OMS	Organisation for the Maintenance of Supplies
PF	Personal File
PV	Positive Vetting
SCR	Society for Cultural Relations with the Soviet Union
SDS	Special Demonstrations Squad
	The unit was originally known as the Special Operations Squad, becoming the SDS in 1972-3. SDS officers were often nicknamed the 'hairies' and adopted false identities,

	often growing beards and long hair to fit in with the groups they penetrated.
Security Service	Britain's domestic intelligence service. Also known as **MI5**
SIS	Secret Intelligence Service. Britain's foreign intelligence service. Also known as **MI6**
SLO	Security Liaison Officer
Special Branch	Department of the police which dealt with intelligence and 'crimes directed against the state'.
SPL	Interdepartmental Group on Subversion in Public Life
StB	State Security. Czechoslovakian Secret Police
STST	Stop the Seventy Tour
SY	Scotland Yard
Transport House	Labour Party Headquarters 1928–80
UCPI	Undercover Policing Inquiry
WRP	Workers' Revolutionary Party
YCL	Young Communist League

INTRODUCTION

In December 1991, Stella Rimington, the Deputy Director General of Britain's domestic intelligence service, MI5, travelled to Moscow.[1] She was part of a team of British officials invited to Russia by the Chairman of the KGB, Vadim V. Bakatin, to discuss and advise on how intelligence agencies work in a democracy. On her arrival in the Russian capital, a few weeks before the collapse of the Soviet Union, Rimington was greeted by members of the KGB—one of whom was clutching a small bunch of red roses—and the talks in the days that followed represented what she later described as the 'strangest experience of my working life'.[2]

The meetings, which were held shortly before Rimington was appointed as the first female Director General of the Security Service, signified a thawing of relations after nearly seventy years of Anglo-Soviet hostility.[3] Rimington noted that until 1991, 'it was inconceivable that I would ever visit the Soviet Union or the countries of Eastern Europe, let alone that I would meet our opposite members there. For someone in my position, travel there, even on holiday, was prohibited until the early 1990s.'[4]

Rimington's visit had been inconceivable because, for almost all of what the historian Eric Hobsbawm had described as the 'Short Twentieth Century' (1914–91), Britain and the Soviet Union were adversaries.[5] Following the Bolshevik Revolution in 1917, a type of 'cold war' developed between the two nations, with Anglo-Soviet relations being marked by a mutual distrust and periods of significant hostility. Setting aside the years where the two allied against Nazi Germany in the 1940s, their relations were decidedly frosty until the Soviet empire began to collapse in the late 1980s.

In Britain, the threat posed by Bolshevik Russia after 1917 was regarded as so significant that both intelligence officials and politicians viewed it as a greater menace than that posed by even Germany, even though Britain and Germany were still at war. One report which influenced such a view was sent from Sidney Reilly, an MI6 agent in Russia, nicknamed the 'ace of spies.' He made clear that there was a significant difference between the Germans and Russians. Whilst the Germans were 'human beings; we can afford to be beaten by them', he said, the Bolsheviks were 'the arch enemy of the human race'. He finished by writing, 'at any price this foul obscenity must be crushed out of existence ... Peace with Germany? Yes, peace with Germany, peace with anybody. There is only one enemy. Mankind must unite in a holy alliance against this midnight terror'.[6]

During 1918, as the First World War approached its conclusion, a belief grew among British statesmen that the Germans were no longer the enemy. The Chief of the Imperial General Staff, Field Marshal Sir Henry Wilson, recorded in his diary after a cabinet meeting on 10 November 1918, 'All the Cabinet agreed. Our real danger now is not the Boches but Bolshevism'.[7] At the same cabinet meeting, Winston Churchill, the Minister of Munitions, argued that the Germans could be a potential future ally against the Russians. 'We might have to build up the German Army,' he declared, 'it [is] important to get Germany on its legs again for fear of the spread of Bolshevism'. Churchill later defined his policy as, 'Kill the Bolshie, Kiss the Hun'.[8] The end of four long years of war with Germany was no time for complacency or celebration. Shortly after the Armistice, the Director of Naval Intelligence, Admiral Sir William Reginald Hall, congratulated his staff on the victory but warned of what was to come. 'Hard and bitter as the battle has been,' he stated, 'we have now to face a far, far more ruthless foe, a foe that is hydra-headed, and whose evil power will spread over the whole world, and that foe is Russia.'[9] In Britain, there were significant concerns about the potential domestic impact of the Bolshevik revolution. There were reasons for such concerns; the Bolshevik leaders Lenin and Stalin believed Britain was the dominant world power at the end of 1918 and, therefore, identified it as their 'primary ideological target'.[10]

In Moscow, the Bolsheviks were also fearful; they were deeply concerned about British intentions to intervene in the Russian Civil War which had broken out following the November 1917 revolution. They were concerned by Allied support for the anti-Bolshevik forces and believed that 'the most dangerous of the anti-Soviet conspiracies was the Lockhart Plot'. Lockhart was Robert Bruce Lockhart, British envoy to Bolshevik Russia who was also working for MI6. The Bolsheviks believed that he had plotted to overthrow their government and kill some of their senior figures. They accused Lockhart of being behind an assassination attempt on Lenin in August 1918, and arrested him, holding him within the Kremlin. Lockhart eventually returned to Britain in October 1918 in an exchange of spies. He was tried in absentia, declared to be one of the 'enemies of the working people', and handed a death sentence if he was ever found in Russia again.[11]

Traditionally, historians have believed that hostility between East and West during the twentieth century, known as the Cold War, began towards the end of the Second World War. The Anglo-Soviet hostility during the twentieth century, however, long predated that. As the authorised historian of GCHQ, John Ferris, has argued, 'for Britain and the USSR, the Cold War began in 1917'.[12] The definition of a cold war is 'a state of political hostility between countries characterized by threats, propaganda, and other measures short of open warfare'.[13] Relations between Britain and Russia during the interwar period fit this definition and they continued to do so until the late 1980s. Whilst it may not be possible to argue that the 1917 Bolshevik Revolution instigated the Cold War, it does appear to have begun a cold war between Britain and Bolshevik Russia.

Individuals within the British establishment certainly believed that some kind of conflict was developing. By 1926, the Permanent Undersecretary at the Foreign Office, Sir William Tyrrell, stated in a memorandum that the Bolsheviks aimed to overthrow the 'present order of things' and promote revolution by 'fomenting disturbance and disorder everywhere.'[14] Indeed, Tyrrell was moved to remark, 'we are virtually at war with Russia'. The Soviets were, he believed, 'discarding the time-honoured practice of force and substituting it for the more invidious weapon of peaceful penetration on the one hand in the internal affairs of other countries, and, on the other, the stirring up of revolution everywhere.'[15]

Members of the British political and intelligence establishment were greatly concerned that the Soviets sought to undermine democracy and export their revolution across the globe. Bolshevism was thought to be spreading like a disease amongst the British public and security officials decided that one way to combat it was to initiate an extensive surveillance programme. One of the key repercussions of the Bolshevik revolution in Britain was that it led to a significant increase in political surveillance. The Bolshevik revolution did not merely have an impact in Britain; as the historian Mark Mazower argues, it 'provided a permanent justification for expanding political policing work in capitalist societies.'[16] In the years that followed the revolution, British politicians and security officials became increasingly concerned about Soviet- or communist-inspired subversion within the country, and subversion rapidly emerged as the primary security threat to the British State.[17] By the early 1920s, intelligence officials had begun to investigate tens of thousands of individuals with real or imagined links to communism or the Soviet Union. Security files were opened on them, with information ranging from basic biographical facts to detailed reports from sources to observation reports, collected on a range of different people.

The Bolshevik revolution was not the catalyst for political surveillance in Britain, but it did turbocharge such intelligence work.[18] The first permanent British intelligence department, the Secret Service Bureau, was created in 1909 and consisted of domestic and foreign branches, which later became MI5 and MI6.[19] In the years that followed, immediately before the First World War, a number of domestic political organisations were closely scrutinised, most notably those campaigning for women's suffrage. The letters and telegrams of suffragettes were routinely intercepted, whilst Special Branch reported on their activities and meetings.[20] Political surveillance became more widespread during the war, although postal censors were said to have 'felt an involuntary deep-seated disgust when [they] first broke the seal of an unknown person's correspondence'.[21]

Although there was initially an uneasiness about such surveillance, the First World War broke the taboo on 'political policing' in Britain. During the conflict, pacifist and 'revolutionary' movements were regularly the subject of Special Branch inquiries.[22] Surveillance expanded to the extent that by 1916, MI5 held detailed records on over 130,000 individuals. The war altered perceptions to such an extent that, by the time of the Armistice, intelligence officials and politicians had begun to believe that it was not possible to return to a time where information was not collected on those suspected of posing a threat to British domestic security. This shift was formalised in 1919 with the creation of the Directorate of Intelligence, a peacetime intelligence organisation designed specifically to collect intelligence on domestic subversion.[23] The Directorate of Intelligence was short-lived, being abolished in 1921. The covert surveillance which began following the Bolshevik revolution did, however, continue for the next seventy years. Both Special Branch and MI5 amassed hundreds of thousands, possibly millions, of records on individuals who included the most fervently pro-Soviet communists, individuals sympathetic to left-wing politics and, later, people who had expressed unease about Britain's nuclear weapons.

Accounts of this large-scale surveillance were hidden for many years. This was, in many ways, because relevant sources have not been available to historians; intelligence history was, for many years, known as the 'missing dimension' of British history.[24] Until the 1990s, this was part of government policy. As will be seen during this work, the operations of the intelligence agencies and information related to espionage or subversion in Britain was more often than not kept secret. The public, it was believed, did not need to know. As the historian Sir Michael Howard wrote in the 1980s, 'so far as official government policy is concerned, the British security and intelligence services do not exist. Enemy agents are found under gooseberry bushes and intelligence is brought by the stalks.'[25]

The level of secrecy that existed before the 1990s does not endure, and it is now a little clichéd to talk of intelligence history as the 'missing dimension'. It is, however, true that some areas of British history have remained somewhat untold due to the previous suppression of information. Histories examining Anglo-Soviet relations during the twentieth century, or the Cold War in Britain, only briefly touch on domestic surveillance, if at all.[26] Accounts that discuss Anglo-Soviet relations in the twentieth century, particularly those examining the post-World War Two era or those which focus on intelligence issues, tend to be dominated by several well-known cases. The understandable interest in the most prominent cases such as the scandals involving the so-called 'Cambridge Five'—Burgess, Maclean, Philby, Blunt and Cairncross—or the British atomic spies Alan Nunn May and Klaus Fuchs has, however, overshadowed a much wider story. The discovery that individuals such as Fuchs or members of the Cambridge Five had been involved in espionage only exacerbated fears which had begun following the Bolshevik revolution about the threat of communism and the Soviet Union. These fears had already led numerous individuals to be caught up in the British State's surveillance net; the intelligence community prioritised surveillance of, and took action against, both political groups and protest groups deemed to have links to the Soviet Union. The fear somewhat distorted their views of people or organisations who had the slightest connection to communism and led to large-scale political surveillance.

This book examines how initial fears about the Soviet threat and the spread of revolutionary and communist ideas led to the large-scale surveillance of a wide range of different political groups in Britain. These not only included the Communist Party of Great Britain (CPGB) and its sympathisers, but also others on the political Left, including the Labour Party, and protest movements such as the Anti-Apartheid Movement (AAM) and anti-nuclear campaigners. Political surveillance in Britain during the 'short twentieth century' was dominated by watching individuals with links to either communism or the Soviet Union. Nevertheless, security officials did not focus solely on such people, and also watched individuals with links to other political movements such as Irish republicanism and fascism or the far-right. This book, however, is not concerned with examining all aspects of the political surveillance that took place in Britain during the twentieth century. It will only examine those groups who were placed under surveillance because of direct or indirect links to either communism or the Soviet Union. It particularly considers the extensive surveillance of people who occupied a 'grey area'—those who were not doing anything illegal and were merely espousing political opinions that were a legitimate part of the democratic debate but could also be viewed as some kind of threat—and debates how necessary and legitimate it was.

There has been a significant amount of literature examining the East-West ideological conflict during the twentieth century, particularly covering the 1945–89 Cold War. This has, however, tended to focus on US-Soviet geopolitics, and has often obscured the uniquely British part of the story. This book explores the impact of the ideological clash in Britain. Not only does it show how a cold war began for Britain and the Soviet Union in 1917, but it also illustrates how it led, domestically, to suspicion of anti-establishment figures and large-scale surveillance. By examining the surveillance of a variety of political and protest groups, it considers how the Soviet Union impacted and influenced British security and counter-subversion policies across more than seventy years.

Until the twentieth century, Britain was long thought of as a place whereby so-called 'political policing' and surveillance of civilians had no place as they were inconsistent with British liberal traditions.[27] Political policing was undoubtedly less extensive in Britain than in other parts of Europe prior to the twentieth century.[28] Some, however, disagree with the idea that surveillance rarely took place and was regarded as un-British; the historian E.P. Thompson has gone as far as to argue that 'spying' was 'an ancient part of British statecraft [and] police practice.'[29] Regardless of such historical debates, this book will show that, during the short twentieth century, political surveillance undoubtedly became mainstream in Britain for the first time. Activity that had been undertaken somewhat cautiously in previous centuries was normalised, as politicians and intelligence and security officials held grave and enduring concerns about the threat posed by the Soviet Union and communism to British domestic security. To misquote Thompson—a man who was, himself, placed under surveillance in the 1940s and 1950s—it could be said that, during the short twentieth century, surveillance became a modern part of British statecraft and police practice.

1

COMMUNISM

THE INSIDIOUS DISEASE

In late 1918, shortly after the end of the First World War, Europe faced two distinct threats. The Spanish influenza pandemic that had emerged earlier in the year was raging, whilst in the East, the Bolsheviks, who had seized power in Russia little over a year before, were trying to spark a global revolution. Bolshevism was frequently spoken of as 'a virus or a plague against which they had to erect a *cordon sanitaire*.'[1] At the time, the British-born Australian journalist Benjamin Hoare, authored a pamphlet, 'The Two Plagues: Influenza and Bolshevism.' Within it, he argued that Bolshevism was 'distinguished from its fellow plague' as a 'moral, mental and spiritual infection' and 'a graver danger than the Influenza plague.'[2]

Influenza had spread across the globe in 1918, infected many—including the British Prime Minister, David Lloyd George, and the American President, Woodrow Wilson—and reportedly killed up to fifty million people.[3] During the pandemic, one health officer stated that it had arrived 'like a thief in the night, its onset rapid, and insidious.'[4] It was feared that Bolshevism could also silently spread across Europe, 'infecting' millions. Many Western leaders held grave concerns about the 'contagion' of the Bolshevik 'disease', and believed the revolution could, maybe would, spread across Europe.[5]

Such concerns were not unfounded, as the Bolsheviks had made it an explicit aim to spread revolution worldwide and had formed the Communist International (Comintern) to help do so.[6] In October 1918, the Bolshevik leader Lenin had written that there was potential for an international revolution to break out 'during the next few days.'[7] By late 1918, this seemed a distinct possibility. Upon visiting Europe in early 1919 to take part in peace negotiations, US President Woodrow Wilson sounded a warning of the looming threat. 'Bolshevism', he stated, 'is moving steadily westward, has overwhelmed Poland, and is poisoning Germany.'[8] On a trip to the continent weeks later, his Secretary of State, Robert Lansing, presented an equally gloomy picture; Europe was 'aflame with anarchy' and 'the Red Armies of Russia are marching westward'. It was time, he stated, 'to stop fiddling while the world is on fire.'[9]

In Britain there was a real anxiety about the potential for the Bolshevik 'virus' to spread throughout the country.[10] Fears of a Russian-inspired revolution had preoccupied members of the British State since the Bolsheviks had seized control in Moscow, even before a formal British Communist Party had been formed. Sir Basil Thomson, the head of Special Branch, was one of the foremost proponents of the idea that Bolshevism was an infectious disease. In October 1918, prior to the Armistice, he was already sounding the alarm, writing in a memorandum, 'people who live under the Bolshevik regime describe it as a sort of infectious disease, spreading rapidly, but insidiously, until like a cancer it eats away the fabric of society, and the patient ceases even to wish for his own recovery.'[11]

Several members of the cabinet, notably Winston Churchill, Lord Curzon and Walter Long, picked up on Thomson's description and continued to use the analogy.[12] Thomson, Churchill, Curzon and Long were fervently anti-communist, yet their remarks did seem out of place.[13] Even the Prime Minister in 1919, David Lloyd George, not a man who was as readily concerned as some of his colleagues, spoke fearfully of how Europe was 'filled with the spirit of revolution.' At home, after widespread social discontent had spread in Britain, he believed that the country was 'nearer to Bolshevism' than it had been at any other time.[14]

In early 1919, fears about the spread of Bolshevism appeared to be being realised. A Bolshevik republic was declared in Bavaria, and a Soviet government took power in Hungary. The British Foreign Office received warnings from a former Austro-Hungarian foreign minister that 'should the sovjet [sic] government acquire real power it will spread further', mentioning 'Austria, Servia [sic], Roumania and Poland'.[15] Further reports also suggested that a 'Communist coup d'état' was very possible, and at one stage likely, in Vienna.[16] The revolutions in Bavaria and Hungary did not last, failing after months, yet the anxiety in Britain endured. Such was the paucity of intelligence about the Soviet Union, it was impossible for officials to form a judgement about the Bolsheviks' ability to successfully export revolution.[17] Much of the intelligence that was received about the Soviet Union was unreliable, meaning that by 1919 British officials could not work out Soviet intentions, whilst being genuinely fearful that revolution could break out.[18]

For those already concerned about the spread of Bolshevism to Britain, events of late 1918 and 1919 would have exacerbated such fears.[19] Over this period, the police went on strike twice and delays in demobilising soldiers following the Armistice led some to mutiny. Strikes in one industry or another led to thirty-five million working days being lost in 1919, with an average of 100,000 men being on strike every day.[20] For some within government, such events were seen as a possible prelude to full-scale revolution in Britain. The second police strike in 1919 was attributed by Home Secretary, Edward Shortt, to 'firebrands in the Force ... working with confessed Bolsheviks',[21] whilst his cabinet colleague, the Secretary of State for Scotland, Robert Munro, stated that a strike in January 1919 over the length of the working week, which led to violent clashes between police and strikers in George Square, Glasgow, should be viewed as a 'Bolshevist rising'.[22]

With hindsight the reasons for so much of the unrest seem obvious. Men who had returned from war made the decision to strike as they would no longer accept poor pay and conditions.

They had been promised 'homes fit for heroes' but were instead faced with shortages of food and housing, wage cuts, and spiralling unemployment.[23] Strikes were nothing new as, in the years preceding the war, walk-outs had occurred in every major industry and across every region of the country.[24] Whilst it can seem extraordinary that senior members of the British establishment were unable to understand the causes of unrest, the events of 1918 and 1919 should be understood in the context of the time. Revolutions did appear to be spreading across Europe; the Bolshevik Grigori Zinoviev had predicted in 1919, 'within a year all Europe will be Communist'.[25] In the words of the esteemed intelligence historian Christopher Andrew, 'apprehension plus ignorance equals exaggerated fears', and this is certainly what happened in Britain.[26] The prospects for revolution in Britain during 1919, whilst slight, should not be entirely dismissed.[27] Fears prompted by unrest at home and revolution abroad meant that action was necessary to protect the nation. In the following years, the British intelligence community increased its surveillance activity and intensified investigations into individuals deemed to pose a subversive threat to Britain.

A Domestic Secret Service

In early 1919, the First Lord of the Admiralty, Walter Long, provided a warning to his cabinet colleagues. 'Elements of unrest, and what we call Bolshevism are,' he said, 'more general, more deep-seated, than many of us believe'. To counter such threats, he recommended that an 'efficient, well-paid Secret Service on the civil side' be established.[28] This led the cabinet to set up a Secret Service Committee to review the role of the various intelligence agencies. The Committee highlighted the 'need for a coordinated domestic intelligence system' and made clear the 'necessity to have a proper mechanism for collecting information about persons engaged in revolutionary or anarchical movements in this country.'[29] By March of that year, the Committee recommended the formation of a new unit to investigate domestic subversion, the Directorate of Intelligence. Sir Basil Thomson was appointed to lead it.[30]

Thomson's role made him principally responsible for collecting intelligence related to seditious meetings and conspiracies, potential disturbances and revolutionary movements. Whilst he made use of a variety of sources, including informants, Thomson particularly relied on local police forces to collect intelligence on such matters.[31] Shortly after his appointment, chief constables were asked to routinely send him confidential reports on incidents in their region relating to 'strikes, impending strikes or labour unrest generally, sabotage and seditious or revolutionary propaganda by meetings or otherwise.' It was also requested that they provide detailed reports on seditious speeches and information on the activities of individuals involved in subversive activity.[32] Thomson also received intelligence from his own agents, who infiltrated organisations regarded as subversive, and a wide variety of informants who reported to him on unrest around the country.[33]

The results of Thomson's investigations were reported on a weekly basis to the cabinet. The reports covered a wide range of issues—in the course of just eight weeks in 1919, Thomson wrote about 'Red Scouts', industrial relations, demobilised soldiers, civil libertarians, the unemployed, 'revolutionary' educators, protest groups and 'revolutionary speakers.'[34] This meant that the reports often lacked a clear focus and could give the impression that danger lurked in every corner of Britain. The reports were also often somewhat contradictory—mentioning that extremists were exploiting the grievances of men for their own ends whilst, on other occasions, stating that working men were against revolution and actively disliked extremists.[35] The fact that subversive individuals were involved in many small, disparate groups meant that the accounts were often chaotic and unfocused. This changed with the formation of the Communist Party of Great Britain (CPGB) on 31 July 1920, which provided a focus for the authorities.[36]

The CPGB was considered to pose a significant threat because it had, in effect, been created by Moscow. The disparate Marxist groups that eventually formed the CPGB had long been unable to unify, having disagreed over policy. The Comintern subsequently ordered the small Marxist parties in Britain to overcome their differences, and within weeks they had united.[37] Moscow's influence on the CPGB was enormous; in addition to playing a crucial role in the formation of the Party, the Soviets provided funding—without which it would almost certainly have ceased to exist—and the Comintern effectively set Party policy.[38] Such was the level of control that Harry Pollitt, who went on to become CPGB General Secretary, once remarked that he believed his 'primary allegiance [was] to Moscow'.[39] The trade unionist Frank Hodges said that British communists were 'the intellectual slaves of Moscow.' Whilst there was greater diversity of opinion within the CPGB than Hodges suggested, his statement was broadly true.[40]

Some security officials believed that Moscow's control of the CPGB only represented part of the increasing influence that the Soviets were exerting in Britain during the early 1920s. For Basil Thomson, a delegation of Russian officials who had travelled to London in 1920 to discuss Anglo-Soviet trade were particularly problematic. In one report he described the delegation as 'a greater menace to the stability of this country than anything that has happened since the Armistice' and believed that 'on instructions from Moscow' it was 'devoting all its energy to revolutionary propaganda.'[41] Intercepted telegrams between the trade delegation and Moscow showed that alongside funding the CPGB, the Soviets also provided subsidies to the left-wing *Daily Herald*.[42] Indeed, it was alleged that all 'extremist organisations' were likely to have received 'financial assistance from Russia'. By September 1920, Thomson reported that at least £100,000 of Russian money had been spent on revolutionary propaganda in England in the preceding nine months.[43]

Despite the wider impact Moscow and its representatives appeared to be having on Britain, Thomson focused his concerns primarily on the CPGB which, he believed, intended to 'fan the already existing flames of discontent, to foment revolution and finally to bring about revolutionary action'.[44] He also linked the emergence of the CPGB to an 'increase in the number of violent speeches [which] advocate revolution by violence and the overthrow of the [British] constitution'.[45] Thomson himself reported on the CPGB for just over a year as, by the end of 1921, the Directorate of Intelligence was abolished.[46] The work of the unit was taken over by Special Branch under its new head, Sir Wyndham Childs. Childs continued to produce weekly reports for the cabinet until 1924 and tended to focus on the dangers of the Party to an even greater extent than had his predecessor.[47] In his memoirs, Childs recalled that 'Communism was a burning question when I took over ... it was ... the most important part of my work.'[48] So extensive were the reports he produced, that one even contained an account of a christening of two young children named Rosa Luxembourg Mackay and Lenin de Valera Mackay at St John's Church, Hurst, Lancashire overseen by the Reverend RW Cummings, a communist vicar.[49]

To keep track of communists, Special Branch used paid informants, wire taps, postal intercepts and attended meetings both covertly and overtly.[50] Special Branch officers routinely attended CPGB meetings and collected information on those in attendance; at times they were spotted taking notes by attendees. On occasion, their presence caused controversy and in 1924, the Labour MP George Lansbury raised the matter in Parliament.[51] Whilst officers attempted to attend meetings covertly, in April 1924 this ended disastrously. At a Communist Party district conference at a London theatre, the chairman, having heard voices from beneath the stage, opened a trapdoor to discover two police officers hiding with a supply of food and taking notes on proceedings. The incident was reported on the front of the CPGB newspaper *Workers' Weekly,* and included photographs of the notebooks which the police, in their haste to leave, had left behind.[52] It appears that this was not the first time officers had secretly attended meetings at the theatre; a Special Branch report on the incident stated that the theatre's manager had allowed officers to do so 'on previous occasions'.[53] The incident did not deter Special Branch from continuing to attend such meetings. Shortly afterwards, Wyndham Childs wrote to John Anderson, Permanent Secretary at the Home Office, justifying the presence of his officers. He stated,

> The Communist Party ... are openly, avowedly, and boastfully seditious and treasonable, and it is, of course, the <u>duty</u> of the Police to take adequate steps to be informed as to the activities of this organisation as well as any other revolutionary organisation.[54]

Special Branch officers were not confined to attending and reporting on meetings. Special Branch compiled its own files on individuals, whilst officers were also stationed at ports around the country and reported on the arrivals and departures of known communists, revolutionaries, and criminals.[55]

Whilst Special Branch took the lead in investigating communists and other 'revolutionaries', information on such individuals also came from other sources. On occasion, members of the public would write letters to the Home Secretary or Prime Minister reporting on the activities of communists and urging the government to do more to prevent such meetings from taking place.[56] MI5 also collected information on communists, although it had been greatly diminished by the formation of the Directorate of Intelligence in 1919 and was restricted to investigating subversion in the armed forces.[57]

The Security Service did not, however, completely confine itself to its remit. The Director General, Vernon Kell, argued that to fully investigate subversion in the military, it was necessary to gain knowledge about civilian subversive movements; in 1923, one MI5 officer successfully joined the CPGB on Kell's instructions.[58] MI5 held files on some of the most prominent CPGB leaders and, by 1925, had information on 25,250 individuals whom it believed to be 'potentially dangerous to national defence.' Its investigations were so extensive that, according to the authorised history of the Security Service, 'between the wars more MI5 resources were devoted to the surveillance and investigation of the CPGB than any other target.'[59] Its small budget, however, meant that MI5 was limited in what it could do compared to Special Branch.

In October 1931, MI5 took over the responsibility for investigating domestic subversion from Special Branch.[60] The Security Service decided not to investigate subversion quite as widely as the Branch had done in previous years; in addition to investigating obvious groups such as the CPGB, Special Branch had also defined organisations such as the Egyptian Association of Great Britain, the Union of Chinese Association in Great Britain and a wide range of anti-fascist groups as 'revolutionary' and warranting investigation.[61] William Phillips, head of MI5's A-Branch, believed that Special Branch officers spent too much time investigating people who were no more than 'Hot Air Merchants', and decided that there was no longer any reason to hold files on Scottish nationalists ('a perfectly sound constitutional movement'), atheists, unemployed marchers, mutinous members of the merchant navy or policemen who had received adverse reports.[62] With MI5 taking prime responsibility, Special Branch was confined to a subsidiary role in supporting MI5 investigations.[63]

The primary focus of MI5's post-1931 counter-subversive investigations was, inevitably, communism and the CPGB; it had first investigated communism in 1915 and 1916, albeit briefly.[64] It appears that merely being in contact with a communist would have been enough for the Security Service to open a file on an individual; in January 1932, they opened one on an Andrew White after discovering a letter he had written to the CPGB. The letter remarked, 'I am very desirous of joining the Communist Party, with whose principles I am entirely in accordance.'[65] After investigation it was discovered that Andrew White was, in fact, an alias used by a 16-year-old schoolboy, Peter Kemp. A fervent anti-communist, Kemp had, remarkably, sought to pose as a member of the CPGB so that he 'could obtain some useful information which he could then pass on to the Government.'[66] Intelligence officials found Kemp's audacity highly amusing, although one did remark, 'if school-boys take to posing as communists, S.10's life is going to become complicated.'[67]

Despite that statement, it does appear that the Security Service did, on some occasions, investigate schoolboys. In January 1933, a file was opened on Martin Pollock, a pupil at Winchester School, after a letter he had sent to the well-known communist Emile Burns was intercepted.[68] After discovering several more exchanges between Pollock and Burns, MI5 sought information from the head of Pollock's house at Winchester. They were informed that Pollock was a 'clever young man' who was in his last few months at the school ahead of university.[69] MI5 regarded Pollock as a communist sympathiser and initially added material to his file on a regular basis. A file remained open on him until at least 1962, although there were few entries post-1934. Pollock eventually became a bacteriologist and Fellow of the Royal Society.[70]

As they had with both Kemp and Pollock, MI5 often discovered information about individuals who were CPGB members or communist sympathisers by intercepting mail sent to senior Communists, or local CPGB parties.[71] Letters were often steamed open using kettles and, once the contents had been copied with a photostat machine, resealed and sent to the recipient. Whilst at the beginning of the 1930s letter-checks provided a crucial way of investigating suspects, as the decade moved on and more people began to use telephones, MI5 began more regularly to tap the phones of those they wished to investigate. Telephone calls were initially transcribed by hand as they were being listened to 'live', resulting in inaccurate accounts that were of limited use. Eventually the problem was resolved using Dictaphones.[72]

Parliamentary Communists

The desire to investigate all communists led MI5 to hold files on several sitting MPs—Cecil Malone, Shapurji Saklatvala, Walton Newbold and William Gallacher. A number of these files, which were opened in the early 1920s, were compiled from second-hand information sent to MI5 and not from MI5's own investigations; in the 1920s, MI5 had neither the resources nor the authority to investigate.

The first MP with evident links to Communism was Cecil L'Estrange Malone, elected as the Liberal MP for Leyton East at the 1918 General Election. At the time of his election, Malone was a highly respected figure, having had a distinguished naval career (which included wartime service), worked as air attaché at the British Embassy in Paris, and been awarded an OBE.[73] He first came to the notice of Special Branch in October 1919 after visiting Russia, where he met senior Bolsheviks.[74] On his return to Britain, he wrote a number of articles about his experience, gave speeches on 'The Truth about Russia', and defected to join the newly-formed CPGB, becoming the first Communist Party MP to sit in the Commons.[75]

In October 1920, Special Branch spotted a Comintern courier, Erkki Veltheim, leaving Malone's flat. In a subsequent search of the flat, officers discovered a training guide for a British 'Red Army', which he was believed to have authored.[76] He subsequently came under much closer scrutiny, and a Home Office Warrant (HOW)—which allowed the State to either open the post or tap the telephone of a suspect—was taken out to intercept his post.[77] The Post Office was instructed to open all letters sent to Malone at a number of addresses, including 'House of Commons.'[78] In November 1920, Malone was arrested and prosecuted after making an inflammatory speech at the Royal Albert Hall, described as 'a deliberate incitement to assassination and revolution by force.' He had remarked to his communist audience, 'what, my friends, are a few Churchills or a few Curzons on lampposts compared to the massacre of thousands of human beings?' After a trial, he was imprisoned for six months.[79] Following his release from prison, Malone rarely came to the attention of the authorities. At the 1922 General Election he lost his seat, having distanced himself from the CPGB. However, he returned to Parliament in 1928 as a Labour MP and became Private Parliamentary Secretary to the Minister for Pensions, before leaving Parliament for the final time in 1931. His MI5 file stayed open until at least 1951.[80]

Shapurji Saklatvala won his seat, Battersea North, at the 1922 General Election as a Labour Party candidate.[81] The authorities had first become aware of Saklatvala in 1910 when they discovered that he was in touch with a number of pro-Indian independence campaigners.[82] In 1911, he was regarded as one of the 'most violently anti-British agitators'.[83] By the time he was elected to the Commons, the intelligence community had compiled a large amount of information on his activities.[84] Attempts had even been made to send him back to the country of his birth, India.[85] Whilst Saklatvala's commitment to communism concerned intelligence officials, what most worried them was his apparent commitment to 'furthering sedition in India.'[86] Applications to intercept his post whilst he was an MP were often instigated by the Indian Political Intelligence Office (IPI), which had an office in MI5's headquarters.[87] The authorities took Saklatvala's commitment to campaigning for Indian self-rule so seriously that, in 1927, a decision was made to prevent him from travelling to India.[88] Saklatvala continued to be monitored after leaving the Commons in 1929 and saw further applications to travel to India turned down by the authorities.[89]

Saklatvala was banned from travelling to India as a result of a policy introduced by Whitehall officials in the early 1920s. The decision to prevent an individual from travelling abroad was only taken in the most extreme circumstances, being seen as a last resort. Officials would only take such action if they had clear evidence that the person was travelling 'for some purpose definitely hostile to the national interest.'[90] Were an individual known to be a communist, their name would be included on a Scotland Yard 'suspect list' and forwarded to the Passport Office. If they attempted to travel to any British Dominions, they would immediately be prevented from doing so, for fear that they would spread revolutionary propaganda around the British Empire.[91] This, officials believed, described Saklatvala's intentions perfectly.

Walton Newbold was the first MP to be elected as an official CPGB candidate when he won the Motherwell seat in 1922. By the time he entered Parliament, he was well known by the intelligence community; in 1920, MI5 had four files on him and regarded him as a 'violent revolutionary'.[92] He was separately described as 'a pure Bolshevist', so extreme that 'even the Irish priests will not support him.'[93] Newbold did not hide his allegiances, and in his maiden speech in Parliament proclaimed himself to 'belong to the same army' and 'rallied under the same flag' as Lenin.[94] He was also recorded as having told a communist meeting that he was 'a British representative of the Russian Communist Party'.[95] As no files have been released on Newbold, it is unclear how often he came to the attention of the intelligence community after 1923, when he lost his seat. He was, however, included on the list of Communists banned from travelling abroad for a time. By 1929, however, he was allowed to travel as he was no longer believed to pose a threat; in fact, he was considered to be ardently anti-communist.[96] It appears that the authorities were sufficiently flexible to change their view on those considered as subversives when the subjects themselves changed their views.

The final MP to be elected as a Communist during the interwar period was Willie Gallacher, who won the West Fife seat at the 1935 General Election. Prior to entering Parliament, Gallacher had long been a prominent member of the CPGB, during which time he was subject to numerous HOWs and featured 'on a Police rosta for intermittent observation'.[97] Gallacher's MI5 file is particularly insightful because he was the first Communist MP newly elected after the Security Service had gained full responsibility for investigating domestic subversion. Shortly after Gallacher had won his Commons seat, MI5 debated whether letters sent to him should continue to be opened. Whilst they initially were, MI5 and the Home Office quickly made the decision to instruct the General Post Office to cease opening correspondence addressed to Gallacher.[98] MI5 also contacted Special Branch and asked for his name to be removed from the Suspect Book of people to be watched at ports 'as he was now a Member of Parliament.'[99] It was decided that records should continue to be kept detailing when Gallacher left and returned to Britain, but that no action should be taken if he was carrying seditious material.[100] Security officials still, however, wanted to gain knowledge about Gallacher as, regardless of his status as an MP, he was still considered to hold dangerous views. After he had spent his holidays in Canada during the summer of 1936, a request was sent to the Royal Canadian Mounted Police for information.[101] Special Branch also continued to report on public speeches he had given, although MI5 were keen to prevent Gallacher knowing that he was being scrutinised. They were likely concerned about the possible fallout if it were known they were investigating MPs.

A Front for Communism

As part of their investigations into communism, the intelligence community sometimes collected information on organisations that may, to many people, have appeared to offer no threat. These so-called 'front organisations' included groups interested in campaigning for the unemployed—The National Unemployed Workers' Movement (NUWM)—and those interested in Soviet life and culture, such as the Society for Cultural Relations with the Soviet Union (SCR).[102] Founded in 1924, the SCR described itself as a non-political organisation which sought 'to maintain cultural relations between peoples of the Soviet Union and Great Britain.' It organised lectures, conferences, and exhibitions to inform those interested on a variety of aspects of Soviet life and, whilst it inevitably attracted members who had links to communism or the Soviet Union, its membership also included highly respectable people such as the economist John Maynard Keynes and the author Virginia Woolf.[103]

Regardless of its proclaimed aims and apolitical nature, the SCR aroused the suspicions of the intelligence community, which thought it to be 'one of the subtler propaganda organisations recently established by the Soviet Government in this country'.[104] By early 1926, intelligence officials had obtained an official list of SCR members; Special Branch determined that 25 per cent of the organisation's 353 members belonged 'to one or other of the Soviet organisations in London.' Eighteen known British communists were also on the list, with it being remarked that 'there are probably a good many more, not taking into account the extreme Left Wingers ... who are Communists in all but name.'[105]

The intelligence community was particularly concerned about the presence of prominent figures within the organisation who had close links to Moscow. One of these was Andrew Rothstein, a founder of the CPGB who worked for the Soviet Information Bureau (ROSTA or TASS) in London.[106] By mid-1925, Special Branch stated that Rothstein 'takes a very active part in the meetings' of the SCR and believed him to be 'an agent of the Soviet government.'[107] Numerous other members of the organisation's executive committee also had links to Moscow, and whilst they could not have been described as 'agents', they often disseminated information provided by Soviet contacts.[108] Although the SCR was not formally tied to Moscow and does not appear to have received financial assistance, it rarely, if ever, criticised the Soviet Union in its publications and often took Moscow's line on controversial issues.[109]

Despite their investigations into the SCR, Special Branch acknowledged that, 'many individuals of undoubted integrity, such as University Professors, are supporters of it in the belief, no doubt, that they are furthering its nominal objects.'[110] Such people were not recorded by the authorities as attendees at SCR meetings, but the details of 'organisers, officials and those seemingly using the organisation as a cloak for revolutionary activity' were documented.[111] Special Branch officers would routinely attend SCR meetings and take notes. Reports described a variety of lectures and debates amongst members on topics such as Russian trade, the rationing system in Russia, women in the USSR and churches and religion in the Soviet Republic.[112] They reveal the extent to which the SCR was tracked, but exactly what the authorities would have learned about the organisation is unclear, other than that it was attracted to Russian culture.

The Menace of Moscow

In retrospect, the attention paid to SCR meetings can appear almost pointless, and lead to the simple question—why was it investigated so extensively? The same question can also be applied to wider investigations into the CPGB. During the interwar period, it only got four MPs elected, never received more than 75,000 votes (less than 0.5% of the vote) and, most importantly of all, was perfectly legal. Its membership barely reached 10,000 in the 1920s and, at its height in the years prior to the Second World War, only reached 18,000. Even then, this was mainly due to people's concerns about war and the threat of fascism rather than their attraction to the communist ideology.[113] Some individuals have, therefore, accused the intelligence agencies of showing a 'paranoid overreaction' to the actual threat posed.[114]

There are a number of reasons why such attention was paid to communism and its offshoots. Firstly, during the early 1920s, there was a slight tendency for the intelligence community to exaggerate the threat for reasons of self-preservation. With intelligence budgets slashed following the Armistice in 1918 and questions being raised about the necessity for intelligence agencies in peacetime, the intelligence services felt compelled to justify their own existence. Providing numerous reports on the grave threat communism and the Soviet Union posed to Britain was a way of helping to safeguard their future.[115]

Intelligence officials also sought to exaggerate the threat, as they believed it was the best way of showing the insidious Soviet influence within Britain. Members of the intelligence community, alongside numerous cabinet members, opposed Britain's having any diplomatic relations with the Soviet Union. They thus promoted the idea of a communist threat to help coerce the government of the day to decisively break off relations. After the Soviet trading delegation was invited to Britain, Basil Thomson's weekly reports to the cabinet regularly argued that revolutionary extremism in Britain had been inspired by the delegation and the CPGB. Over many months, Thomson produced stories to feed the narrative that Britain would be much safer if the Soviets had no presence in the country. On one occasion he opined that 'if the supply of money from abroad could be stopped communist activity in this country would, for all practical purposes, cease to exist.'[116]

Cabinet ministers such as Lord Curzon, Winston Churchill and Walter Long, who were strongly opposed to Anglo-Soviet diplomatic relations, used Thomson's intelligence reports as evidence of the need to take a harder line against Moscow. In 1920, unhappy about the presence of the Soviet trade delegation in Britain, they forced the Prime Minister, David Lloyd George, to release intercepted Soviet diplomatic telegrams revealing that the delegation was providing subsidies to the CPGB and the *Daily Herald*. Fortunately, the Soviets did not appear to notice the revelation that the British were reading their communications, but hardliners displayed a cavalier attitude towards protecting the sources of secret intelligence time and again.[117] In September 1920, Thomson, Sir Henry Wilson, Chief of the Imperial General Staff, and the Director of Naval Intelligence, Admiral Sir Hugh Sinclair, urged, albeit unsuccessfully, for further intercepts to be published.[118] Three years later, in 1923, the Foreign Secretary, Lord Curzon, sent a diplomatic note to Moscow protesting about the activities of the trade delegation, in which he directly quoted from intercepted Soviet communications and 'taunted the Soviet government with Britain's success in decrypting their communications.'[119]

Such indiscretions reached their height in 1927, after a police raid on the headquarters of the All-Russian Co-operative Society (ARCOS), which shared a building with the trade delegation.[120] Having been informed that the ARCOS building would contain documents which detailed Soviet espionage against Britain, the cabinet decided to break off diplomatic relations. When no incriminating material was found, ministers sought to justify the diplomatic breach by quoting from intercepted Soviet diplomatic telegrams in Parliament during a debate on Anglo-Soviet relations.[121] In the authorised history of MI5, Christopher Andrew described this as 'an orgy of governmental indiscretion about secret intelligence for which there is no parallel in modern parliamentary history.'[122] The victory for the hardliners in ejecting the Soviets proved to be pyrrhic; having been alerted that their communications were being intercepted, the Soviets adopted an almost unbreakable form of communication—'one time pads'[123]—leaving Britain unable to decrypt almost all high-grade Soviet intelligence until the Second World War.[124] By exaggerating the threat communism posed to Britain over a number of years, individuals such as Thomson laid a path which enabled ministers to argue that the Soviet influence was dangerously extensive and eventually led to their objective of ending Anglo-Soviet relations.

The Communist Threat

The threat communism posed to Britain may have been exaggerated by individuals with an ulterior motive. It was the case, however, that communism could still potentially have posed a threat; it was necessary, therefore, to place communists under surveillance. MI5's reasoning for investigating the CPGB can be found in an internal history of the Security Service, *The Security Service*, written by the MI5 officer, John Curry, during the Second World War. Whilst this history was never intended for public consumption, it was published in 1999 and provides an insight into how the Service viewed the threat of communism.[125] Curry wrote that of particular concern to MI5 was the fact that the aim of Communist Parties around the world was to seize power through revolutionary methods. Even if violence was not the desired way of achieving such a revolution, he wrote, the CPGB would be committed to using 'conspiratorial' or subversive methods to be successful.[126]

The MI5 position, according to Curry, was that even if the CPGB was not able to achieve a revolution in the short-term, it was still important to investigate the Party in order to be prepared should circumstances change in the future. Surveillance would have enabled the Security Service to better understand the aims and policy of the CPGB and an 'adequate appreciation' of both its strength and ability to achieve a revolutionary situation.[127] Much of the information collected was, according to Curry, 'often dull and [would] remain so as long as the CPGB remains [a] small and insignificant force.' However, he stated that it was 'impossible to ignore [the CPGB's] potential importance as a factor making for disintegration in the life of this country.'[128]

Fears that communists could use subversive or conspiratorial methods to harm Britain led officials to focus particularly on their presence within the Civil Service. There were concerns about communists infiltrating government departments, particularly those which gave civil servants access to privileged information. By the mid-1920s, this led senior civil servants to conclude that some form of action needed to be taken. In March 1926, having discovered that twenty Post Office workers were members of the CPGB, Sir Evelyn Murray, Secretary to the General Post Office, expressed concern about the potential for 'revolutionary agitators' to be in control of 'the transmission of Government communications in times of crisis, and especially their secrecy'.[129] After further concerns were expressed about the presence of communists in War Departments and Naval Establishments, in 1927, it was decided that restrictions should be placed on communists working in government departments. Those 'shown by reasonable evidence to be actively engaged in the dissemination of anti-constitutional and revolutionary propaganda, either oral or written' were to be immediately dismissed. Communist sympathisers, who did not take 'any active part in the furtherance of Communism' should be removed from their jobs, ministers believed, when an opportunity arose.[130]

In October 1928, two men working for the Admiralty at Woolwich were challenged about their communist beliefs. One decided to give up communism and remained employed, but the other refused and was dismissed.[131] Somewhat ironically, the man who was dismissed, Percy Glading, would later go on to be jailed in 1938 having been convicted of spying for the Soviet Union. In 1928, his dismissal was challenged by the Amalgamated Engineering Union who argued, 'it was intolerable in the 20th century that a man should be denied employment in a Government establishment because of his political views.' The Civil Lord of the Admiralty explained that such a policy was enacted as communists believed in revolution and were potentially dangerous, as 'they may attempt sabotage such as blowing up ammunition'.[132]

Individuals who were believed to be communists were initially given a warning that there was a policy in place not to employ communists in government establishments. 'Active' communists would be informed that unless they gave up their communism, they would be dismissed; those who were communists but took no active part 'in the furtherance of communism' would be 'warned accordingly' that communists would not be employed by the government. The policy of providing a warning was, however, later discontinued as MI5 believed it revealed to communists that the authorities were aware of their activities and had the potential to drive communist activity underground.[133] In 1936, further action was deemed to be necessary in dealing with the problem of 'untrustworthy employees' in Defence Departments after several cases of sabotage were suspected to have been carried out by communists. This led to the introduction of an early form of security vetting, whereby MI5 would check the details of new employees working in Defence Departments.[134]

The policy of preventing communists from being employed in certain roles was painstakingly designed by civil servants and other establishment officials, most of whom were keenly aware of the need to protect both security and civil liberties. For hardline anti-communists within the intelligence community, however, the action taken to curb communists did not go far enough. On separate occasions, Basil Thomson, Wyndham Childs, and MI5 DG Sir Vernon Kell lobbied the government to curb CPGB activity and possibly even ban it.[135] Correspondence from the King's Private Secretary, Lord Stamfordham, in 1925 suggests that even George V believed the government should act; Stamfordham told the Prime Minister that the monarch wondered if the time had come 'for a more vigorous and drastic policy against these enemies of law and order whose avowed object is the subversion of our whole social and political order.'[136]

In his memoirs, Childs recorded his disappointment that the governments he worked under 'refused to strike one overwhelming and final blow against the Communist organisation'. He wished to be allowed to use the 'full force of the Law' to 'smash' the Party, and suggested that the Prime Minister, Stanley Baldwin, prevented decisive action from being taken.[137] Childs was correct. During the interwar years, Britain was largely led by moderate characters, in the shape of Baldwin, Lloyd George and James Ramsay MacDonald, who did not subscribe to the more extreme views held by hardliners about the threat communism posed. Senior Whitehall mandarins also played a key role in restraining the excesses of the most virulent anti-communists in government and persuaded them to pursue less hardline policies.[138] It was believed better to tolerate and monitor communists than ban them. Outlawing the Party would most likely have driven communists underground, making it more difficult for the authorities to track, and may even have drawn more sympathy to its cause.[139]

The Wrong Target?

Although intelligence officials undertook extensive investigations into communism, their actions were focused too narrowly—on rank-and-file members of the CPGB. They overlooked individuals who were committed to the ideology of communism but were not members of the CPGB, and such people were thus able to cause significant damage to British security. Wyndham Childs wrote in his memoirs that the CPGB was made up entirely of 'wasters, work-shies, half-wits and professional agitators', and that he did not believe that a rational person could be attracted by communist ideology.[140] It was commonly thought that communism would only be attractive to the less-educated and the working class. The authorities did not believe that those educated at public schools, middle-class individuals, and those in professional jobs were disposed to believe in communism.[141]

These attitudes meant that during the 1920s, Special Branch was entirely unaware of the existence of two Soviet informers within its midst. Two Special Branch officers, Inspector Hubertus van Ginhoven and Sergeant Charles Jane, had been recruited in the early 1920s by William Norman Ewer to provide 'inside information'. Ewer, an avowed communist and foreign editor of the *Daily Herald*, ran a network of communist agents, using his organisation, the Federated Press of America, to 'provide journalistic cover for espionage'.[142] One of the members of Ewer's network, a former Special Branch sergeant known by the pseudonym 'Albert Allen', made clear that 'any move that [Scotland Yard] was about to make against the Communist Party or any of its personnel was nearly always known well in advance to Ewer who actually warned the persons concerned'.[143] It was further discovered that the informants had given Ewer the location of the headquarters of MI5 and MI6, thereby making it possible for his network to track intelligence officers. The informants were also asked to get access to the index cards in the Special Branch registry, to provide information on the 'suspect list' of names sent to the ports and to find out the names of individuals whose correspondence was intercepted.[144] MI5 concluded in a 1930 report that, as a result of the information provided,

> Ewer was enabled to give warning to suspects and subversive operations of suspicions entertained or of projected police action, to nullify the effect of security measures, to cripple

enquiry and thus positively enhance the successful operations of the Communist conspiracy in the UK and its promotion from abroad.[145]

Ginhoven and Jane were dismissed from Special Branch but not prosecuted.[146] The penetration of Special Branch contributed to its being stripped of the primary responsibility of countering communist espionage and subversion in Britain in 1931.[147]

The Security Service also missed the most subversive communists whilst focusing on those who posed little threat. MI5's investigations into the Party were not without success—most notably their discovery of the espionage of CPGB member Percy Glading—but were too narrowly focused.[148] More time should have been spent on communists who were not rank-and-file Party members, particularly those in higher social classes who were attracted to communism at a younger age, particularly at university. Such people had the ability to pose a much more significant threat to the British State through infiltrating its institutions—the prime example of this being the notorious Cambridge Five. The five—Guy Burgess, Donald Maclean, Kim Philby, Anthony Blunt and John Cairncross—were recruited to spy for the Soviets whilst at Cambridge University during the 1930s and subsequently worked in various branches of the British State, including MI5, MI6 and the Foreign Office, which enabled them to gain information to pass on to Moscow. Despite their associations with communism, the early security vetting procedures in the 1920s and 1930s had no impact upon them since the procedures focused only on individuals working in Defence Departments and did not include 'black-coated' office workers.[149]

In retrospect, it is obvious that intelligence agencies should have spent longer directing their investigations towards individuals of a greater social standing. There was evidence that communist groups were forming at elite universities as early as 1920. In 1921, Basil Thomson included accounts of developing communist cells at both Oxford and Cambridge in his reports to the cabinet.[150] In November of that year, Thomson reported on correspondence between Arthur Reade, a communist leader at Oxford, and Arthur

Nott, chairman of the Young Communist League (YCL). In the letter, Reade made the goals of the Oxford communist group very clear,

> Our object is to stir up a communist nucleus among the Varsity men, who will be going out as schoolmasters, scientific workers, literary men and professional and 'intellectual' workers in general that may take their place in the Revolutionary working class movement.[151]

Such a declaration is even more notable when it is considered that in September 1920, correspondence had been intercepted which showed British communists calling for 'Government Departments and public offices, the Army, the Post Office, the Telegraph Service, wireless stations and newspaper offices' to be covertly infiltrated.[152]

The CPGB made serious moves to attract 'people who are capable'— intellectuals, students, authors, doctors and other professionals—to the Party in the early 1930s. Willie Gallacher visited the Communist Party group at Cambridge University in 1934 and made clear, 'we want ... good scientists, historians and teachers ... We want you to study and become good students.' The Security Service did not take note of this, and thus did not investigate the relevant type of people. Action was only belatedly taken at the end of the 1930s, when one of MI5's chief spymasters, Maxwell Knight, sought to penetrate the communist movement at Oxford University.[153] Knight was particularly aware of the threat covert communists could pose. A colleague later revealed that he had talked of how the Russians would 'recruit a young man at university with Communist views, tell him to dissociate himself from the Party, watch him and keep him on ice for years. Then one day they will come to him and say: "Now we want you to do this..."'[154]

Although he would not have known at the time, Knight was describing almost exactly what had happened with the Cambridge Five. He was, however, an isolated voice, and his analysis gained little traction within the intelligence establishment. Intelligence officials had chances from the early 1920s onwards to concentrate their investigations on the communist subversive influence within the upper classes and the establishment. However, in the words of Christopher Andrew, they 'remained curiously traditional in their search for [subversion], concentrating their attentions on the labour movement, the armed services, the CPGB apparat and agents from abroad'.[155]

The men charged with keeping Britain secure at the time simply could not comprehend that individuals of a background similar to their own were capable of posing a threat. George Carey Foster, who later became head of security at the Foreign Office stated that 'for centuries the Office had operated on trust and in that family atmosphere they couldn't conceive that there was a wrong 'un amongst them.'[156] Kim Philby believed that officials had a 'genuine mental block which stubbornly resisted the belief that respected members of the establishment could [spy for Russia]'.[157] Another of the Cambridge spies, Guy Burgess, suggested that 'class blinkers' prevented officials from ever suspecting he could be a spy. Born to a middle-class family, attending Eton and being an 'intellectual' meant, he believed, that 'people like me are beyond suspicion.'[158]. These 'class blinkers' meant that officials did not have their views challenged and, according to the historian Hugh Trevor-Roper, led 'the British Secret Service ... [to become] divorced from the "public" bureaucracy'. As those present within the intelligence community had '[been] recruited by patronage', he believed it 'acquired some of the character of a coterie; and it preserved, as such coteries easily do, outmoded habits of thought.'[159]

'Behind Socialism Stands Communism'

The unchallenged groupthink that pervaded much of the establishment during the 1920s and 1930s not only led officials to miss the threat posed by their 'own', but also led them to be over-suspicious of individuals who did not come from the same class or hold the same political views. Many within the intelligence community as well as the wider establishment were deeply suspicious of differing views. Such opinions are best exemplified by the words of Admiral Sir Reginald 'Blinker' Hall, wartime

Director of Naval Intelligence, 'everyone who is not a Tory is either a German, a Sinn Féiner or a Bolshevist'.[160]

This deep-seated suspicion of those who had more left-wing political views meant that, when the first Labour government was formed in January 1924, many within the British intelligence community and wider establishment were not merely suspicious of their new political masters, but also fearful. The trepidation many held about communism encouraged concerns about the overtly socialist Labour Party. There was a widely held belief that socialism was not much different from communism. Winston Churchill expressed such a view, saying, 'behind socialism stands communism; behind communism stands Moscow, that dark, sinister, evil power which has made its appearance in the world'.[161] The Labour Party was perceived to be little different from the Communist Party and, in 1922, Wyndham Childs wrote that the differences between the two were 'in regard to methods rather than aims.'[162] Many feared that the Labour Party was a wolf in sheep's clothing; the Conservative Lord Birkenhead said as much when he stated that those who led Labour came across as 'moderate men' but were merely fronts for the 'avowed extremists' from which the Labour movement 'derives its vitality and driving power'.[163]

The view that the Labour Party was a threat to constitutional government in Britain was widely held amongst traditionalists. When the Party gained power, taking office, as a minority administration, on 22 January 1924 (ironically the day after Lenin's death) such fears exploded.[164] The Earl of Derby, Secretary of State for War, 1916–18, felt compelled to write to the King imploring that he 'should not let Labour take office.' The King's Private Secretary, Lord Stamfordham, responded, stating, 'His Majesty ... was not in the least alarmed ... at the prospect of a Labour government ... never doubted their loyalty or patriotism and felt that the best interests of the country would be the primary aim of their policy'.[165] This more sanguine position was also taken by Stanley Baldwin and another former Prime Minister, Herbert Asquith. Baldwin believed that the election of a Labour government at some time was inevitable and merely represented democracy in action, whilst Asquith simply did not view the new Prime Minister Ramsay MacDonald's politics as in any way revolutionary.[166]

Despite the position of the King and former Prime Ministers, much of the reaction to the new government bordered on hysterical. The *Daily Mail* wrote that since Labour was now in power 'Britain would sink to the position of an outlaw State, like Soviet Russia, and would be viewed by all the free nations with well-deserved dislike and distrust'.[167] For Churchill, the election of a Labour government was 'a serious national misfortune such as has usually befallen a great state only on the morrow of defeat in war',[168] whilst one of Baldwin's former cabinet ministers, Sir William Joynson-Hicks, referred to the new administration as being 'interlopers' who were 'against the Constitution.'[169]

With historical distance, this hysteria appears to be overdramatic. The Labour Party was a fully constitutional political party, and its leadership was fervently anti-communist. These fears were not, however, entirely without basis, especially in the context of the global political atmosphere at the time. In an intelligence report in 1920, Basil Thomson wrote that a bloody revolution was unlikely in Britain and judged that if a revolution was forthcoming, it would be through 'gradual evolution through the ballot box.' As the Communist Party was never popular enough to gain any ground during elections, members of the intelligence community worried that Communists could gain power via the Labour Party.[170] Indeed, this is exactly what Moscow had instructed British Communists to do. In 1920, Lenin urged the CPGB to support the Labour Party 'in the same way a rope supports a hanged man' and, ahead of the 1922 General Election, the Comintern issued a message to the British working men and women, urging them to vote for Labour to force it into becoming a more radical and revolutionary party.[171]

Although the Labour Party rejected attempts by the CPGB to affiliate with it in the early 1920s, other actions it took may have indicated that it was not as tough on communism as it claimed.[172] Communists were allowed to stand as official Labour Party candidates in elections until 1924 and were not banned from attending the Party conference until 1928.[173] Some of the fringes of the Labour Party also expressed solidarity with communists and their aims and, at a local level, several district Labour Parties were happy to work with communists.[174] Minority elements of the Party may have tolerated communism, but the Labour leadership was fervently anti-communist, loathed the ideology and would not have countenanced any alliance with it. The most senior men in the Labour Party in the 1920s—James Ramsay MacDonald, Phillip Snowden, Arthur Henderson, JR Clynes and Jimmy Thomas— were, in the words of one historian, 'democratic socialists, refusing absolutely to flirt with extremism'.[175] They saw no comparison between socialism and communism, believing that socialism respected democracy whilst communism believed in violence and dictatorship.[176]

Henderson, who would serve as Home Secretary under MacDonald, led the Labour Party twice during the 1910s. He was a Methodist who enjoyed playing lawn bowls and had served in the War Cabinet.[177] In 1918, as Labour leader, he had stated, 'If you want me to lead the Labour Movement as a Bolshevist I give you notice I am done with the job. Would to God some of our people who are espousing the Bolshevik cause knew what it was'.[178] Clynes, who preceded MacDonald as Labour leader and then served as his deputy leader and Lord Privy Seal, declared that 'a communist is no more a left-wing member of the Labour Party than an atheist is a left-wing member of the Christian Church'.[179] Yet, even such strong denunciations would not have mollified the intelligence community when the Party took office in 1924. The two most senior men in the new government, Prime Minister Ramsay MacDonald and his Chancellor, Phillip Snowden, had long been on the radar of MI5 and Special Branch. Both organisations were likely to have held security files on the occupants of Number 10 and Number 11 Downing Street, as well as on a number of other members of the government.[180]

Suspicions appear to have been raised about MacDonald at the beginning of the First World War. A pacifist, he was observed making an anti-war speech in Birmingham, and whilst no action was taken against him, the Director of Public Prosecutions believed that the speech 'was one for which he richly deserved prosecution'.[181] MI5 also considered recommending MacDonald's prosecution for seditious oratory during the war, but decided against it.¹⁸² During 1919, MacDonald's name appeared in a number of Basil Thomson's weekly reports. One account suggested that he had attempted to organise a general strike simultaneously in France, Italy and Britain as 'a mark of sympathy with the Soviet form of government.'¹⁸³ Such an account is, however, highly questionable as, according to MacDonald's biographer David Marquand, by the summer of 1919 he 'had come to the conclusion … that the cruelty and fanaticism of the Bolsheviks were not accidental excesses, but the inevitable consequences of the Leninist creed'.¹⁸⁴

MacDonald's movements do appear to have been extensively tracked by intelligence officials, and he was seemingly aware of it. In August 1919, Thomson reported an account from 'a Frenchman who met Mr Ramsay MacDonald at Lucerne.' MacDonald was quoted as having told the source that 'he was under strict surveillance' and 'that the English government was seeking for the flimsiest pretext on which to accuse him'.¹⁸⁵ Thomson's report also quotes from 'a recent letter' written by MacDonald which suggests that his correspondence was also intercepted.¹⁸⁶ No files have been released which detail the surveillance on MacDonald, but it was hinted at in an article published in *John Blunt* magazine by Horatio Bottomley in 1928. Headlined 'The "Yard's" Secret Report on Ex-Premier', Bottomley's article alleged that he had seen a copy of a 'confidential Report by Scotland Yard dealing with the activities of Mr Ramsay MacDonald from the year 1916 down to 1921'. It is likely that the document was leaked to Bottomley, and his article detailed a number of times in which MacDonald had come to Special Branch attention. Notably, Bottomley reported that the file was closed in 1921, with the conclusion from an intelligence officer that,

> Events in 1920 … have proved MacDonald to be a Constitutional Socialist, and not a Bolshevist. He has opposed, actively and successfully the Reds in the ranks of his own Party, and it is largely due to his leadership that the Independent Labour Party has not become affiliated to the Third International.¹⁸⁷

The detail of Bottomley's report suggests he had probably seen an official document. Although a past dislike of MacDonald and conviction for fraud may lead to Bottomley's account being treated with the utmost scepticism, there are two factors that make it likely that his account of the document was true. Firstly, the article contains information on MacDonald's movements in 1919 that appear very similar to accounts chronicled in Basil Thomson's weekly reports.[188] Secondly, Home Office files show that the article led to a probe within the department as to the veracity of the information in Bottomley's account and the source of the leak.

After investigating the matter, Home Office officials discovered that the information in Bottomley's report quoted, almost verbatim, from 'a book of biographies of persons who came into prominence during the war largely on account of their pacifist tendencies.' Although the investigation did not prove the existence of a specific Special Branch file on MacDonald, it seems highly likely that one would have been opened because of his pacifist beliefs; as one civil servant wrote in 1928, 'in view of the nature of R. MacDonald's activities during the war a dossier must have been compiled'.[189]

Intelligence officials' concerns about MacDonald may have dissipated by 1920, but it is still likely that a significant number were apprehensive about him and his government in January 1924. During the war, notice was also taken of the activities of Philip Snowden due to his own links to the pacifist movement. The Home Office held a large file detailing the 'pacifist activities' of both Snowden and his wife. Reports were routinely produced on Snowden's speeches and the authorities discussed prosecuting him under the Defence of the Realm Act on a number of occasions, believing his declarations to be 'deliberately mischievous'.[190] The Home Office also held a file on the pacifist activities of another cabinet member, Charles Philips Trevelyan.[191] Trevelyan was also a notable opponent of the security and intelligence services, which he believed should be dismantled.[192]

Unsure about the new men in power, the intelligence community would not have been calmed by some of the government's actions. MacDonald's relationship with Wyndham Childs was fraught from the start and he saw his request to view his own Special Branch file refused.[193] The Prime Minister also made clear to Childs his scepticism of the need for weekly intelligence reports, suggested that they should include reference to fascism as well as communism, and declined to circulate them to the cabinet.[194] Within weeks of taking office, the new government provided further reason for intelligence officials to be alarmed when it provided de jure recognition of the Bolshevik regime, becoming the first government in the West to do so. Although this was not as radical as it first appeared, the Foreign Office was so concerned about the new government that they declined to notify MacDonald of the GC&CS's intercepts of Soviet traffic for several months.[195] The final incident that raised doubts about Labour's attitude towards communism came in August 1924, when the government decided to withdraw charges, issued under the Incitement to Mutiny Act, against a communist, John Ross Campbell.[196] The government was accused of intervening in the law, and many Conservatives suggested that the real reason the prosecution was dropped was due to pressure from the communists.[197] The so-called 'Campbell case' caused the government to fall, as MacDonald's administration lost a vote of confidence in the Commons, and led to a general election being called for 29 October 1924.

Despite fears to the contrary, the first Labour government proved to be moderate and capable of holding high office. The government respected and continued traditions, wearing court dress at official functions with the King.[198] Ministers worked well with civil servants—having secretly pledged 'not to annoy the Civil Service'—and the Prime Minister enjoyed a jovial relationship with Cabinet Secretary Maurice Hankey. Even the most radical member of the cabinet, John Wheatley, was described by the Assistant Cabinet Secretary, Thomas Jones, as being 'Pale Pink rather than Turkey Red.'[199] Although there was an initial reluctance by both MacDonald and some ministers to engage with the intelligence community, the two eventually found some common ground.[200] Eventually, the Prime Minister took notice of weekly intelligence reports after Childs had included evidence of communist attempts to subvert the Labour Party.[201] The Home

Secretary, Arthur Henderson, defended Special Branch in the Commons and, 'to MI5's relief', continued to authorise HOWs on leading Communists.[202] The government even responded to industrial action in a way which differed little from the manner in which previous governments would have responded. It reactivated the strikebreaking organisation, the Supply and Transport Committee, during a dock strike in February and in March, and went as far as to proclaim a state of emergency during a London transport dispute.[203] The cabinet later set up a committee on industrial unrest to consider the communist influence on a wave of strikes, during which it viewed and accepted the legitimacy of MI5 and Special Branch reports.[204] Whilst the government's actions proved it was fit to hold office and was moderate in nature, events during its dying days make it clear that not all of those working in intelligence were convinced.

The Zinoviev Letter

Four days before the 1924 General Election, on 25 October, the *Daily Mail* published a letter purporting to be from the head of the Comintern, Grigori Zinoviev, to the CPGB. The letter appeared to suggest that the government had been coerced by communists and radicals into normalising relations with the Bolshevik government.[205] It was, MacDonald later said, a 'political bomb' designed to influence the election campaign. Although there is a consensus among many historians that the leak was not a part of an orchestrated establishment plot, it seems that rogue elements of both MI5 and MI6 leaked the letter in an attempt to damage Labour's electoral prospects. As Christopher Andrew has argued, 'those responsible intended ... to sabotage Labour's prospects of [electoral] victory.'[206]

The Labour Party lost the 1924 General Election, with Baldwin's Conservative Party winning 412 seats and a large majority in the House of Commons. For many politicians on both the Right and the Left, the Zinoviev letter had played a crucial role in the result. The proprietor of the *Daily Mail*, Lord Rothermere, who had published the letter, believed it had cost Labour 'something like

100 seats.'[207] Yet, this may not have been quite the case. Although they lost seats, the Labour vote increased by over one million. It was the decline of the Liberal Party, which lost 118 of its 158 seats, which ensured a strong Conservative victory.[208]

Although the impact of the Zinoviev letter in deciding the results of the general election may, therefore, be overstated, it was still important. Not only was there a consensus at the time that its impact was significant, but the letter appears to have been leaked in an effort to damage Labour in the election. In 1998, after decades of speculation, the then Chief Historian of the Foreign Office, Gill Bennett, was commissioned to investigate the case. In her report, Bennett concluded that the letter was almost certainly a forgery and stated that it was very likely to have been deliberately leaked.[209]

Although there is no definitive evidence, it is possible that members of the intelligence services who were suspicious of the Labour Party deliberately leaked the letter to ensure damage to the Party and the government. Christopher Andrew raises this in his authorised history of the Security Service, stating that those responsible 'convinced themselves that they were acting in the national interest—to remove from power a government whose susceptibility to Soviet and pro-Soviet pressure made it a threat to national security.'[210] According to Bennett, certain members of the intelligence community had a clear allegiance to the Conservative Party—notably Joseph Ball of MI5 and Desmond Morton of SIS—and they may have leaked the letter.[211] Ball is also mentioned by Andrew, who states that his 'subsequent lack of scruples for using intelligence for party political advantage strongly suggests, but does not prove, that he was willing to do so' in 1924.[212] Ball is a particularly significant character in the affair, not least because after retiring from the Security Service, he went on to become Director of Publicity for the Conservative Party in 1927.[213] There is some evidence that he had previously considered leaking information to the press when dealing with a case of 'suspected treachery by British left-wingers'. When working for the Conservatives, Ball described the Labour Party as the 'enemy' and opined that the 'revolutionary tail wags the Labour dog'. Whilst there was no definitive evidence to suggest that Ball leaked the letter, 'such an action would have suited his *modus operandi*'.[214] Ball likely did not act alone, and fingers have also been pointed at Admiral 'Blinker' Hall and Lieutenant-Colonel Freddie Browning, both of whom had worked in intelligence, as being involved in the publication of the letter.[215]

If intelligence officials were involved in the Zinoviev affair, they were most likely rogue elements working on their own. Although many intelligence officials may not have felt entirely easy about Labour being in office, it seems unlikely that the majority would have believed in plotting to bring the government down. Whether or not they would have mourned the collapse of the government is, however, another story. As one Whitehall official wrote in November 1924, 'as you know the civil service has no politics, but I fancy they would contribute heavily to a statue to Zinovieff and Mr Campbell, for the effect they had on the election'.[216]

In the years after the Zinoviev affair, Whitehall officials appear to have been acutely aware of the need to avoid any allegations of political bias against the intelligence community.[217] During a meeting of the Prime Minister's Secret Service Committee in March 1927, Sir William Tyrrell, Permanent Under-Secretary of State for Foreign Affairs, recalled a recent conversation he had had with Stanley Baldwin, the Prime Minister at the time. He stated that Baldwin was fearful that the work of Special Branch 'might at any moment give rise to a scandal, owing to the Labour Party obtaining some plausible pretext to complain that a government department was being employed for party politics'. Tyrrell went on to say that 'Home politics were tending more to a contest between Conservatives and Socialists and there was a grave danger that the government of the day might sooner or later turn to Scotland Yard for information needed in the party struggle'.[218] The concern about the way in which the Labour Party would view the intelligence community's work was also expressed in 1928, after the article in *John Blunt* revealing the existence of a file on Ramsay MacDonald. A note from September 1928 stated, 'the article is certain to lead to Questions when the House meets and the Labour Party will probably allege that it appears evident that the police are being used for spying on their legitimate activities'.[219]

The General Strike

Members of the British establishment in the early-to-mid 1920s were wary of the Labour Party, not only because of its supposed links to communism but also because it was perceived to challenge the status quo. Labour's actions in government did not suggest that it was anti-establishment and wanted to break up the old order of Britain, but the perception that it did greatly clouded the judgement of those working within the British State. For many of these individuals, an alternative political outlook was not simply seen as indicative of people with different backgrounds and experiences having a different attitude as to how to improve British society; instead it was seen, in some way, as being suspect.

There are numerous examples from 1920s Britain of establishment figures appearing to feel threatened by apparent challenges to the status quo. The attitude of some British officials suggested that only dangerous revolutionaries opposed the old order. The inability to distinguish between legitimate democratic dissent and a revolutionary challenge meant that those who challenged traditional British policies were, too often, immediately written off as insurgents. This kind of attitude was displayed by Basil Thomson in 1920. Discussing apparent 'home grown revolutionaries', he opined that the description fitted anyone who was 'pro anybody by whom it could be shown that his country was in the wrong'. He said that this type of person would be pro-Boer, pro-Indian, a pacifist, or a conscientious objector. In effect, Thomson suggested that anyone who opposed the policy of the government should be viewed as revolutionary.[220] Whilst it was not wrong to suggest that radical agitators would always oppose the policies of the British government, his analysis dismissed those with legitimate opinions who disagreed with governmental policy. This not only displayed a lack of empathy with or understanding of different opinions, but helps to show why those who challenged the old order were often perceived as being fundamentally dangerous. In addition to this, the belief that communists were ubiquitous and making every effort to subvert British democracy meant that many establishment members tended to view any challenge as being communist-inspired. Communism was too often seen as responsible. In the words of the former cabinet minister, Lord Crawford, 'we naturally ascribe all of our ills to this horrible phantom ... always lurking in the background, and all the more alarming because it is tireless and unseen.'[221]

The combined concerns about communism and a challenge to the status quo meant that in May 1926, when a General Strike began, many British establishment members thought the country was facing insurrection. The dispute was fundamentally over wages and working hours but was portrayed by the government as something which threatened British democracy.[222] On this, King George V fundamentally disagreed with his ministers. Prior to the outbreak of the strike, one coalmine owner told the King that the miners were 'a damned lot of revolutionaries.' Feeling sympathy for their plight, the monarch replied, 'try living on their wages before you judge them.'[223]

Throughout the dispute, the government produced a daily newspaper, the *British Gazette*, which declared that 'Constitutional Government is being attacked'.[224] Some members of the cabinet had preconceived ideas about the strike; hardliners such as the Home Secretary, Sir William Joynson-Hicks, were, according to Christopher Andrew, 'emotionally incapable of seeing the General Strike as anything other than a deep-laid plot'.[225] Yet even the more moderate Baldwin sought to draw attention to the danger the strike posed and spoke of how it 'imperilled ... the freedom of our very constitution.'[226] By being framed in such a manner, the strike was stripped of its legitimacy.

The reaction of intelligence officials to the outbreak of the strike was to form a temporary emergency section of MI5, based in the War Office and known as MI(B). The new unit, commanded by MI5 Deputy DG, Eric Holt-Wilson, was staffed by current and former MI5 officers—some of whom had to be brought out of retirement. It also recruited a number of temporary agents to collect intelligence during the strike through infiltrating unions, communist cells and the armed forces.[227] Agents were deployed around the country to report on various aspects of the strike, including the policy, plans and intentions of strikers, strikers' resources and morale, public sentiment, troop morale and any communist activity linked to the strike.[228]

The agents sought to ascertain the mood of the public in different regions of the country and regularly sent reports back to MI(B). One report detailed the minute-to-minute movements of a well-known socialist in Stratford-upon-Avon.[229] Other reports make clear that agents frequently posed as communists or acted as agents provocateurs to gain information. In the East End of London, one agent was able to discover how to obtain arms without a police licence.[230] Despite this, what was most striking from many of the reports was the lack of revolutionary or violent intentions amongst the men. Reports from Birmingham suggested that men were not inclined to strike, were keen to get back to work, and would even be prepared to volunteer for the emergency services if they received protection.[231] In Aldershot, agents visited bars and eating houses that were popular with soldiers and sought to start political arguments. They found, however, that when they expressed subversive opinions, they did not gain any support from the soldiers, who displayed no 'disloyal feelings'. Working men and labourers were also found to be 'perfectly loyal.'[232]

The strike did not develop in the way in which some members of the establishment feared, ending after only nine days on 12 May. Almost immediately afterwards, most people could not understand why there had been such concern; the strike never had any revolutionary aims, and those who led it, such as the TUC General Secretary, Walter Citrine, had no intention of subverting the constitution.[233] It is, however, important to note that concerns about the strike were not confined to right-wing anti-communists. Some within the Labour Party, such as MacDonald and the unionist Jimmy Thomas, had worried that radicals could gain some control. Even Citrine himself confided in his diary, at the beginning of the dispute, a fear that if the unions lost control, the dispute could turn into a revolutionary situation.[234]

Communists did attempt to interfere in the strike, but the influence they had was negligible.[235] Despite this, the day after the strike had ended, the head of MI6, Admiral Hugh Sinclair, sent a memorandum to Wyndham Childs purporting to prove 'beyond doubt' that the General Strike had been 'conceived many months ago at Moscow'. He also wrote that the Soviet 'directors of the movement' had 'found facile accomplices' in British trade unionism, and that 'through the combined efforts of these unscrupulous people, the responsible Trade Union leaders have been exploited and swept along'.[236] Childs himself wrote in his memoirs that the Strike would never have happened 'but for Communism.'[237] There is little evidence, however, that such statements were true. It is correct that money was sent from the Soviet Union, apparently to support the families of those on strike, but the donations were rejected by the TUC.[238]

Apparent evidence of communist or Soviet involvement in the strike was seized upon by hardline cabinet ministers such as Joynson-Hicks. In June 1926, he circulated a memorandum in which he stated that the Soviets were 'without doubt providing money on the first day of the General Strike for the financing of the strike.'[239] Although he later retracted such a falsehood, Joynson-Hicks and other hardliners made use of the evidence as an opportunity to argue for firmer action against the Soviets.[240] They used the fact that the Soviets had sought to influence the strike as further evidence of their insidious involvement within Britain and of the need to sever Anglo-Soviet diplomatic relations.[241] The General Strike began the process that resulted in the diplomatic breach following the ARCOS raid in May 1927.

The strike was merely another example of the way in which the British establishment saw opposition as inevitably inspired by Soviet-backed communism. Such was the fear of communism, the authorities were willing to use almost anyone to help counter it. In the months before the strike broke out, volunteers were recruited for the Organisation for the Maintenance of Supplies (OMS) to help maintain essential public services and render industrial action impotent.[242] Volunteers included members of right-wing patriotic groups and fascists.[243] The presence of fascists was not an oversight; the government was well aware that they were signing up to the OMS and expressed few reservations. In September 1925, whilst discussing the types of people he expected to volunteer, Joynson-Hicks wrote, 'the Fascists [and] the Crusaders ... are well known, and, I think to be depended upon. I have seen their leaders several times.'[244] Weeks later, he addressed the topic again, informing the cabinet that 'various unofficial organisations had been formed' to provide volunteer labour in the event of a strike, 'including the OMS, the Chambers of Commerce, the Fascisti and the Crusaders, and it was understood that the persons who volunteered under these unofficial organisations would, in case of emergency, be at the disposal of the Government'.[245] A further acknowledgement of the role fascists would play in the strike appears in cabinet minutes from April 1926, days before the strike began. The minutes state, 'the Cabinet agreed: To take note that the main Fascist movement had been broken, and that the best of the so-called Fascists had attached themselves to the OMS'.[246]

It should be noted that people who were known as fascists in the 1920s were not identical, in their political outlook or methods, to those who gained prominence in the 1930s. Fascists were also prevented from joining the OMS collectively under the banner of their own organisation, and were only accepted as long as they temporarily ended their association with fascist movements.[247] Nevertheless, the very fact that people who, at the very least, held extremely questionable views, were accepted as part of what was, in some way, an anti-communist crusade says a great deal. The establishment's profound fear of communism not only led it to take strong action against the legal far-left but appears to have resulted in a greater degree of leniency towards the legal far-right.

Conclusion

Throughout the 1920s and into the 1930s, politicians and members of the intelligence community were highly fearful of communists subverting the British constitution and threatening the defence of the realm. Whilst it is true that there was potential for communists to pose a threat, those officials charged with investigating the danger did not focus their inquiries correctly. They tended to overestimate the threat posed by rank-and-file communists whilst underestimating, and even overlooking, the much graver threat posed by secret, more well-to-do communists.

Often the reasons for investigating communism were motivated by a sincere fear by officials who believed that society in post-Armistice Britain was decaying. They believed this was prompted by communist influences and thus sought to investigate the ideology to deal with the root cause. These officials had reasons to be fearful, and their anxieties were understandable, but their lack of knowledge about the motivations of many of the working-classes who were attracted to radical politics prevented investigations from being successful. The lack of diversity of opinion within the intelligence establishment prevented officials from understanding the reasons behind the involvement of many working-class people in radical politics. Had they better understood these motivations, they would have realised that only a small number of individuals were fully committed to radicalism in Britain, and that many had only temporarily turned to radical politics because they were unhappy with their personal circumstances.

The inability of numerous intelligence officials to understand different viewpoints meant that they often undertook surveillance operations that were, in all likelihood, unnecessary, and had deep suspicions about people and organisations who did not pose a subversive threat. Officials regarded any opinions and ideas different from their own as a threat to the State. Such challenges to the 'old order' were, in fact, a result of the ideas of individuals who had no revolutionary aims and believed things should be done differently to improve British society. The kind of groupthink that led to an overreaction towards the Labour Party and the General Strike meant that intelligence officials failed to notice the members of the establishment who were committed to communism. Communism was simply not seen as something by which well-educated individuals from a good background could be seduced.

Communism posed a genuine threat in interwar Britain, and the Soviets did wish to subvert and damage the country. Whilst surveillance of communists during the interwar period did have some successes, often it merely revealed information to intelligence officials that they would likely have already known. Investigating the communist threat to Britain was an extremely difficult task, but the way in which intelligence officials went about it led them to overreact and over-investigate what were minor threats. The misdirection of surveillance operations meant that, whilst the intelligence agencies had amassed large amounts of information about the activities of British communists by the 1930s, they remained unaware of the most threatening aspects of the communist subversion in Britain.

2

FRIEND OR FOE?

FASCISTS IN INTERWAR BRITAIN

On 27 November 1923, Lord Stamfordham, Private Secretary to King George V, wrote a letter to H.R. Boyd, a civil servant at the Home Office. Replying, on Buckingham Palace-headed notepaper, to Boyd's correspondence from the previous day, he wrote, 'Your letter about the "British Fascisti" takes away my breath'.[1] Stamfordham was shocked, having been informed by Boyd that the founder of the newly-formed British Fascisti (BF), a Miss Lintorn-Orman, had told a police inspector that there would be no problem in obtaining the permission of the King to use the Royal Crown on the organisation's emblem. She explained this was because Stamfordham was 'a personal friend of hers and a friend of her organisation.'[2] Stamfordham stated, 'for the life of me I cannot imagine who Miss Lintorn-Orman can be—as to her being a personal friend of mine and my being a friend of her organisation, she must be under some painful delusion.' The BF dropped the idea of using the Crown as part of their emblem.[3]

The BF was founded in May 1923 by Lintorn-Orman and portrayed itself as the defender of Britain and Empire against communism and socialism.[4] The most prominent members of the BF were upper-middle class people and those of an aristocratic background, but members also comprised ex-military and naval officers, and 'lower ranks of loyal working-class toughs.'[5] Some of the more prominent members included Conservative MP Patrick Hannon, England Cricket Captain (1924–5) Arthur E.R. Gilligan and Colonel Sir Charles Burn, a former aide-de-camp to the King.[6] The BF stated that it had at least 100,000 members at one time, though such claims appear exaggerated; membership peaked in the mid-1920s with 'several thousand active members.'[7]

Although the BF boldly claimed to be defending Britain against the communist menace, it was not taken seriously by many of the population. It rarely appeared on the radar of the intelligence establishment and, when it did, it was mocked. One Special Branch memo on the movement stated that 'the BF was formed for the purpose of protecting the British Public from the machinations of the Communists!', whilst another report described Lintorn-Orman as 'a crank'.[8] Those on the Left were untroubled by the movement, whilst the wider public were bemused by it. Often the initials BF were said to be an abbreviation for 'Bloody Fools'.[9] Quite simply, when the BF did attract attention, people saw it as an organisation of eccentrics, an adult version of the Scout movement 'for those who had not grown up.'[10] They were, according to one Foreign Office official, 'treated with the derision and contempt they deserve'.[11]

In this context, it is understandable why the first formal extreme right-wing organisation in interwar Britain attracted minimal interest from security officials. Shortly after its formation in 1923, one Home Office official stated that it was 'hardly worth inquiry in its present stage.'[12] The lack of attention paid to the BF, especially in comparison with that paid to communists, is clear from Special Branch's weekly reports to the cabinet. Whilst communists were regularly mentioned in the reports, there were few references to fascists. When the BF was mentioned, it was only in the context of its relations to communism; it was noted that BF meetings had been interrupted by 'extremists'.[13] The only concern the authorities appeared to have about the Fascisti was that its members might cause a public order issue in clashes with 'extremists'. In October 1923, MI5's DG Vernon Kell wrote, from what we know of the BF I have no reason to imagine that they are anything but loyal. At the same time, I do not consider that the Fascisti would be desirable in this country. They would rather tend to create "breaches of the peace" and thus come into collision with the police.[14]

Writing months later to the Chief Constable of Gloucester Constabulary, Kell played down the BF's threat. He stated that the organisation was small and disorganised, although he admitted that the Security Service only had 'rather vague' information on the movement. In the short letter, Kell gave so little credence to the BF that he spent a paragraph writing about MI5's Christmas cards.[15]

Despite underplaying its threat, at the beginning of March 1924 MI5 did take out a HOW on the offices of the BF as it was believed that BF leaders were 'developing an organisation for the utilisation of force in the event of civil disturbance in this country.'[16] It is not entirely clear what information the HOW revealed about the BF. Despite the presence of undesirable individuals within the organisation, security officials did not seem to consider it capable of posing a significant threat and believed many of the BF's aims were implausible.[17] If it could pose any threat at all, it was thought to be to law and order and not through subversive activities.

'On our side'?

The BF portrayed itself as opposing Bolshevism and socialism and being strongly committed to 'defending the British Constitution and Empire.'[18] During the 1924 General Election campaign its members offered to police meetings for both the Conservative Party and, despite the BF's opposition to socialism, the Labour Party. The offer was, however, refused by Labour.[19] The BF also sought to prove its apparent commitment to constitutional order by proposing to attend political meetings of an 'extreme nature', 'heckle the speakers to their fullest extent without creating a breach of the peace' and organise counter-revolutionary meetings.[20]

The BF was particularly concerned about the emergence of communism in Britain, and shared, with much of the establishment, a loathing for the ideology. Fervent anti-communism made some of the BF's members useful allies for the State in combatting the so-called 'Red Menace.' As previously mentioned, BF members who had disaffiliated themselves from the movement played a part in strikebreaking during the 1926 General Strike. The BF's apparent support, however, went much further than mere strikebreaking; it also supplied the intelligence community with information it had collected on those active within the communist movement on an ad hoc basis. By late 1924, an MI5 correspondence stated that 'SCOTLAND YARD is in close touch with the B.F.'[21]

The section of the BF which collected information that was passed on to Scotland Yard was known as 'K'. It was said to have been formed by some of the 'wilder or more youthful [BF] members' who wanted stronger action to be taken against communism and were 'determined to meet force with force'.[22] One MI5 document from 1924 explicitly stated that K had collected 'some fairly good' information which was 'of use to the police and led to an arrest'. This enabled the Fascisti to establish a closer liaison with Scotland Yard.[23] The same report detailed some of the activities of K, stating,

> "K" organised the heckling and breaking up of communist meetings ... They have raided some of the Communist HQ and have a store of arms in London. They are well organised and efficient and have done some quite good work from an intelligence point of view.[24]

Although the group had a store of arms—something which would usually cause alarm—it does not appear that the authorities were in any way concerned. Perhaps this was because of K's 'good intelligence work.' Indeed, it appears that on several occasions the authorities either turned a blind eye to, or were very lenient towards, members of K. In March 1925, K members were arrested and prosecuted after kidnapping the prominent communist, Harry Pollitt. In court, the kidnappers were acquitted after being defended by Sir Henry Curtis-Bennett, KC, a former MI5 officer. One of the kidnappers later wrote in a private letter, 'in the strictest confidence I can inform you that the police and the govt and all concerned are all on our side'.[25] Another K member made a similar statement after being arrested for breaking into a CPGB office in Glasgow, ransacking it, and stealing documents. Joseph McCall, who was convicted of the crime, told a court that the police had known about his undercover work before his arrest. The fact his sentence was so light after being found guilty—seven days imprisonment and a £3 fine—suggested that the authorities knew all about, and tacitly approved of, K's anti-communist crusade.[26]

Later in 1925, members of the National Fascisti, an offshoot of the BF, hijacked a *Daily Herald* delivery van.[27] The hijackers were initially charged with larceny, but this was downgraded by the Public Prosecutor to a charge of breaching the peace. Having bound over the defendants, the magistrate dealing with the case was moved to remark that the Public Prosecutor had been 'extremely lenient in the matter.'[28] The incident was all the more controversial as it happened around the same time as twelve communists were convicted under the Incitement to Mutiny Act and jailed for several months. The trial involving the communists has long been regarded as a purely political prosecution and, by late 1925, the belief that fascists were being treated leniently was growing.[29] In the Commons, one MP argued that there was a 'serious danger that such action may destroy public confidence in the impartial administration of justice'.[30] The prominent socialist intellectual, George Bernard Shaw, remarked ironically that 'a mere withdrawal of the [larceny] charge ... was ... a very poor acknowledgement of their services to the Government; I think that they might at least be given the OBE at the first opportunity.'[31] Whilst it may have been simply the case that State officials believed fascists posed a minimal threat, the fact that they were fiercely anti-communist and apparently provided good intelligence may have led the authorities to treat BF members less severely than they should have done.

A Web of Ties

The BF was far from the only private organisation that provided the British intelligence community with information on communists during the 1920s. After the 1918 Armistice, intelligence budgets were vastly reduced, and intelligence officials found it cheaper and more effective to occasionally outsource some of the intelligence work on communism to private right-wing groups. Such groups on the radical Right had provided the authorities with information during World War One and these informal relationships continued into the interwar period.[32] The use of such groups was raised by Basil Thomson in 1920. 'It may be possible', he wrote, 'to use some of the unofficial agencies for combatting Bolshevism to expose the [communist] conspiracy and turn it into ridicule; to follow the [communist] conspirators about and question them at their own meetings'.[33]

The boundaries between private groups and the intelligence community became blurred during the interwar years. If any one individual epitomised the closeness between the intelligence community, the BF and other anti-communist right-wing groups, it was Maxwell Knight. In the 1930s, Knight was primarily responsible for MI5's investigations into fascism yet, somewhat paradoxically, during the 1920s, he had been a BF member. In his memoirs, Knight wrote that he had joined the BF in 1924, undercover at the behest of Sir George Makgill, a wealthy industrialist, fervent anti-communist and founder of the private Industrial Intelligence Bureau (IIB).[34] The IIB, financed by the Federation of British Industries and the Coal Owners' and Shipowners' Associations, collected intelligence on industrial unrest and subversion from communists.[35] Intriguingly, Makgill was a close friend of MI5's DG, Vernon Kell, and it is said that he had been encouraged by Kell to set up the IIB.[36]

Knight maintained throughout his life that he had never been a fascist, and that his association with the BF was purely professional. It is, however, doubtful that this relationship was as benign as he suggested. Writing in the authorised history of MI5, Christopher Andrew argues that at the time he was a member of the BF, 'Knight's political views had more in common with the BF than he was later willing to acknowledge'. Indeed, his first wife was the director of the BF Women's Units whilst, according to a young MI5 officer who worked closely with Knight after the Second World War, he 'had no time for democracy and believed that the country should be ruled by the social elite'.[37]

Knight may not have been a fascist when he joined the BF but appears to have had sympathies with the fascist cause by the time he left the organisation many years later. In his insightful biography of Knight, Henry Hemming has argued that he initially had to be 'in character' as an 'enthusiastic young fascist' as part of his undercover work. However, as time went by, it became harder 'to maintain the inner division between the fictional personality he had created and his inner self.'[38] During his time in the BF, Knight developed significant relationships, even friendships, with fellow members and these bonds increased his sense of loyalty to individual members.[39] Shortly after joining the BF, Knight became the organisation's Deputy Chief of Staff and Director of Intelligence; these roles made him responsible for collating intelligence reports on communists, running fascist agents inside Trade Unions and organising counter-espionage and sabotage operations.[40] Knight was also a prominent member of the K organisation and participated in a number of break-ins of CPGB offices.[41] He was fervently anti-communist and his actions displayed not only a firm commitment to the fascist cause but also a deeper sympathy with, and commitment to, the BF itself.

Knight's ties to the BF do not appear to have concerned the intelligence community; intelligence officials received reports from him even when he was a BF member. By the end of 1924, Knight was not only reporting to Makgill's IIB, but also provided intelligence to Special Branch and Desmond Morton of MI6. Some of his reports were even seen by MI5.[42] In 1925 Knight was invited by Kell to meetings of his Intelligence and Police dining club. At one of the dinners, Kell asked Knight if he would be interested in joining a reserve list of intelligence officers who could be used in an emergency.[43] Despite his fascist background, Knight was clearly viewed as a useful ally in the fight against communism. Although he gave up his position as BF Deputy Chief of Staff in 1927, he did not sever all ties with the BF, and made clear in print that he was still committed to his 'other fascist activities'.[44] In 1929, Knight began working more formally for Morton and officially became an MI6 agent. Seeking to combat communism, he ran a network of subagents who were embedded in the CPGB.[45] Despite this more formal arrangement with MI6, Knight remained a BF member, and it seems that he did not ultimately resign from the organisation until 1932, by which time he was working for MI5.[46]

Knight was not the only individual originally employed by Makgill's IIB who provided intelligence on communists to the British State. One of Knight's close associates, a man named James McGuirk Hughes, also worked for the IIB. Hughes was said to have had 'a peculiar gift' for street corner propaganda, intelligence work and sabotage inside left-wing organisations, and may well have collaborated with BF members in anti-communist activity.[47] Between 1920 and 1924, he was the Liverpool district secretary of another anti-communist Makgill organisation—the British Empire Union (BEU)—and he organised the infiltration of communist organisations, forgery, break-ins and the removal of confidential documents.[48] Hughes' anti-communist activities are notable because they appear to have been actively encouraged by Scotland Yard. In one report, Hughes wrote,

> we have the complete confidence and help of Scotland Yard, and in fact we have received payment from them ... our relations with the provincial police continue to be good ... We had placed under us a number of the plain cloths [sic] men of the Glasgow police.[49]

MI5 noted that Hughes was 'suspected of working with SY' and had been 'seen to visit SY on occasions.' One Security Service official wrote, 'there is reason to believe that he is also in receipt of money from SY; this however is not yet confirmed.'[50] MI5 files state that the Security Service itself received information from Hughes— '[he] has occasionally given oddments of information to us, but we have never felt fully satisfied with him'. It was noted that he had been known as a 'windbag' and was 'not considered the type of man who could safely be trusted with confidential information.'[51]

The BEU, which Hughes worked for whilst he was undertaking his most prominent anti-communist activities, was later integrated into a larger private anti-communist organisation, the Economic League (EL).[52] The EL was founded in 1919 by Admiral 'Blinker' Hall, Conservative MP and former Director of Naval Intelligence

(DNI).[53] Initially known as National Propaganda, the EL was supported by anti-labour industrialists and other sympathetic businessmen and funded by wealthy supporters.[54] Hall had links to power not only through his Parliamentary seat and former position as DNI but also through a close relationship with Basil Thomson.[55] Hall was said to have 'exploited' his connections with contacts in the intelligence community for the benefit of the EL.[56]

Officially, the EL claimed to be countering the socialist beliefs of the working classes by using propaganda to make the case for capitalism.[57] However, some of its activities were somewhat more covert. The EL collected information on certain organisations and compiled a blacklist of individuals whom it considered to be 'dangerous subversives.' It aimed to ensure these people were not employed in British industries and, when requested, provided employers with detailed records on both the individuals and organisations it deemed to be a threat. During the General Strike, the EL also helped to provide the government with information on coal stocks, the availability of transport and the organisation of strikebreaking organisations.[58]

In 1926, the EL appointed John Baker White as its Director, leaving him with responsibility for the day-to-day running of the organisation.[59] Baker White was one of the key figures in the State intelligence-private intelligence networks during the 1920s. Prior to joining the EL, he began his career working for the Makgill organisation, running agents and infiltrating communist organisations.[60] As part of his work for Makgill, Baker White acted as a talent spotter; he played a significant role in recruiting Knight for the IIB.[61] Baker White was, himself, closely involved in the BF at the time, and referred to himself as a BF 'unit officer'.[62] He was particularly close to the prominent BF member, Nesta Webster, who was a friend of his mother's and, reportedly, the inspiration for his own strong anti-socialist beliefs.[63] It is not clear what Baker White's relationship with the BF was once he became Director of the EL, although the two organisations do appear to have been closely intertwined.[64]

As Director of the EL, Baker White was closely involved with anti-communist activities. He regularly offered information to

MI5 that his sources within the CPGB had collected. Frequently, he would meet Con Boddington of MI5—another former Makgill operative—to pass on such intelligence.[65] The EL also sent information to the police.[66] Baker White later worked for the State as part of the Political Warfare Executive during the Second World War and, in 1945, was elected as the Conservative MP for Canterbury.[67]

The BF: An 'intolerable nuisance'?

John Baker White epitomised the tangled networks that emerged in the 1920s. At the time, many individuals within the State, the BF, the Conservative Party and private right-wing groups were convinced that every effort should be employed to tackle what they believed to be the great menace of communism. Due to their shared anti-communist feelings, such people would often attend the same meetings and started to mix with one another. Baker White and Knight, for example, met at an anti-communist event organised by the BEU. From there, relationships and networks grew and the boundaries between private organisations, political organisations and the intelligence community itself were broken down. Anti-communism meant that the lines between such organisations became blurred, and some people became involved in more than one of the organisations. Those who collected intelligence about communists for the BF or one of the right-wing groups such as the EL would often have their reports sent to the State's own intelligence agencies, whilst many who began their crusading in right-wing anti-communist groups that preceded the EL often ended up as members of the BF.[68]

The organisation with the ability to bring the anti-communist message to the greatest number of ears in 1920s Britain was the Conservative Party. Seeing potential allies in the fight against communism and socialism within the private right-wing groups, the Conservatives began to develop relationships with these groups. In 1929, Conservative Party Chairman, JCC Davidson, suggested raising funds for anti-communist groups. He made it clear that 'a very large sum of money can be raised in the country [to fight socialism] which wouldn't be available for normal, local party requirements.' In a further letter, Davidson stated his belief that it would be quite easy to raise 'a quarter of a million from the great manufacturing firms and from other sources which stand to lose most if a socialist government gets into power'.[69]

The Conservative Party also had relationships with the intelligence community—as mentioned previously, individuals such as Joseph Ball and 'Blinker' Hall, who had worked in intelligence, went on to work in Conservative Central Office and became a Conservative MP respectively. Several links were also forged between the Conservatives and the BF. Initially, one of the major aspects of the BF relationship with Conservatives was that members of the BF would steward Conservative meetings.[70] A significant number of people held dual membership of both the BF and the Conservative Party; in March 1925, the BF secretary for the West Kensington district had said 'the majority of the local residents who were members of the Conservative Association were now members of the Fascisti'.[71] The Conservatives had no formal procedure to deal with dual membership of the Party and other political organisations, so links to the BF were often simply overlooked.[72] Indeed, several Conservative MPs were involved with, or were members of, the BF.[73]

At first glance, the apparent embrace of fascists because of their anti-communist beliefs by elements of the British intelligence community, as well as the Conservative Party, appears inexplicable. The situation was, however, more complex; there is a degree of consensus among historians that the BF, during its initial incarnation at least, was not a fully-fledged fascist organisation in the way that the term would commonly be understood today.[74] The BF did, however, display some fascist tendencies. Maxwell Knight later wrote that the 'experience gained' in the BF 'probably had a considerable effect' on the overtly fascist British Union of Fascists (BUF) in the 1930s.[75] Indeed, several individuals who played important roles in the BUF, most notably William Joyce (later better known as 'Lord Haw-Haw'), had their first taste of the radical Right as members of the BF.[76] The BF's paramilitary elements, use of forceful stewarding methods and authoritarian ideas arguably set a precedent for the way the BUF acted. The BF also made clear it admired Mussolini and Italian Fascists.[77]

One of the most common reasons scholars have argued that the BF was not itself fascist is because, whilst it may have modelled itself on fascist movements abroad, ideologically it did not commit to particularly 'fascist' beliefs.[78] In simple terms, the BF did not commit to revolution and instead sought to defend the King and the British Empire against what it saw to be the evils of communism. Fascism was seen as a foreign concept, something that was neither suitable nor particularly relevant to Britain.[79] Many of the British public in the 1920s did not understand fascist ideology and often equated fascism with strikebreaking.[80] Arnold Leese, who later led the pro-Nazi Imperial Fascist League, had a brief involvement with the BF but left because he did not believe it was truly fascist. He asserted 'there was no Fascism, as I understood it, in the organisation, which was merely Conservatism with Knobs On'.[81]

In many ways, whether or not the BF was fascist is almost immaterial because the State did not perceive it to be so. Official reports and memoranda from throughout the 1920s show that if the BF was ever perceived as posing any threat it was to law and order, and not to the security of the British State itself. At times, alarms were raised about the BF encouraging, and being involved in, violent disorder, but it was not considered to be a radical, subversive, political organisation as the CPGB was. Fundamentally, the BF's focus on the threat posed by communism and the Soviet Union meant that it was primarily viewed as an ultra-Conservative, anti-communist organisation.

Although it does appear that the BF's anti-communism gained it allies in high places and allowed it to get away with its worst excesses, it must be said that many within the British State expressed deep disquiet about the movement. Special Branch officers attended and reported on numerous BF meetings, whilst its head, Wyndham Childs, described the Fascisti as 'an intolerable nuisance … a menace to the peace of this country.'[82] In his memoirs, Childs wrote that they 'took the Law into their own hands under the sacred name of patriotism. Their object was laudable, but their methods damnable and illegal. I never ceased to let the Fascisti know exactly what I thought of them.'[83] Childs also criticised the intelligence-gathering by private groups such as the EL for producing 'alarmist' and exaggerated reports on the extent of the communist threat.[84]

Concerns about the BF were also raised by Whitehall officials, who questioned whether members of the organisation should be allowed to work within the Civil Service, especially as moves had been made to prevent communists from doing so. Sir John Anderson, permanent secretary at the Home Office, made clear that,

> Everything possible should be done to discourage Civil Servants from associating themselves with the Fascisti and similar movements. Some of these movements are harmless and even praiseworthy; others decidedly mischievous. The only safe line for a Civil Servant is to keep clear of them all ... I feel so strongly on this subject that I should be in favour of a definite pronouncement by the Government except for the fact that awkward questions would arise in regard to such a body as the OMS which has had a sort of Government recognition.[85]

Whilst it is unclear what action was taken against civil servants who were members of the BF, they would have been strongly advised against being members of the organisation. Officials separately stated, 'it is most inadvisable that members of H.M. Forces should have any connection with the Fascisti as ... it is equally undesirable for a member of H.M. Forces to become a member of a communist organisation'.[86]

Sir John Anderson was a particularly strong voice opposing the State using members of the BF and showed his concerns about the matter in 1931. During a meeting with MI6's chief, Admiral Sir Hugh Sinclair, Anderson made clear his grave concerns that one of the 'principals in [MI6] was, or had been, connected with the British Fascisti and was under suspicion of working for political organisations such as the Conservative Party'. At the time Maxwell Knight was working for MI6, and Anderson was undoubtedly referring to him.[87] Indeed, by the early 1930s, Knight had left the BF which was, itself, in a terminal decline. The months preceding the General Strike had marked the high point of the organisation. The failure of the strike itself made it difficult for fascist leaders to sustain their argument that Britain faced a grave threat from revolutionaries and communists. As the BF membership declined in the years following the General Strike, the movement became much more recognisably fascist, embracing totalitarianism and anti-Semitism.[88]

The British Union of Fascists

In October 1932, a new fascist movement emerged in Britain, the British Union of Fascists (BUF). It was founded by Sir Oswald Mosley, and quickly usurped the BF as the primary fascist movement in Britain. Mosley, who described the BF as 'three old ladies and a couple of office boys', had been involved in politics for many years prior to forming the BUF and, at different times, had sat in Parliament as a Conservative, Independent, and Labour MP.[89] In the 1920s, he had been regarded as a rising star within the Labour Party and, ironically, found himself under sustained verbal attack from fascists.[90] Although considered to be firmly on the left of the Labour Party, Mosley was fiercely anti-communist.[91] Following Labour's victory in the 1929 General Election, Ramsay MacDonald is said to have considered appointing Mosley as his foreign secretary, before eventually appointing him Chancellor of the Duchy of Lancaster. Within a year, however, Mosley became disillusioned and resigned his post before leaving the Labour Party shortly afterwards.[92] By the time he launched the BUF, Mosley's political ideology was clearly fascist.

From the very beginning, the BUF was much more overtly fascist than the BF had ever been. Mosley had a deep admiration for Mussolini and decided his new organisation would wear a uniform of black shirts. BUF policy was distinctly revolutionary, and the movement prioritised forming a Fascist Defence Force. If the Party ever won power, Mosley aimed to introduce a Corporate State, outlaw all other political parties and end democratic elections in Britain. He believed that 'effective government was impossible within the existing framework', and stated that in a new fascist

Britain, the only permissible criticism of the government would be 'the constructive criticism of technicians.'[93]

Despite such overtly revolutionary proposals, the formation of the BUF did not immediately lead security officials to develop more significant concerns about fascism. The ideology was still not fully understood by many working within the British State, and the BUF was not considered overly significant. Even the emergence of fascists in Europe did not lead MI5 to worry about any potential domestic repercussions. John Curry wrote in his in-house history of the Security Service, 'the Nazi threat attracted practically no attention in the Security Service between 1931-33 and very little when Hitler and the Nazi Party came to power in Germany'.[94] It should not, however, be said that the British State received no information on foreign fascism. As early as 1930, James Marshall-Cornwall, British Military Attaché in Berlin, reported to the Foreign Office that fascism posed a significant threat in Germany. He wrote,

> The National-Socialist Movement is a real danger, and far more of a menace to the present constitution than is Communism. The trouble about the "Brown Shirts" is that their principles and theories are entirely *destructive*. They wish to destroy the present fabric of the State but have no constructive programme with which to replace it, except a sort of mad-dog dictatorship.[95]

Marshall-Cornwall's words appear to have had little, if any, impact back in Britain. For many officials, not least those within the intelligence community, fascism was not in any way a threat comparable to communism. This was particularly evident in March 1933, when Guy Liddell, deputy head of MI5's B-Division, accompanied by the head of MI6's Berlin station, Frank Foley,[96] visited Berlin to 'establish contact with the German Political Police' (which would be reformed as the Gestapo within weeks). During the visit, Liddell examined files seized from the German Communist Party and, although he considered them to be 'disappointing', arrangements were made with Rudolf Diels, the soon-to-be head of the Gestapo, for files to be copied and forwarded to MI5.[97] Whilst Liddell departed Germany 'with no illusions about the brutality of the Nazi regime', he still believed that they could potentially be of use in the fight against international communism.[98] In his report on his trip he concluded by writing,

> The Berlin Police ... are in possession of extremely valuable records, which if placed virtually at our disposal will be of great assistance in establishing how the Comintern's work in Western Europe and in the Colonies is being reorganised. There is no doubt that the moment chosen to establish contact with the present regime has been a good one. Those in authority are persuaded that they have saved Europe from the menace of Communism ... In their present mood, the German police are extremely ready to help us in any way they can.[99]

Several months later, in November 1933, Whitehall officials decided that MI5 should begin to examine fascism in Britain 'in the same way as they look after communism.' The work was, however, not a priority for MI5, and the Security Service only agreed to undertake this added responsibility if it could be delayed until April 1934, 'and then only provided that adequate funds were forthcoming to pay for the necessary staff.'[100]

Once MI5 had begun the work in 1934, Kell wrote to all chief constables asking them to provide any information on the fascist movement in their individual regions. The letter, however, somewhat downplayed the fascist threat and sought to emphasise the continuing threat communists posed. The 'Fascist Movement [is] a natural re-action to Communism', Kell wrote, 'programmes and policies of various Fascist organisations are open, not secret, and loyalist rather than subversive.'[101] It is clear that Kell simply did not believe that fascists posed a threat. The letter contained the following paragraph,

> It is perhaps of more immediate interest to observe that some of the individuals whose names have come before us in connection with the Fascist Movement have previously been known to us on account of their connection with the more extreme left wing of political thought. In some cases, no doubt, they are Communist agents in Fascist circles, while some are merely persons of shady or eccentric character, who drift from one thing to another.[102]

Many of the reports on fascism produced by MI5 in the preceding months also sought to compare fascism to communism. The Security Service's first in-depth report on fascism in Britain stated, 'while communism is international and preaches class-warfare, fascism insists on the common interest of all classes in an intensified economic nationalism inspired by patriotic sentiment'. The report even sought to diminish the term 'fascist' and stated, 'every man and every movement in any way opposed to communism is now apt to be branded as fascist'.[103] After many years of regarding fascism as a radical but constitutional movement, members of the intelligence community appeared to have struggled to modify the way they viewed it. It was only at the end of the report that any warning was sounded about the BUF, 'while the Fascists maintain that they aim at obtaining power by means of the ballot box, we cannot be certain that they do not contemplate the use of methods involving force'.[104] This echoed another memorandum, written several months previously, which stated that the BUF had 'the intention of entering the Parliamentary world with the ultimate object of capturing its machinery' and warned that most BUF members 'are not of the type to behave particularly constitutionally should any opportunity for doing otherwise occur'.[105] It went on to state,

> the [BUF] is an organisation well worth investigation, as although in a very disorganised and loose state at the moment ... it will be more than possible to weld it into a very formidable organisation, and there can be no doubt that the interest in Fascism at the moment is greater than at any other time since the initial Italian experiment.[106]

Despite these substantial warnings, strong action was not taken to counter the BUF. The simplest reason for the reluctance of the Security Service to expend great resources on watching the organisation was that it was seen to be too small to carry a threat. The first report on the movement stated, 'we are not concerned with the political situation and Fascist prospects at an Election, or with the political aims of Sir Oswald Mosley and the British Union of Fascists, so long as these aims are pursued by strictly constitutional methods.'[107] Similar reasoning was also used by the

Met Commissioner, Lord Trenchard, in 1933 when discussing Special Branch surveillance of the BUF. Trenchard wrote, 'I do not quite agree that Fascism has become dangerous yet; it may become so but we are watching it ... frankly it has not yet become an important organisation.'[108] As later became evident, Trenchard was not someone who was willing to display leniency towards the Fascists. At the time, however, this kind of response seemed perfectly rational considering that the BUF was a minor party whose rhetoric seemed more threatening than its actions. Other than a peak in mid-1934, the membership of the BUF was consistently small and many of those members were 'passive' rather than active. The movement also failed to make ground nationally, with much of its membership confined to London and the South-East, and did not have a single MP or local councillor elected during the interwar period.[109]

Pro-Fascist or Anti-Communist?

As the BUF was politically insignificant, failing to gain popular support in the early-to-mid 1930s, security officials believed it reasonable to merely maintain an awareness of its activities. At the same time, the CPGB also had a relatively small membership and failed to gain ground politically, but it was viewed very differently by the authorities; the CPGB was subject to large-scale surveillance, the BUF was not. This difference was perhaps most starkly displayed by the Home Office's refusal to authorise HOWs on all of the most prominent BUF members.[110] Remarkably, successive Home Secretaries refused applications for a HOW on Mosley for several years, even after his close personal relations to the Nazis were obvious when he was married to his second wife, Diana, at the residence of the Nazi, Joseph Goebbels, in 1936.[111]

As surveillance was conducted covertly, the most obvious public demonstration of the way in which the authorities treated fascists differently from other radical political movements was the policing of their marches and rallies. In the early 1930s, Special Branch had actually been proactive in collecting intelligence on the BUF.[112] It frequently produced reports on the movement; one even contained extensive detail on the first 'Fascist wedding' in December 1933 of the BUF Chief of Staff, Ian Hope Dundas.[113] The policing of fascist marches in the years that followed, however, resulted in accusations of a pro-fascist bias in the police, with officers said to have 'openly tolerated' and 'shown a remarkable indulgence' of fascists.[114]

Fascists appeared to be treated very differently from anti-fascists and communists.[115] On one occasion, a BUF procession was allowed through the West End of London, despite internal police documents admitting that 'we always deny this route to the Communists'. Separately, the BUF was allowed to hold a large march in Regent's Park, but when anti-fascists requested permission to hold a smaller meeting in the same place just days later, the police intervened to prevent it.[116] The authorities were also much more lenient about the use of 'violent' language by fascists. Communists would routinely be hounded for using phrases perceived to be inflammatory and offensive on the basis that this could create confrontation; the police rarely, however, took action against fascists who would use offensive and provocative language in their speeches.[117] The disparity in treatment meant that some on the Left developed a belief that fascism had been able to grow 'with the direct connivance with the state', and thought that the State potentially viewed fascists as part of an 'irregular army to preserve capitalism'.[118]

Accusations that the police treated fascists and anti-fascists or communists differently became commonplace after the BUF meeting at Olympia in London on 7 June 1934. The meeting was particularly important because it attracted a crowd of 15,000 people and was almost regarded as a social occasion. Up to 150 MPs attended, alongside clergymen and a significant number of the press.[119] During the meeting, BUF stewards brutally attacked any hecklers before forcibly ejecting them from the hall. So severe was the violence that one observer declared that it had been a miracle that no one had died and that they had never seen 'so much blood in all my life'. Other witnesses reported seeing barely conscious men with ripped clothes bleeding profusely, while some stated that Blackshirts brutally kicked and punched those who were removed from the hall. Many were injured, and some were even hospitalised.[120]

Despite the violence, the police did not enter the meeting hall to intervene and stated that they had no authority to enter public meetings held on private premises. In a government meeting after Olympia, the Attorney General explained, 'the law was explicit that the Police could not go in except on the invitation of the protesters, unless they knew that an offence had been or was being committed'.[121] Subsequent evidence makes it clear, however, that there were a number of officers within the hall during the Olympia meeting. A review of the event in 1936 made this clear but warned that this information could not be made public—'we must die in the last ditch before we disclose any report made by any Special Branch Officer.' Those officers were present 'not primarily as Police Officers at all but in order to give us confidential information from the political side'.[122] Seven hundred officers were also stationed outside the hall to deal with anti-fascist counter-protesters and made twenty-three arrests—the majority of whom were anti-fascists or onlookers attempting to help the injured.[123] Although nothing was done to break up the Fascist procession prior to the meeting, the police made plans to disperse a communist counter-march.[124]

The authorities were acutely aware that in some quarters they were being accused of having a pro-fascist bias. This was noted in an MI5 report, written after Olympia, which mentioned that such a claim had arisen because 'disturbances at Fascist meetings have often been followed by the arrest of working class opponents while Fascists have not been arrested'. The report countered such accusations, arguing, 'the fact that Fascists have never made an organised attempt to break up their opponents' meetings, while they have suffered in that way themselves, is not stressed'.[125] Although it appeared that the police were protecting the Blackshirts when they provided a large number of officers for fascist meetings, the authorities justified this by stating that the BUF should be free to hold a procession as long as it was peaceful. One Home Office memorandum stated, 'the police should take steps to clear a path through the crowd for the Fascist procession to their meeting place. The Commissioner said that he would take similar action if any attempt were made by political opponents to prevent a May Day gathering in Hyde Park', and that 'if the fascists were prevented by their political opponents from holding an open air meeting in Hyde Park, strength would be given to their claim that it was not possible to obtain free speech in this country'.[126]

The authorities did not look kindly on anti-fascist activities at Olympia because they believed that the anti-fascists made deliberate attempts to cause the maximum level of disruption possible. One Special Branch report recorded that communists had been encouraged to apply for tickets for the Olympia meeting and that they had planned to masquerade as members of the BUF by wearing black shirts.[127] A further report stated that leading members of the CPGB had inspected the neighbourhood of Olympia prior to the meeting and had communicated that 'there were many old bricks, of which use could be made, lying about'.[128] This may well have been true, but the authorities still ignored the fact that the Blackshirts adopted violence as part of their culture, something which played a significant role in the clashes at Olympia.[129] Although they may not have found specific evidence of BUF plans for violence at the event, it does appear that the authorities were more willing to turn a blind eye to the Blackshirts' involvement in violent incidents.

It is notable that the police also appear to have questioned the veracity of some witness statements which were taken after Olympia; police files indicate that background checks were done on individuals who provided evidence about the violence. Some of the statements came from doctors who had seen or treated the injured and subsequent police reports linked some of the doctors to radical organisations, referring to their 'communistic tendencies'.[130] Despite the fact that even police officers had attested to the level of violence at Olympia, there still appears to have been an attempt by some police officials to, in some way, see a communist-inspired conspiracy behind the statements provided by some witnesses.[131]

In the eyes of the police, a major difference between the fascists and communists was that whilst the fascists worked with police to organise processions and followed instructions, the communists were antagonistic towards, and uncooperative with, officers.[132] On one occasion, the BUF even offered to help police in Sussex to search for the perpetrator of a shooting of an officer.[133] In contrast, the anti-fascists' relationship with the police was summed up in one report after Olympia. It stated that the 'general attitude of demonstrators towards police was very hostile, loud remarks being made to the effect that police were showing partiality towards the Blackshirts'.[134] In this context, it is easier to understand why the two were policed so differently. It was not the fact that the police displayed a partiality towards the fascists, but rather that they behaved differently towards people who were less aggressive, hostile and insulting. The BUF made every effort to establish a positive rapport with the police and, inevitably, this meant the police were less likely to treat them harshly.

The accusations that the police were pro-fascist appear less convincing when the private opinions of those charged with making decisions within the police force are considered. Lord Trenchard, Metropolitan Police Commissioner 1931–35, was fiercely critical of the fascists.[135] After Olympia, he wrote that the 'one and only' reason why disputes over freedom of speech deteriorated into violence was 'the existence of the Fascist organisation'.[136] Trenchard found an ally in John Gilmour, Home Secretary 1932–35, and both agreed that something needed to be done to limit the fascists' excesses. Even before Olympia, Gilmour had argued that 'Fascists are responsible for a substantial amount of disorder'. He believed that it was necessary to place restrictions on the wearing of political uniforms because they encouraged the fascists to be more aggressive, created more disorder and gave 'what would otherwise be harmless evolutions a semi-military appearance which causes considerable resentment'.[137]

After Olympia, Gilmour made his position even clearer and argued that there was a definite need to ban political uniforms and give the police more powers to intervene in fascist meetings at the point when they believed violent disorder was likely.[138] Whilst Trenchard agreed with the need to ban fascist uniforms, he went one step further than Gilmour and argued that there was a need to ban the BUF itself.[139] Home Office officials declined to ban the BUF, believing, as they had with the CPGB, that organisations with extremist beliefs were acceptable provided their policies did not break the law.[140]

Gilmour's concern about the BUF did, however, signal that the establishment had begun to believe fascists could pose a distinct threat. In the 1920s, Gilmour believed that fascism in the form of the BF was harmless and advocated using BF members to provide help to the State in an emergency.[141] In the 1930s, however, he held much greater concerns about Mosley and the BUF, and echoed Stanley Baldwin's belief that 'Mosley was a cad and a wrong un'.[142] Not all of those who sat on the government benches endorsed such a sentiment, however, and several Conservative MPs professed admiration for the BUF. Colonel Thomas Moore, MP for Ayr, wrote that 'The Blackshirts have what the Conservatives need' and suggested that there were no fundamental differences in outlook between 'the Blackshirts and their parents, the Conservatives'.[143] The intelligence community noted that other Conservative MPs were sympathetic towards the BUF, and Special Branch even discovered that one, Henry Drummond Wolff, had donated money to the BUF.[144]

The number of backbench MPs who supported the Blackshirts was, however, small. Some sympathisers became more hostile to the movement after the violence at Olympia.[145] Indeed, Olympia changed a number of establishment figures' minds about the BUF, most notably that of the proprietor of the *Daily Mail*, Lord Rothermere. In January 1934, Rothermere had professed support for the BUF with the headline, 'Hurrah For The Blackshirts!' and was said to have played a role in encouraging support for the movement.[146] The BUF reached peak-membership in the months after the *Mail* expressed its own support, and MI5 noted in the summer of 1934 that Rothermere's advocacy was 'an important factor' in the bolstering of Mosley's reputation.[147] The *Daily Mail*'s backing only lasted for six months and, in July 1934, after Olympia, Rothermere formally withdrew his support for the movement.[148] A retrospective analysis of the Rothermere-BUF relationship by the Security Service in 1941 noted that 'there is little doubt that Rothermere's Fascist sympathies arose from that obsessive fear of communism from which he appears to have suffered during the last twenty-five years of his life'.[149] The report mentioned Rothermere's 'obsessive fear of communism' unironically, but many others within the intelligence community and wider establishment had such a 'fear' of communism during the 1930s that they had underestimated the true threat of fascism themselves.

Time for Action

For many establishment figures, the events of 1934 not only revealed the true nature of the BUF but also led them to believe that action would need to be taken against the organisation. For Vernon Kell, however, the opposite was true. In the autumn of 1934 he wrote, 'it is becoming increasingly evident that the conditions which led to the success of the Fascist movement in Italy, or of the Nazi movement in Germany do not exist in England ... at Olympia Mosley suffered a check which is likely to prove decisive'.[150]

MI5 attitudes towards the BUF only began to change after it was discovered that the organisation was receiving money from abroad. In early 1935, the Security Service reported that 'the question of contributions from the German and Italian ruling parties is still an open question but the balance of probabilities is against any such subvention'.[151] However, by October 1935, MI5 stated that new information had been received which left 'no room for doubt' that the BUF was receiving Italian money. The report went on to state,

> These facts [put] the Fascist Movement in Great Britain in an entirely new light. Where it seemed to have roots in this country, these roots now appear to be very much frailer and to have been kept alive by artificial means. Thus, both the Communist Movement and its re-agent, Fascism, are for all practical purposes dependent on foreign funds. Without such funds Fascism, at any rate, would probably cease to exist.[152]

It was further reported that the BUF 'receive a monthly contribution of £3000 payable through the Italian Embassy in

Paris'.[153] Little action was taken against the BUF in 1935, however, since its membership was declining, and it had failed to put forward any candidates to stand during the 1935 General Election; it was increasingly regarded as irrelevant. Foreign subsidies could not prevent the decline. Although the Security Service continued to monitor aspects of the movement closely, it did not believe that fascism had either the ability to generate mass support or create a significant threat to British security.[154]

Politically, the BUF may have been largely irrelevant but, from time to time, it still had the capability to gain attention through its rallies. In March 1936, one BUF meeting at the Albert Hall created significant headlines. Unlike at Olympia, police officers were present and helped to 'escort' hecklers out of the meeting. This led officers to, once again, be accused of policing in a manner that favoured the fascists; even the previously pro-fascist *Daily Mail* declared 'Police Guard Blackshirts'.[155] Later in 1936, the fallout from another fascist rally led the authorities to take decisive action to deal with the BUF. On 4 October 1936, Mosley and his party planned a provocative march through a largely Jewish area in the East End of London. Anti-fascists mobilised 100,000 people—described by Special Branch as 'undoubtedly the largest anti-fascist demonstration yet seen in London'—to counter the BUF.[156] Police attempted to clear a route for the BUF, but anti-fascists assembled barricades and, with their route blocked, the Fascists were eventually forced to abandon their march to avoid violent clashes. The anti-fascists proclaimed a great victory and celebrated the fact that they had prevented the Fascists from passing.[157] Although the Fascists and anti-fascists did not clash, significant confrontations between anti-fascists and police at Cable Street resulted in seventy-nine anti-fascists being arrested.[158]

The events at Cable Street served as a catalyst for the State to take legislative action. The Met Commissioner, Sir Philip Game, subsequently argued that there was a need to 'declare the Fascists an illegal organisation'. He believed such action was the only plausible solution to control public order disturbances.[159] The Home Secretary, John Simon, also believed action was necessary, and produced a memorandum for the cabinet recommending new legislation to preserve public order.[160] The subsequent Public Order Bill was presented to Parliament in November 1936, and the 1936 Public Order Act became law on 1 January 1937.[161] The Act banned political uniforms—except on ceremonial occasions—gave the police power to either ban or re-route processions and prohibited quasi-military organisations.[162] Simon argued that it worked like a 'charm', whilst the Labour MP, Herbert Morrison, later a member of the War Cabinet, declared, 'it ... commenced the undermining of fascism in this country'.[163] Plans to introduce legislation which would help to limit the activities of the BUF had been considered before 1936—most notably in 1932 and 1934—but never came to fruition as the government did not believe that they had cross-party support. The Public Order Act was introduced as, after the clashes at Cable Street, politicians from all parties became convinced that the police did not have adequate powers to deal with violent disorder.[164]

It was not legislation alone which restricted the activities of the BUF after Cable Street. Mosley was also prevented from being able to broadcast his views.[165] Combined with the limitations imposed on the BUF rallies, this helped to suppress fascism in Britain almost entirely. By mid-1937, MI5 believed that the movement was struggling to survive and faced a 'financial crisis' after Mussolini's subsidy was greatly reduced.[166] Vernon Kell wrote that it 'has either ceased to exist, or has lost practically all its importance throughout the provinces ... only in London has BUF given any trouble to police'. Whilst the movement was far too weak to pose a substantial subversive threat, the Security Service was concerned that the movement could potentially do so if war broke out. An MI5 informant within the BUF believed that there were 'a certain number of young people—possibly only a few hundred—who have been so hypnotised by Fascist propaganda that in the event of a war against Italy or Germany their sympathies would lie with the enemy.'[167]

Moves were therefore made to mitigate against this possibility, and Kell's Deputy, Eric Holt-Wilson, drafted an amendment to the 'War Book' of legislation—regulations and other measures to be introduced in wartime—to enable the internment of British citizens in wartime if they were a threat to public safety or the 'Defence of the Realm'. This was approved by the Committee of the Imperial Defence in July 1937.[168]

A Front for Fascism

With the BUF struggling for its own survival, MI5's main investigations into fascism in Britain in the second half of the 1930s tended to focus on front organisations. Interest was taken into the activities of the Auslands Organisation and the Fasci all'Estero—organisations which were, respectively, arms of the German and Italian State working in Britain to promote their countries. Whilst the Security Service had some difficulty collecting information on the Italian Fasci all'Estero, significant information was collected on the Nazi Auslands Organisation, the association of Nazi members living abroad.[169] The activity of the Auslands Organisation—referred to as the 'Nazitern' by Churchill—was at the whim of Hitler, and MI5 believed it to be 'a ready-made instrument for intelligence, espionage, and ultimately sabotage.' Intelligence officials also discovered that there was some close personal contact between members of the Auslands Organisation in London and some of the most senior BUF members who sympathised with the organisation.[170]

One of the home-grown front organisations into which MI5 took an interest was the 'January Club'. Formed in 1934, it concerned the Security Service because it claimed not to be fascist, was more secretive than other fascist organisations and 'brought Fascism to the notice of a large number of people who would have considered it a lot less favourably if its activities had been confined to [the BUF]'.[171] One of the organisation's founders was Sir Donald Makgill—son of Sir George Makgill—and those who attended its dinners included Conservative MPs, individuals who already had involvement with the BUF and members of the upper classes including the Gentleman Usher to the King, Commander Louis Greig.[172] It is clear from reports that intelligence officials were aware of discussions at January Club dinners, but did not appear to find much of interest from an intelligence point of view.[173] The impact the club managed to have is impossible to quantify, although its limited membership suggests that its influence was not likely to have been far-reaching.[174]

Unlike the January Club, many of the other front organisations watched by MI5 were overtly pro-German. These included the Anglo-German Fellowship (AGF), Anglo-German Academic Bureau, the Hitlerjugend (Hitler Youth), and the Link. The AGF, which was founded in 1935, was believed by MI5 to be approved by the German authorities and 'sponsored by prominent National-Socialist Party members in Germany'.[175] The senior Nazi, Joachim von Ribbentrop, was reported to have played a 'prominent part' in its foundation.[176] Although the organisation did not champion the Nazi party publicly and claimed merely to be wishing to promote better Anglo-German relations, it ensured, at the very least, that it did the Nazis' bidding for them.[177] The AGF had numerous prominent members and Lord Mount Temple, who had been a Conservative MP and Transport Minister in Baldwin's 1924–29 ministry, served as its chairman.[178] An MI5 agent infiltrated the organisation in 1937 and proposed 'to take as active a part in the proceedings of the Fellowship as it is possible for him to do so'.[179] The impact of the AGF until its decline in 1939 was, however, questionable, especially because the majority of members came from the upper classes and it made no impression on wider society.[180]

The Anglo-German Academic Bureau was often viewed as a 'clearing house for Anglo-German cultural relations.' The basis of its work was described by *The Times* in 1938 as, 'the exchange of students and teachers between British and German educational institutions.'[181] MI5 believed, however, that the organisation was 'the main centre for Nazi propaganda and movement'.[182] In his in-house history of the Security Service, John Curry stated that 'there was evidence that German teachers and students were encouraged to deliver lectures of a political and semi-political nature in this country.'[183] A significant number of people belonging to the bureau resided in the UK; Kell reported in November 1937 that there were seventy German teachers and a number of 'exchange' teachers and students at various schools and colleges throughout the country. He asserted that 'all these persons are required to conduct propaganda on the lines laid down by the party.' The lectures would have to be approved prior to delivery by a Nazi official, and reports would have to be sent back to Germany detailing the reception it had received and subsequent discussion it provoked.[184] On one occasion, MI5 reported that a member of the bureau had given lectures to the Civil Service Clerical Association.[185] The intelligence community tracked both students and teachers to discover the content of their lectures.[186] Surveillance was also carried out because members of the bureau in the UK were viewed as potential spies. MI6 reported that the German SS was 'making use of young people who come to England as students to a considerable extent for providing information as to what is going on in this country'.[187]

Young people also came to the notice of the authorities when they took part in activities linked to the Hitlerjugend. In November 1937, it was discovered that the founder of the Boy Scouts' Association, Robert Baden-Powell, had met with the German Ambassador to the UK, Ribbentrop, and the leader of the Hitler Youth, Hartman Lauterbacher.[188] Baden-Powell, in a report to the Scouts' International Commissioner, stated that Ribbentrop had insisted that 'true peace between the two nations will depend on the youth being brought up on friendly terms together in forgetfulness of past differences' and that the Scout Movement would be 'a very powerful agency for helping bring this about'. The Ambassador had also suggested that Baden-Powell meet Hitler. The founder of the Scouts made clear that he was 'in favour of anything that would bring about a better understanding between our two nations'.[189] The discovery of the Scouts' links to the Nazis is somewhat ironic since, in the 1920s, the authorities had been concerned about its links to communism. MI5 attempted to obtain information on the '"Red" Boy Scout Movement' in 1920 and reported in 1925 that the CPGB was attempting to 'insert their people into the Scouts and Guides'.[190] This infiltration does not appear to have been successful.

The Link was founded by Admiral Sir Barry Domvile in September 1937, supposedly for the purposes of promoting friendly Anglo-German relations. It quickly became regarded as more important than the AGF in the eyes of the Nazis, and the more extreme members of the AGF transferred to the Link.[191] It was reported that leading BUF figure Neil Francis-Hawkins attempted to get every pro-German member of the BUF to join the Link.[192] Surveillance was routinely carried out on meetings of the organisation, and agents were instructed to infiltrate it on the orders of Maxwell Knight.[193] In July 1939, Kell described the organisation as 'nothing more nor less than an instrument of Nazi propaganda in this country' and stated that there was evidence that some money had been passed from the German government in order to fund it.[194] Indeed, such was the fervency of pro-German feeling amongst members of the Link that one intelligence source, embedded within the organisation, was described in one report as being 'amazed at the attitude of the audience and the amount of enthusiasm shown for a pro-German cause'.[195]

Anti-Nazis and Refugees

In the second half of the 1930s, MI5 did not merely monitor pro-German or pro-Nazi groups but also investigated anti-Nazis and others fleeing Germany. Primarily, such groups were subject to surveillance because security officials were concerned that some of those opposed to the Nazi regime may also have had communist sympathies. Initial investigations into anti-Nazis in the early-to-mid 1930s, however, appear to have been partially prompted by a desire to maintain cordial Anglo-German relations. In October 1935, for example, Special Branch opened a file on the Non-Sectarian Anti-Nazi Council after the German Embassy had drawn the attention of the Foreign Office to a demonstration planned by the group.[196] On another occasion, in January 1936, after a complaint by the German Embassy about anti-Nazi posters, a Home Office official 'accordingly asked Scotland Yard for a report'.[197] The Special Branch report identified the creator of the posters as 'an English Jew named Alfred Abraham WOOLFSTEIN' who was said to be 'actively engaged in organising a publicity campaign to the prejudice of Hitler and Mussolini, and against war'. It stated that he was a friend of the pacifist former Labour Party leader, George Lansbury, and 'is regarded as a "peace crank"', before concluding that he was working independently of any political organisation.[198] Whilst such investigations were essentially inconsequential, the mere fact that they even took place is notable. In April 1936, the Home Office and Foreign Office resolved to deal with future complaints by informing foreign embassies that the freedom of expression and liberty of the press was fundamental to Britain and advised that '"foreign nationals" would be best to ignore such verbal attacks.'[199]

Such investigations may have been both unimportant and short-lived, but the authorities did carry out more significant surveillance against other critics of the Nazi regime—most notably German exiles in Britain. In 1937, it appeared that attempts were being made to create an organisation which would coordinate groups of German exiles and opponents of Hitler in various countries across Europe. MI5 believed 'that the general intentions of the organisation can only be hostile to the German Government' and argued that the establishment of a branch in the UK had the potential to 'be something of an embarrassment'. Nothing appears to have resulted from these initial suggestions and, in fact, inquiries into the organisation died down in June 1937.[200]

The Security Service also investigated several organisations formed by refugees in the UK, partly because of concerns that they were communist front organisations. One such group was the Free German League of Culture which was ostensibly set up to 'preserve and advance Free German Culture'. MI5 used exiles to join the organisation to provide detailed information on its workings and placed its leading members under surveillance because it believed that the organisation was spreading communist propaganda.[201] Surveillance was also carried out on the Czech Refugee Trust Fund, an organisation which aimed to provide support and security for political refugees from Czechoslovakia threatened by Nazism. Although it was created by (and initially partially funded by) the British government, MI5 investigated extensively, believing the organisation to have been penetrated by communists. Communists were among the people most threatened by the Nazi regime and thus were present amongst the refugees who fled to Britain.[202]

Better Communism than Nazism?

In the late 1930s, intelligence officials believed that the fascists capable of posing the greatest threat were those who were part of front organisations. Individual fascists were considered to be so unthreatening that they appear to have been utilised by intelligence officials to counter communists. In August 1937, four members of the BUF stole documents from the home of a civil servant, Major Wilfrid Vernon, who worked at the Royal Aircraft Establishment (RAE) in Farnborough.[203] The men who burgled Vernon's house were caught by police and were found guilty of larceny. Vernon had strong left-wing sympathies and the defendants alleged at their trial that MI5 had sought to obtain evidence that he was spreading communist propaganda amongst troops.[204] Vernon was subsequently dismissed from his position after being charged under the Official Secrets Act for the illegal possession of 'sensitive' documents which he had taken home to work on.[205]

The case is particularly notable because the fascists who were caught informed police that they had been told, by a 'senior intelligence officer', to steal the documents and take them to the Intelligence Department at Scotland House.[206] It is certainly the case that in 1937, MI5 were gravely concerned about Vernon working at the RAE and considered him to be 'an extremely bad Communist.'[207] Efforts had been made to remove him from his post prior to the burglary, in March 1936, but the case built against him was not considered sufficiently strong to lead to his dismissal.[208] Following this decision, the authorities may well have been active in seeking evidence that would justify dismissing Vernon from the RAE, as subsequently happened. The evidence suggests that he may have been subjected to a sustained campaign to remove him; in September 1936 his property was also burgled, although the culprits were not caught.[209]

In 1941, evidence came to light which suggested that the secret State may have been involved in the 1937 burglary. At the time,

John Charles Preen, who had been convicted of robbery, was in prison, having been interned without trial in 1940 as a result of his membership of the BUF. During a hearing to discuss his potential release, Preen revealed that P.G. Taylor (an alias of James McGuirk Hughes), whom he believed to be an MI5 officer, had told him to break into Vernon's house and find evidence which proved his disloyalty.[210] Whilst his assertions cannot be substantiated, they are nonetheless interesting and, if true, once again show the concerns intelligence officials had about communists as late as 1936–37.[211]

The decisive shift MI5 made from viewing communism as the major domestic subversive threat to regarding fascism as such does not appear to have happened until shortly before the outbreak of war in 1939. If any particular individual's views epitomised the way in which the establishment had regarded communism during the interwar years, it was those of Winston Churchill. Following the 1918 Armistice, he continually warned of the dangers of communism, but in 1939 his view had changed. 'Let Germany become Bolshevik', he said, 'Better Communism than Nazism'.[212]

One of the authorities' most pressing concerns at the outbreak of war was the possibility of there being a 'Fifth Column' of fascists in Britain who were willing to support the Germans and undermine the country from within. Such fears were, according to John Curry, exacerbated by the fact that MI5 had 'no definite knowledge whether there was any organised connection between the German Secret Service and Nazi sympathisers in [Britain], whether of British or alien nationality.'[213] Reports of the supposed role fifth columnists had played in the successful Nazi invasions of Norway, Belgium and Holland only increased security officials' concerns and led MI5 to advocate the need for decisive action to be taken to neutralise the BUF and its leadership.[214]

At cabinet on 22 May 1940, Home Secretary John Anderson reported that MI5 believed 25 to 30 per cent of the BUF would be 'willing, if ordered, to go to any lengths' on behalf of Germany. Subsequently, the cabinet agreed to allow the internment of 'those showing sympathy with foreign powers.' They also approved the arrest and detention of Mosley and thirty-two leading members of the BUF; by July 1940, 753 members of the BUF had been detained without trial.²¹⁵ Internment effectively killed off organised fascism in Britain. Most of those who were detained were released in 1941, with Mosley eventually being moved to what was effectively house arrest in 1943.²¹⁶ The authorities did, however, continue to scrutinise British fascists closely even after their release and compiled 'suspect lists' consisting of the names of those to be interned in the event of an invasion until September 1944.²¹⁷ One of the internees released in 1944 was Archibald Ramsay MP. Remarkably, having been released, he was able to retake his seat in the Commons. He wrote that upon his return, many fellow MPs 'have been very nice to me ... some have gone out of their way to do so.'²¹⁸

Even after the mass internment of 1940, the intelligence community continued to watch those it believed capable of posing a threat to British security.²¹⁹ One of those closely scrutinised was Arthur Donaldson, a Scottish Nationalist, who subsequently went on to lead the Scottish National Party (SNP) during the 1960s. An MI5 report stated in early 1941 that Donaldson was positioning himself as a 'Scottish Quisling' in preparation for a possible invasion.²²⁰ It was reported that he had alluded to working with Germany, saying on 5 January 1941, 'you can be sure that Germany will give us every possible assistance in our early struggle. The time is not yet ripe for us to start a virile campaign against England, but when fire and confusion is at its height in England, we can start in earnest'. The intelligence report concluded 'he firmly believes that a German conquest of England would be to his own and Scotland's advantage'.²²¹ Donaldson was interned for six weeks during 1941.

Internment demonstrated that, for the first time since 1918, security officials did not consider communism to pose the primary subversive threat to Britain. Despite the signing of the Molotov-Ribbentrop pact, members of the CPGB were not interned.²²² With its resources stretched in the fight against fascism, MI5 eventually had to cease keeping a record of each member of the CPGB—something it had long considered necessary—and confined itself to investigating only the most important members of the Party.²²³

Fascists were interned during the Second World War not because of their political beliefs per se, but instead because the authorities believed that they would 'act against Britain in the name of their beliefs'.²²⁴ Some scholars have, however, questioned whether fascists would have been able to cause significant damage to Britain, and have dismissed the idea that members of the BUF would ever have been capable of forming a 'Fifth Column' if they had been left at liberty.²²⁵ This may underestimate the potential threat as, although the number of potential fifth columnists was undoubtedly quite small, they could still have been capable of causing damage to Britain. A wartime undercover operation carried out by Eric Roberts, a bank clerk then working for MI5, indicated that there were 'scores and probably hundreds' of people in Britain willing and able to help the Nazi cause.²²⁶

A Change in Priorities?

Whilst the danger posed by fascism was the main focus for intelligence officials during the war, by 1943–44 Whitehall officials began to consider what their priorities would be in a post-war world. They believed that communism would again become a significant subversive threat to British security. As ever, Churchill summed up the fear held by many establishment members about the Soviets and communism in general. The Soviet Union may have been an ally, but it was not entirely trusted. The wartime Prime Minister reflected this inherent suspicion when he declared to the cabinet, after the Tehran Conference in late 1943, 'trying to maintain good relations with a Communist is like wooing a crocodile, you do not know whether to tickle it under the chin or to beat it on the head. When it opens its mouth you cannot tell whether it is trying to smile, or preparing to eat you up'.²²⁷

Despite significant concerns about the Soviets, opinions within the British State as to the extent of their threat were very mixed. The major division was between the diplomatic and military minds within Whitehall.²²⁸ The diplomats believed that cordial relations with the Soviets could be maintained, whilst the military advocated making plans to deal with a potentially hostile Soviet Union after the war had ended. The Chief of the Imperial General Staff, Field Marshal Sir Alan Brooke, concluded as early as 1943 that the Soviets would become Britain's next enemy. He even wrote in his diary that work should be done to 'foster Germany, gradually build her up, and bring her into the Federation of Western Europe.'[229] This view was not unique to Brooke; it was commonly held in military circles. Even before the defeat of Germany, thoughts began to turn to a possible future war with the Soviets, in which the Germans would potentially be a Western ally.[230]

For some intelligence officials, there was a concern that any shift in priorities at the end of the war may lead to investigations into fascism being neglected. With fascism defeated and no effective advocate of the doctrine in Britain, MI5 officers admitted that the reason for investigating the ideology would be 'not so obvious'. Tommy Shelford of MI5's F-Branch advocated the need to continue investigating fascism after the end of the war and believed it would be 'prudent' to devote a significant number of officers to do so.[231] He found support from Victor Rothschild, Head of MI5's Counter-Sabotage Department, and Graham Mitchell of F-Branch, both of whom believed the threat would be significant post-war.[232] MI5's Director General, Sir David Petrie agreed that fascism would have to continue to be monitored, although he questioned how extensive this would need to be as, after several years of war, fascists would struggle to gain any traction for their ideas.[233]

Consideration was given to banning fascism permanently after the war and, although this never happened, prominent fascists were closely investigated into the 1950s.[234] In 1945, however, some at MI5 began to regard communism once again as the primary subversive threat to Britain. In January of that year, Petrie wrote, 'I have long thought ... that, with the end of actual hostilities [communism] would leap up to first place in importance of all the subjects we deal with.'[235] Despite this, communism was not immediately the priority once war had ended; many establishment figures were aware of the threat the Soviets could pose in peacetime but still hoped that Anglo-Soviet relations could remain cordial. Churchill summed up this confusion best. In early 1945, he argued that 'as long as Stalin lasted, Anglo-Russian friendship could be maintained'. Yet, after VE Day months later, he ordered plans to be drawn up for a military conflict with the Soviets, codenamed Operation Unthinkable.[236]

There was such confusion about Soviet post-war intentions because Britain simply did not have sufficient intelligence to make an informed judgement. For MI5, moving from war to peace led to a change from 'intelligence feast to intelligence famine'.[237] The unit within the Security Service which dealt with the Soviets was composed of a small number of officers and was still being 'run down' even at the end of 1945.[238] It was virtually impossible to obtain any information from within the Soviet Union; Britain did not have a single source or a single agent in Moscow and GCHQ was deciphering very few Soviet communications.[239] Britain was in the dark, and was struggling to obtain the most basic information concerning Soviet intentions and Soviet intelligence agencies. Dick White of MI5 believed that the Security Service had become complacent after the wartime successes. 'No one had sufficiently thought about the communist threat', he later admitted, '…the moment I thought about the Russians I realised it was a completely new and uncharted territory.'[240] The Security Service only reverted to investigating communism with real fervour in late 1946 or early 1947. After this, communism again began to dominate its work.[241]

Conclusion

For most of the interwar years, fascism and communism were indelibly linked in the minds of British intelligence officials; there was rarely a discussion on fascism which did not involve a comparison to communism. Such was the all-pervading fear of communism amongst members of the British State that almost all action against any other extreme political organisation took a back seat. During the interwar years, fascists were primarily seen through the prism of their opposition to communism. This was most notable during the 1920s, when the BF's anti-communist activities were, tacitly or expressly, endorsed by elements of the British establishment. Fascists were often regarded as 'useful idiots' in the battle against the all-encompassing foe of communism. During the 1920s, BF members were often violent and broke the law but appear to have been dealt with leniently. The authorities did not view their activities as subversive and believed the greatest threat the BF posed was to law-and-order; this judgement was probably correct. The BF's activities should not, however, be completely underplayed, as they provided some inspiration for the more overtly fascist, subversive BUF.

The surveillance of fascists, in particular members of the BUF, in Britain during the interwar period was nowhere near as extensive as the surveillance of communists during the same time. This was not, however, because State officials had fascist sympathies, but rather because they were so fervently anti-communist. There may have been some within the British establishment who were pro-fascist, but they represented a tiny minority. The authorities were not necessarily too soft on the fascists; rather, the communists were perhaps dealt with too harshly. When the BUF did pose a threat to law-and-order, legislation was introduced to severely limit its activities. In peacetime, the BUF was politically irrelevant and, after the introduction of the Public Order Act in 1936, it held little ability to influence the British public, meaning limited surveillance was consistent with the threat faced.

Until the onset of war, fascists were simply not considered capable of posing a great enough threat to British domestic security by intelligence officials. It was felt that the only way in which fascists could pose such a threat was in the event of war; by the end of the so-called 'phoney-war' in May 1940, fascists were rounded-up and interned en masse. Fascists had only begun to be viewed as a significant subversive threat in the late 1930s, once war with Germany became a probability and evidence pointed to the ties some British fascists had with fascist movements abroad.

Fascism did pose a threat to Britain in the later 1930s and the authorities took proportionate action to deal with this threat. For much of the interwar period, fascism compared favourably with communism in the eyes of officials. Communists posed a subversive threat, whereas fascists did not. The anti-communism of many fascists may have meant that officials were less likely to take action to limit fascist activities but, fundamentally, fascists were not subject to extensive surveillance because they were not believed capable of threatening Britain in peacetime. Concern about communism dominated the thinking of intelligence officials and, even before the end of the war, they again began to see communism as the imminent threat. The Second World War effectively provided a decade-long hiatus in seventy years of Anglo-Soviet hostility and meant that communism was only temporarily not considered as the primary subversive threat to Britain. For some intelligence officials, the need to concentrate on fascists during wartime was a 'dangerous interruption of the Service'.[242] By the end of the war, they could again direct their full focus on the long-term foe—the Soviet Union and communism.

3

A 'RELIGIOUS DOGMA'

COMMUNISM IN POST-WAR BRITAIN

On 4 September 1945, Konstantin Volkov, deputy chief of Soviet intelligence in Turkey, arrived at the British consulate in Istanbul, offering information in exchange for asylum and £50,000. Volkov had promised to reveal the names of hundreds of Soviet agents, most notably, '9 agents in London one of whom was said to be the "head of a section of the British counter-espionage service"'. Unfortunately for Volkov, the case was put in the hands of Kim Philby—'almost certainly' one of those Soviet agents in London he was referring to. Philby, head of the section responsible for Soviet and communist intelligence at MI6, immediately informed his own Soviet handler of Volkov's planned defection. Before the British could safely relocate Volkov to the West, Soviet 'diplomatic couriers' had arrived in Istanbul, sedated Volkov and his wife, and taken them back to Moscow onboard a military aircraft.[1]

One day after Volkov had appeared at the British consulate in Istanbul, 5 September 1945, Igor Gouzenko, a cypher clerk at the Soviet Embassy in Ottawa, left work with over 100 classified documents concealed beneath his shirt. He went to the offices of the *Ottawa Tribunal* offering information on a Soviet spy ring in Canada but was turned away by a reporter who 'thought the story too hot to handle'. After later visiting the Canadian Justice Department, Gouzenko was again rebuffed and told that he was 'in possession of stolen documents.' The Canadian authorities took no action until they were called to Gouzenko's flat on the evening of 6 September after it had been broken into by four Russian men. Fortunately for Gouzenko, he had realised that his home was being watched and had hidden in a neighbour's flat. Following this incident, the Ottawa police intervened, taking Gouzenko and his family to a place of safety. Gouzenko subsequently provided evidence to the Canadian authorities which revealed that the Soviets had penetrated the atomic bomb project and had also recruited spies from the Canadian parliament, governmental departments and intelligence agencies.[2]

Gouzenko's information about the atomic bomb project was of particular significance to Britain. It revealed that the British atomic scientist, Alan Nunn May, had passed atomic secrets to the Soviets during the war.[3] After a prolonged MI5 investigation, Nunn May confessed to his espionage. At his subsequent trial at the Old Bailey in May 1946, he pleaded guilty to breaching the Official Secrets Act and was jailed for ten years. Prosecuting the case, the Attorney General, Sir Hartley Shawcross, told the judge, 'I ought to make it abundantly clear that there is no kind of suggestion that the Russians are enemies or potential enemies.'[4] Within months, however, his statement no longer rang true. The revelations that emerged from Gouzenko's documents had a profound impact on East-West relations; in Britain, they alerted many officials to the severity of the threat that was posed by the Soviet Union.[5] In September 1946, the Joint Intelligence Committee (JIC) stated that the communist threat to Britain was already considerable. Referring to it as 'a serious menace to the interests of the British Commonwealth both outside British territory, and to a lesser extent inside it', the JIC recommended that 'some immediate counter-action should be taken against this danger.' Communism was, the Committee believed, 'the most important external political menace' to Britain and the West, and its threat would likely endure for the 'foreseeable future'.[6]

The JIC report was swiftly followed by a report by a Royal Commission in Canada which had investigated Gouzenko's allegations. The Royal Commission revealed the extent of the Soviet penetration of Canadian public life and, along with JIC warnings, helped to persuade the British Prime Minister, Clement Attlee, to establish a Cabinet Committee on Subversive Activities. In early 1947, at its first meeting, the committee received a report from its working party that made clear, 'what was done in Canada might be attempted with comparable if not equal success in any other democratic country, including our own'. The report pointed out that the Nunn May case suggested a Soviet espionage network already existed in Britain and, if not, attempts would likely be made to establish one. Evidence from Canada indicated that the greatest threat to Britain, therefore, came from the 'Communist organisation'—the CPGB.[7]

The Surveillance of Communists

During wartime, many within the British intelligence community had continued to regard the CPGB with a deep suspicion. Despite the fact that MI5 believed the Party was likely to be involved in espionage, investigations into communists were scaled back.[8] Once the war was over, the Security Service tracked communist activity closely but did not revert to collecting information on all communist sympathisers, as it had done during the interwar years. This was in part due to the attitudes of Clement Attlee, Labour Prime Minister from 1945, and Sir Percy Sillitoe, who took over as MI5 Director General in 1946. Whilst Attlee strongly supported investigating communists, he made clear his belief that MI5 should not hold files on individuals who did not pose a direct subversive threat to Britain.[9] Sillitoe himself had 'trenchant views on the danger of police states' and 'would rather see two or three traitors slip through the net of the Security Service, than be party to the taking of measures which could result in a [totalitarian] regime'.[10]

Although the opinions of Attlee and Sillitoe had some impact, a major impetus for reducing the number of individuals on whom MI5 kept records was a report produced in November 1945 by a retired civil servant, Sir Findlater Stewart.[11] Whilst relatively content that most of the information MI5 held on individuals was justifiable on security grounds, during his inquiry, Stewart came across a number of files in the Security Service registry which concerned him. On one visit to MI5's file registry, he noticed a number of records on individuals whose names were familiar to him; one was the tennis player Eileen Bennett, the other General Martel, a tank expert.[12] He regarded the presence of such files as evidence of the unnecessary surveillance MI5 sometimes carried out and, in his subsequent report, stated that records must only be kept for security reasons and that the registry should be 'cleared periodically of matter which has become obsolete'.[13] The major conclusion of the report was that the Security Service should be 'concerned with the Defence of the Realm from external and internal danger, and with nothing else.'[14] He recommended that MI5 'should be kept absolutely free from any political bias or influence and nothing should be done that might lend colour to any suggestion that it is concerned with any particular section of the community'. Sillitoe was advised to tell staff to have 'no connection whatever with any matters of Party-political character.'[15]

Following the report, MI5 made clear that it was not interested in communism as a 'political creed' but merely 'in its subversionary tendencies in so far as they may act prejudicially on the defence interests of the realm'. By late 1946, MI5 records contained reference to more than 250,000 communists and sympathisers.[16] Intelligence officials felt that, as they only had finite resources, they needed to prioritise who to put under surveillance. In 1947, MI5 rejected a request from the Admiralty to watch the Navy and keep them informed about morale, believing that such work was 'not our business'.[17] Such was the change of impetus in the immediate post-war years that MI5's Deputy DG, Guy Liddell, even went as far as to assert that MI5 was a 'restraining hand' on 'all Government departments'.[18]

The move towards a less exhaustive examination of the CPGB did not, however, last long. By the end of 1948, as the threat posed by communism became clearer, MI5 decided that it would again be necessary to keep a record of all CPGB members.[19] The collection of information on CPGB members was hugely successful; by 1952, the Security Service had managed to identify between 80 and 90 per cent of the CPGB and the YCL.[20] MI5 did not simply track CPGB members, it also collected information on the nominators and assentors of CPGB Parliamentary candidates.[21] It has even been alleged by former South African intelligence officer, Gordon Winter, that the details of all people who voted for the CPGB in General Elections were recorded by intelligence officials. This was determined by examining roll numbers on ballot papers and gave the Security Service further evidence of individuals sympathetic to communism. This claim has not, however, ever been substantiated.[22]

The Security Service used a variety of methods to discover information about the CPGB, with the most common being letter checks and telephone taps.[23] The Security Service also employed surveillance officers ('watchers') to gain information on certain communists.[24] HOWs and watchers helped the Security Service to collect a significant amount of information on the CPGB, but other means—euphemistically referred to as 'elaborate arrangements' in official correspondence—were required to discover the full extent of CPGB activities and to obtain Party records.[25] Most notably, MI5 placed four hidden microphones inside the CPGB's King Street headquarters, which provided an insight into the private thoughts and discussions of CPGB officials.[26] The microphones revealed that members of the Party were concerned that they were being listened to; on one occasion communists even removed the floorboards at King Street to search for bugs, although they did not find any. In the 1960s, the Party sought to safeguard against any listening devices by creating a 'safe room'. Ironically, however, this room was also bugged.[27]

During the 1950s, MI5 also acquired information during a series of covert operations, codenamed STILL LIFE, whereby intelligence operatives broke into CPGB offices and obtained a huge number of records.[28] Such operations were possible because the Security Service had 'quite a number of agents' inside the Party who could give 'good coverage'.[29] Undoubtedly the most important of these was Julia Pirie. Having initially been instructed by MI5 to join the CPGB as a typist, Pirie eventually became personal assistant to the Party's General Secretary, John Gollan. She regularly reported back to her MI5 handlers and met them during cricket matches at the Oval, leaving her with 'a lifelong love of the game'.[30]

Pirie was 'highly likely' to have provided 'information that allowed MI5 to obtain the entire secret membership of the Party'.[31] The Security Service was informed that many Party records were stored at the house of the member, Ronald Berger. Under one of the STILL LIFE operations—Operation PARTY PIECE— the house was watched and the Security Service discovered that Berger's wife would leave the key under the doormat.[32] An MI5 officer made an impression of the key and, when the occupants went away for the weekend, intelligence officials were able to enter the house and copy all of the secret files, gaining an invaluable amount of intelligence.[33] Pirie is also likely to have informed MI5 that the Party had moved some meetings to a safe room in King Street to avoid being overheard by any eavesdropping devices. This led the Security Service to instigate Operation TIE PIN to bug the room. It was possible to access the room from an old coal chute on the pavement outside CPGB headquarters. One Saturday evening, a number of MI5 officers acted as drunken revellers passing King Street in order to create a distraction whilst an MI5 technician placed a false door containing a microphone over the chute.[34]

MI5 employed a variety of methods to counter communism. Break-ins were common; according to the former MI5 officer Peter Wright, 'for five years we bugged and burgled our way across London at the State's behest, whilst pompous bowler-hatted civil servants in Whitehall pretended to look the other way.'[35] Indeed, the Security Service had experts in 'lock picking, burglary, telephone-tapping, placing bugs, opening sealed letters, organising surveillance, photographing targets in compromising circumstances and blackmailers.'[36] Intelligence officers were encouraged to do all that they could to disrupt subversive organisations. On at least one occasion they were said to have 'impregnated lavatory paper with an itching substance at halls hired by communist organisations.'[37] In order to counter communists, there were almost no limits.

Although MI5's work was carried out covertly, many communists were aware that they were being spied upon. In 1948, one of the listening devices within King Street picked up John Gollan saying as much.[38] On another occasion, during a meeting of 'Science for Peace', a Special Branch officer reported that the communist scientist J.B.S. Haldane explicitly referred to the 'representative of MI5 in the audience'.[39] By 1951, mindful of surveillance, communists had become more security-conscious, making telephone and letter checks much less effective.[40] Despite this, the Communists were not always aware of the extent to which they had been penetrated; one time the CPGB's industrial organiser was heard stating that 'MI5 coverage of the Party was extremely haphazard'.[41] Crucially, the Communists appear to have had no knowledge of MI5 officers working within King Street. Julia Pirie seems never to have been suspected and she continued to receive a Communist Party pension, paid from a bank in Italy, until her death in 2008.[42]

E.P. Thompson and Eric Hobsbawm

The surveillance of communists in Britain was substantial in the decade or so immediately following the Second World War, despite the fact that the CPGB had relatively few members and was electorally unsuccessful (it received fewer votes than the left-wing Common Wealth Party in 1945 and did not win a parliamentary election after 1950).[43] Intelligence officials believed that it still 'had the capacity to punch far above its numerical weight'.[44] As one MI5 report stated, whilst the CPGB membership 'represents no more than about one in a thousand of the total population of the country ... the importance of the Party as a subversive movement, as an espionage organisation and as a potential Fifth Column is considerably greater than such a small proportion would suggest.'[45]

The prospect of British communists acting as a 'Fifth Column' in the event of a war with Russia was taken very seriously by security officials. MI5 kept a record of CPGB members 'so that in case of war they could be dealt with speedily and efficaciously'.[46] By the early 1950s, significant plans had been put in place to intern communists if such a war occurred. The use of two sites on the Isle of Man as permanent internment camps was arranged, whilst the Home Office requisitioned Ascot and Epsom Racecourses and a holiday camp in Rhyl to hold detainees temporarily.[47] By 1954 the authorities had identified around 3,000 people to be detained in the event of war, 1,000 of which were 'British subjects' and the rest 'aliens'.[48]

Although reference is given in MI5 documents to a 'master list of potential detainees known as the Everest List', it has never been released.[49] It is, however, possible to find information on some of those individuals on the list from documents contained in their PFs. In the file of E.P. Thompson, best known as an historian, is a note from April 1953 stating that he had been added to the Category 'A' detention list.[50] This was dated just days after MI5 had received a report that he had been elected a member of the Yorkshire District Committee of the CPGB.[51] Within a week of Thompson resigning from the District Committee in April 1956 he was demoted from the Category A list, suggesting that MI5 was most concerned about those who held positions of power in the Party.[52] As soon as they stepped down from such positions, they were seemingly considered to be less of a threat.

Thompson's file is also insightful in showing the deep divisions within the CPGB following Khrushchev's denunciation of Stalin in February 1956 and the brutal repression of the uprising in Hungary, by Soviet troops, later that same year. Intercepted letters made it clear that Thompson had lost faith in the leadership of the Party.[53] The Security Service was particularly interested in a letter Thompson sent to Bert Ramelson, Secretary of the Yorkshire Communist Party, in May 1956. He wrote,

> All I can say is, Thank God there is no chance of this [Executive Committee] having power in Britain: it will destroy in a month every liberty of thought, conscience and expression, which it has taken the British people 300 odd years to win.[54]

In the margin of a copy of the letter an MI5 officer scribbled '!!'. Intelligence officials were undoubtedly jubilant to discover such a message, which was described as 'interesting and helpful as an indication of the attitude of one of the leading party intellectuals in this county.'[55]

MI5 discovered that Thompson had resigned from the Communist Party in November 1956.[56] Within days, intelligence officials began to re-examine his security significance and, by the end of November 1956, his name had been completely removed from the list of those to be detained in the event of war with Russia.[57] Despite this, Thompson's file remained open, and the Security Service would occasionally add material to it that had little significance from a security point of view. It is clear from his file that Thompson never posed a threat to the British State. The reasoning behind continuing to collect information on him over such a long period is, therefore, questionable.

Thompson was representative of intellectuals who became more prominent in the CPGB after the war. Along with several other well-known scholars, notably Christopher Hill and Eric Hobsbawm, Thompson was a member of the Communist Party Historians' Group.[58] The group concerned MI5 because it was believed to be encouraging all CPGB members to 'take an interest in the Marxist interpretation of local history'.[59] Hobsbawm, widely regarded as one of the leading British historians of the post-war age, first joined the CPGB in 1936 as a student at Cambridge, and was watched by MI5 from 1942.[60] In his memoirs, Hobsbawm wrote that he was certain he had been tracked by the Security Service. Wondering 'did I already have an intelligence file when I was at Cambridge?', he stated that he was certain he had one by the middle of 1942, after 'a friendly sergeant in Field Security told me that I was supposed to be watched'.[61] He made huge efforts to discover details about his file and in 2009, aged 91, made a request to view it. This request was, however, rejected and the file remained classified.[62] The Security Service rarely, if ever, releases PFs when the subject of the file is still alive. The file was only released after his death.

Hobsbawm's own views on how he believed the intelligence community perceived him—recorded in his memoirs—can be compared with the details contained in his MI5 file. During the war, he served in the Royal Engineers and the Army Education Corps. In

Interesting Times, he writes how he 'was clearly seen as a suspicious character, to be kept out of sensitive areas such as abroad, even after the USSR became Britain's ally and the Party devoted itself to winning the war.' Indeed, he writes that he did not leave the British Isles during the whole war, 'the longest period I have ever spent without crossing some land or sea frontier'.[63] The MI5 file proves that he correctly assumed he was prevented from travelling abroad; a report from 1944 made clear that he was 'introducing strong partisan views' into his unit and propagandising on behalf of the Communist Party. MI5 recommended that steps be taken to prevent Hobsbawm being sent abroad as, 'it is very likely that he might cause similar trouble ... he would be far better kept under our eye in this country'.[64] Towards the end of the war, in April 1945, Hobsbawm applied for a job at the BBC and was considered to be 'a most suitable candidate'. He was, however, rejected for the role after MI5 warned the BBC that he was 'not likely to lose any opportunity he may get to disseminate propaganda and obtain recruits for the Communist Party'.[65] The BBC agreed not to accept him, but he did contribute to the Corporation's output on an ad hoc basis until the early 1950s.[66]

After the war, intelligence officials continued to collect information about Hobsbawm. In December 1950, Special Branch described him as a 'self avowed communist ... one of the intellectuals of the Party', and reported that he had held a number of meetings at his flat which had been attended by 'well known communists', including the scientist J.D. Bernal.[67] In January 1952, the Security Service decided to take out a HOW on Hobsbawm, 'to establish the identities of his contacts, and to unearth overt or covert intellectual communists who may be unknown to [MI5]'.[68] Some of the letters intercepted were written in French and had to be translated for MI5.[69] MI5 discovered very little from a security perspective through their surveillance of Hobsbawm; checks on him only showed what they already knew—that he was a communist who was active within the Party. One of the few challenges security officials faced in investigating him was the fact that, for many, his name was difficult to spell; documents within his file refer to names such as 'Hogspawn', 'Hobsthorn', 'Hopsbaum' and a variety of other spellings.[70]

Although MI5 do not appear to have learned anything from a security perspective from their surveillance of Hobsbawm, they did gain knowledge about his personal life.[71] One intercepted letter showed that he had been suffering with jaundice, whilst a source reported that he had suffered an 'emotional breakdown'.[72] The Security Service also discovered that Hobsbawm and his wife had a significant difference of opinion over communism.[73] Further surveillance revealed that he was not liked within the CPGB; one report stated that Hobsbawm was 'out of date with his Communism' and 'would probably not survive if the Russians came'.[74] Despite his absolute dedication to communism, in 1956, MI5 discovered that, like E.P. Thompson, Hobsbawm was dissatisfied with the way in which the CPGB leadership reacted to Khrushchev's denunciation of Stalin and the Soviet response to the Hungarian uprising. Together with a number of communists, he signed a letter which condemned the way the CPGB leadership had provided 'uncritical support' to the Soviet action in Hungary.[75] However, unlike Thompson, Hobsbawm did not leave the Party. He remained a member until its dissolution in 1991, although was less committed to the Party, and thus continued to be of interest to MI5.[76]

The most striking feature from the files of both Hobsbawm and Thompson is the banality of the material that was collected on them. The surveillance of both men appears, at first, to have been a waste of MI5 resources. During the 1990s, however, Hobsbawm gave two media interviews in which he was questioned about his commitment to communism. In both, he seemed to suggest that the deaths of millions in the Soviet Union would have been justified if they had resulted in the formation of a 'communist utopia.'[77] Whilst he never blindly accepted communist dogma and was privately critical of the CPGB, his comments allude to his deep commitment to the ideology. In this context it is hard, therefore, to be critical of the Security Service for collecting information on him. It should be noted, however, that MI5 do not seem to have ever picked up that Hobsbawm believed in a communist utopia so fervently. Whilst it was clear that he was deeply committed to communism, MI5 never discovered, as a result of surveillance, that he was as dedicated as his later comments suggested.

A New Type of Communist

Thompson and Hobsbawm were representative of prominent individuals who came to the notice of MI5 in the 1940s and 1950s as a result of their communist beliefs. Investigations into communists post-war differed from those carried out during the interwar years; MI5 found itself focusing on a very different type of person after 1945. Pre-war, the Party consisted of an 'almost exclusively' working-class membership but, during the war, 'considerable numbers of clerical, intellectual, professional and scientific workers, who before harboured no more than left-wing political tendencies, were drawn into the communist fold.'[78] Whilst the Party still mainly consisted of working classes, by 1945 it contained a small, but significant, number of 'intellectuals' or 'professionals'.[79] The changing nature of the type of people attracted to communism meant that during its investigations into the Party, MI5 found itself scrutinising high-profile individuals. Files were held on individuals such as the folk singer Ewan MacColl, the actor Michael Redgrave and the novelist Doris Lessing because of their membership of the CPGB or sympathy with communism. Information was also collected on Kingsley Martin, Editor of the *New Statesman*, and the playwright J.B. Priestley, as they moved in left-wing circles, although their links to communism were tenuous.[80]

Whilst such prominent individuals were strongly committed to the communist cause, they posed little, if any, danger to the security of the British State. In the immediate post-war years, however, there were some professional, intellectual, individuals who believed in the ideology of communism that did have the capability to threaten British internal security. Those who had become attracted to communism during wartime were said by security officials to comprise 'university students and graduates, civil servants and members of the professions.' These individuals posed a different threat to that posed by rank-and-file CPGB members as, officials believed, their loyalty lay mainly with the 'the ideological conception of international communism' rather than with the Party itself.[81] One official argued that 'this type of enthusiast was far more dangerous than the known Communist acting under direction of the party'.[82] As a report from 1948 stated,

> If there were any subversive activity on behalf of a foreign power carried out in peacetime, one would expect it to be carried out by individuals of the intellectual group acting on their own initiative. The working-class group is unlikely to be the source of peace-time espionage.[83]

Communism began to be seen more as an ideology than a political viewpoint; as Christopher Warner of the Foreign Office wrote, communism, 'must be viewed ... as a religious dogma and faith which can inspire such fanaticism and self-sacrifice as we associate with the early Christians and the rise of Islam, and which in the minds of believers transcends all lesser loyalties to family, class or even country.'[84] Alan Nunn May exemplified this kind of person, a man willing to betray Britain due to his devotion to the communist ideology. The fact that Nunn May had also concealed his communist beliefs greatly concerned intelligence officials, particularly as many of those discovered in Canada, as a result of Gouzenko's information, had done something similar.[85] Roger Hollis of MI5 believed that 'one of the most alarming points of the Canadian case was that most of the agents recruited by the Russians were not people with open and obvious communist connections.'[86] It was thought that many communist sympathisers, both in Canada and elsewhere, had been discouraged 'from joining the [Communist] Party openly.'[87]

If this was worrying enough to MI5, evidence from Canada also suggested that certain people were deliberately chosen by Soviet recruiters because of their ability to acquire secret information.[88] This was certainly understood by Attlee, who wrote in 1948, 'the Russian technique in all countries is to infiltrate their sympathisers into key positions in all circles, official and non-official, and by this means to influence policy'.[89] These types of people had the ability to cause a great deal more damage than ordinary CPGB members, as one MI5 memo made clear,

> The higher social status of the present membership has brought a new danger to the fore as the scientists and professional workers, who are now in the Party ranks, have access to far more secret information than had the pre-war membership. The danger of leakage of information to the Soviet Union is thus very much greater than it was previously.[90]

There is evidence that the CPGB took an active role in ensuring that its young members with an intellectual background gained influential positions in the British State. An unnamed former Cambridge University student later told Peter Hennessy that, towards the end of World War Two, the CPGB General Secretary, Harry Pollitt, instructed communist undergraduates to gain First Class Degrees in order to secure influential posts. As Hennessy writes, 'it would be intriguing to know if MI5 was aware of the pitch.'[91]

The fallout from the espionage cases in Canada and, particularly, Nunn May's conviction, led the Attlee government to formalise security procedures. In March 1948, the Prime Minister announced in the House of Commons the introduction of negative vetting of individuals 'employed in connection with work, the nature of which is vital to the security of the State.'[92] Negative vetting, or the 'purge procedure' as it became known, involved submitting the names of individuals employed in such roles to MI5 to see if any information had been recorded against them. If the Security Service had a record that they were either a CPGB member, a communist sympathiser or associated with a fascist organisation, the individual would be removed from their role and either transferred to non-secret work or dismissed.[93] The policy of vetting and removing communists from positions allowing them access to secret information was not entirely new; during the interwar years an informal system was introduced.[94]

By the end of the 1940s, MI5's perceptions of the threat communists and communism could pose had changed significantly. Before the war, the intelligence community feared that communists would cause 'unrest in the industrial sphere and in the Armed Forces of the Crown, leading possibly to political strikes and even revolutionary outbreaks.'[95] In early 1950 it was stated that 'it is most unlikely that the Party leadership has any faith in its ability to bring about a successful revolution by its own efforts in the near future.' The Party itself remained worthy of consideration because, although it was no longer directly tied to Moscow and had not joined the new Communist International, the Cominform, it was still seen as subservient to and slavishly admiring of Soviet Russia.[96]

MI5 expended significant resources investigating the CPGB, but its most important post-war work was to scrutinise the 'intellectual' communists in Britain who could potentially cause the most damage. In July 1950, MI5's John Marriott wrote, 'it should be regarded just as important to identify convinced Marxists, particularly among educated people, as it is to identify card-holding members of the Communist Party.'[97] By 1951, the Security Service 'allocated special staff to a study of communism among the professional classes; and this study will include, so far as is practicable, a search for intellectual sympathisers with communism as well as actual party members.'[98] Having learned from the Canadian case, MI5 was particularly concerned about potential subversives in jobs that allowed them access to secret information. This meant that they sought to investigate more widely those who worked for the State, particularly in the field of atomic energy, most notably, atomic scientists.

Surveillance of Scientists

During the war, a significant number of scientists who were communists or communist sympathisers had been given security clearance. Such individuals would normally have been refused clearance, but winning the war was prioritised.[99] Post-war, this meant that numerous scientists, recorded as having communist sympathies, were working in roles which gave them access to classified information.[100] The problem this created was articulated by MI5's John Collard, who wrote that Britain was left with 'a number of individuals whose loyalty to this country ... must be considered dubious owing either to their alien origin or their political sympathies.'[101] In the months following Nunn May's conviction, MI5 re-examined the information they held on atomic physicists who were foreign-born or who were believed to have held far-left political views.[102] In July of that year, Guy Liddell advocated placing informants in 'all laboratories where work on atomic energy was going on'. Such informants, he stated, should 'make it their business to know as much as possible about the general mode of living and political views of young scientists.'[103]

In early 1950, another British atomic scientist, Klaus Fuchs, confessed to having passed secret information to the Soviets whilst working on the Manhattan Project during the war. His conviction for espionage inevitably led MI5 to increase their scrutiny of atomic scientists. One of Fuchs' closest colleagues, Professor Rudolf Peierls, was tracked so closely by intelligence officials that one surveillance report detailed his 'travelling to Paddington station, where ... he [took] a bath in the Gents Toilet on No. 1 Platform'.[104] MI5 even intercepted, and included in his security file, a letter to Peierls from his young son Ronnie.[105]

The Security Service also investigated Fuchs' boss at the Atomic Energy Research Establishment (AERE) at Harwell, Herbert Skinner, and his wife, Erna Skinner. The Skinners had never previously come to MI5's attention but a file was opened on them, and their phone was tapped in the hope of learning more about Fuchs' activities.[106] Despite not having found any incriminating evidence against them, intelligence officials continued to watch the couple closely for many months after Fuchs' conviction. MI5 was particularly concerned about Erna, largely because she had previously been Fuchs' mistress, but also because of both her German-Austrian origin and her having a number of left-wing friends.[107] In July 1950 James Robertson of MI5 made an assessment of the Skinners. He wrote,

> Since the SKINNER's, on their own admission, have Communist friends, they may share these friends views, and that Professor SKINNER's [move] from Harwell to Liverpool University should not therefore be a ground for the Security Service ceasing to

pay them attention. I suggested, for example, as one possible measure, that enquiries should be made periodically through sources in the University, as to whether or not they continue to have associations with Communists, and if so with whom; also that an occasional visit from a member of the Security Service might have a salutary deterrent effect.[108]

MI5 continued to watch the couple although Herbert Skinner had left Harwell and was not, himself, considered to represent a security risk.[109] They kept a file on the Skinners until at least 1953.

Herbert Skinner was not the only one of Fuchs' colleagues at Harwell who felt the pressure in the weeks and months following Fuchs' arrest. Members of the scientific community became suspicious of each other. Professor Brian Flowers, who eventually succeeded Fuchs as head of Harwell's theoretical division, spoke of how the case was a 'dreadful morale breaker.'[110] The wife of one AERE employee later wrote that following Fuchs' arrest,

> there were a series of "purges" in Harwell. Security was tightened to an extent that nearly amounted to panic. Anyone with the smallest suspicion of Communist activities in their past lives was under scrutiny, and all those vulnerable to blackmail, or with a secret to hide, came into the category classed as "unreliable". If one had ever been seen reading a copy of the "Daily Worker", it seemed one was to be marked for life.[111]

Members of the theoretical division were rigorously investigated; some were transferred to administrative jobs and others left Harwell permanently.[112] Fuchs' actions also impacted the morale of his former wartime colleagues. Norris Bradbury, who had worked alongside Fuchs at Los Alamos, perhaps best articulated the effect of his actions saying, 'For the first time Fuchs raised the question among the scientists, "Who can you trust?" We felt as if we'd all been betrayed.'[113] A member of the British team in wartime America, Frank Kearton, simply described it as 'the worst time in my life.'[114]

One of the most important repercussions of Fuchs' espionage was the introduction of even stronger security measures and investigations into individuals working in the atomic energy field.

Shortly after Fuchs' conviction, Clement Attlee took the first steps to strengthen security by establishing a Committee on Positive Vetting (PV).[115] British officials not only felt that there was a need to tighten security procedures, but also deemed that they needed to be seen to be tightening security procedures by their American counterparts.[116] Fuchs' actions had a hugely detrimental effect on Anglo-American relations and 'led to a crisis in the Special Relationship'.[117]

Almost immediately after Fuchs' arrest, the Cabinet Committee on Atomic Energy acknowledged that 'there might be a demand [from the US] for change in security clearance policy'. By March 1950, this was made clear when the General Manager of the US Atomic Energy Committee, Carroll Wilson, informed the British Ambassador in Washington that, 'unfortunately as a result of the Fuchs case nobody over here would believe that' British security was up to the required standard.[118]

Prior to Fuchs' arrest, the British had been on the verge of reaching an agreement to resume sharing classified atomic material with their American counterparts, which had ceased following the passage of the 1946 Atomic Energy Act in the USA. The Act, commonly known as the McMahon Act, banned the sharing of classified atomic information with foreign powers.[119] The revelations of Fuchs' espionage ended any potential agreement, and led Attlee's government to realise that they needed to prove to their American counterparts Britain's commitment to improving security. The government moved to introduce much more intrusive security procedures after receiving a report from the PV Committee.[120]

The Committee sought to ensure that individuals with 'access to cosmic [nuclear] documents' were beyond reproach. In order to do so, it recommended that more substantial investigations—positive vetting—should be undertaken into the reliability of individuals in around 1,000 posts.[121] The introduction of positive vetting led security officials to conduct much more intrusive inquiries into the lives of individuals, which involved a security questionnaire, character references and an interview process with either the subject or referees.[122] Although the process was originally intended to cover only 1,000 jobs, it quickly expanded to 11,000 before increasing steadily in the following years.[123]

The fallout from the Fuchs case and the disappearance of another atomic scientist, Bruno Pontecorvo in September 1950, made officials much more reluctant to accept the employment of individuals about whom they had even minor concerns. Lord Portal, Controller of Production (Atomic Energy) at the Ministry of Supply, argued that there was a need 'to get rid of anyone who is tainted' working within the atomic energy field with only one month's notice.[124] In the years that followed Fuchs' conviction, however, many more scientists found themselves caught up in an increasingly security-conscious environment. One scientist at Harwell, a British national, was placed under extensive surveillance and eventually removed from his post because he had been born in Russia and had parents still living in the Soviet Union. This was despite the fact that security officials judged him to be entirely trustworthy.[125]

By the summer of 1953, foreign-born scientists were considered too great a security issue and, according to the *Daily Express*, Harwell had decided that 'all scientists recruited ... must now be British born of British parents.'[126] In 1964 it was revealed in Parliament that a total of twelve individuals (civil servants and government-employed atomic scientists) had been moved from their posts since the Fuchs case, 'in the interests of national security because they were foreign-born, or because they had relatives living behind the Iron Curtain or because of a combination of both these circumstances.'[127]

In the years that followed Fuchs' conviction, security officials did not merely concentrate their efforts on investigating atomic scientists. Investigations became more wide-ranging and scientists from a variety of disciplines came under their scrutiny. MI5 was very concerned about scientists; not only did they have access to the most secret information, but they also appeared to be unusually receptive to communist ideology. The Cabinet Secretary, Norman Brook, noted this in a report on the Security Service. He wrote,

> Even more dangerous, and more difficult to identify, are the intellectual-Marxists who for various reasons refrain from

joining any Communist organisation, but are strongly influenced by Communist doctrine and propaganda and may develop intellectual loyalties to these ideas that would override their national duty. These ideas evidently have a strong appeal to a certain type of intellectual; and scientists and artists, in particular, seem to be especially susceptible to them. It is significant that it was in this class that Fuchs and Pontecorvo were found. There is an undoubted gap in our knowledge of potential agents for the Russian intelligence service or of people who might be willing, and able, to convey useful info to the Russians.[128]

In the post-Fuchs environment of early 1950s Britain, and with Anglo-American security cooperation on the line, the decisions security officials deemed necessary were understandable. Unfortunately, this resulted in many cases where the individual concerned was effectively regarded as guilty until proven innocent. In 1956, this shift in policy was formally articulated by a Committee of Privy Councillors, appointed to conduct an inquiry into security procedures in the public services. They made clear that, in the case of any doubt as to a person's connections to communism, it was essential to 'incline in favour of the State rather than the individual'.[129]

The Security Service was faced with a very complex task in assessing individuals. Whilst it was possible for them to prove a positive (that a person was a Soviet agent) it was impossible for them to prove a negative (that a person was not a Soviet agent). The difficulty facing the Security Service was identified by MI5's Ronnie Reed. He wrote that the only way to be certain about an individual's loyalty was to have him under continuous observation and to run letter and telephone checks, which was obviously 'impracticable'.[130]

Whilst some scientists were removed from jobs with access to secret information, it is also highly likely that other innocent individuals were unable to pursue their chosen careers in atomic science due to security restrictions. In the decades that followed Fuchs' conviction, talented foreign-born scientists were likely prevented from taking up certain posts. The stringent security measures enacted may have made Britain safer in denying some individuals access to secret information. However, these measures may also have meant that Britain failed to benefit from the expertise of those who posed no security threat.[131]

A Security Risk?

The British State could not afford to take risks by employing people about whom there were security concerns. This did not merely include those employed directly by the State, but also affected government contractors. In 1953, concerns were raised about the reliability of Joseph Poliakoff, who had installed and checked Churchill's deaf-aid apparatus in No. 10. His employment was said by MI5 to 'constitute a risk' as he was Russian-born and his company had previously both employed known communists and sold equipment to the Russian Trade Delegation in London. Although the Security Service had no information suggesting that Poliakoff had made 'improper use of the opportunities he had had in servicing the equipment', it was agreed with Churchill that he should be replaced.[132] The Prime Minister's hearing difficulties nearly caused another security problem shortly afterwards when microphones and loudspeakers were installed around the cabinet table so that he could hear his colleagues. Shortly after the equipment was fitted, officials were informed that a local taxi driver had said that he was picking up the ministerial discussions on his radio. As one minister later said, 'that was the end of that experiment!'[133]

The government had the ability to demand that private firms, engaged on secret government contracts, remove certain employees if MI5 had adverse information about them. Unlike the 'purge' of individuals in the public sector, this was not publicly announced.[134] In 1954, the topic was raised in the House of Commons when it was discovered that Rolls Royce had dismissed an employee after government officials had expressed concerns about the individual's 'reliability' working on a secret contract. The Minister of Supply, Duncan Sandys, defended the policy by stating, 'national security requires us to guard very zealously our technical defence secrets. We try to be as fair as possible to the individual, but we also have to be fair to the community.'¹³⁵ The authorised history of MI5 states that the dismissal of private employees was 'rare.'¹³⁶

The government policy to 'purge' communists had unintended consequences. Some private companies introduced their own politically-motivated 'purges'. Two individuals employed by the Eastern Growers Marketing Association were reportedly dismissed in September 1948, after the managing director had made clear 'we cannot have people in this office with extreme views, whether Fascist, Socialist or Communist.'¹³⁷ In April 1949, the John Lewis Partnership asked employees to sign a statement saying that they were not members of the CPGB or sympathisers to communism; those who refused would be dismissed.¹³⁸ The case drew attention to the practice and led to a debate in Parliament; the Minister of Labour, George Isaacs, clarified that the government strongly opposed the action of John Lewis, and suggested that they should drop the policy. Isaacs stated that 'no good purpose can be served by trying to pursue a man for his political opinions, because one would only get into the region of religious opinions and so on.'¹³⁹ Vetting was necessary, but the climate created by the government's policy encouraged some employers to discriminate against their staff on political grounds.

When vetting was initially introduced, investigations were limited to examining an individual's political views. However, after the defection of Burgess and Maclean in 1951 other factors began to be considered.¹⁴⁰ Individuals were considered a potential security risk if they had certain 'character defects' such as 'drunkenness, addiction to drugs, homosexuality or other forms of loose living.' These 'defects', security officials believed, could 'make a man unreliable or expose him to blackmail or influence by foreign agents.'¹⁴¹ Indeed, it was discovered in 1962 that John Vassall, an Admiralty clerk, had been blackmailed into spying for the Soviets. Vassall, a gay man, was lured into a honeytrap by the KGB in 1955 whilst clerk to the British Naval Attaché at the British Embassy in Moscow. After being confronted by the KGB with 'compromising' photographs which had been taken secretly and showed him with other men, Vassall agreed to provide the Soviets with secret naval documents. He was arrested in September 1962, admitted his espionage, and was jailed for eighteen years.[142] Homosexuality was illegal in Britain until 1967 and, therefore, gay men were of particular concern to British security officials. Despite this, MI5 rejected a proposal from the Treasury in 1965 to bar any known homosexuals from working in a role which required positive vetting. By 1969, almost half of all the 'character defect' cases involved homosexuals. It is, however, unclear how many men were transferred or removed from their posts.[143]

Although the majority of those vetted worked directly or indirectly for the State and had access to secret information, MI5 also secretly investigated and vetted those who worked at the BBC.[144] BBC employees were vetted as a result of concerns that they could, in some way, spread their communist beliefs across the airwaves. For similar reasons, some within the British State worried about the capacity of teachers to preach communist views to students in classrooms.[145] Despite these concerns, during the 1950s, the State created no rules to ban or discipline communist teachers and preferred to leave this to Directors of Education and HM Inspectors. In 1951, Middlesex County Council decided to take more formal action and passed a resolution stating no person should be appointed as a school headteacher if they had any association with communism or fascism. Although this was met with objections, the Middlesex Education Authority was adamant that it intended to proceed with the policy.[146] It is unclear whether any teachers were removed or denied promotions because of their political views and, after the early 1950s, the government does not appear to have been too concerned about the issue.[147]

Even though Whitehall may never have formally introduced a policy to encourage the removal of communists within the education sector, it does appear that they were informally excluded where possible, particularly in higher education. In his memoir, Eric Hobsbawm wrote that whilst it was 'neither as hysterical nor as thorough-going as in the USA ... it was a bad time to be a communist in the intellectual professions'.[148] He asserted that, between the late 1940s and late 1950s, 'to the best of my knowledge, no known communists were appointed to university posts, nor, if they were already in teaching posts, were they promoted'. Indeed, Hobsbawm believed that he himself was subject to this informal procedure, as he was 'turned down for several posts in economic history at Cambridge and did not get a promotion to a Readership in London until 1959'.[149] Hobsbawm was by no means the only communist who complained of finding their career progression in academia blocked. There are numerous stories of others who found themselves rejected for promotion.[150] Although they may not have been removed from their posts, it seems that some academics were quietly discriminated against because of their political beliefs.

In 1960, the Security Service decided that, in exceptional circumstances, they would make inquiries in schools. Rather than investigating teachers, however, they mainly focused on pupils. Graham Mitchell, MI5's Deputy DG, believed this was necessary because 'childhood indoctrination is part of international Communist Practice', and due to the fact that several prominent communists had 'acquired their political consciousness while at school'.[151] This was a significant turnaround as, when vetting was first introduced in 1948, a youthful indulgence in communism was not considered important.[152] The authorities seem likely to have changed their opinion on this issue after having discovered that Burgess and Maclean had developed their communist beliefs at Cambridge and then apparently distanced themselves from communism in order to conceal their true beliefs. In October 1960, plans to investigate a small number of pupils at schools were formalised; MI5 agreed with the Home Office that inquiries could be made in cases where it was impossible to find information in any other way, and that each inquiry would require the Home Secretary's prior consent.[153] The extent of, and results from, such investigations remain unknown.

British McCarthyism

It is undeniable that, as the 1950s progressed, the British State increasingly discriminated against individuals because of their political views. Positive vetting procedures which prevented communists from working in jobs with access to secret information have been described as a 'silent', inherently British, version of McCarthyism.[154] Whilst in the strictest sense it may be possible to argue that a 'purge' of communists in the public sector did bear a resemblance to aspects of McCarthyism, Britain was not the only country which decided such action was necessary. Switzerland was another that excluded communists from jobs which gave them access to sensitive material.[155]

The introduction of vetting in Britain was deliberated over at great length by both politicians and officials who sought to protect both civil liberties and security whilst avoiding overt political discrimination.[156] In America, communists were hounded and publicly exposed but, in Britain, when action was taken against suspected communists it was done discreetly, and attempts were made to find them alternative employment. As Douglas Hyde, former news editor of the *Daily Worker*, said when comparing the two countries, 'the British witch-hunt seemed pretty 'civilised' … [Britain] set out not to make martyrs whereas McCarthy made them left, right, and centre.'[157]

Between 1947 and 1956, in America, 2,700 federal employees were dismissed and 12,000 resigned. The British 'purge' bore no resemblance to that seen across the Atlantic. Even accounting for the differences in population size, the British numbers were much smaller; some figures state that only 124 people were dismissed from the Civil Service across the same time period, with a number of those individuals probably reassigned to non-sensitive work.[158] Whilst the number of people affected by the 'purge' in Britain was relatively small, it is likely that numerous other individuals were either rejected before they gained a job with the State or discouraged from applying for Civil Service posts altogether.[159]

Britain and America were worlds apart in the way in which they treated individuals believed to have communist sympathies. Indeed, so different were the two nations that some American actors, writers, and members of the film industry, moved to Britain to continue their careers after being blacklisted in their own country because of their political beliefs.[160] One such individual was the actor and director Sam Wanamaker, who moved to Britain in 1951. Wanamaker, a member of the Communist Party of the USA, left America before he was subjected to a hearing by McCarthy's House Un-American Activities Committee. In February 1955, he compared life in the US to that in the UK; whilst 'freedom' in the US was 'non-existent', he said, in Britain there was a 'tolerance towards Communism ... in the true spirit of democracy.'[161] Ironically, such comments are only known about because they were reported by 'a reliable source' to Special Branch and placed in a file MI5 held on Wanamaker. Although he sought to avoid associating himself with communism too directly after moving to Britain, Wanamaker was still considered worthy of some investigation by MI5.[162] The Security Service collected information on him when he sought to apply for permanent residence in Britain. Whilst he was never placed directly under surveillance, MI5 did recommend that Wanamaker should be added to a list of individuals to be interned 'in the event of an emergency' because of his communist background.[163] Life was far from perfect in Britain for individuals like Wanamaker who held communist sympathies, but it was much preferable to life in the US. Wanamaker was free to work as an actor and, as his biographer Diana Devlin has written, 'Sam and [his wife] Charlotte were free to associate with theatre people who were members of the Communist Party of Great Britain, or firm supporters of the Labour Party'.[164] Indeed, despite the investigations into him by MI5, Wanamaker was granted permission to stay indefinitely in Britain by the Home Office in 1957, continued his acting career unobstructed, and was later awarded an honorary CBE for his work.[165]

The type of witch-hunt seen in the United States was simply not possible in Britain; it was anathema to British values.[166] Across the British political spectrum, there was a consensus that policies to combat communism should be rational and effective. Occasional demands from dissenting backbench MPs for the CPGB to be outlawed failed to gain traction and were easily dismissed.[167] Neither Attlee nor Churchill had any desire for Britain to follow the American course, and both were dismayed by McCarthy and his politics. In 1953, freed from the constraints of high office, Attlee made his feelings clear. After receiving criticism from McCarthy, he stated that he would not be 'instructed by a beginner like

A 'RELIGIOUS DOGMA'

Senator McCarthy' on how to handle communists.[168] Churchill, on the other hand, was still Prime Minister in 1953, and thus had to be more circumspect in criticising the McCarthyite excesses. It is said that such was his dislike of what was happening in America that he inserted an anti-McCarthyite passage into Queen Elizabeth II's coronation speech.[169]

Despite the distaste for the way the Americans dealt with communists, Britain continued to work closely with them on security matters. This included responding to requests from the American authorities for information about individuals who were believed to be a security threat. In late 1953, J. Robert Oppenheimer – who had played a crucial role in the development of the atomic bomb during the war as head of the Los Alamos research laboratory – travelled to London. He had been the subject of McCarthyite investigations in the USA for several years due to his past communist associations. MI5 were asked by the FBI to track Oppenheimer's activities whilst he was in Britain and provide 'any pertinent information concerning [his] activities and contacts ... that may come to your attention'.[170]

In response, MI5 contacted Special Branch and Harwell – where Oppenheimer was due to visit – asking for reports about any adverse information on him that came their way.[171] Although the investigations revealed very little, MI5 provided the FBI representative at the American Embassy in London with 'the gist' of Oppenheimer's movements – including information that he had attended a dinner party in Oxford – 'but no details'. Apart from asking for reports, MI5 believed that there was 'no justification for taking any special surveillance action.'[172]

Whilst the British authorities did provide the Americans with some information on individuals when requested, it appears that they were reluctant to send detailed reports. This was made clear on one occasion when the FBI asked for help in proving that the actor Charlie Chaplin had associated himself with communism. An internal MI5 memo stated, 'I think it better not to volunteer the information ... this is [scarcely] of any security significance'. As a result, the Americans were only given the barest details.[173] Often, it seems, the British authorities disagreed with the premise of such investigations. Special Branch privately described some American requests for information as 'dangerous and stupid' and MI5 appear to have agreed.[174] They may have continued to respond to requests for information, but this did not mean they were, in any way, endorsing the American way of doing things.

Britain never really had a McCarthy-type figure in political life. Two public figures did, however, develop a name for advocating similar policies—Sir Waldron Smithers and Lord Vansittart. Smithers, Conservative MP for Orpington, was a vociferous anti-communist, actively involved in anti-communist organisations and propaganda. In 1947, his request for the government to set up a 'Committee on Un-British Activities' was swiftly rejected.[175] Smithers routinely made anti-communist speeches in the Commons and, on a number of occasions, requested that the CPGB be outlawed.[176] In 1951, he demanded that the government prosecute the so-called 'Red Dean of Canterbury', Hewlett Johnson, and stated that, when Johnson was inevitably convicted, he should be 'publicly hanged' to show the sincerity of the government's anti-communism.[177]

The positions Smithers took were extreme and he was very much a lone voice in the Commons. He was not taken seriously and was instead viewed by those in power as nothing more than an irritant. He regularly wrote to Churchill imploring him to do more to counter communism, yet it appears that the Prime Minister paid little, if any, attention to such letters.[178] On one occasion, however, Churchill himself dismissed Smithers during a Commons debate, declaring, 'I very much doubt whether it is the communists in this country who are the root of all our troubles'.[179] Smithers was not only spurned by fellow politicians, but also by members of MI5. In his diary, Guy Liddell wrote that he was a 'silly old blimp' who had been nicknamed 'Sir Waldron Blithers'.[180]

If Smithers was easily dismissed as an eccentric, a more credible McCarthy-type figure was Lord Vansittart, a former Permanent Undersecretary at the Foreign Office. In March 1950, he warned in the House of Lords that communists had 'infested' the BBC, universities, the Church and the Civil Service.[181] Although he sought to distance himself from McCarthy, the *Manchester Guardian* drew comparison between the two, writing, 'We should hate to see Lord Vansittart becoming another Sen. McCarthy, although naturally he would do his smearing with much more artistry and wit'. Vansittart found himself derided from all quarters; the press mocked him as 'Lord VanWitchhunt' and the House of Lords almost censured him for libelling people he accused. The greatest dismissal of his ideas came in 1950 from the Lord Chancellor, Viscount Jowitt, who made clear, 'In trying to deal with evil ... we must not fall into the error of adopting those very methods which we condemn in totalitarian countries ... You cannot cast out Satan by means of Beelzebub.'[182]

The concept and practice of McCarthyism was distasteful to almost all British officials. Even the most uncompromising anti-communists within the British establishment viewed the reactionary tendencies present in America as repugnant. One hardliner, John Peck, head of the Foreign Office's secret anti-communist propaganda unit, the Information Research Department (IRD), made clear that Britain should not follow the American example. In a brief for the Foreign Secretary, Anthony Eden, in 1953, he wrote, 'we regard propaganda issued by right-wing elements designed to appeal only to other right-wing elements as dangerous to us and helpful to the enemy ... we regard the quest for perfection in security and for ideological purity of public opinion, as unattainable and greatly favouring Communist interests.'[183]

Peck's words highlight the fundamental nature of the differences in the way in which the British and Americans viewed and dealt with communism. This gulf was perhaps most clearly displayed in the way the two nations handled individuals who had once professed an attachment to the communist ideology. The American approach was summarised by Sir Frederick Hoyer Millar of the British Embassy in Washington in 1950. He wrote that 'Americans think no man who has ever been a Communist or has professed Marxist views, is to be trusted, even if he publicly recants his Communist leanings and associations.'[184] In Britain, even those individuals who had been 'purged' due to their political beliefs were not blacklisted for life. Officials left open the possibility of re-employing people who had previously been removed from jobs with access to secret information if it was determined that they were no longer a security risk.[185]

One example of the State revising its view about an individual with a chequered past is the case of W.N. Ewer. During the 1920s Ewer was believed by MI5 to have run a secret intelligence network that had collected information on the intelligence community which was 'passed to the Russians'.[186] Ewer was never prosecuted and was believed to have severed his ties with the CPGB in the early 1930s. In 1941, MI5 stated, 'we have no interest in him now that he has apparently turned over a new leaf'.[187] After the war, Ewer became a trusted contact of the IRD, a secret unit within the Foreign Office charged with planning and organising anti-communist activity both in Britain and abroad. Formed in 1948 and the brainchild of the junior Foreign Office minister, Christopher Mayhew, the IRD produced non-attributable material designed to reveal the 'truth' about communism.[188] Some of the information included in IRD material came from the Security Service, although it was never attributed as such.[189] IRD material, Mayhew later revealed, was 'offered to, and accepted by, large numbers of selected MPs, journalists, trade union leaders, and was often used by the BBC's External Services.'[190] The IRD was greatly successful and would effectively 'plant' stories in the press to try to influence public opinion about communism and the Soviet Union. By the early 1960s, about three or four articles in the British press per week were based on information provided by the IRD.[191]

Ewer has been described as one of the IRD's 'hardest working and most dependable client[s]'. He wrote numerous anti-communist articles in the *Daily Herald*, contributed to IRD-sponsored books, and broadcast regularly on the BBC.[192] The British State was willing to make use of him despite the fact that the Security Service clearly believed he had spied for the Soviets in the 1920s. Ewer's past was briefly reviewed post-war when MI5 were examining past espionage cases. In January 1950, Maxwell Knight interviewed him, but Ewer gave little away and denied that his group had been involved in espionage in the 1920s.[193] He continued to be a reliable IRD client in the years that followed and was awarded a CBE in 1959. Upon his retirement as the *Daily*

Herald's diplomatic correspondent in 1964, Ewer was invited to a lunch held in his honour at the Foreign Secretary's official residence and was presented with lifetime access to the Foreign Office's press facilities.[194] The Ewer case illustrated the British ability to reassess an individual and not stigmatise them based on their past communist beliefs.

Another individual utilised by the IRD, despite a past involvement with espionage, was David Floyd. In 1951, shortly after the disappearance of Burgess and Maclean, Floyd, then a Foreign Office diplomat, voluntarily told his superiors that he had been a communist when at Oxford University in the early 1930s.[195] In a subsequent interview with MI5's chief interrogator, Jim Skardon, he admitted that at Oxford he had met and become friendly with Arthur Wynn, a recruiter for the KGB. Floyd admitted that this had 'led to his meeting a Russian on some twenty occasions.'[196]

During the war, Floyd had been employed on the British Military Mission in Moscow, and he subsequently worked at the British Embassy. In his interview with Skardon, 'he maintained he had never imparted any information, although the Russian had pressed him hard about the personnel of the mission.'[197] The case was put to the Director of Public Prosecutions who quickly decided not to prosecute, 'since there was no evidence of any information passed by FLOYD to his Russian contact'. MI5's Deputy DG at the time, Guy Liddell, wrote that the Security Service had recommended against a prosecution as it would 'do nobody any good.'[198] In his diary, he expanded, 'since the man came forward voluntarily ... to penalise him would discourage others from volunteering a statement about their past. Apart from this, a successful prosecution seemed extremely unlikely.'[199]

During a subsequent interview with MI5, Floyd was said to have admitted passing 'very low-grade' information to the Russians, but said that he had 'become disenchanted with Soviet-style communism after the 1948 coup in Czechoslovakia.' Whilst he was not prosecuted, his passport was temporarily confiscated and he was made to resign from his job in the Foreign Service. Shortly afterwards, however, a Foreign Office memorandum stated that 'he is already in touch with MI5, who want to find him a job.'

In 1952, he became the communist affairs correspondent of the *Daily Telegraph*, appointed by the paper's deputy editor, Malcolm Muggeridge; both Muggeridge and the *Telegraph* editor at the time, Colin Coote, had previously worked in intelligence.[200] In his role at the newspaper, Floyd wrote articles critical of communism. He was also in touch with the IRD, which considered him a 'prominent anti-communist journalist' and a 'useful contact'.[201] Prior to Floyd's becoming an IRD contact, Whitehall officials examined his reliability 'pretty thoroughly'. Although some expressed concern about using him, Floyd remained an IRD contact until at least 1974.[202]

'Discover him and control him'

Floyd's case was not unique, and there are several other individuals who were not prosecuted for espionage in the 1950s and 1960s. Often, it appears, British officials preferred to keep such cases quiet rather than publicise them. Fundamentally, many officials believed that prosecuting individuals involved in espionage had few benefits and many drawbacks. They did not wish to see the kind of public exposure of such figures as had been seen in the US, which risked martyring an individual. The British way was more pragmatic. Publicising cases could create a hate figure in the short term but, in the long-term, exposed the State to both embarrassment and severe criticism. Officials worried about the reputational damage such spy scandals could cause to the British intelligence community and the inevitable questions about the trustworthiness of British security measures. Writing about the Nunn May and Fuchs cases, the novelist and wartime MI6 officer, Graham Greene, argued that 'the real value of the two scientists to the Soviet Union was not the benefit they received from their scientific information, but from their capture, and the breakdown in Anglo-American relations which followed. A spy allowed to continue his work without interference is far less dangerous than the spy who is caught.'[203]

Although there was no formal policy in Britain to suppress potential spy scandals, it does appear that official attitudes were

A 'RELIGIOUS DOGMA'

often in favour of secrecy. The timing of the Floyd case is notable, coming weeks after the disappearance of Burgess and Maclean and months after the conviction of Fuchs and the disappearance of Pontecorvo. It happened at a time when the authorities had already faced multiple scandals and wanted to avoid more. This was not always the case, however, and at the beginning of the 1960s, several individuals were prosecuted and convicted of having been involved in espionage. In March 1961, five members of a spy ring at the Admiralty Underwater Weapons Establishment in Portland, Dorset, were convicted of being involved with the passing of secret information to the Soviet Union.[204] In May that same year an MI6 officer, George Blake, confessed to having passed secrets to the Soviets and was jailed for forty-two years. In 1962, the Admiralty clerk John Vassall admitted spying for the KGB.[205] Although such spies were exposed publicly, some believed that they should not have been. Harold Macmillan, the Prime Minister, argued that Blake's case should not go to trial as it would cause too much damage, whilst some within MI6 expressed disquiet about revealing that Blake, a serving MI6 officer, had been involved in espionage. Dick White, the head of MI6, insisted that Blake should be prosecuted as 'the cost of doing nothing would be enormous.' Even White, however, considered not prosecuting Blake. 'If he isn't prepared to plead guilty', White said, 'we'll just put him on a plane to Moscow.'[206]

In the years that followed the slew of scandals, officials seemed inclined, once again, towards avoiding prosecutions. In 1963, MI5 received information finally proving that Kim Philby had spied for the Soviets and decided to offer him immunity from prosecution if he cooperated and confessed.[207] Although he partially confessed, Philby did not take the offer of immunity and instead decided to defect to the Soviet Union.[208] It has been suggested in some quarters that the authorities let him slip away. His defection did not become public for many months and, although his disappearance created negative headlines, they were largely short-lived. Had he returned to Britain, his presence would only have created a prolonged amount of 'adverse publicity' for the government and intelligence community.[209] The following year, in 1964, the two remaining members of the Cambridge Five, Anthony Blunt and John Cairncross, separately confessed to their own involvement in espionage. Both admissions came after they were, like Philby, offered immunity from prosecution. Neither, however, defected and they were not publicly outed for decades.[210] Indeed, to maintain the pretence, Blunt was even allowed to remain in his job as Surveyor of the Queen's Pictures at Buckingham Palace for a further eight years until he took early retirement at the age of 65.[211]

Questions have been raised, most notably by George Blake himself, about why Philby, Blunt and Cairncross were offered immunity when others were not. Some have suggested that the reason for this was that the establishment wanted to protect members of its own class.[212] Whilst this may have been a factor, there appear to be two reasons that explain why prosecutions did not take place—a lack of evidence and, again, because of a desire to avoid the inevitable and damaging fallout. Dick White regularly remarked that espionage was 'a crime often devoid of disclosable evidence'. The evidence against certain individuals was frequently based on secret sources and could not be used during a trial.[213] Without a confession, therefore, intelligence officials did not see any way of achieving a successful prosecution.[214] The information that revealed the espionage of Klaus Fuchs and several other spies, including the Cambridge Five, had come through decrypted Soviet telegrams which became known as the VENONA messages.[215] Had Fuchs not confessed to passing secrets to the Soviets, he would not have been prosecuted. Indeed, prior to his confession, officials had discussed finding him a university post which did not have access to secret information.[216] Even the cases that did lead to trial, such as Fuchs', contained an element of secrecy and cover-up. Before such cases, the prosecution and defence would consult each other to ensure the most damaging information would not be disclosed in open court.[217]

Following several spy scandals, in the early 1960s British officials were increasingly unwilling to see 'dirty linen' aired in public. Several espionage trials had resulted in severe criticism of the State and a media storm. Secrecy and cover-up, therefore, became even more appealing. The Prime Minister, Harold Macmillan, expressed such a view after the discovery and conviction of John Vassall in 1962. He said,

> When my gamekeeper shoots a fox, he doesn't go and hang it up outside the Master of Foxhounds' drawing room; he buries it out of sight. But you just can't shoot a spy as you did in the war. You have to try him ... better to discover him, and then control him, but never catch him ... There will be a terrible row in the press there will be a debate in the House of Commons and the government will probably fall. Why the devil did you 'catch' him?[218]

Very simply, the discovery of a spy did not represent a success but, instead, a failure of intelligence. It caused embarrassment to the government and led to questions as to why the intelligence community had not previously discovered them. Spy scandals were, Macmillan said, 'dangerous and bad for our general national interest'.[219] As his official biographer Alistair Horne stated, Macmillan believed that the actual information spies had passed to the Soviets was 'less damaging than the demoralisation caused by the *fact* of their treachery'.[220] He believed that 'a spy causes more trouble when he's caught', and was far from alone in seeing things in such a way.[221] Certain figures in both MI5 and MI6 argued against prosecution of spies during the various scandals in the 1950s and 1960s; Maurice Oldfield, deputy-head and head of MI6 during the 1960s and 1970s, believed control of a spy was much better than capture and conviction.[222] Such attitudes amongst intelligence officials were not unique to the post-war era and can be traced back to at least as early as 1909—the year of the founding of MI5—when Vernon Kell discouraged arrests which led to open trials of suspected spies. Such action, he believed, would do more bad than good—revealing sources and 'other confidential information' as well as alerting the 'enemy'.[223]

The British way of doing things was to encourage secrecy, and to prevent information reaching the public arena if possible. Although this may have meant that several individuals involved in espionage were not held accountable for their actions during the first two decades of the post-war era, it also helped Britain to avoid the kind of witch-hunt that had occurred in the US. For British officials, avoiding a witch-hunt was the pragmatic, sensible thing to do.

Conclusion

In the first twenty years following the Second World War, the danger posed by communism to Britain was greater than ever. Ironically, the CPGB was less important than it had previously been. The twin events of 1956—Khrushchev's denunciation of Stalin and the brutal repression of the uprising in Hungary by Soviet troops—had fatally damaged it. CPGB members left in their thousands and, though the Party's threat was greatly reduced, MI5 continued to monitor it and its members.[224]

For security officials, communism remained a concern because it was believed that 'the communist faith overrides a man's normal loyalties to his country and induces a belief that ... it is justifiable to hand over secret information to the Communist Party or the Russians'.[225] Although they initially took some time to realise the extent of Soviet penetration of different parts of the British State, by the beginning of the 1950s officials and politicians accepted that much more extensive security measures needed to be introduced. Whereas during the interwar years, a fear of communism may have been overblown, in the immediate post-war years that fear was perfectly understandable. The steady stream of intelligence revealing that yet another individual had spied for the Soviets increased intelligence officials' concerns about the extent of the Soviet penetration of British society. The Security Service, therefore, felt the need to investigate countless individuals with the slightest links to the far-left.

The introduction of security measures in the late 1940s and early 1950s was undertaken in a manner that was quietly effective. In Britain, individuals who were placed under intensive surveillance by MI5 rarely knew about it and were able to go about their lives without restraint. Although the intelligence community was still inherently suspicious about left-wing political views, compared to the 1920s and 1930s the action taken was much more understandable and justifiable. The threat posed by some individuals committed to the ideology of communism was a real one, and the intelligence community could not afford to risk overlooking any potential security threats. The Security Service was faced with 'known unknowns'—they knew that some communists would be willing to betray Britain, but did not know who they were because such people had loose ties, if any, to the CPGB.

The stringent vetting measures taken to combat communism were a last resort resulting from the discovery of the espionage of Fuchs, Burgess, and Maclean. With the benefit of hindsight, it appears that the penetration of the British State by Soviet spies was not as extensive as intelligence officials may have feared. This does not mean that the threat posed by communism to the British State at this time should, however, be dismissed. At the time, such a threat was credible and communist penetration appeared to be deep-rooted. The authorities were left with a real dilemma, needing to protect the security of the nation whilst, simultaneously, preserving civil liberties. This balance appears to have been maintained. Vetting measures were only introduced after painstaking deliberations and, as the Lord President, Herbert Morrison, stated in 1948, action taken against communists was not because of their political views 'but because experience had shown that Communists were commonly expected or used, perhaps unconsciously, to provide information for the benefit of Russia.'[226]

Although the action taken may have sometimes been a little excessive and occasionally affected people who posed no threat to the security of the State, it would have been unthinkable to have continued to allow communists or communist sympathisers access to top secret information. Individuals whose employment was affected by the purge procedure were not 'named and shamed', they were often found alternative employment. The secrecy applied to both purge cases and spy scandals was partly motivated by a desire to avoid the embarrassment which could result from any revelations of espionage. Such exposés could have made Britain look weak on security matters and threatened Anglo-American security relations. Nonetheless, secrecy also meant that Britain avoided what had happened in the US. In the UK, there was no witch-hunt and security procedures did not create martyrs.

The introduction of security measures was undoubtedly belated. However, by the mid-1960s, their effect had greatly reduced the ability of communists to pose a subversive threat to Britain. Individuals committed to the ideology found it a lot harder to gain access to, and leak, highly classified information. The actions of the Labour government led by Clement Attlee to introduce both negative and then positive vetting started a process which made it much harder for subversives to gain significant influence in British society.

4

SUBVERSION AND THE LABOUR PARTY

In the early evening of 16 October 1964, a black Daimler carrying Britain's new Prime Minister arrived in Downing Street. Harold Wilson had been driven from an audience with the Queen at Buckingham Palace, where he had become the first Labour Party Prime Minister for thirteen years.[1] Wilson was commonly known by his middle name, Harold, rather than by his first name, James. To MI5, however, he was known as 'Norman John Worthington' — the pseudonym under which the Security Service held a file on him due to its 'unusual sensitivity.' MI5 had first opened a file on Wilson in 1945, shortly after he had been elected as the Labour MP for Ormskirk. When he became a member of the cabinet in 1947, MI5's Graham Mitchell wrote that the justification for opening a file 'derives from comments made about him by certain Communist members of the Civil Service which suggested an identity or similarity of political outlook'.[2]

In the 1950s, whilst the Labour Party was in opposition, Wilson took up a role as an economic consultant for a company which imported Soviet timber.[3] As a result of this work, which led him to make regular visits to Moscow, he developed relationships with people known by MI5 to be either communists or KGB officers.[4] In 1956, due to Wilson's frequent trips to the east, the KGB decided to open an 'agent development file', codenamed 'OLDING', in the hope of recruiting him. According to the former KGB archivist, Vasili Mitrokhin, the OLDING file recorded that Wilson had previously provided information that was considered valuable enough to be passed on to the Politburo. The file did, however, state that 'the development did not come to fruition'.[5]

The file MI5 held on Wilson has not been released, but part of its contents was revealed by Christopher Andrew in his authorised history of the Security Service. He writes that whilst MI5 did not suspect Wilson of being a secret crypto-communist or fellow traveller, intelligence officials 'looked askance at some of the Communist connections he developed in the course of his Russian travels'.[6] Andrew states that 'allegations that Wilson was ever a KGB agent derive not from credible evidence but from unfounded conspiracy theories.'[7] This is backed up in KGB files. Any information Wilson shared with the Soviets appears not to have been of a confidential nature and was, instead, mostly 'political gossip.' Indeed, by the time Wilson became Prime Minister, the Soviet Embassy in London commissioned articles attacking his policies; by 1964 the KGB did not regard him as a friend of the Soviet Union.[8] Nonetheless, suspicion surrounded Wilson. Shortly before he became Prime Minister, the CIA also opened a file on him under the codename 'OATSHEAF' after receiving information from a Soviet defector, Anatoly Golitsyn, which led them to believe Wilson was a Soviet agent.[9]

Wilson was not a Soviet agent, but he was certainly someone who attracted both gossip and suspicion within the intelligence community. It is, therefore, a little surprising that his government was able to work smoothly with the intelligence community on his taking office. Although the Labour Party and the intelligence community had a degree of mutual distrust when Wilson arrived at Downing Street, the two were able to develop a reasonable working relationship. Coming to office almost exactly forty years after the first Labour government had fallen in 1924, Wilson did not face the difficulties in dealing with intelligence agencies that James Ramsay MacDonald had experienced. This can partly be explained by the fact that, by the 1960s, the Labour Party was a much more established political party and thus intelligence officials had more respect for them. In many ways, however, it was due to the fact that the Labour Party had developed such strong relations with the intelligence community during the leadership of Clement Attlee, particularly during the Attlee government between 1945 and 1951.

The Attlee Government and the Development of Labour-MI5 Relations

Having won the General Election in July 1945, Attlee's incoming government was in a position to work well with the intelligence community. In contrast to 1924, when the Party and its personalities were an unknown quantity to security officials, senior Labour Party figures were familiar to Whitehall mandarins in 1945. The wartime coalition government had contained several Labour members who were able to develop a good knowledge of the world of intelligence. Attlee had served under Churchill as Deputy Prime Minister which, he said, gave him 'full experience of high and responsible office', notably allowing him to work closely with MI5.[10] Herbert Morrison, who served as Lord President of the Council in the Attlee administration, also frequently interacted with the Security Service as wartime Home Secretary and regularly read their reports on fascism and communism.[11] Most notably, Hugh Dalton was appointed by Churchill to run the Special Operations Executive (SOE). Dalton, who would later serve as Chancellor of the Exchequer under Attlee, effectively became the Labour member of the coalition most closely involved with intelligence on a day-to-day basis.[12]

Almost all the members of Attlee's new administration had experience of working in government. Of those members of the cabinet appointed in the summer of 1945, only two were taking ministerial office for the first time.[13] Despite this, questions were raised about the Labour Party taking power. During the General Election campaign, Churchill expressed doubts about the trustworthiness of Attlee's party. In a radio broadcast he declared that a Labour government 'would have to fall back on some form of Gestapo'.[14] Rather than damage the Labour Party, Churchill's pronouncement backfired and instead led him to be heavily criticised. Even his wife, Clementine, cautioned him against the use of such language, and had pleaded with him 'to delete the odious and invidious reference to the Gestapo' before the speech was transmitted.[15]

Churchill's speech was pure electioneering, and he did not truly believe the Labour Party would pose a threat.[16] He knew the Labour leadership well and, after losing the election, worked constructively with Attlee's administration as leader of the opposition, meeting with ministers to discuss the growing threat posed by the Soviet Union.[17] Some Whitehall officials were, however, genuinely concerned about the Labour Party taking power. Upon hearing the news of Attlee's victory, the Permanent Under-Secretary of the Foreign Office, Orme Sargent, was said to have predicted a 'Communist avalanche over Europe, a weak foreign policy, a private revolution at home and the reduction of England [sic] to a second class power'.[18] Others still viewed Labour as the untrustworthy Party of the past. One GCHQ official, William Clarke, stated that a Labour government posed a 'potential danger' to Britain's ability to read overseas traffic; 'our first Director had grave trouble ... when the last Labour government was in power', he wrote.[19] Within weeks, the new administration had allayed any potential Whitehall fears. The Foreign Office official, Patrick Reilly, made this clear in a letter. 'I don't think you need to worry', he wrote to his parents, 'These chaps have proved their worth these last five years and I truly think they are better equipped to bring us through the exceedingly difficult period that lies ahead.'[20]

Within MI5, the initial reaction to a Labour victory may not have been as extreme as it was in some quarters, but there still would have been a wariness about their new political masters. The Security Service held files on a number of members of Attlee's cabinet. There is evidence that files were opened on Ellen Wilkinson, Minister of Education, and Aneurin Bevan, Minister of Health, although they have never been declassified.[21] The files on some ministers—notably Stafford Cripps, John Strachey and Manny Shinwell—have, however, been released to the National Archives. The file held on Cripps is particularly illuminating. It shows that intelligence officials seem to have been apprehensive about any potential questions as to why there was a file on a member of the government. An MI5 officer wrote in the file in September 1945,

> Sir Stafford Cripps was a leading figure in the Popular Front Movement before the war which had a very close Communist interest, and could hardly object if we had records of his activities in regard to this. The same applies to his more recent interest in Communist controlled youth movements.[22]

The Security Service provided similar justifications for maintaining a file on Strachey. Shortly after he was elected as MP for Dundee at the 1945 General Election, an MI5 officer wrote in the file, 'there is now no longer any justification for its continued existence and that, on what I conceive to be a strict view of the circumstances which justified our having a file at all, it really ought to be destroyed'.[23] The file was, however, kept open.[24] Material was added to it even after he became a minister, although this appears to have been an error and 'horrified' MI5.[25] Strachey had been closely associated with the CPGB in the 1930s and this formed a large part of the reason for retaining his file. As an MI5 officer wrote shortly after he had been elected, 'it is convenient to have available material which enables us without making undue enquiries to express a favourable opinion about him'.[26] It is most likely that MI5 made use of the file in such a way after attention was drawn to Strachey's previous communist sympathies by American officials when he became Secretary of State for War in 1950.[27]

Although there was disquiet in the US about Strachey's links to communism after his appointment to the War Office, MI5 had no particular concerns about him or the wider Labour government. Not all intelligence officials were comfortable with the Labour Party, however. On one occasion a Special Branch officer passed information to a Conservative MP revealing that 'there were several Trotskyists in the local Labour Party'. The apparent attempt to sully Labour was unsuccessful, though, as MI5 made it clear to Attlee that it was in no way concerned about the issue.[28]

The politics of the Labour Party were still alien to traditional establishment figures; Guy Liddell remarked in his diary that 'state socialism differs little if at all from Communism'.[29] This represented a misunderstanding of left-wing ideology. The leadership of the Labour Party was fiercely opposed to communism, and well aware of its potential threat. To Attlee, communists were the 'enemy within' and he regarded the CPGB as 'merely the dummy of the ventriloquist Stalin'.[30] His Foreign Secretary, Ernest Bevin, was similarly uncompromising in his attitude towards communists. As a former Trade Unionist, Bevin had experience of battling with communists and thus developed a fierce hatred of communism.[31] He was particularly strong in his opposition to the Soviet Union, believing Stalin and the Soviet Foreign Minister, Vyacheslav Molotov, to be 'evil men'.[32] To direct its opposition to communism, the government formed the secret IRD unit within the Foreign Office. Designed to expose the 'true nature' of Soviet communism and eventually unify worldwide opinion against the Soviet government, the IRD was initially confined to carrying out anti-communist propaganda abroad.[33] Attempts to allow the IRD to use anti-communist propaganda in the UK were resisted on the basis that government funds should not be used to attack a legal political party, the CPGB. In 1951, however, a decision was made to create a 'Home Desk' or 'English section' for the IRD to coordinate anti-communist propaganda in the UK. This was justified as it was said that the CPGB was not committed to democracy and because communism in the UK was, in some way, directed by Moscow.[34]

The Attlee government was strongly committed to both the defence of Britain and Europe. The Prime Minister and Foreign Secretary believed passionately that Britain should acquire its own atomic bomb. In early 1947, Attlee formed a secret cabinet committee, consisting of only five ministers, to force through a decision to develop a British atomic weapon without having to involve the wider cabinet or Parliament.[35] The government also played a key role in the formation of NATO in early 1949, believing it was vital to defend Europe against the growing threat posed by the Soviet Union. Britain and the West were, Attlee believed, in a 'conflict between two ideologies—the totalitarian ideology and the democratic ideology' and democracy needed to be defended.[36]

Both Attlee and Bevin made clear, in their meetings with intelligence officials, their belief in the necessity of tackling communism. In the summer of 1945, shortly after taking office, Bevin met with Nicholas Elliott of MI6. During their lunch, the new Foreign Secretary stated, 'Communists and communism are vile. It is the duty of all members of the service to stamp upon them at every opportunity.'[37] Attlee worked particularly closely with the post-war MI5 Director General, Sir Percy Sillitoe—so closely, in fact, that he later wrote the foreword to Sillitoe's memoir. Sillitoe was said to 'inspire greater confidence in Number Ten than in his own staff', and they met more times than any subsequent Prime Minister and Director General. Indeed, such was Attlee's commitment to MI5 that, during his term in office, he became the first Prime Minister to visit MI5's headquarters.[38]

The closeness of the Attlee-Sillitoe relationship can perhaps be explained by the fact that both were outsiders to the intelligence establishment. Attlee had little in common with those who worked for the Security Service whilst Sillitoe had a background in policing, most notably as the Chief Constable of Kent. His appointment was not supported by intelligence insiders; MI5's Dick White remarked that Sillitoe did not 'understand intelligence'. Some members of the Security Service deliberately conversed in Latin around Sillitoe to expose his inferior education.[39]

Subversive MPs

Some of Sillitoe's MI5 colleagues may not have been impressed with him, but they do appear to have been struck by Attlee's willingness to take up the fight against communist subversion. According to Liddell, Labour 'were far more interested to make use of our services' than the Conservatives had been previously.[40] In 1946, the Prime Minister asked to 'be informed in every case where we had positive information that a Member of Parliament was a member of a subversive organisation', no matter which party the MP belonged to.[41] He also asked Sillitoe to notify him about 'signs of subversion among Ministers' families.'[42] Indeed, the Attlee years established a tradition that continues to the time of writing, whereby MI5 informs any new Prime Minister if they have evidence that any potential minister is a security risk.[43]

Following Attlee's request for information on MPs, Liddell remarked in his diary,

> I gathered he felt that he had a responsibility to the House and the country to see that such members did not get into positions where they might constitute a danger to the state. They might either be ... as members of the Government, or if they were in the Opposition as members of Royal Commissions or Parliamentary Delegations.[44]

The Security Service met with Attlee to inform him about individuals on whom they held information. Much of the Security Service's interest in MPs was focused on the Labour backbenches; it is said that 'about a dozen' of the 393 Labour MPs elected in 1945 were 'either secret CP members or were close to the CP'.[45] Attlee was given the names of Labour MPs whom MI5 had identified as 'crypto-communists'—John Platts-Mills, Lester Hutchinson, Bessie Braddock, and Leah Manning. Having received such information, Attlee, in turn, gave MI5 the names of MPs he was certain were CPGB members—Norman Dodds, Stephen Swingler and Denis Pritt.[46] Liddell told Attlee that MI5 could only confirm for certain the names of Hutchinson, Platts-Mills, Manning, Braddock, and Geoffrey Bing, MP for Hornchurch.[47]

MI5 watched Bing throughout his time as an MP. Despite his election as a Labour MP, the Security Service were in no doubt that his true loyalties lay with communism.[48] This was based on intelligence garnered from surveillance of the CPGB; it was reported that various Communist leaders discussed and approved his standing as a Labour candidate.[49] Bing caused MI5 considerable concern in 1947 when it was reported from a trustworthy source that he would be part of 'an open and concerted attack on MI5' during a Debate on the Army Estimates.[50] Whilst nothing materialised, this highlighted MI5's fear that, once a communist was elected to Parliament, their platform for espousing their opinions was enormous; as they had been voted in by the public, it was much more difficult to suppress them.

Whilst MI5 continued to collect information about Bing once he was elected as an MP, they tried to be as discreet as possible. In 1949 SIS asked for information on him, but MI5 could not provide it—'since the subject of the enquiry was evidently the MP, it was difficult for us to put a summary down for transmission'.[51] The following year, Bing travelled to the British Colony of the Gold Coast 'to contact and check up generally on local nationalist and Left Wing agitators.' Although one MI5 officer suggested sending information about his trip to the Security Liaison Officer (SLO) in the Gold Coast, it was eventually decided not to; Dick Thistlethwaite of MI5 warned, 'there is every reason to be cautious in sending reports about MPs to the field'.[52]

MI5 was clearly uneasy about investigations into sitting MPs, realising the potential controversy this could cause if such information ever became public. This may have been the case with Bing, but was even more so in the case of Wilfrid Vernon, elected Labour MP for Dulwich at the 1945 General Election. Vernon had first come to MI5's attention in the early 1930s as a communist sympathiser working at RAE Farnborough. In 1937 his house was burgled by fascists who found sensitive documents in the property. Vernon was subsequently convicted under the Official Secrets Act of illegally possessing the documents and dismissed from his position.[53]

After this incident, Vernon barely came to MI5's attention until 1944, and only a handful of notes were added to his file after he became an MP in 1945. In 1948, however, MI5 obtained information from a source, Ernst David Weiss, which led them to investigate Vernon more extensively. Weiss, who had previously been part of a Soviet espionage network in Britain, claimed that in 1936 and 1937 Vernon had passed him secret documents, including a set of blueprints of an Avro-Anson aircraft.[54] After examining the case, the Security Service concluded that Vernon's association with the network ended in 1937; they decided not to investigate any further due to Vernon's status as a Member of Parliament.[55] Dick White of MI5 wrote in Vernon's file in May 1948, 'the fact that a Labour

MP worked in a Russian spy ring at that time is surely something which the Prime Minister should hear about, even though it is probable that no action will be feasible at this juncture'.[56] Attlee was eventually informed about Vernon in October 1948 and was reported to be 'shocked' about Vernon's past which 'came to him as a complete surprise'.[57]

As the case against him was of an historic nature, the Security Service took no action. However, after Vernon lost his seat in the 1951 General Election, things changed. A note was made in his file, stating,

> You will recall the Director General's decision, after his interview with the Prime Minister about the case of Vernon, that it would not be possible to interrogate this former spy. Vernon was not re-elected to the present Parliament. I should therefore like to recommend that he should now be interrogated.[58]

The case was again raised with the Director General who also agreed 'now that Vernon had ceased to be a member of the House of Commons we were entitled to proceed to interview him without obtaining any further sanction'.[59] MI5 imposed both telephone and letter checks on Vernon prior to interviewing him.[60] He was interrogated by Jim Skardon in early 1952 and admitted his guilt. Following two interviews, Skardon assessed that Vernon 'was not currently engaged in any activity which might be described as subversive' and stated, 'I am certain that he has no current interest for the Security Service'.[61] The authorities decided to take no further interest in Vernon, in part as he was now nearly 70 and seemingly at the end of his career, but also because they believed they could not gain any further insight into his past.[62]

Lost Sheep

The Security Service closely but discreetly watched some Labour backbenchers, opened their mail and tapped their telephones.[63] In this, they were not alone. The leadership of the Labour Party also investigated its own MPs who were considered to be on the extreme Left or crypto-communists. The Labour Party General

Secretary, Morgan Phillips, kept a 'Lost Sheep' file on pro-Soviet MPs,[64] who were described as having 'used their positions and prestige ... in support of policies which, time and again, had been rejected by the Annual Party Congress'.[65] These MPs were harshly dealt with; Herbert Morrison took action against those who did not conform to the anti-communist line, whilst Bevin often confronted left-wingers and warned that he 'had them under observation'.[66]

Certain MPs on the left of the Party were constantly in conflict with the leadership and continually attacked the government. In 1947 Attlee confided in a colleague that he thought 'about six of our cryptos should be sacked'.[67] The following year, after Bevin had been heckled by some backbenchers when he made a speech strongly condemning the Soviet Union, Attlee criticised those MPs who continued to support the Soviets, accusing them of '[shutting] their eyes to the absence of human rights when they look to Eastern Europe.'[68] Things came to a head later in 1948 and during 1949 when the Labour National Executive Committee (NEC) took decisive action against a number of MPs who 'persist[ed] in acting as a group in organised opposition to Party policy'.[69] Several were severely reprimanded and four—John Platts-Mills, Konni Zilliacus, Leslie Solley and Lester Hutchinson—were expelled from the Party.[70]

Very little of the intelligence material collated by the Labour Party appears to have survived. Many of the files were said to have been burned by Ron Hayward when he became General Secretary in the 1970s, making it difficult to examine how extensive the dossiers were.[71] The one file which does endure, and gives a tantalising insight into the information collected by Party officials, is the Morgan Phillips' 'Lost Sheep' file held in the Labour Party archives. The collection of information is referenced in a letter sent to Phillips about Konni Zilliacus, which contains a note scrawled on it questioning 'have we got a dossier on him?'.[72] The Lost Sheep file also contains a seventeen-page document compiled from speeches and writings of Zilliacus detailing all of the occasions that he had displayed pro-communist views.[73] Zilliacus' fellow MPs also informed on him and one, Desmond Donnelly, notified

Phillips that Zilliacus had written an article attacking the Labour leadership in the Soviet publication, *Pravda*.[74] Whilst giving a small insight into the kind of information collected, such a file shows only the tip of the iceberg.

After the Attlee government was defeated at the October 1951 General Election, the Labour Party began to develop stronger relations with the IRD in order to tackle those within the Party who were believed to be subversive. IRD files state that the English Section of the department was 'in regular touch with officers at the Labour Party at Transport House since at least 1952', whilst an IRD member was invited, as a private visitor, to the Party's annual conference every year between 1953 and 1967.[75] The IRD provided Labour officials with a significant amount of information that helped the Party to proscribe several radical left-wing organisations.[76] It was even asked by Gerry Reynolds, Labour MP for Islington North, to help with an investigation into his Constituency Party (CLP) which, he believed, 'was slowly passing into the grip of a well-organised group of extreme left-wing malcontents'. The IRD passed a limited amount of information on to Reynolds about a number of members of the CLP.[77] IRD information was widely circulated to people involved with the Labour Party, including Transport House Staff, MPs, members of the NEC and Labour members of the House of Lords.[78]

The IRD also helped the Labour Party to build up information about a number of their own MPs. It had a strong relationship with Herbert Bowden, Labour's Chief Whip in opposition, and appears to have supplied him with material.[79] At one IRD meeting, attended by a member of MI5, it was made clear that 'any additional information which the Security Service might wish to pass indirectly to [Bowden] on this subject would, of course, be welcomed, and the English Section would ensure that it reached its destination.'[80] It appears, therefore, that senior Labour Party officials may have been covertly sent material on Party members and MPs by MI5. However, no other files currently released give any further insight into this.

Information gained from the IRD and other sources helped the Labour Party in compiling dossiers on some of its members and

MPs. Regional Labour officials would often inform counterparts in other areas of the country on known or suspected Trotskyists and other individuals who had the potential to cause the Party harm. Regional officials also obtained information from a network of agents, party officers and Trade Unionists; some were also provided with intelligence by Special Branch officers which could then be sent on to Transport House.[81] One MP on the left of the party, Ian Mikardo, asserted in his memoirs that 'our leaders were using the National Agent's Department in Transport House and the Regional Organisers out in the country to compile MI5-type dossiers on us, and on some of our supporters in the constituencies'. Ahead of the 1955 General Election, Mikardo was part of a Party sub-committee which met to consider prospective parliamentary candidates. During one meeting, Mikardo objected to the deselection of Konni Zilliacus. In response, Sara Barker, the Labour Party National Agent, produced several files detailing the reasons why Zilliacus should not be able to stand. Mikardo wrote that they were 'an eye opener' and that 'no MI5, no Special Branch, no George Smiley could have compiled more comprehensive dossiers.' The files consisted of 'not just press-cuttings, photographs and document references but also notes by watchers and eavesdroppers, and all sorts of tittle-tattle'. He believed that the information contained in them had some input from 'government sources' and from Labour attachés at the American Embassy.[82]

By the early 1960s, the leadership of the Labour Party was particularly concerned about possible communist infiltration. Although the Party had received information from the IRD and, indirectly, from the Security Service, there was a desire to open a formal channel of communication with MI5 to identify crypto-communists within the Parliamentary Party. In 1961, the Labour leader Hugh Gaitskell agreed with his deputy, George Brown, and Patrick Gordon Walker, the shadow Home Secretary, that they should approach the Security Service. However, in a tragicomic manner, they did not know how to initiate contact. They eventually decided to go through the journalist, Chapman Pincher, who provided contact details for both the heads of MI5 and MI6.[83]

Gordon Walker met with MI5 Deputy Director General, Graham Mitchell, in September 1961, and gave him a list of twenty-five Labour MPs. He thought sixteen 'were in effect members of the CPGB pretending to be Labour members or under Communist Party direction', and nine were 'possible' crypto-communists.[84] Mitchell did not, however, confirm or deny these suspicions, and told Gordon Walker that 'it was incumbent on the Security Service to be very careful to do nothing which could be represented as partaking of a party political nature.'[85] Internal MI5 files show that they believed that the MPs listed posed little threat and had limited influence. According to the Security Service's authorised history, no investigations were made into the MPs.[86]

'Politically motivated men'

The episode demonstrated how, after a decade out of power, the Labour leadership was out of touch with the intelligence community and security matters. Indeed, when Harold Wilson became Labour leader in 1963, following the death of Gaitskell, he admitted that he had never heard of 'C', the head of MI6.[87] When Wilson became Prime Minister in October 1964 it is therefore unsurprising that both the government and the intelligence community felt a little uncertain about one another.

In his first meeting with Wilson after his election victory, MI5 Director General Roger Hollis sought to assure the new Prime Minister that the Security Service strictly adhered to the limitations of its directive and avoided 'party political matters'. It is likely that the Security Service would have been concerned when, in early 1965, Wilson began to ask questions regarding the extent of MI5's surveillance. He specifically queried how many MPs' telephones were being tapped and, despite assurances from his Home Secretary Sir Frank Soskice that MI5 only tapped MPs' telephones 'in the most exceptional circumstances', the Prime Minister made it clear to Hollis that he was 'very strongly opposed to tapping the telephones of MPs.' At the time when Hollis and Wilson met to discuss the matter in March 1965, Soskice had approved a HOW on the Labour MP Bob Edwards. Wilson, after discovering this, decided that it should immediately be cancelled. Edwards was later revealed to have been a KGB agent, and Christopher Andrew argues that Wilson's actions 'probably delayed Edwards's discovery by over a decade'. After the HOW had been cancelled, Edwards became chairman of the Defence, Foreign and Commonwealth Affairs Sub-Committee of the Parliamentary Estimates Committee, and later vice chairman of the Western European Union Defence Committee. Once Edwards' ties to Moscow were discovered years later, the Security Service concluded that his roles on the committees 'would have been of interest to the KGB' and there was 'no doubt' that he would have passed on to them 'all he could have got hold of'.[88]

Wilson's opposition to HOWs taken out on MPs was such that, in November 1966, he told Parliament that he would not permit the telephones of the members of the House of Commons or the House of Lords to be tapped in future.[89] The notion that MPs' phones are not tapped has since become a custom known as the 'Wilson Doctrine', and survives at the time of writing.[90] Whilst Wilson was strongly opposed to the interception of MPs' phone communications, he did leave a loophole allowing it to take place if absolutely necessary.[91] As one study of the Wilson Doctrine emphasises, the 'timing of this announcement would be governed by considerations of national security and might, indeed was likely to be, some time later'.[92]

The 'Wilson Doctrine' may have given the impression that Wilson and his government were strongly opposed to surveillance. In practice, however, this was not the case. George Wigg MP, Wilson's 'intelligence scout and security enforcer', took an extremely hard line on security matters.[93] He requested that ministers of state, parliamentary secretaries and parliamentary private secretaries in departments involved with foreign and defence policy be positively vetted. Although Wilson agreed not to pursue the idea after Whitehall objections, he later requested that MI5 provide him with 'chit-chat' on ministers. His request was dismissed by DG Martin Furnival Jones, who clarified that he would not wish to 'report on information on the morals of Ministers unless there was some security aspect to them'.[94]

Wilson was a keen consumer of intelligence and was particularly interested in information on industrial disputes. During the 1966 strike by the National Union of Seamen he received regular reports from the Security Service; it has been said that 'no previous Prime Minister had shown such enthusiasm for regular up-to-the-minute Service reports during an industrial dispute'.[95] MI5 surveillance revealed that the strike had communist involvement. This led Wilson to denounce the strike leaders in the Commons as a 'tightly knit group of politically motivated men' and reveal that they 'have been able to dominate the majority of that otherwise sturdy union'.[96] Wilson's disclosures signified the first time a Prime Minister had so clearly reproduced Security Service intelligence to Parliament since the 1927 ARCOS raid.[97] MI5 fully supported the statement, which it helped to draft; one MI5 man was present in the Commons chamber, in a seat below the Speaker's chair as Wilson spoke.[98] The strike was called off within weeks.[99]

Wilson displayed an uncompromising attitude to what he perceived to be subversive activity in industrial relations. Indeed, he has been described as 'more security minded than MI5 on union politics and left-wing entryism'.[100] In 1969, Wilson's Home Secretary, James Callaghan, asked Furnival Jones for damaging information on the left-wing union leader, Hugh Scanlon, to help unseat him. Both Furnival Jones and the Permanent Undersecretary of the Home Office, Sir Phillip Allen, later agreed that such a 'ploy' was 'rather alarming'. Wilson and Callaghan may have been keen recipients of intelligence about pro-communist Union leaders, but they refused to sign HOWs on such people, as they were aware of the political fallout if ever it became known that a Labour government was endorsing the surveillance of Union leaders.[101]

Soviet Penetration of the Labour Party

During Wilson's time in office, MI5 held files on a number of Labour MPs and some members of the cabinet. Some ministers, such as Lord Gardiner, the Lord Chancellor, were convinced that the Security Service held files on them and made unsuccessful attempts to view them.[102] Whilst it is not clear if MI5 ever held a file on Gardiner, they did hold one on Stephen Swingler, a junior minister in the Department of Transport and later in the Department of Health and Social Security. By the time Labour took office in 1964, it is likely that MI5 would have compiled a significant amount of information on Swingler; in May 1947 Attlee informed MI5 that he was 'certain Swingler was a CP member' and in 1961, his name was on the list that Gordon Walker passed to MI5.[103] Despite this, Wilson had a great deal of confidence in Swingler and regarded him as 'one of our most successful ministers.' During his time in the Department of Transport, Swingler worked under Barbara Castle. Castle lobbied Wilson to promote Swingler, whom she believed to be a highly capable minister, to a cabinet post. She recorded in her diaries that the Prime Minister had told her, 'the trouble was security', and that Swingler had been doing some 'very stupid things ... dabbling in Eastern Europe'.[104]

It seems likely that MI5 would have warned Wilson about Swingler. The Security Service greatly feared the possibility of MPs whom they regarded with suspicion gaining cabinet posts. As Furnival Jones, who became MI5 DG in 1965, cautioned, 'if the Russian Intelligence Service can recruit a backbench MP and he climbs to a ministerial position, the spy is home and dry.'[105] Although it is unclear whether the Security Service played a part in Wilson's decision not to promote Swingler to full cabinet status, they did get involved in the cases of other ministers earmarked for a cabinet position. One of those in whom they took an interest was Niall MacDermot, a Treasury minister. MacDermot later revealed that MI5 blocked his promotion 'on the grounds that they thought my wife was a security risk'.[106] In 1966 MacDermot had married a half-Russian, half-Italian woman, Ludimila Benvenuto. The following year, Wilson informed MacDermot that MI5 wished to interview his wife as 'there were allegations from abroad'.[107] MI5 are said to have subsequently placed the MacDermots under surveillance and interviewed Ludimila; their primary objection was that she had worked on an ad hoc basis for a Soviet Embassy official in helping to distribute Soviet films in post-war Italy. The official for whom she had worked turned out to be a KGB officer and the distribution business was a cover, although it was said that she had no knowledge of this. Whilst Wilson asked MacDermot if he had passed confidential material to his wife and was prepared to trust his minister, MI5 advice won out. In September 1968 with his career prospects fading away, MacDermot resigned as housing minister. Realising he would never reach the cabinet, he retired from politics at the 1970 General Election.[108]

The concerns MI5 held about frontbenchers such as MacDermot were, in many ways, surpassed by their disquiet about individuals on the Labour backbenches. Security officials often had more substantial evidence about backbenchers and believed that by the mid-to-late 1960s there was 'almost certainly Soviet penetration of the Labour Party'.[109] MI5 were particularly concerned about Bernard Floud, MP for Acton. Floud had first come to MI5's attention during the 1930s when at Oxford University and was reported to have been a 'most ardent Communist'.[110] Having sporadically investigated him in the decades that followed, MI5 began to scrutinise Floud more comprehensively shortly after he was first elected as an MP in 1964. At this time, the Security Service was investigating the possibility that there had been a spy ring at Oxford in the 1930s similar to that belatedly uncovered at Cambridge.[111] During their investigations, intelligence officials discovered that Floud had advised fellow communists to hide their political allegiances while at Oxford and gain positions in the Civil Service after graduating. When part of the Civil Service, they would be able 'to obtain information of value to the CPGB'. He was said to have put one such communist in contact with a 'Central European', later identified as Arnold Deutsch, who had recruited the Cambridge Five.[112]

MI5 believed it 'highly possible' that Floud 'may have worked for the Russians as a talent spotter, when an undergraduate' at Oxford. Security officials also thought 'it may be postulated that as a member of Parliament, although as yet only a back-bencher, FLOUD has a potential as an agent of influence'.[113] By May 1966, after much debate, MI5 decided to interview Floud to try to resolve the case after gaining permission from the Home Secretary and Prime Minister.[114] He was interviewed several times with MI5 officers believing him to be reluctant to tell the whole truth.[115] Floud mentioned during the interviews that he wished to resolve the case as he had political ambitions and did not wish to have a 'black mark' against his name.[116] In the final interview, Floud was effectively told by MI5's Peter Wright that the Security Service remained concerned about his past and would be unable to provide him with security clearance should he ever be appointed to a ministerial post.[117] After the final interview, Furnival Jones made clear to the Home Secretary that he would 'be uneasy if [Floud] were given a position of trust by the Government'.[118] No further action was forthcoming as Floud committed suicide in October 1967.[119]

Several contemporaries of Floud's on the Labour backbenches in the 1960s were also believed to have been recruited by foreign intelligence services. The name of Ray Fletcher, MP for Ilkeston 1964–83, appeared in KGB archives as having been recruited in 1962. However, the Soviets apparently severed ties with him in 1964, having learned that he was also 'co-operating' with the Czech intelligence service, the StB. Shortly before his death in 1991, Fletcher admitted contact with Czech Embassy staff who 'it was later claimed were intelligence personnel', but said that he had reported all meetings to the Foreign Office.[120] In response to the discovery of Fletcher's name in KGB archives, his widow claimed that he had acted as a conduit between MI6 and Czech dissidents.[121] The lack of any conclusive evidence about Fletcher makes it difficult to judge the case. It is unclear whether MI5 ever investigated him or were even aware of his foreign contacts.

Another Labour MP who reportedly had contacts with the Czechs was Barnett Stross, MP for Hanley and later Stoke-on-Trent. Stross was included on both Morgan Phillips' list of 'Lost Sheep' and Gordon Walker's 1961 list, and clearly provoked suspicion amongst the Party officials. It is known that he had a strong relationship with Czechoslovakia, having taken in Czech refugees who had escaped from Nazism, and later becoming a prominent fundraiser to help rebuild the Czech village of Lidice, which was destroyed during the war. He was awarded the Order of the White Lion by the Czech government—the highest honour recognising an individual's contribution to Czechoslovakia. It was reported by a Czech defector that the StB saw Stross as 'a sympathetic contact within the British parliament', but there is virtually no information available on him, and his name was not mentioned in MI5's authorised history.[122]

Stross' case illustrates the difficulty in deciding whether someone was or was not a Soviet 'agent'. It is known that the term was fluid and did not necessarily mean a 'spy' in the conventional sense. Crucially, the only evidence for such allegations comes from the archives of Eastern bloc intelligence services, which are believed to contain exaggerations. The Soviet defector, Oleg Gordievsky, has since stated that officials would sometimes overstate the level of control they had over certain contacts. Anyone who had spoken to Soviet intelligence officers on a number of occasions could be listed as a 'contact' or eventually an 'agent', although Gordievsky admitted that they were in no way 'spies' and their usefulness was limited. It would have been possible for some MPs to have had Soviet sympathies, have contacted Soviet-bloc embassies, and have developed relationships without ever revealing secrets. Despite this, they may still have been classed as an 'agent'.[123]

It may be difficult to arrive at firm conclusions about whether or not Stross and Fletcher did spy for the Soviet Union, but there are other backbenchers about whom much more is known. In 1969, a Czech intelligence and security officer, Josef Frolik, defected to the West and revealed that two MPs, Will Owen and Tom Driberg, had provided information to the StB.[124] Owen, MP for Morpeth, had been included on the list passed to MI5 by Patrick Gordon Walker in 1961. At the time, the Security Service had concluded that Owen was 'not known to be CP but CP officials say he has no hesitation about being in touch with CP'. They did not regard him to be 'of most significance'.[125] Frolik stated that Owen was paid £500 a month and provided 'top secret material of the highest value'. Whilst he was only ever a backbencher, Owen was a member of the Commons Estimates Select Committee; the Security Service believed that this gave him access to some material classified 'SECRET'. During his time on the committee, it received seven 'SECRET' documents from the Ministry of Aviation and a further six from the Ministry of Defence.[126] When informed of the allegations against Owen, Wilson described him as 'a drip ...

an ineffective member of the House, moderately intelligent but very naïve'. The Prime Minister was 'not in the least surprised' that Owen would pass on information but refused the Security Service permission to tap his telephone.[127] Owen was arrested and admitted receiving money from the Czechs but denied passing on classified information to them.[128] He resigned his seat and was tried on official secrets charges in May 1970. Although Owen was acquitted, in MI5's authorised history, Christopher Andrew states that he was 'almost certainly, guilty as charged'.[129]

In the late 1960s, Wilson was said to have been informed that Frolik had named Driberg as being paid by the StB.[130] Driberg served as Chairman of the Labour Party in the late 1950s and was a prominent backbencher in the 1960s. As well as working for the StB, he was also involved with the KGB; files in KGB archives state that they recruited him in 1956. Described as 'one of the most promiscuous homosexuals in British public life', Driberg was recruited after the Soviet authorities collected compromising material on him during a trip to Moscow. He had journeyed to Moscow to interview his old friend, Guy Burgess, and the Soviets blackmailed Driberg to work for them during his visit.[131] As a Soviet agent, Driberg reported information from inside the Labour NEC and gossip about the dynamics of the parliamentary party. He was also utilised to write a biography of Burgess, *Guy Burgess: A portrait with background*, that was essentially a propaganda piece, censored by the KGB.[132] He broke off contact with the KGB in 1968.[133]

No MI5 files have been released on Driberg, and there is no mention of him in Andrew's authorised history of the Security Service. He was, however, on the list of dubious Labour MPs that Patrick Gordon Walker handed to MI5 in 1961.[134] The case of Driberg is particularly intriguing because he had worked for the Security Service in the interwar years. He was recruited by MI5's Maxwell Knight when he was a student communist and provided the Security Service with information from inside the CPGB until being discovered and expelled from the Party in 1941.[135] It appears that Driberg continued to be in contact with Knight for many years after he had left the CPGB. Prior to Driberg's trip to Moscow in 1956 to interview Burgess, he had received 'some preliminary briefing' by the Security Service. He also appears to have informed Knight about Burgess' life in Moscow after further trips to visit the Russian capital in the following years.[136] The intelligence historian Nigel West claims that Driberg even reported every contact he had with Czech intelligence back to MI5.[137] This appears to be very possible. He may well have continued to be an MI5 agent; his story remains unresolved.

The most significant individual named by Frolik as being in the pay of Czech intelligence was John Stonehouse, Labour MP for Wednesbury. In 1968, Wilson appointed Stonehouse as Postmaster General before making him the Minister of Posts and Telecommunications the following year. It does not appear that Stonehouse had ever come to the notice of the Security Service prior to Frolik's revelations but, following them, they interviewed him. Stonehouse denied that he had ever helped Czech intelligence; MI5 reported to Wilson 'there is no evidence that [he] gave the Czechs any information he should not have given them, much less that he consciously acted as an agent.'[138] Stonehouse left office when Labour lost the 1970 General Election and, when Labour returned to government in early 1974, he remained on the backbenches. Just weeks after being re-elected to a new constituency of Walsall North at the October 1974 General Election, Stonehouse went missing on a beach in Miami and was presumed drowned. Wilson made a statement to the Commons on 17 December, whereby he confirmed that allegations had been made against Stonehouse in 1969, but the Security Service found no evidence to support them, nor had any evidence emerged since.[139] Just over a week later, Stonehouse was discovered in Australia having faked his own death after facing catastrophic business debts. He was returned to Britain and jailed for seven years in 1976 for fraud.[140]

The Stonehouse case had the most extraordinary ending in 1980, when the Security Service received information from a second Czech defector who asserted that 'Mr Stonehouse was a conscious paid [StB] agent from about 1962'. The defector revealed that, as a minister, Stonehouse had 'provided information about the Government plans and policies and about technological subjects including aircraft', for which he was paid 'about

£5,000 in total'.[141] Margaret Thatcher's government considered prosecuting Stonehouse, but decided against it as the Attorney General believed that the new evidence 'would not be sufficient to sustain a successful prosecution'.[142] After this decision was made and endorsed by the Prime Minister, consideration was given to whether he should be interviewed again. The Security Service believed there was nothing to gain, and the matter was left to lie.[143] Whilst Stonehouse never confessed to his actions, he hinted at his treachery when he wrote a spy novel following his release from prison, about a civil servant who had been entrapped and recruited by East German intelligence.[144] He died in 1988. After his death, a file held in Czech archives showed he had been a Czech agent but significantly stated that the StB had been disappointed by the intelligence he provided as a minister.[145]

Stonehouse is one of only two men known to have worked for a foreign intelligence agency whilst holding ministerial office. The other, Ray Mawby, Conservative MP for Totnes 1955–83, also worked in the office of the Postmaster General. StB files show that he met with Czech intelligence officers from 1960 and provided information about politics and trade unions, although such information was said to be 'of only limited interest'. Mawby's contacts with the StB continued after he had joined the government in 1963, serving as assistant Postmaster General—a post he held until 1964. The files show that he handed over information from inside the Conservative Party and provided his contacts with plans of the Prime Minister's office in the House of Commons and its security.[146] His relations with the Czechs ended in 1971 and it is unclear whether Mawby ever came to the attention of MI5. He died in 1990, and his espionage was only revealed in files held in Czech archives in 2012.

The Wilson Plot

Despite the successful attempts by Eastern bloc intelligence agencies to subvert British democracy by recruiting MPs, during the 1960s Anglo-Soviet relations improved to the extent that Harold Wilson was able to proclaim them as being at an 'all-time high.' Britain had become one of the Soviet Union's leading capitalist trading partners and even briefly became their leading supplier.[147] Nonetheless, caution was still required. As the Foreign Office made clear,

> So long as the Communist Party of the Soviet Union regards itself as obliged to conduct a non-military but otherwise comprehensive struggle against us, our relations with the Soviet government cannot be those of friendship or trust. Nor can they be stable.[148]

Political relations may have improved during the late 1960s, a time of East-West détente, but for those working in intelligence, suspicions of the Soviets remained substantial. The long-term Soviet attempts to recruit spies from within the British establishment had had a corrosive effect. Although Soviet attempts to penetrate British society had peaked by this stage, some within MI5 became almost paranoid that many other Soviet agents were present within the establishment but remained undiscovered. By the early-to-mid 1970s, the paranoia that had developed led some within MI5 to begin to suspect their own colleagues of being Soviet agents. Two officers, Peter Wright and Arthur Martin, began an almost-obsessive hunt to uncover the supposed moles within their midst. Most notably, they suspected Roger Hollis and Graham Mitchell, DG and DDG respectively, although an internal investigation cleared both men.[149]

Such a level of paranoia was not confined to intelligence officers. As one scholar has written, 1970s Britain was 'experiencing a paranoid political style'. The 'belief in plots and parallel networks of one kind or another' gripped the State, the government, Parliament, and the media.[150] Those on both sides of the political spectrum began to fear for democracy; there were concerns that Britain would either be subjected to a right-wing military coup, as had happened in Chile, or was being taken over by Marxist ideas and was in danger of falling to communism. As an election loomed in 1974, the novelist Kingsley Amis went as far as to opine that it would mark Britain's 'last free election'.[151]

By the time Harold Wilson returned to Downing Street for a second period as Prime Minister in March 1974, after four years in opposition, it seemed as though the British establishment was having a collective nervous breakdown. In such circumstances, Wilson not only became a focus for the paranoia, but also began to develop suspicious thoughts himself. Although he had worked relatively well with the intelligence community during his first spell in office, some security officials felt uneasy about his return.[152] Relations declined to the extent that by 1975, Wilson had become 'convinced that there was a plot to destroy him and his government'. He worried that MI5 was 'conducting some sort of vendetta against him' and that he was 'being watched or monitored, observed by both hostile and some friendly intelligence services'.[153] Wilson's insistence that there were people in the shadows plotting against him was often written off as the rantings of a man who had become extremely paranoid.[154] This may have been the case, but some evidence suggests that Wilson's concerns were not without basis. Wilson's own personal home, his office, the offices of his lawyer and the homes of at least six of his aides were all broken into over several months in 1974 when private papers were stolen.[155] This could have been a coincidence, but at the very least makes it understandable why he had started to become concerned. It has also come to light that the Cabinet Room, its waiting room, and the Prime Minister's private study at Number 10 were all bugged. Microphones were introduced at the request of Prime Minister Harold Macmillan in 1963 when Downing Street was being refurbished and remained in place until 1977.[156] Files as yet unreleased at the time of writing are said to suggest that the microphones were not monitored, but Wilson was correct to have had suspicions.[157]

During the Wilson years, treacherous remarks often passed the lips of establishment members. Some London-based CIA officers were said to have expressed shock at the 'openly scurrilous and disloyal remarks' made by MI5 officers about Wilson.[158] Certain other members of the British establishment with connections to the intelligence community even went as far as to talk casually about mounting a military coup.[159] Some members of the Security Service, such as Peter Wright, believed Wilson was possibly, maybe probably, a Soviet agent. In his memoir, *Spycatcher*, Wright wrote that some in MI5 thought Wilson to be 'a menace' and that a plan had been devised where 'MI5 would arrange for selective details of the intelligence about leading Labour Party figures, especially Wilson, to be leaked to sympathetic pressmen'. The information was intended to show 'that Wilson was considered a security risk'. Wright stated that 'it was a carbon copy of the Zinoviev letter'.[160] Wright's claims were, however, somewhat exaggerated. In an interview he admitted that in his memoir he had overstated the number of MI5 officers who approved of the plot, stating that 'the maximum number was eight or nine. Very often it was only three'. When asked how many would have joined him in plotting 'when all the talking had died down', he replied, 'one, I should say'.[161]

John Hunt, who served as Cabinet Secretary during Wilson's second spell in office, said many years later that 'a few, very few, malcontents in MI5 ... a lot of them like Peter Wright who were right-wing, malicious and had serious personal grudges—[who] gave vent to these and spread damaging malicious stories about the Labour government'.[162] Discussing the matter on another occasion he stated, 'I don't think the group [in MI5] were in any sense evil. They were people on the whole who followed a train of thought: the Russians used to try and entrap everybody, they must have tried with [Wilson], they must have succeeded.'[163] A small number of 'malcontents' undoubtedly existed within MI5 at the time; the head of MI6, Maurice Oldfield, personally told Wilson that there was an 'unreliable section' in MI5.[164] If some members of MI5 were willing to suspect their own bosses of being Soviet agents, it seems likely that they would have been willing to believe the same about a Labour Prime Minister. If they truly thought this, they would have reasoned he must be removed from office for the sake of the country. Although the truth about what went on will likely never be known, it does seem unlikely that there was an organised plot against the Prime Minister. A small number of rogue individuals existed but were unrepresentative of the wider Security Service at the time. In 1987, MI5's Director General, Sir Antony Duff, ordered an internal inquiry in an attempt to investigate rumours of a plot against Wilson. After examining all the evidence possible, and interviewing all relevant MI5 people, it 'concluded unequivocally that no member of the Service had been involved in the surveillance of Wilson, still less in any attempt to destabilise his government.'[165] By the 1970s, most within MI5 fully accepted the legitimacy of the Labour Party, although a small faction still saw it as a subversive threat.

Trotskyist Entryism

Wilson resigned as Prime Minister in April 1976 and was replaced by his Foreign Secretary, James Callaghan. At the time, MI5 was becoming concerned about the increasing number of Trotskyists within the Labour Party. In 1973, the Labour NEC had abolished its list of Proscribed Organisations, which had been crucial in preventing elements of the far-left from gaining influence within the Party.[166] Abolishing it was symptomatic of a shift to the left within Labour and particularly the NEC and, MI5 believed, encouraged subversive organisations to attempt to infiltrate the Party.[167]

For much of the post-war era until the 1970s, MI5 had been relatively sanguine about the threat Trotskyism could pose, whilst the Labour Party had been much more concerned.[168] By the mid-1970s, these stances had been somewhat reversed. In 1976, whilst MI5 alarm about Trotskyists was growing, the Labour NEC declined to act against the increasing number of Trotskyists who had infiltrated the Party. Even though a 1975 report by the Party's National Agent, Reg Underhill, warned that Trotskyist groups had a clear strategy for infiltration, the left-dominated NEC would not allow its publication and tended to be dismissive of the issue.[169]

Despite the attitude of the NEC, many senior figures within the Labour Party were concerned about the matter. Members of Callaghan's new government expressed grave concerns about political subversion. In November 1976, during his first meeting with the MI5 DG, Michael Hanley, the Home Secretary, Merlyn Rees, asked for information about Trotskyist penetration of the Labour Party. Hanley later noted that, unlike the Labour NEC, Rees 'fully seized the importance of subversive penetration of the Labour Party.'[170] The Security Service provided him with details which revealed Trotskyists had penetrated numerous local Labour Party branches.[171] For the first time, therefore, MI5 believed that Trotskyism posed a significant danger, not only to an established political party but, with Labour in government, potentially to the British State.

The Security Service believed the major Trotskyist entryist group within the Labour Party was the Revolutionary Socialist League (RSL), better known as Militant or Militant Tendency (MT). By using entryism, Militant was following a strategy advocated by Trotsky himself in the 1930s—that of entering a social democratic party and transforming it from within.[172] As early as 1959, Militant founder, Ted Grant, spoke of how the 'historical justification for the policy of entryism' was to transform the Labour Party, and that eventually Labour would become 'a revolutionary party'.[173]

MI5's ability to investigate Militant was hampered by the secrecy of the organisation. For many years, Militant refused to admit its own existence, with its leading figures stating that it was merely an informal group managing the production and sale of the *Militant* newspaper.[174] Their annual conferences were closed to the public and security was said to be 'very impressive'. Precautions taken to protect secrecy were typified by the fact that any paperwork handed out during the event was numbered and collected in at the end of each session.[175] Despite this, the intelligence agencies did manage to infiltrate Militant's annual conference; intelligence officers were able to covertly attend Militant conferences from their inception in 1976.[176] At the 1977 conference, intelligence operatives recorded a speech by Peter Taaffe, the deputy leader. He stated that Militant cadres would be the 'spinal column of the future mass revolutionary organisation' and 'an indispensable weapon of the Revolution in Britain'.[177] MI5 investigations into Militant were highly successful; by the late 1970s, through a combination of telephone checks, eavesdropping on annual conferences and agent penetration, they had identified about 75 per cent of the Tendency's membership.[178] In the mid-1980s, the overall number of Militant members was believed to be in excess of 6,300.[179] It has been said that MI5 recruited up to thirty Militant members as informants.[180] These successes came with one caveat; the Security Service never felt it had absolute knowledge of Militant. As one report in January 1985 made clear, 'there were a number of limitations in the intelligence available on MT which was a clandestine organisation.'[181]

Militant was able to grow and gain significant influence not only due to the lax disciplinary procedures in the Labour Party, but also because of the dedication of its members and its strong internal discipline—a characteristic which most other Trotskyist groups had lacked.[182] It was this commitment that enabled it not only to gain influence in the youth sections of the Labour Party, but also at a local and national level. Most notably, Militant had a considerable impact on the Labour-led Liverpool City Council during the 1980s. It is likely that the Security Service would have taken interest in the activities of members of the Council during the 1980s. Although no files have been released, a former Special Branch officer admitted in 2002 that a file was held on the deputy council leader and Militant member, Derek Hatton.[183]

At national level, Militant managed to have several members of the Tendency selected as Labour parliamentary candidates. Two were elected as Labour MPs at the 1983 General Election—Dave Nellist for Coventry South East and Terry Fields for Liverpool Broadgreen.[184] Merseyside Police later confirmed 'they had collected some material' on Fields 'for the purpose of investigations', whilst a former Special Branch officer admitted that MI5 had asked for an agent to infiltrate the Coventry Labour Party to monitor Nellist when he was an MP.[185] The agent was instructed to 'cultivate' Nellist, and developed a close relationship with him, 'helping him with a lot of things' and 'going around with him to a lot of meetings.' A former Special Branch officer later justified the surveillance by arguing that MI5 was not monitoring any specific individuals and instead monitoring Militant. Reports were produced on Nellist, the officer stated, because 'he was at a [Militant] meeting.'[186]

Had it been known at the time that the Security Service was closely tracking the activities of an MP, this would have caused uproar. However, intelligence agencies' interest in the pair can be more easily understood when it is recognised that, by being

Militant members, they were committed to its constitution and were, therefore, bound to prioritise Militant's needs ahead of Labour's.[187] Nellist and Fields were, in some ways, Labour MPs in name only. This was evidenced in the 'rapturous reception' they received at a Militant rally after the 1983 election, despite the Labour Party having suffered its worst election defeat for 65 years.[188] Although it was not unreasonable that both were watched, it would be interesting to view the information collected by the intelligence community on Nellist and Fields as neither seems to have been involved with any subversive activity. Their conduct was not that of apparently revolutionary MPs. Whilst Fields was jailed for sixty days in 1991 for his refusal to pay the poll tax, both were popular constituency MPs. Nellist was even chosen as 'Backbencher of the Year' by the conservative *Spectator* magazine in 1991.[189] Both also donated over half of their salary to charity for the nine years that they served in the House of Commons.[190]

Nellist and Fields were deselected as Labour candidates in 1991 ahead of the 1992 General Election and failed to be re-elected after standing against official Labour Party candidates.[191] The action taken against the pair was part of wider disciplinary action to purge the Labour Party of Militant. In 1982, the Proscribed List was revived, and Militant was added to it.[192] Numerous Militant members were expelled from the Labour Party between 1983 and 1986, most notably those on Liverpool Council, including Hatton. By 1991 over 200 people were believed to have been expelled from the Labour Party because they had links to Militant.[193] Unable to work within the Labour Party from the mid-1980s onwards, Militant's influence rapidly waned and its threat slowly dissipated.[194]

Once the Labour Party began to deal with Militant, the attitude of the intelligence community towards MT changed. By 1985, Militant was in decline nationally[195] and, although it continued to have a stronghold in Liverpool, officials believed that the organisation's subversive threat had diminished. In January 1987, the inter-departmental group on Subversion in Public Life (SPL) reported that Militant had 'no immediate spring-board for disruptive activity'.[196] The report recommended that any further action should be proportionate to the limited threat, stating, 'it would be sufficient in this area to monitor and report from time to time on the state of subversive, including in particular MT, influence on local Councils.'[197]

'A new and disturbing form of subversion'

Security Service concerns about Militant were not confined to its activity in politics. Newly released files show that there was significant unease about members of the Tendency working in Civil Service and other public sector roles.[198] In October 1984 an unnamed civil servant nearing promotion was identified as a Militant sympathiser. MI5 advised that he 'should not have access to information classified CONFIDENTIAL'; it appears likely the individual was not promoted.[199] The reasoning—that subversives threatened classified information—had long been used to exclude communists or communist sympathisers from certain posts. It appears, however, to have been rarely used to deal with Militant members. The subversive threat they posed was believed to be different and was described by the Cabinet Secretary Sir Robert Armstrong as 'a new and disturbing form'. In January 1985, a meeting of senior Whitehall staff commented that 'the MT threat was not to the security of classified information but the creation of the maximum disruption to the effective operation of the government'.[200]

Concerns had been raised after a strike by computer staff at the Newcastle offices of the Department of Health and Social Security (DHSS) in 1984. The strike, which severely disrupted pension and child benefit payments to millions of people, was believed to have been organised by Militant activists in Civil Service unions.[201] Whitehall officials believed that Militant members involved in the strike wished for it to continue indefinitely because of the disruption that it would cause to government services. Militant members were believed to have infiltrated one of the main Civil Service unions, the CPSA, and it was feared that they could cause even greater disruption unless action was taken.[202] In November 1984, the Permanent Secretary at the Department of Health and Social Security, Sir Kenneth Stowe, argued that the rise of Militant members in Civil Service unions may have been because of the policies of Margaret Thatcher's government. He wrote that the threat they now posed 'could be said to be an indirect result of [government ministers] losing the loyalty and commitment of the moderate centre in Civil Service unionism through the policies they have pursued towards the Civil Service since 1979.'[203]

Recognising the significance of the subversive threat Militant members posed to the Civil Service, in early 1985, the Cabinet Secretary Sir Robert Armstrong commissioned an investigation into it.[204] In August, SPL reported that Militant members were 'active and adept at exploiting real or imagined grievances amongst [Civil Service] staff' and that their activity during disputes had allowed Militant to increase its membership among civil servants. The report stated that there were 1,420 people with subversive records in the Civil Service.[205] Of these, 733 had Trotskyist records, 284 of whom were members of Militant.[206] SPL stated, however, that the numbers 'probably understate the real figures' as Militant was 'known to be a clandestine organisation and details of all its members are not known'.[207]

Vetting had been largely successful in denying civil servants with a communist record holding positions from which they could threaten State security. However, the threat posed by Militant members was considered by Whitehall officials to be a great deal more difficult to counter. Many of the Militant members worked in non-sensitive jobs, and it was not considered feasible to extend vetting for such positions.[208] In an attempt to counter the new subversive threat, governmental departments were required to work with the Security Service to maintain an up-to-date list of subversives working within the Civil Service. In this way, the information could be quickly accessed when necessary and acted upon accordingly. Each department was advised to develop procedures to ensure that 'subversives are not posted to work in Key Areas' and 'persistent troublemakers, whether members of subversive organisations or not, are identified and removed from work in Key Areas'.[209] Signing off the new policies in December 1985, Thatcher made clear her belief that Civil Service management should 'be very ready to sack subversive troublemakers if they showed any cause under the Civil Service rules.'[210] No further information on subversives in the Civil Service has been released, but it is extremely likely that a number of Militant supporters were prevented from taking up certain posts, redeployed, or possibly prevented from continuing to work within the Civil Service.

Conclusion

In the second half of the twentieth century, the Labour Party emerged as an important part of Britain's fight against subversion. Under the leadership of Clement Attlee, the Party positioned itself as strongly anti-communist and took decisive action to prevent subversive individuals from infiltrating the British State or the Labour Party itself. Attlee's government often worked well with the Security Service to identify crypto-communists within Labour and prevent such individuals gaining influence within the parliamentary party or the wider party membership.

During the Attlee years, senior figures based at the Labour Party headquarters, Transport House, also developed close relationships with the British secret State, most notably with the IRD, to help counter subversives. Information provided by the IRD helped the Party to build up dossiers of information on Labour MPs who advocated pro-Soviet or pro-communist positions and take appropriate disciplinary action against them. The Labour Party General Secretary between 1944 and 1961, Morgan Phillips, had very little tolerance for MPs whose views on communism and foreign affairs conflicted with the Party leadership. The relations between Transport House and the IRD survived after Labour had left government in 1951. Throughout the 1950s, information provided by the IRD—which often came, indirectly, from intelligence sources—allowed the Party to expel members and proscribe radically left-wing organisations.[211]

The government of Harold Wilson, which came to office in 1964, continued to work well with the Security Service to identify subversives not only in the parliamentary Labour Party but also in the trade union movement. Wilson was particularly keen to counter the influence of communists and other subversives within unions, and he worked closely with the Security Service to expose their growing influence. Although Wilson appeared less eager to investigate politicians, and sought to prevent MI5 from tapping MPs' telephones, he requested intelligence on his ministers and appears to have considered Security Service intelligence when deciding on the appointments of certain MPs to cabinet posts. The Wilson years, however, marked the beginning of a decline of Labour-intelligence relations. The Prime Minister himself was suspected by a small number of intelligence officials of being a security risk and, despite Labour's importance in helping to combat subversion, suspicions about the trustworthiness of the Party began to grow.

By the early 1970s, intelligence officials had every reason to express concern about the Labour Party after its NEC moved to the left. The abolition of the proscribed list in 1973, which had previously been successful in denying oxygen to the far-left, increased the ability of subversives to pose a threat to Britain by making it much easier for them to join and influence the Labour Party. The subsequent emergence of Trotskyists within Labour, and the influence they gained in the 1970s and 1980s, illustrated how crucial the Party had been in denying left-wing subversives room in British politics. MI5 briefly believed that Trotskyists were capable of posing a significant subversive threat to the British State but, as soon as the Labour Party re-introduced stronger disciplinary and security procedures, which resulted in the expulsion of more than 200 individuals, the threat began to dissipate. Nothing demonstrated more clearly the key role played by Labour in the post-war era in combatting subversion in Britain.

Trotskyism was able to gain a degree of prominence and pose a subversive threat in the 1970s and 1980s not only because of the laxity of Labour security procedures, but also because the influence of communism had begun to decline. As MI5 had reported in the late 1960s, the subversive threat to Britain, which had for a long time been dominated by communism, had 'diminished in gravity' and was becoming 'more diffuse'.[212] Investigating communism continued to be a priority for the Security Service but, by the early 1970s, MI5 began to turn its attention towards different political groups in its counter-subversion operations—not only taking a closer interest in Trotskyists but also in other movements, most notably groups involved in industrial disputes and single-issue protest organisations.[213]

5

ENEMIES OF THE STATE OR ENEMIES OF THE GOVERNMENT?

In 1969, the Conservative Leader of the Opposition, Edward Heath, invited five trade unionists to dinner to try to get to know them better. Heath had been acquainted with one, Jack Jones, for over thirty years. The two had met in Spain in 1938 during the Spanish Civil War; Jones was fighting for the Republican cause, whilst Heath was visiting as part of an anti-Franco student delegation from Oxford University. Writing in his memoir about the dinner at Heath's Albany flat, Jones recalled 'a pleasant evening', with,

> Heath talking of his yacht and musical interests. At one stage he showed us a new piano he had bought and at our invitation played one or two short pieces. Then Vic Feather [TUC General Secretary] called out, 'Play the "Red Flag" for Jack' and the leader of the Tory Party cheerfully played Labour's national anthem.[1]

The following year, in June 1970, Heath became Prime Minister. Although he attempted to maintain convivial relations with union leaders during his time in office, his premiership was dominated by industrial action.[2] Within weeks of coming to power, his government was forced into agreeing a settlement with striking dockers. Having granted their demands, Heath asked MI5 to provide advance warnings about future strikes. He believed that the strikes were organised by groups of 'evil men' who intended to harm the government and was determined not to be caught unawares again. The Security Service did not share his belief that most strikes were as a result of sinister forces and, rather than providing him with information, Whitehall officials instead sought to delay the matter by setting up two new governmental committees to examine industrial disputes.[3]

In December 1970, power workers went on strike and Heath again requested information from MI5. The Home Secretary, Reginald Maudling, asked that the Security Service place a listening device in a room where a key meeting of the Unions involved in the strike was being held. Maudling was informed by MI5's Deputy Director General, Anthony Simpkins that 'it would be a departure of great significance to seek intelligence from a target which could not properly be regarded as subversive'. The bugging did not take place.[4] The Security Service made it clear to the government that industrial action in itself should not be viewed as subversive— 'leaders of Unions ... are performing the task for which they were elected and, though that may be damaging to the State, they cannot be described as subversive'.[5]

In early 1971, MI5 DG Martin Furnival Jones made it clear to Maudling that the Security Service would not automatically investigate industrial disputes. He regarded union leaders' desire to seek wage increases as a legitimate activity and argued that they were motivated principally and 'perfectly properly' in 'ensuring that their members do not lose ground in the inflationary race.' If the Security Service were to investigate an industrial dispute it would need to have firm grounds for doing so because, Furnival Jones wrote, the links between Trade Unions and the Labour Party meant that 'seeking intelligence about Trade Union affairs could very readily be construed as work "in connection with matters of a Party-political character"'.[6]

Despite the Security Service's reluctance to investigate strikes, it did scrutinise trade unions when it considered communists were exerting influence within them. Although the subversive threat posed by communists had reduced by the early 1970s, MI5 did believe that 'in the industrial sphere the [CPGB] is still capable of causing grave damage.'[7] By this stage, the CPGB was no longer part of the 'direct parliamentary political struggle' and had instead decided to focus its efforts on extra-parliamentary activities, notably the penetration of the trade union movement.[8]

At the beginning of the 1970s, MI5 investigated the leaders of two major unions, Jack Jones and Hugh Scanlon. It was noted that both 'have Communist records, are prepared to work closely with the Communist Party on particular issues and stand well to the left of the trade union movement.'[9] The Security Service took out a HOW on Jones, tapping his phone to investigate his connections with the CPGB, but made clear that it 'was not concerned with his industrial activities.'[10] They also wished to examine if he was 'being manipulated or under the strong influence of the Russians'. The HOW on Jones was cancelled after a year as MI5 judged that there was no evidence of his being influenced by either the Russians or any British communists.[11] The Security Service also concluded that the CPGB had little influence on Hugh Scanlon.[12] Intelligence provided many years later, by the MI6 agent Oleg Gordievsky, revealed that Jones had met Soviet intelligence officers on several occasions and was regarded by the KGB as an agent. This was, however, an ambiguous term, and whether Jones would have viewed himself as an 'agent' is open to question.[13] The authorised history of MI5 states that 'Jones was not being manipulated by the Russians.'[14]

The Russians may not have recruited Jones but remained very keen to gain as much information as possible from British sources. MI5 believed that 'there is virtually no information about this country or indeed about any country in the west which the Russian Intelligence Service is not anxious to obtain.'[15] In 1971, a decisive step was taken to try to combat the influence of Soviet intelligence officers working, under official cover, out of the Soviet Embassy in London. There was increasing concern about the sheer number of Soviet officials present in Britain and, after months of discussion, the Heath government took the decision to expel nearly 100 officers present at the London Embassy, in an operation codenamed FOOT.[16] It represented the largest single diplomatic expulsion in history and helped to successfully counter Soviet espionage operations in Britain. For Dick White, the expulsions 'levelled the field: 1951 had been the highpoint of Soviet espionage in Britain. They never had it so easy again. After that it was downwards for them and upwards for us.'[17] After 1971, it is said, the KGB 'found it more difficult to collect high-grade intelligence in London than any other Western capital'.[18]

A Subversive Conspiracy?

Heath had worked well with MI5 to carry out Operation FOOT successfully. Nonetheless, he continued to disagree with intelligence officials about the subversive influence in industrial disputes. For MI5, in the early 1970s, communists were simply not capable of directly influencing national industrial disputes; industrial action 'may be exploited by subversive organisations, [but] has not been created by them.' The major reason for CPGB activity in unions, MI5 believed, was 'to win political power' and thus 'any industrial unrest which may result from its activity in trade union movement the CPGB tends to regard as a bonus.'[19]

In early 1972 the National Union of Mineworkers (NUM) voted to go on strike for the first time since 1926. The press expressed sympathy with their position; the *Daily Express* opined that 'these men do a hard, dirty, dangerous job. All they ask for is a decent wage. They deserve it. They should have it.' The *Daily Mail* called on the government to meet 'the just demands of the lower-paid miners.' In this, the newspapers were reflecting public opinion. Even though the strike eventually led to power outages and a three-day week, opinion polls showed that a majority of the public believed the miners were justified in striking for higher wages. The government was determined not to agree to the NUM's demands but was eventually forced to grant large pay rises for the miners.[20] Heath was convinced that the strike had been influenced by subversive organisations. After the strike had ended, it was made known to MI5 that he found 'it hard to believe that the way in which the [strike] developed was unplanned' and wished to see 'an analysis to show who was responsible for the organisation of this episode'.[21] In response, MI5's Deputy Director General, Michael

Hanley, explained that the strike was perfectly legitimate and that there was 'no evidence that [the CPGB] exercised a decisive influence either in planning the strike or during its course.'[22]

The Security Service was able to reach such a definitive conclusion due to intelligence it had previously collected. The leader of the Scottish miners, Mick McGahey, was already the subject of a phone tap as he was a member of the CPGB.[23] Information would also likely have been provided by the NUM president at the time of the strike, Joe Gormley. A former Special Branch officer revealed years later that Gormley had a 'very close working relationship' with intelligence officials. Alongside Gormley, it was said that '22 or 23' senior trade unionists provided information to members of the intelligence community about industry.[24]

Heath's disagreement with the intelligence agencies on the matter of subversion of industry is laid bare in a document he received from the Security Service in March 1972 entitled 'Subversion in Britain'. The report made clear that 'the Communist Party does not yet control any union or exercise a decisive influence on the TUC. Its attitude to industrial disputes is tactical and it exploits rather than creates them'. Referring specifically to the 1972 miners' strike, MI5 reported that 'the efforts of subversive groups represent a small part of the general momentum. While not insignificant, their efforts have not been decisive'. Heath scribbled on the report, 'I don't agree'. The report contains a number of Heath's annotations. Even when MI5 sought to play down the influence of subversives by stating that there were about 40,000 people, 'or well below 0.1% of the population', who 'could be described as committed supporters of the various subversive organisations', he scrawled on the report—'a hell of a lot'.[25]

According to Peter Wright, writing in *Spycatcher*, 'the miners' strike of 1972 and a succession of stoppages in the motorcar industry had a profound effect on the thinking of the Heath government. Intelligence on domestic subversion became the overriding priority.'[26] The government continued to push the Security Service for more information and, whilst profound disagreements remained over what was and was not subversion, Heath did eventually gain some concessions from intelligence officials. In late 1972, Whitehall mandarins were pressurised by the Prime Minister to change MI5's terms of reference to enable the Security Service to collect more intelligence on industrial disputes. Officials, notably Sir Philip Allen, Permanent Secretary at the Home Office, and the Cabinet Secretary, Sir Burke Trend, resisted these attempts, but MI5 did ultimately agree to produce more information. The Director General, Michael Hanley, stated that he was prepared to 'stretch the Charter as far as it would go' but would not agree to watching an individual on whom there was no adverse security information.[27] Throughout the miners' strike in 1972, a combination of Whitehall and Security Service officials did not indulge the Heath government's paranoia about subversives. The officials sought to differentiate between opposing the government on the one hand and subversion on the other; as it was made clear in October 1972, 'opposition to the industrial policies of the government of the day is not in itself subversive.'[28]

The attitude of the intelligence community in the early 1970s contrasted strongly with the attitudes held in the 1920s, when intelligence officials had pressurised the government to take stronger action against communists only to be dismissed by more moderate ministers. MI5's analysis of the miners' strike was both calm and rational. Intelligence officials did not seek to create hysteria merely because communists had a degree of involvement.

Red Under the Bed

At the end of 1972, the Security Service reviewed the industrial disputes that had broken out in Britain during the year. The subsequent report stated, 'it is doubtful whether the Party's activity has had a decisive impact on the outcome of any major disputes [during 1972] outside the building industry.'[29] The National Building Strike, which began during the summer, was highly successful and led to significant pay rises for workers in the building industry.[30] MI5 took an interest in the dispute as they believed its success had been down to the organisation of flying pickets by a rank-and-file movement controlled by communists, the Building Workers' Charter.[31]

ENEMIES OF THE STATE OR ENEMIES OF THE GOVERNMENT?

In September 1972, 250 flying pickets travelled to Shrewsbury to close down building sites. The former Special Branch officer, Tony Robinson, later described the strike as being 'very violent' and revealed that some of those involved in the flying pickets were monitored by intelligence officials. Such individuals, he said, 'used to travel the length and breadth of the country and ... intimidate building workers who insisted on carrying on working or who wouldn't go on strike'.[32] For Sir Robert Mark, the Met Commissioner in 1972, the Shrewsbury pickets 'committed the worst of all crimes, worse even than murder, the attempt to achieve an industrial or political objective by political violence.' It was, he later wrote, 'the very conduct which helped to bring the National Socialist German Workers Party to power in 1933.'[33] One of the picketers at Shrewsbury was Ricky Tomlinson, who later became a well-known actor. By the early 1970s, Tomlinson had been a WRP member for several years; Robinson detailed that he had been closely monitored by the authorities and was regarded as 'a left-wing agitator ... prone to violence and basically speaking ... a political thug'.[34]

Although there were a number of violent disturbances in Shrewsbury, no arrests were made.[35] In November 1972, however, a number of pickets were arrested, apparently on the direction of the Home Secretary, Robert Carr.[36] Months later, in January 1973, the Attorney General, Peter Rawlinson, wrote to Carr making clear he believed that 'proceedings should not be instituted'.[37] The prosecutions went ahead anyway. Twenty-four of the pickets were charged with conspiracy to intimidate and three, including Ricky Tomlinson, were found guilty of the charges in December 1973 and jailed.[38] In 1974, Tomlinson and his fellow jailed picket, Des Warren, attempted to overturn their convictions. Rejecting their appeal, the Lord Chief Justice, Lord Widgery, stated that 'the deterrent effect of the original sentence has contributed to a period of relative peace.'[39] This was exactly what the Heath government had wanted.

The Heath government undoubtedly wanted to deter further strikes and would have privately welcomed the convictions. Files that have subsequently been released suggest that Heath took a good deal of interest in the case. Legal proceedings continued despite the advice of the government's top legal adviser and, most interestingly, ITV broadcast a programme, *Red Under the Bed*, about communist infiltration of the trade unions on the day the jury retired to consider its verdict. The programme contained footage of two of the defendants, a march through Shrewsbury and images of violence and damage alleged to have been caused by pickets during the building strike.[40] Files on *Red Under the Bed* state that the IRD had a 'discreet but considerable hand in the programme.'[41] Heath's Principal Private Secretary, Robert Armstrong, wrote several weeks after the broadcast that 'the Prime Minister has seen the transcript of [the] television programme ... He has commented that we want as much as possible of this sort of thing.'[42]

Although the memos may suggest government involvement in the television programme, it remains unclear whether Heath or any of his ministers did directly participate in its development. It is also far from clear if, as some have argued, *Red Under the Bed* had any influence on the jurors in the trial. Indeed, in March 2021, the Court of Appeal dismissed the impact of the programme ruling 'we are confident that any juror who saw this programme would not have been prejudiced against the appellants as a consequence'. The Court did, however, overturn the convictions of fourteen men convicted for involvement in the dispute, after accepting that the destruction of original witness statements by police, ahead of the trial in 1973, made the convictions unsafe. Lord Justice Fulford remarked, 'what occurred was unfair to the extent that the verdicts cannot be upheld.'[43]

Edward Heath's time in office was plagued by strikes in several different sectors. Unsurprisingly, his premiership ended against the backdrop of industrial action. In February 1974, another miners' strike was called.[44] On this occasion, unlike in 1972, the Security Service provided the Prime Minister with information about the strike, believing that 'Communists in the [NUM] were largely responsible for framing the pay claim which is the subject of the present dispute. This originated from the communist-controlled Scottish Area and was subsequently endorsed by the NUM's National Conference in July 1973.' The Security Service thought Mick McGahey to have been highly influential. Heath had, himself, met McGahey during discussions between the government and the NUM in November 1973. The Prime Minister alleged that McGahey 'proclaimed that he wanted to bring down the government.' The memorandum which MI5 sent to Heath about the strike was, according to the Security Service's authorised history, 'drafted with a possible Commons statement in mind.'[45] Rather than taking on the miners and revealing MI5's analysis in Parliament, as Harold Wilson had done in 1966 with the Seamen's strike, Heath decided to call an election on 'Who governs?'— positioning the government against the unions.[46] He lost.

'The Enemy Within'

In the years after Heath's departure from Downing Street, MI5 became more concerned about the involvement of subversives in industrial disputes. By April 1976, it believed that 'the main subversive threat to the authority of Government is directed through the trade union movement'.[47] As the number of strikes increased towards the end of the 1970s, the Labour government led by James Callaghan requested intelligence about disputes, notably about the picketing outside the Grunwick photo-processing plant in London.[48] A former trade union official himself, Callaghan was concerned about the confrontation between pickets and police at Grunwick. He believed it had the potential to bring the government down and asserted that 'the government was not dealing with respectable unionism but rent a mob.'[49] The Prime Minister asked to be kept 'informed about [the] movements' of one of the key organisers of the pickets, Arthur Scargill, and is likely to have received intelligence about the dispute.[50]

Intelligence officials may have believed that the subversive involvement in industrial disputes had increased, but they continued to conclude that not all strikes were controlled by subversives. Callaghan was concerned about a potential police strike in 1977 but was not provided with any intelligence as the Security Service did not believe the unions involved to be subversive. Callaghan's government, like Edward Heath's, was effectively brought down by industrial disputes, with numerous strikes occurring during the so-called 'Winter of Discontent' of 1978–9. The Security Service did not provide the government with intelligence that would potentially have enabled it to counter such action.[51] With many strikes unresolved for months, the Conservative Party was able to defeat Callaghan at the 1979 General Election arguing, very simply, 'Labour Isn't Working'.[52]

One of the major industrial disputes of the late 1970s occurred in the car industry. MI5 believed the senior shop steward at British Leyland's (BL) main Longbridge Plant, Derek Robinson, had coordinated the strikes. Robinson, branded 'Red Robbo' by the press, was an avowed Communist and had long been known to MI5. Having joined the Communist Party in 1951, he stood as the CPGB candidate for Birmingham Northfield in four General Elections from 1966 to 1974.[53]

Robinson was, according to one Special Branch officer, regarded as a 'noisy agitator'. At the time of the strikes MI5 believed he posed a significant threat, and they recruited an individual who was both a 'very close' colleague of Robinson's at Longbridge and a highly placed official within his Union, the AUEW, to report on him. Codenamed '910', the individual regularly provided MI5 with 'very highly valued' information on the intentions of union officials at Longbridge and the strikes they were going to call.[54] The most crucial piece of information he passed to the Security Service were the minutes of a CPGB Midland District Committee meeting, held to discuss opposition to a BL 'restructuring' plan and attended by Robinson.[55] According to Michael Edwardes, Chairman of British Leyland, who was shown the minutes, those present at the meeting intended 'to break the company' and 'talked about bringing the company down ... bringing the country down.'[56]

Robinson opposed the restructuring plan even after a ballot of BL workers showed that, despite proposed job losses and plant closures, 80 per cent were in favour. On 19 November 1979, after refusing to withdraw his opposition, he was sacked for 'deliberately undermining the company's recovery programme, threatening both the market share and confidence in the company's future'. His dismissal led to a mass walkout amongst Longbridge workers, with 30,000 striking to demand his reinstatement. Within days, however, the AUEW refused to back the strike, and most employees returned to work.[57] The President of the AUEW, Terry Duffy, appears to have felt he could not legitimately support continued industrial action after he was shown MI5's information which confirmed Robinson's contact with communists.[58]

The dispute at BL took place only months into the premiership of Margaret Thatcher, who had taken office in May 1979.[59] One of the most pressing concerns of the new Thatcher government was dealing with industrial disputes. Thatcher had herself been a member of Heath's cabinet in the early 1970s and thus attributed most of the strikes to 'wreckers' and subversives; as one account puts it, 'those who had lived through the Heath government at No. 10 were especially prone to see it that way.'[60] Following her election victory in 1979, MI5 provided Thatcher with a memo on subversion in the UK. It concluded by stating, 'though the threat from subversion is serious and in some ways more evident, it is not greater than 10 years ago'. Thatcher questioned such an assessment and wrote 'doubt this' on the report.[61] In her first meeting with the MI5 Director General, Sir Howard Smith, Thatcher asked to be provided with more information on strikes. Smith noted that 'Mrs Thatcher assumes a greater role and influence on the part of the Communist Party and Trotskyists in the trade union and industrial field than they did in fact enjoy'. Her requests for the identification of those behind strikes were rebuffed and the Director General emphasised that the Security Service would only provide information on strikes which involved people previously identified as subversive.[62]

The major clash between the Thatcher government and industry resulted in the miners' strike of 1984–5.[63] The strike, which began on 6 March 1984, differed from the strikes of the 1970s in that it was not about wages but about pit closures and job losses.[64] As had happened during the General Strike of 1926, the government sought to portray the 1984 miners' strike as a grave threat to the British nation. In May 1984, the Energy Secretary, Peter Walker, argued that it was 'a battle enthusiastically supported by Marxists to see whether or not the mob, using mob violence, can rule.'[65]

Pickets were routinely referred to as 'extremists' that threatened the way of life of the British people and democracy itself.[66] This was not mere public posturing; the government genuinely believed it. In July 1984, John Redwood, head of the Downing Street policy unit, wrote to the Prime Minister warning that 'the extreme Left is mounting an extra parliamentary challenge to the Government on a number of fronts.' He made clear to Thatcher that the strike was a battle that could not be lost, warning that settling on terms favourable to the miners 'would be the end of effective government.'[67]

Just over a week after Redwood's comments, at a meeting of the 1922 Committee of backbench Conservative MPs, the Prime Minister herself referred to the miners as the 'enemy within' who were attempting to circumvent democracy.[68] Thatcher never made such remarks in public, but her private papers suggest that she had planned to use the phrase during her speech to the Conservative Party Conference in October 1984. She intended to warn that Britain was facing an 'insurrection'. The speech was, however, never made after the IRA bombing of the Grand Hotel in Brighton during Conference week.[69]

Thatcher and her ministers were not wrong to view the strike as a significant threat, but this threat was of a political rather than a security nature. In the opening weeks of the dispute, the Security Service reported that there had been no significant subversive involvement. Thatcher and her government disagreed and pushed to obtain more information from MI5. Whilst MI5 did collect significant intelligence during the first few months of the strike, it decided not to provide such information to the Prime Minister. Initially, only senior Whitehall mandarins received the regular reports that the Security Service produced on the strike and they do not appear to have been forwarded to Thatcher. In June 1984, she became aware of the existence of such reports and subsequently insisted that they were sent to her on a regular basis.[70] The Prime Minister, however, remained far from satisfied and, in October 1984, was said to be 'disappointed' at the 'little action by the Security Service.'[71]

During the initial period of the strike, much of the information which was collected resulted from investigations carried out by the police. Officers were seeking to understand the tactics and movements of pickets to be able to control mass picketing. In July 1984, a Home Office memo stated that the police had acquired information through 'observation, listening to miners' CB radios and by surveillance methods'. This was 'extremely successful' in alerting them to where mass pickets would be moving to and any last-minute changes of plan.[72] In time, however, such surveillance became less successful as pickets became more cautious and curtailed their use of CB radios. As the police found it much more difficult to learn about their movements in advance, officials proposed alternative ways to gain information.[73] David Hall, Chief Constable of Humberside Police and Controller of the National Reporting Centre,[74] went as far as to ask if more could be done 'by way of telephone intercepts to get information about potentially violent incidents.' It was, however, made clear to him that whilst the police could apply for warrants to tap phones for matters categorised as 'serious crime', they 'would certainly not be available to the police for the purposes of gathering intelligence'.[75] Nevertheless, files do show that one arm of the police force—Special Branch—did collect intelligence during the strike. In a memo in August 1984, Home Secretary, Leon Brittan, wrote that Special Branch obtained intelligence from covert operations, including surveillance.[76]

The police role during the strike was not confined to collecting tactical intelligence. Anecdotal reports suggest that some officers policed in an overly aggressive and provocative way.[77] Questionable policing practices particularly took place in June 1984, when pickets and police clashed at Orgreave in South Yorkshire. Indeed, after images of clashes between pickets and police on horseback were televised, Queen Elizabeth II was said to have remarked, 'Oh that's awful! Oh! we shouldn't do that!'.[78] It seems that the clashes may have been deliberately provoked by police officers. Speaking anonymously many years after Orgreave, one former police officer said that the police had been 'anticipating trouble' and had 'a licence to do what we wanted'. He said that police attacked people 'even if they weren't doing anything'.[79] The violent clashes were initially blamed on the miners, ninety-five of whom were charged with a variety of offences including riot or unlawful assembly. Their trial, however, quickly collapsed and they were cleared of the charges.[80]

The way the strike was policed often overstepped the mark. Numerous police officers appear to have bought into the claim that striking miners were the 'enemy within' and treated them accordingly. During the strike, the *Sunday Telegraph* journalist Peregrine Worsthorne had fervently supported the government's defeat of the miners, yet he later reflected on the way it was policed. 'The physical methods adopted by the Thatcher revolution to put down the Scargill miners were', he wrote in 2005, 'alien, owing more to France's brutal revolutionary tradition of treating all protests as incipient insurrections ... than to Britain's preference for beer and sandwiches in Downing Street.'[81]

The police appear to have been encouraged by the government to take the strongest action possible against the pickets. One chief constable later recalled a meeting at the Home Office where police chiefs were informed that Thatcher was convinced that 'a secret communist cell ... was orchestrating the strike in order to bring down the country'. She urged the police to intensify their own intelligence gathering by 'infiltrating and monitoring groups and activities which threatened order'.[82] Home Office officials were acutely aware that the way the dispute was policed could make it appear that officers were doing the government's bidding. In November 1984, the Permanent Secretary at the Home Office, Sir Brian Cubbon, wrote that 'internal questions' needed to be asked about how 'the Home Office relay[s] to the police service the political influence on operational policy which was wanted in the early days of the dispute'.[83] His concerns were shared by the Chief Inspector of Constabularies, Sir Lawrence Byford, who raised the need for 'the police to be distanced from the stance of the political party in power.' Referencing the strike, Byford wrote that 'there is a body of opinion within the Service which believes that whilst the support of Ministers was appreciated greater evidence of neutrality on their part might have been helpful.'[84]

ENEMIES OF THE STATE OR ENEMIES OF THE GOVERNMENT?

In January 1985, after questions had been raised about Special Branch's investigations into strikers, Leon Brittan defended its conduct. He argued that 'where picketing may pose a threat to public order it is entirely right that a chief officer should have access to any relevant information that his Special Branch can provide to help him determine an appropriate level of policing.'[85] During the strike, Special Branch undertook significantly more surveillance than MI5. Whilst MI5's directive restricted it to only investigating subversion, the limits on Special Branch were less specific; in 1978, the then Home Secretary, Merlyn Rees, stated in the Commons that 'the Special Branch collects information on those whom I think cause problems to the State.'[86]

A Limited Role?

MI5 arguably had a greater independence than Special Branch had from the government. This enabled intelligence officials to resist ministers' demands when they believed they were being asked to do too much. Although the Security Service reportedly confined itself to investigating the role of subversion during the dispute, one account has claimed that MI5 tapped the phones of 'every single NUM branch and lodge secretary ... the entire national and area union leaderships, as well as sympathetic trade unionists and support-group activists all over the country'.[87] In MI5's authorised history, Christopher Andrew strongly refutes such allegations, describing them as 'fanciful'. He acknowledges that there was a degree of phone tapping during the strike but argues that it was not indiscriminate. The Security Service, he writes, only targeted 'leading Communist and Trotskyist militants and those judged to have close links to them'.[88]

Home Office files appear to support Andrew's judgement. In July 1984, a memo discussing the collection of intelligence on the miners' strike stated that the reports provided by the Security Service were merely about subversion and did not provide 'the sort of tactical intelligence' that police were keen to obtain.[89] Another Home Office official, writing a number of days later, made clear that the only way to discover who was organising the picketing 'would be by interceptions directed at NUM headquarters or by the areas, but these would not be within the Security Service's guidelines'.[90]

In her memoirs, Stella Rimington, who worked in MI5's counter-subversion F-branch during the strike, sought to argue that their operations were strictly limited. 'Accusations that we were running agents or telephone interceptions to get advance warning of picket movements are wrong,' she wrote, 'we in MI5 limited our investigations to the activities of those who were using the strike for subversive purposes.'[91]

She was adamant that such surveillance was both legitimate and strictly limited, making clear, 'we certainly did not work as tools of Mrs Thatcher in her battle to break the miners' strike and destroy the NUM.'[92] Officials across Whitehall were, however, acutely aware of the fallout that would result from MI5 operations being made public. When discussing the collection of intelligence about NUM intentions for the strike, one Home Office official warned, 'we have to be very careful how we proceed, in view of the allegations already about telephone interception, which have been mentioned in Parliament and are to figure prominently at Lab Party Conference in October.'[93] There was, it seems, a fear that information about MI5's investigations into the strike would become public.

One area of the strike that the Security Service did examine was the NUM's funding. In October 1984, the High Court confiscated the Union's funds—over £10m—following the NUM's decision not to pay a fine of £200,000 for contempt of court.[94] NUM President Arthur Scargill subsequently made attempts to obtain money from abroad to finance the strike and specifically sought funds from the Soviet Union. Soviet miners decided to each donate a day's wages to the NUM. Although such money was not sent directly from the Soviet government, it would have been necessary for the Soviet Ministry of Finance to authorise any transfer of money out of the country.[95] The transfer of $1.4m was authorised by Mikhail Gorbachev, the Soviet 'heir apparent'. Intelligence provided by the MI6 agent, Oleg Gordievsky, working in the Soviet Embassy in London, revealed to British intelligence officials that the decision to send the money had been made by the Central Committee of the Soviet Communist Party, against the advice of the KGB.[96]

The NUM never ultimately received funds from the Soviet Union. At a meeting in December 1984 between Thatcher and Gorbachev, the Prime Minister challenged her counterpart about Soviet attempts to send funds. Although Gorbachev denied this had occurred, once he had returned to Moscow, he ensured that no money should ever be sent to the miners.[97] Stella Rimington, speaking in 2002, stated that MI5 regarded attempts to send money from abroad to help the miners as 'interference by a foreign power in the internal affairs of this country.'[98] The Soviets undoubtedly wished to send funds to British miners, but their desire to get involved in the strike may not have been quite as extensive as may be assumed. As one scholar has pointed out, 'the Soviet Union conspicuously failed to do the one thing that might have helped the NUM during its strike—prevent the export of Polish coal to Britain.'[99]

The Security Service was perfectly justified in investigating NUM funding if it believed that it came from abroad. As Stella Rimington articulated, foreign interference could not be ignored. In February 1985, the Cabinet Secretary, Robert Armstrong, wrote, 'I think, that it was a legitimate use of interception to seek to discover what assistance the NUM was receiving from overseas.'[100] Armstrong was, however, particularly concerned that the information MI5 had collected by intercepting NUM communications about its funds had also been used to help sequestrators searching for NUM funds. This, he believed, 'would be more difficult to justify'. Armstrong and 'an unnamed man'—an MI5 officer—had met with a representative of the sequestrators, a Mr Larkins, and sought to provide him with 'information which might help them in their search.' In return, it was hoped that Larkins might have information which would help MI5 in their own investigation into money the NUM might receive from abroad. Writing after the meeting, Armstrong expressed concern 'about the conclusions that will be drawn about the involvement of the Security Service and about the activities in which it was engaged in connection with the NUM dispute' if such information became public.[101]

Despite such fears, the Security Service always sought, internally, to justify its operations during the strike as part of legitimate work—be it investigating the NUM's funding or investigating subversives who happened to be involved with the dispute.[102] Concerns expressed inside Whitehall about some operations, however, represented a tacit acknowledgement that, at the very least, some MI5 investigations strayed very close to the line. In reality, they crossed the line. As Armstrong acknowledged, helping the sequestrators was 'difficult to justify', whilst investigating individual subversives helped intelligence officials to gain significant knowledge about the strike. Such operations particularly enabled MI5 to collect intelligence on two individuals who played a key role in the NUM. The communications of the NUM Vice President, McGahey, were intercepted on the basis that he was a communist, whilst MI5 also closely watched the NUM President, Arthur Scargill.[103] Scargill, who had long been the *bête noire* of the Conservative Party after playing an influential role in the 1972 miners' strike, was portrayed throughout the 1984–5 dispute as the epitome of the 'enemy within'.[104]

By the time the strike began in March 1984, Scargill had been on MI5's radar for many years. It is likely that he first came to notice in the 1950s when he had joined the YCL in Barnsley. He left the YCL in 1961, but files show that he continued to attract Security Service attention.[105] In November 1973, MI5 took out a HOW on him as he was regarded as a communist sympathiser, and this continued to be renewed for at least the next decade.[106] In March 1984, however, MI5 did not consider that his contact with the CPGB was particularly significant, despite the fact that the Party supported the strike and had an influence within the NUM.[107] Remarkably, one senior MI5 official believed that the CPGB had unsuccessfully sought to exert a 'moderating influence' on Scargill.[108] As Scargill could thus not be listed as a communist sympathiser, MI5 classed him as an 'unaffiliated subversive' in order to justify continuing to watch him. This special category was defined as 'UK citizen or foreigner who is not a member of, or sympathetic to, one subversive organisation, but who threatens parliamentary democracy'.[109]

ENEMIES OF THE STATE OR ENEMIES OF THE GOVERNMENT?

Security Service officers justified classifying Scargill as an 'unaffiliated subversive' for two reasons—he had called the strike without balloting NUM members and had repeatedly said, in public and private, that he aimed to bring down the Thatcher government through strike action.[110] Many years later, when questioned about this, he argued that he 'wanted at all times to get rid of a Conservative government' but would only do so by 'legitimate means.' Scargill stated that his opposition to the government had been perfectly reasonable, and claimed, 'it's because of my views, because of my passion, that they regard me as an enemy of the state. I'm an enemy of capitalism, I'm a supporter of socialism and it's for that reason that it doesn't surprise me that the state and its security services have always targeted me as subversive.'[111] Scargill's opposition to the government was not, however, as benign as he later claimed. Following the 1983 General Election, he had declared that 'a fight back against this Government's policies will inevitably take place outside rather than inside Parliament'. Referring to the government as being 'elected by a minority of the British electorate', he made it clear that, 'faced with possible parliamentary destruction of all that is good and compassionate in our society, extra-parliamentary action will be the only course open to the working class and the labour movement.'[112] In this context, intelligence officials' view of him as a threat is understandable. Scargill's inability to have a decisive impact on the strike means that, in retrospect, he may appear to have been nothing more than a provocative firebrand. To the Security Service at the time, however, he would have been viewed as a significant threat.

As no files have been released on Scargill, it is impossible to know exactly what the surveillance of him did reveal. The surveillance may have been of limited value during the strike, however, as he was aware that his phone was tapped and 'occasionally shouted abuse into the phone at the people who were tapping him'.[113] This caused the intelligence community some problems; as Home Office officials noted in July 1984, 'Security Service sources are now drying up, because NUM leaders are becoming more circumspect in what they say to each other and tending to use methods which we find it difficult to tap'.[114] Despite this, the intelligence community would still have gathered information on the strike as a result of their investigations into people classed as communists, Trotskyists or unaffiliated subversives. In August 1984, Leon Brittan noted that through such investigations, intelligence officials had obtained some picketing plans. These were, however, 'not of great value' as they were vague plans that the police had previously discovered themselves through their own methods.[115]

Scargill may have been aware that his phone was being tapped, but the Security Service was able to gain intelligence about his intentions by other means. An agent, codenamed 'Silver Fox', was recruited within the NUM. The agent was said to have been close to Scargill and the leadership of the NUM, and provided 'very, very specific and precise [information] that was correct every time' on the whereabouts of 'violent' pickets.[116] Other MI5 investigations provided some useful intelligence too. One report by an MI5 officer gave a gloomy picture on the level of information that was being obtained, but still made clear that they 'would expect to pick up any change in Scargill's overall strategy' and 'would probably get wind of another Orgreave'—information that would certainly have been useful.[117] Leon Brittan even admitted in a note to the Prime Minister that investigations into subversives 'might throw some light on the way in which picketing is being organised at either area or national level'.[118] Targeting subversives seems to have provided a useful way for intelligence officials to collect material on things or people that were not subversive.[119]

Protest and Survive

Investigating communists and subversives not only allowed the intelligence community to gain a good deal of knowledge on the miners' strike, but also gave them an insight into various other movements in the 1960s, 1970s and 1980s. As a result of such investigations, intelligence agencies held significant information on organisations that were not, in themselves, subversive. One group on whom information appears to have been collected was on one of the 'No' campaigns in the 1975 Referendum on Britain's membership of the European Economic Community (EEC).

Several local branches of the 'No' campaign contained communists; in Merseyside, communists had such a presence in the movement that Labour Party activists felt unable to join with the campaign.[120]

Richard Body, joint chairman of the council of the 'Keep Britain Out' campaign, later stated that during the campaign he spoke to 'a long-time friend, a man who I trusted totally ... who had intelligence connections' and was told that 'MI5 was tapping the phones of anyone connected with former Labour MP Ann Kerr.' Kerr was part of the 'No to the EEC' Campaign group during the referendum and, according to Body, 'MI5 thought that [she] was a fellow traveller and that the Soviets were supporting the No vote to leave Europe weak.' As a senior member of the 'No' campaign, Body believed that he 'was contaminated by having contact with her'; he was told by his long-time friend that he, 'or any of my committee must expect to have our phones tapped.'[121] There has never been any mention of the intelligence agencies taking an interest in the referendum from other sources. However, the presence of communists in the 'No' campaign makes it likely that MI5 gained some knowledge of their activities, and thus acquired information on the campaign, even if it was unintentional.[122]

The presence of communists in legitimate protest groups, such as the Campaign for Nuclear Disarmament (CND) and the Anti-Apartheid Movement (AAM), often meant that such groups were also subject to significant surveillance. CND, which primarily advocated unilateral nuclear disarmament, had two periods of prominence—1958–64 and again in the 1980s. The organisation was publicly launched in February 1958 and organised meetings and marches, most notably the annual 'Aldermaston march' held over the Easter weekend. The first of these marches—from Trafalgar Square to the government's Atomic Weapons Research Establishment at Aldermaston—was held in April 1958 and involved, but was not formally organised by, CND.[123] The march appears to have been the first occasion that the authorities took notice of anti-nuclear protesters. Special Branch produced a detailed fifteen-page report which concluded by stating that proceedings were moderate in tone and 'no untoward incidents occurred'.[124] According to two former Special Branch officers,

Ray Wilson and Ian Adams, the documenting of peaceful protests was routine since mass demonstrations were believed to 'always have the potential for violence.'[125]

Although the authorities kept records of CND meetings, it does not appear that they were overly concerned by the activities of anti-nuclear protesters in the late 1950s and early 1960s. The movement was not affiliated to any political party or ideology and attracted support from many different groups of people. In 1959, David Spedding, who became chief of MI6 in the 1990s, wrote an anti-nuclear article in his school magazine and participated in the Aldermaston march.[126] CND had few, if any, links to communism; when it was first launched, the CPGB opposed CND because of its attachment to unilateralism.[127] Whilst the CPGB never privately dropped its opposition to unilateral nuclear disarmament, in 1959 it attempted to support CND for 'purely tactical reasons'—namely an attempt to gain a voice in a growing peace movement.[128] By the early 1960s, therefore, MI5 believed that although CND was a 'non-political organisation' led by non-communists, it was 'liable to communist penetration.'[129] Security officials did not exaggerate the communists' influence on CND, making clear in May 1962 that it was insignificant and that, although communists were present at CND demonstrations, such support was 'unsolicited'.[130]

In the years that followed, some anti-nuclear protesters split from CND, forming more radical organisations such as the Committee of 100 and Spies for Peace.[131] Security officials began to re-examine the threat anti-nuclear protesters could pose and believed that 'there may now be a substantial security risk in employing a supporter of CND or the Committee of 100 in a post [with access to classified information].'[132] Committee of 100 members were subsequently prevented from being allowed to work in a Civil Service post which required positive vetting. CND members, officials believed, should only be employed if it could be certain that their beliefs would not affect their loyalty to the State.[133]

This change in policy—never publicly announced—meant that officials who undertook positive vetting enquiries would need to know if a potential employee was a member of either CND or the Committee of 100. By October 1963, therefore, MI5 began to document all members and supporters of the Committee of 100 and all leaders of CND. Privately, officials acknowledged that recording any CND members and preventing them from taking certain jobs would be controversial; it could be seen to imply that 'a sympathiser of CND' was a 'potential traitor'.[134] CND was regularly described by officials as a perfectly legal organisation, supported by many law-abiding citizens, that was 'not, and never has been, a Communist front organisation'.[135] Despite this, Whitehall officials justified the policy on CND members as it was believed that individual members could possibly assist the Committee of 100, and that sympathy with CND 'may give rise to strain upon the loyalties of persons in official employment with access to classified information.'[136] The numbers of CND supporters who were either rejected for Civil Service roles or removed from their jobs with access to sensitive information are not available. It does, however, seem likely that several individuals would have been moved to a job within the Civil Service not requiring positive vetting, and several applicants would have been rejected because of CND links.

By the late 1960s, the anti-nuclear movement had begun to decline.[137] The idea of unilateral nuclear disarmament failed to resonate with public opinion, and the activities of the Committee of 100 and Spies for Peace negatively affected public support for CND.[138] The Committee of 100 was disbanded in October 1968 and, whilst CND remained active, it began to associate with fringe protest movements and to embrace their causes.[139] In March 1971, a security assessment of CND concluded that, whilst it had gained members who were communists, it was not a subversive organisation. Indeed, MI5 believed that the threat posed by CND had declined to such an extent that it recommended that CND members should only be barred from working on classified work in the area of defence, as opposed to all work involving classified information.[140]

CND's Revival

In the early 1980s, a changing global political climate and escalating East-West tensions led CND to regain prominence following over a decade of relative obscurity. Issues such as the renewal of the British nuclear deterrent and the deployment of American Pershing II nuclear missiles across sites in Britain and other parts of Western Europe, led CND membership to surge from 9,000 in 1980 to 110,000 in November 1985.[141] The Thatcher government, which had strongly supported the deployment of American missiles, was particularly concerned about CND and the wider anti-nuclear movement, believing it to pose a subversive threat. Thatcher herself believed the movement was significantly influenced by communists both in Britain and, most importantly, in Moscow.[142]

The organisation attracted widespread support, transforming 'from a hobbyists' club to a nationwide movement.' In York, Alec Howe, son of the Chancellor Sir Geoffrey Howe, became the press officer for his local CND branch.[143] Thatcher's concerns about those involved with the movement were not, however, entirely without foundation. CND's National Council included several communists, whilst the Soviet Peace Committee had some contact with senior CND figures.[144] The MI6 agent, Oleg Gordievsky, who worked in the KGB London residency at the time, revealed that the Soviets viewed the British anti-nuclear movement as a 'natural ally' and 'believed [they] could exercise considerable influence over it'. Intriguingly, MI5 initially chose not to share these revelations with Thatcher as it believed the KGB claims to be exaggerated. MI5 judged that the Soviets had very few contacts and little influence within CND, and that any attempts to contact leading figures within the movement had come to nothing.[145] Briefings given by intelligence officials to the Prime Minister routinely dismissed Soviet attempts to influence the peace movement. Instead, they emphasised the failures of the KGB and highlighted the fact that CND leaders were both fiercely independent of, and critical of, Moscow. MI5 made clear that CND was not and 'has never been considered a subversive organisation.'[146]

Publicly, the government may have criticised the anti-nuclear movement, but it did accept the right to protest.[147] In private, ministers sought to encourage the Security Service to investigate it more extensively. The authorised history of MI5 states that the government put pressure on the intelligence officials to provide information on CND and the wider peace movement, although such investigations would 'go beyond the terms of its charter'.[148] This was something that Whitehall officials acknowledged. In November 1983, the Security Service and Special Branch were both asked to provide information on the way in which the anti-nuclear movement was planning to 'conduct its campaign' the following year. Joe Pilling, the Home Office official requesting information from MI5, did not pressurise the Security Service. Noting 'the properly narrow focus of your service's interest in the anti-nuclear movement' he stated, 'if you have nothing to add ... I shall quite understand.'[149]

The request for more information on the anti-nuclear movement did not only come from the government. The police regularly sought details on the plans of future demonstrations so that they could make early preparations to defuse protests.[150] Pressure to provide more information on CND also came from the Army Intelligence Corps (9 Sy Coy). They wanted greater knowledge of CND because its activities were considered to be directly impinging on military interests. Whilst acknowledging that 'the presence of many well meaning people in CND and some of its more innocuous aims have given it a 'respectable' image', 9 Sy Coy made clear that 'some elements of CND are subversive and the organisation is at least at variance with the interests of the state.'[151] It was suggested that a greater interest should be taken into CND activity, and that both Special Branch and MI5 should be asked to provide information if future investigations revealed that any CND activity was impinging on the military.[152] Major P.W. Snell of 9 Sy Coy also argued that CND should be monitored because 'some of its activities are in direct conflict with HM Governments policy and plans'.[153] There is no evidence that such views were widely held within the British establishment. Having seen the Sy Coy report, one Ministry of Defence (MoD) official derided it as exaggerating the threat and remarked, 'clearly we are all subversives now!' The official was sceptical about the subversive nature of CND and commented that the Intelligence Corps 'always propose a cure infinitely worse than the disease.' Realising that Sy Coy's assessment could cause outrage, he asked the UK Land Forces to 'have as many copies of 9 Sy Coy's paper destroyed as possible'.[154] The opinions of 9 Sy Coy demonstrate that certain individuals within the British establishment believed that opposing government policy immediately rendered an individual or organisation subversive.

Other than the Prime Minister herself, the member of the cabinet who was most keen to obtain information on CND was the Defence Secretary, Michael Heseltine. The MoD was deeply concerned about anti-nuclear protests—many took place at military bases across Britain—and regularly produced reports on the activities of anti-nuclear and peace movements.[155] In 1983, Heseltine set up a special unit within the MoD known as Defence Secretariat 19 (DS19), to combat anti-nuclear propaganda.[156] MI5 was pressurised by the MoD to provide 'ammunition' against CND but an internal MI5 investigation stated, 'our response was very cautious ... we appear to have resisted [political pressure]'. The Security Service does, however, appear to have provided DS19 with unclassified material—obtained from publicly available sources—on some leading CND figures, much to the 'discontent' of at least some Security Service officials.[157]

DS19 also appears to have received information on CND from private intelligence services. The Thatcher government, believing that the Security Service was not providing adequate intelligence on such movements, encouraged private individuals and organisations to infiltrate the anti-nuclear movement. One of the bodies it supported, the Coalition for Peace Through Security (CPS), infiltrated CND. The CPS had close ties to the Conservative Party, and two of its leading figures, Dr Julian Lewis and Edward Leigh, later became Conservative MPs.[158] The CPS regularly produced material that took a strongly anti-CND line, and attempted to portray CND as both being in the pay of Moscow and full of 'Communists, Neutralists and Defeatists'.[159] Although links between the Coalition and the Conservative Party were denied, in 1985 *The Guardian* reported that the Coalition had confessed to infiltrating CND and passing information they had collected to Heseltine and DS19.[160] MI5 officials were said to have been 'amazed by the scale and audacity of the operations launched by privateers, which included stealing documents from CND's headquarters.'[161]

Conservative backbenchers, notably Winston Churchill MP (grandson of the wartime prime minister), also conducted their own campaigns against unilateralists through the Committee for Peace with Freedom.[162] Indeed, it appears that the Conservative Party directly conducted investigations into CND itself; files from Mrs Thatcher's personal archive show that Conservative staffers attended CND meetings and reported back their findings. In June 1982, Peter Shipley of the Conservative Research Department wrote about a demonstration that had attracted at least 150,000 people. Having observed proceedings, he stated that CND seemed to be 'a very middle class movement', describing the event, from which he had collected pamphlets, as having 'a rather folksy, relaxed atmosphere' with many of the attendees being 'the archetypal Guardian reading parents eating their nut cutler [sic] picnics under the trees.'[163] Such reports showed that many of those who supported CND were harmless, and the threat the organisation could ever pose was not as great as many politicians may have feared.

Mrs Thatcher may have taken a firm stance against CND but for some in her party this was not strong enough. The Conservative peer, Lord Beloff, wrote to the Prime Minister urging her to take stronger action to 'publicly discredit' the anti-nuclear movement. He advocated using the intelligence agencies to provide further information on the sources of funding for the anti-nuclear movement. Only then, he stated, could the 'Soviet-inspired anti-patriotic groups' be properly countered. 'I will not be content', Lord Beloff wrote, 'until it becomes as hazardous to wear a CND badge on the streets of London as it would be to sport a swastika in Tel Aviv.'[164]

'You have to inquire'

Despite its disagreements with the government over whether or not CND was subversive, MI5 did investigate elements of the anti-nuclear movement on the basis that they were not investigating the movement itself but, instead, investigating subversive elements within it. Stella Rimington, a member of the counter-subversion F-branch at the time, explained such operations from an MI5 point of view in her memoirs. She wrote,

> the anti-nuclear movement, in its own right an entirely legitimate protest movement, was of great interest to the Soviet Union ... Soviet officials encouraged Western communist parties, like the Communist Party of Great Britain, to try to infiltrate CND at key strategic levels by getting their members elected as officers. The idea was that they could then direct the activities of the organisation to suit their own long-term objectives. Our job, and what we were doing, was to monitor those activities, not to investigate CND, which on its own was of no interest to us.[165]

As a result of their investigations, the Security Service did collect significant information on all leaders of CND regardless of whether they could truly be classed as subversive. In 1977, MI5 opened a file on Monsignor Bruce Kent when he became chairman of CND, describing him as a 'possible anarchist'. In MI5's authorised history, Christopher Andrew concludes that the reasons for opening a file on Kent were 'distinctly dubious'.[166] Kent's successor as CND chair, Lord Hugh Jenkins, inferred many years later that he may also have been investigated during his own chairmanship.[167] A file was also eventually opened on Jenkins' own successor, Joan Ruddock. When she first became chair, MI5 could find no reason to open a file on her as she had 'no subversive affiliation.'[168] Justification was found in 1982 after she had met with a Soviet man whom she believed to be a journalist. Ruddock was, according to Christopher Andrew, 'doubtless unaware [he] was a KGB officer', but MI5 still decided to classify her as a 'contact of a hostile intelligence service'.[169] When the existence of Ruddock's file was later revealed by a whistleblower, the Shadow Home Secretary, Gerald Kaufman, alleged in the Commons that MI5 had 'deliberately and wrongfully classified [her] as a subversive so they could open a file on her'.[170]

Evidence from that whistleblower, the former MI5 officer, Cathy Massiter, suggests that the Security Service often wrongly alleged persons within CND to be subversive in order to investigate their activities. In 1985, after becoming concerned that the Security Service was exceeding its remit, Massiter made details about the surveillance of CND members public. She claimed that there was a file on Roger Spiller, a vice-chairman of CND, because of reports that he had been in the YCL as a student. Although MI5 believed the reports to be false, this claim was used to justify his being recorded as a 'member of subversive organisation.'[171] The most serious of Massiter's revelations involved CND Vice-President John Cox. In an affidavit, Massiter stated that Cox was subject to a telephone tap because he was also a member of the CPGB and implied that Cox's membership of the CPGB provided the Security Service with a convenient excuse to gain greater knowledge on CND. Cox had frequent phone contact with CND headquarters as he lived in Wales. MI5 was thus able to gain a great deal of knowledge about CND, without tapping the phones of CND HQ, on the basis that they were investigating a communist. Massiter stated that the investigation revealed little about Cox that was not already known, and that he worked within CND 'because he was a committed CND member rather than working in CND in order to further the interest of the Communist Party.'[172]

Massiter's allegations led to an internal MI5 inquiry. According to the authorised history of the Security Service, an unnamed future Deputy Director General, having reviewed the evidence, concluded, 'I feel in retrospect that Massiter may be right in questioning whether the warrant was strictly justified'. Internal MI5 files do, however, state that the phone check on Cox provided MI5's 'most important source on Communist involvement in the peace movement and a useful source of intelligence on Trotskyist activities within CND and on Soviet attitudes towards CND.' One MI5 officer noted that information collected as part of the surveillance enabled them to conclude that the CPGB was not influential within CND; the warrant on Cox was cancelled in 1985 when the Security Service had sufficient material to 'make a full assessment on the level of CND and, in that light, reduce our coverage.'[173] Similar reasoning also appears to have been used for MI5's investigations into the Greenham Common Peace Camp.

The Greenham Common protesters were based outside an airbase in Newbury, Berkshire, and a file was opened on the peace camp because it was believed to be 'subject to penetration by subversive groups.' As a result of their investigations, MI5 was later able to conclude, 'with some authority', that 'the subversive influence on the founding and continuing life of the camp has been slight.'[174] Investigating anti-nuclear groups may well have been beneficial in allowing the Security Service to judge their subversive threat. Yet this suggests that some within MI5 believed in a principle articulated by the Chief Constable of West Midlands Police, Sir Philip Knights. 'Unless you inquire', he said, 'you don't find out.'[175] However true such a statement may have been, using it as a guiding principle in a democracy committed to legitimate protest and civil liberties was surely questionable.

It is not known if Knights' comments reflected a view that was held widely within security circles. By the mid-1980s, however, opinions had started to change about the surveillance of a group such as CND. In 1985, Sir Antony Duff took over as MI5 DG and began to question the Security Service's extensive counter-subversion operations. Reviewing the investigations into CND, he remarked that a paper on the subversive influence within the movement concentrated 'rather too much on CND activities as such'. He also implied that, had he been in charge years earlier, he would not have approved the HOW on John Cox.[176] Very simply, Duff believed that MI5 spent too much time investigating subversion and he therefore made a conscious effort to move the service away from counter-subversion operations.[177]

It is undoubtedly true, as Duff commented, that the Security Service spent far too long investigating elements of CND that were in no way subversive. It is, however, also understandable, why investigations into the anti-nuclear movement took place. During the early 1980s, a nuclear conflict between East and West appeared to be eminently possible.[178] It would have been indisputably to Moscow's advantage for the West to unilaterally renounce its nuclear weapons. Security officials, therefore, would have held concerns about groups advocating unilateralism. Not all investigations into groups or individuals holding anti-nuclear sentiments were, however, as understandable. Some were slightly sinister.

In the early 1980s, Madeline Haigh—a housewife and former teacher who had previously taught Mrs Thatcher's own daughter—became concerned about the presence of nuclear weapons within Britain and decided to act. She joined a Quaker peace group and wrote several anti-nuclear letters both to newspapers and the MoD. In 1981 she wrote a letter to a local paper after an anti-nuclear rally had been cancelled. Shortly after it was published, two men visited her home and said that they were investigating mail order fraud. Suspicious of the men and their motives, Haigh decided to pursue the matter, first contacting the police and then her local MP in an attempt to clarify what had happened.[179] Her persistence led to the revelation that the two visitors to her house were actually Special Branch officers who were investigating her letter to the newspaper. Remarkably, she was told by the police that 'it was quite normal to follow inquiries about people who write to the press on controversial topics.'[180] When the case was raised in the Commons in 1983, the Minister of State at the Home Office, Douglas Hurd, stated that West Midlands Police had begun their investigation into Haigh because 'she might be a person who was prepared to support, or get involved in, public protests which were likely to become violent'.[181]

Many years later, when discussing the Haigh case, Sir Philip Knights, Chief Constable of West Midlands Police 1975–1985, stated that anyone who had attended an anti-nuclear demonstration during the 1980s 'unfortunately' had the potential to be investigated. 'You can't just pick it out of thin air whether somebody is a subversive or not. You have to inquire' he said.[182] If Haigh could be investigated on such spurious evidence, it seems unlikely that she was the only one.

Further Protest

CND and the anti-nuclear movement were not the only protest groups that were subject to investigation by the authorities during the 1960s, 1970s and 1980s. Security officials became increasingly concerned about protests during the late 1960s after large demonstrations against the Vietnam War were held in London in 1967 and 1968. Violent clashes between protesters and police during a demonstration at the American Embassy in Grosvenor Square in March 1968 alarmed intelligence agencies.[183] According to one former Special Branch officer, it led to a recognition that the intelligence community was 'totally inept at both the information we gathered and the way we dealt with that information.'[184] The urgent need for a remedy resulted in the forming of a new Special Branch unit—the Special Demonstration Squad (SDS)—in September 1968.

The SDS initially consisted of ten officers who became long-term penetration agents and infiltrated numerous radical left-wing groups. By living amongst the groups, the officers were able to gain intelligence and covertly report it back to their Special Branch handlers.[185] SDS officers were responsible for gathering intelligence on demonstrations by 'left-wing extremists' and identifying both the organisers and those participants who promoted disorder or violence.[186] The activities and excesses of the SDS became public in the years after it had been disbanded (in 2008).[187] In 2015, the Home Secretary, Theresa May, ordered a public inquiry into undercover policing practices between 1968 and 2008. The inquiry, known as the Undercover Policing Inquiry (UCPI), is expected to report by the late 2020s.[188] It has been reported that over 1,000 political or protest groups were infiltrated by SDS officers.[189] According to Sir John Mitting, chair of the UCPI, very few of these groups should have been infiltrated.[190]

One of the first groups infiltrated by the SDS was 'Stop The Seventy Tour' (STST), an anti-apartheid campaign set up to protest against and disrupt the South African Springboks rugby tour of Britain and Ireland in 1969–70.[191] Informants revealed information on the group's plans for certain protests and said that the 'extremist elements' had planned to use tear gas during one demonstration.[192] In November 1970, Detective Inspector Phil Saunders of the Met sought to justify the infiltration of STST. He wrote,

> When there was a sufficiently emotive issue—such as the 'Stop the Seventy Tour' campaign which guaranteed broad-based support and the attention of the mass media [-] the extremists

were able seriously to threaten the maintenance of order, making it imperative that advance information of their plans was available.

Reviewing Saunders' report in the UCPI interim report of June 2023, Sir John Mitting stated that 'his observation is difficult to understand or to justify ... it is not an accurate reflection of what in fact occurred.[193]

Alongside the reports from informants, Special Branch also received information on STST from its own officers who were present at demonstrations. In November 1969, a Conference of Chief Constables accepted that the protesters held sincere views that were held by 'most people in this country'. It did, however, warn that 'as on other occasions, the processions of demonstrators are often taken over by other bodies, like anarchists, who are seeking other objectives which include confrontation with the police and the introduction of violence.' Although believing that stopping the demonstrators may be necessary to 'protect the peace', the chief constables did acknowledge that such action could lead to the police being 'accused of supporting a political standpoint'.[194]

It seems likely that the police sought to gain prior knowledge of STST to police their protests effectively. It is also, however, relevant that Special Branch noted in 1970 that the Communist Party was 'taking an active interest in STST matters.'[195] Officers routinely collected STST pamphlets and produced detailed reports on the protesters' activities including details of their movements and of their chants.[196] The particulars of protesters appear to have been regularly collected by Special Branch. By March 1970, they had created an album containing the photographs and descriptions of a number of demonstrators which acted as a reference for Constabularies to identify protesters.[197]

In 1970, following the rugby tour, STST sought to oppose a tour of England by the South African cricket team, scheduled for June. Once again Special Branch reported on STST meetings and, on one occasion, they detailed a speech given by the Middlesex cricketer and future England Cricket Captain, Mike Brearley. His name was, however, spelt incorrectly and the report noted that there was 'no trace' of him in Special Branch records.[198] The same report recorded that another future England Cricket Captain, David Gower, was also in attendance.[199] From April 1970, reports on STST opposition to the tour were produced fortnightly and detailed the movement's plans and exploits. The reports also revealed the extent of the investigations into the anti-apartheid activist Peter Hain. As a result of 'discreet enquiries', information was even gained about his parents and their previous life in South Africa. The subsequent document stated that Peter Hain's mother, Adelaine was 'the real instigator behind [him].' The information on the Hains' activities in South Africa and their links to the South African Communist Party is so detailed that it seems likely that it came from sources in South African intelligence.[200] This should be seen in the light of comments made in the memoir of the former South African intelligence agent, Gordon Winter. He wrote that British and South African intelligence 'feed each other information about known Communists in both countries.'[201] Although it is impossible to verify Winter's account, the report on the Hains suggests that this probably happened.

The investigations into the STST came as part of a wider inquiry into the AAM. MI5 held files on the Chairman of the AAM between 1960 and 1964, David Ennals, and his brother, Martin, a founder of the movement. Special Branch officers also regularly attended and reported on public AAM meetings and demonstrations.[202] In January 1970, after receiving complaints from members of the AAM about the presence of both police officers and plain-clothes officers at meetings, Special Branch sought to justify its attendance at such meetings in a report to the Home Secretary. It was made clear that officers would usually attend in order to preserve public order, following incidents of disorder involving anti-apartheid protesters. The report stated that the police merely sought 'to obtain information on future events' which threatened public order, to 'detect possible offences by those participating' and identify 'likely troublemakers' at future protests. It made clear that no private AAM meeting would be attended by the police.[203]

Although Special Branch sought to justify their surveillance of the AAM as being merely a part of their law-and-order role, it seems likely that officers also attended to report on communist influence on the movement. By the late 1960s, intelligence officers believed that despite the AAM having more non-communist than communist members, such was the power of the communists that the movement 'must therefore be assessed as under Communist influence.' As a result of its investigations into the CPGB, the Security Service did, however, discover in 1969 that the leadership of the Party itself was 'dissatisfied with [the] present [communist] influence on AAM policy and activities.'[204]

The extent of MI5's investigations into the AAM is not entirely clear. Few files have been released on it, and the movement is notable by its complete absence from the Security Service's authorised history. The AAM was also investigated by a number of private security companies. In 1970, a private detective agency admitted investigating members of the AAM on behalf of 'people who represented commercial organisations' in what was described as 'preemployment screening.'[205] One of the leading private groups which investigated the AAM was the Economic League (EL). Having been a prominent anti-communist organisation both pre- and post-World War Two, the EL evolved into an organisation chiefly concerned with providing vetting services for private companies in the second half of the twentieth century. The EL was funded by the private companies who subscribed to its services. It developed an extensive index of people it deemed to be subversive and provided information to subscribing companies on their employees. Its judgement of 'subversives' was highly subjective and often led to people who had done little wrong being potentially denied employment.[206] Members of the Thatcher government notably recommended use of the EL to investigate subversion. The authorised history of MI5 records that, at the beginning of Thatcher's premiership, the Secretary of State for Trade and Industry, Sir Keith Joseph, urged the Security Service to warn any companies of any subversive individuals applying for jobs with them. After MI5 had rejected this idea, Joseph proposed using the EL to provide the warnings to employers.[207]

The AAM was infiltrated by the EL as it was considered to be a 'vehicle for extremists', and 'a revolutionary campaign masquerading as a bona fide cause.' People would be added to the EL blacklist after attending AAM meetings, even if they were not members of the movement. At least one individual was blacklisted after writing to a newspaper supporting Edinburgh City Council's purchase of a Nelson Mandela portrait.[208] Private companies such as the EL faced few constraints on the way in which they investigated protest groups like the AAM as, unlike agencies of the state, they did not have a charter limiting the scope of their enquiries.

Although private organisations may have taken the upper hand, British State intelligence did continue to monitor the AAM well into the 1980s. Investigations were extensive; Special Branch regularly reported on AAM meetings, including one attended by only seven people. Files even show that Surrey Special Branch recorded the name of a student working part-time at Sainsbury's in Croydon after receiving information 'from a reliable source' that a student was 'actively passing anti-apartheid literature to other members of staff.'[209] In 2001, after apartheid had ended in South Africa, more information about MI5's own investigations into the AAM came to light. The Security Service's then Director General, Stephen Lander, met with Peter Hain, then a Labour MP and Foreign Office minister. Lander admitted that Hain had been kept under surveillance during his time in the AAM and that the Security Service had held a file on him.[210] Despite believing that communists had a degree of influence within the movement, MI5 never regarded the AAM as a communist front organisation since it contained many non-communist elements and attracted support from people holding a wide range of political views.[211] It is likely that MI5 would have sought to justify any investigations into the AAM in the same way that it justified its study of organisations such as CND; it was not investigating the organisation in itself, but rather any communist involvement within it.

Black Power

The AAM was not the only movement concerned with racial inequality in which British intelligence officials took an interest. During the 1950s and 1960s, black rights groups were regularly watched by security officials as it was believed that they were fronts for communists and therefore threatened British security.[212] One of the most prominent organisations placed under observation was the British Black Power Movement (British Black Panthers). The Security Service had a dedicated 'Black Power desk', whilst Special Branch officers regularly reported on it.[213] Special Branch investigations into Black Power were, however, hampered by an inability to gain sources within the black community—a problem which was greatly exacerbated by lack of black officers within the police force.[214]

Investigations into Black Power were stepped up ahead of an August 1970 demonstration organised by the movement to protest about police raids on the Mangrove restaurant in Notting Hill. The Mangrove was a hub for the Notting Hill black community. Police regularly raided it in the belief it was a 'drugs den' or a 'hive of criminality' but found no evidence to justify such claims.[215] The demonstration led to violent clashes between the police and protesters and resulted in nine senior Black Power members being charged with incitement to riot.[216] Special Branch produced a report on the demonstration which included lists detailing the banners and slogans used during it.[217]

A Special Branch appraisal of the Black Power movement, composed shortly after the Mangrove demonstration, provides some insight into why those within the British State were so suspicious of the movement. It stated that Black Power advocates were 'potentially dangerous' because 'they have set out deliberately to manufacture complaints of white oppression'. Referring to them as 'black separatists', the report made clear that their aim was to 'bring about direct confrontation with the police in order to sow the seeds of racial friction and thereby advance the cause of "Black Power".' It is notable that despite these warnings, the report sought to downplay the threat posed by Black Power because 'the philosophy of black separatism has been largely ignored by the vast majority in this country.'[218]

After a ten-week trial in late 1971, the 'Mangrove nine', as they became known, were acquitted of incitement to riot.[219] Four of the nine were, however, found guilty of the lesser offences of either assault or affray. Evidence suggests that, following the trial, the intelligence community intensified their investigations into Black Power.[220] In early 1972 the Home Office requested and received information from the Security Service on the 'nine.' The reports included security information obtained from 'delicate sources requiring protection', which suggests the possibility that they had at least one informant inside or close to the movement.[221] Black Power continued to be watched well into the 1970s and was regularly included in MI5's biannual reports on 'current security matters.'[222] By 1976, it had become less of a priority as the Security Service believed that 'the exploitation of racial issues by extreme Left (including Black Power) organisations does not in the short term pose a substantial threat.'[223] MI5 did, however, believe that Black Power had the potential to pose a threat in the future, so is likely to have kept an eye on the movement for several more years.

Black Power came to prominence at a time when Whitehall officials were frequently discussing the employment of black people in public sector jobs that involved access to classified information. Prior to 1964, successful applicants to the Civil Service who were black were automatically barred from taking up a role in any of the Defence Departments—the Ministry of Defence, the Service Departments, the Ministry of Aviation, GCHQ, the Atomic Energy Authority and the Cabinet Office—for security reasons.[224] Minutes from a Personnel Security Committee meeting in December 1963 reveal some of the thinking behind such a decision. The Committee believed that black people 'presented an obvious target for subversion' and were 'especially vulnerable because of instability of temperament and because racial tension between the white and coloured peoples might produce a conflict of loyalties.' The most remarkable conclusion from the meeting stated, 'the fact that a man was coloured was in itself a security risk. This was not a question of prejudice or discrimination but of fact, and this must be faced realistically.'[225]

In February 1964, reviewing the policy, the Official Committee on Security agreed that 'any discrimination on grounds solely of colour was politically indefensible and therefore unacceptable.'[226] A further report stated that Defence Departments did not have any objection to black people 'as such', but highlighted that there were three reasons as to why they should not be employed:

a) It is difficult to pursue vetting enquiries when the antecedents of the individual concerned are mainly overseas, and in countries where security arrangements are minimal.
b) Many of these people will have two loyalties, one to the United Kingdom and one to their place of origin.
c) It is of special significance that these people are coloured, and thus liable to have been subjected to racial tensions; as a minority group they are open to pressures from those who would subvert them.

The report concluded that Defence Departments would, in the future, consider employing black people in such roles when the 'assimilation of the coloured peoples of this country into the normal flow of its life would lead to a position in which the difficulties foreseen would no longer be real.'[227]

Whitehall officials were distinctly aware that such a policy, if publicly known, would be heavily criticised. Correspondence from June 1964 acknowledged that reason (c) was the 'most cogent', but 'since it relates solely to the colour of the candidate's skin it is clear that the exclusion of coloured staff could not rest on this argument without exposing Ministers to extreme political embarrassment.' They, therefore, sought to introduce a policy that would automatically exclude black people without overtly referencing their colour.[228]

By 1964, officials acknowledged that since the Civil Service was receiving applications from a significant number of black people, the policy of automatically banning them from working in Defence Departments was unsustainable. It was therefore decided that a person could not be employed until they had shown that they had 'assimilated into this country'. This would be shown by 'a substantial period of residence in the United Kingdom', and it was decided as a 'working rule' to be living in the UK for at least ten years.[229] In July 1964, the change of policy was officially approved by the Ministerial Committee on Security but was not publicly announced.[230]

Reviewing the policy in April and May 1967, officials recognised that it still had flaws and noted that 'discrimination on the grounds of colour was a practical effect [of the ten-year rule] though not its purpose.'[231] Such a policy, they believed, could only be defended if all jobs in Defence Departments required positive vetting, which they did not. (Later in 1967, it was decided that posts requiring only negative vetting would be subject to a 'five-year rule.'[232]) The Official Committee on Security did, however, note that because of the introduction of the residency rule, the policy did not merely discriminate against black people—it 'applied as much to a Cypriot, or indeed to a French Canadian, as to a Nigerian.' Despite all of this, MI5 was far from comfortable with the new rule. The Director General, Martin Furnival Jones, stated that intelligence officials objected to black people accessing classified information. He told the Official Committee on Security that concerns 'stemmed simply from the colour of a man's skin, which gave him a chip on his shoulder.' The minutes of the Committee reveal the extent of the Security Service's prejudices about black people, stating,

> It would be a long time before this chip was removed. Even when a man was placed in a position of trust which ought to remove the chip, he and his wife and family might be subject to public humiliation on grounds of colour in such a way as to make the chip reappear. It must be assumed that Communist intelligence services were fully aware of the possibilities of recruiting agents from among disaffected coloured people in this country. The security risk of employing coloured staff was therefore a serious one, and one which should be brought to the attention of Ministers.[233]

In 1968, ministers sought to strengthen legislation on racial equality, making it unlawful to discriminate against anybody on grounds of race, ethnic or national origin in matters of employment. The Race Relations Act (1968) was seen by Whitehall officials as potentially problematic because, although it contained exemptions on the grounds of national security, it could lead to difficult questions about the policy, since individuals rejected for employment were able to take their cases to the Race Relations Board.[234] Nonetheless, it was believed that the policy could be justified to the Race Relations Board by arguing that 'we do not discriminate against people because of their colour, race, ethnic or national origin, but because of their lack of assimilation into our way of life.'[235] In June 1968, this justification was expressed publicly for the first time by the Financial Secretary to the Treasury, Norman Lever, in a written answer to a parliamentary question.[236]

It is unclear if defence departments began to employ a greater number of black people in jobs involving access to secret information as time progressed.[237] Very few figures relating to this have been released to date. Whilst it is likely that the numbers would eventually have increased, the process would have taken a long time. In 1966, for example, out of nearly 700 black people recruited to the Clerical and Executive classes of the Civil Service, only ten were assigned to security departments.[238] Figures are not available for the years that followed, so it is not known how long it took for a significant number of black recruits to be able to take up jobs in security departments. Perhaps more pertinently, the number of black candidates who had their applications rejected because of the policy is also unknown. Some security departments simply did not recruit black people. It is notable that the recently published authorised history of GCHQ states that the agency 'followed Foreign Office policy for personnel, and until around 1980 adopted a de facto colour bar.'[239] The author of the authorised history, John Ferris, also records that 'British intelligence and security services generally did not employ British Jews' between the mid-1950s and 1980. The discrimination against Jews may not have been as pervasive—certain Jews were seemingly allowed to work at GCHQ if they had 'scarce skills'— but existed, nonetheless. In GCHQ, concerns were also raised about individuals who were citizens of the Republic of Ireland, had previously been an Irish citizen, or were married to an 'alien'. The Civil Service commission agreed to prevent some such applicants being sent to work for GCHQ.[240] The fear that an individual's racial characteristics might have led them to undertake subversive activities meant that selection for some jobs in State security was based on discriminatory assumptions for many decades.

Conclusion

Throughout the 1970s and 1980s, British State intelligence agencies investigated several organisations who were not, in themselves, believed to be subversive. Despite undertaking some questionable investigations, British intelligence officials routinely found themselves in conflict with the government of the day. Ministers had come to expect detailed information on subversives and were often dissatisfied with the information that they were receiving from the intelligence community on strikes or protest movements. Disagreements about those who were and those who were not subversive meant that the Security Service often rejected government requests for intelligence on industrial disputes or protest groups.

It is apparent, however, that MI5 undertook some investigations into communists and subversives that provided them with information on organisations that were not, themselves, considered to be subversive. The Security Service could argue that it was not going beyond its remit, that such information was a by-product of legitimate investigations and that it was not seeking to investigate the organisations themselves. The former MI5 officer Cathy Massiter admitted, however, that it was impossible to 'just concentrate on the subversive elements of CND' because 'you had to be able to answer questions on the non-subversive elements.' This made investigations more problematic, she said, because 'the whole thing began to flow out into a very grey area.' She stated that this showed the 'extreme ambivalence between what the Security Service is there to do—what it perceives itself as being there to do: to study subversion—and what actually happens in practice, which is in effect to broaden this study quite a long way beyond these basic guidelines.'[241]

Whilst MI5 sought to justify such investigations as being within its charter, in reality, aspects may have been outside their remit.

ENEMIES OF THE STATE OR ENEMIES OF THE GOVERNMENT?

In her memoirs, Stella Rimington wrote that investigations into individuals concentrated solely 'on hostility to the democratic process itself [and] never included political dissent'. The 'activities of organisations or individuals with subversive intent was of concern to us', she wrote, 'the right to set up and join pressure groups and protest was not.'[242] However, in a later interview, she appeared to admit that the intelligence community went too far in some investigations. She said, 'files might have been opened on people who would not now be regarded as falling firmly within a recording category ... looked at from the point of view of the twenty-first century, we could say that in some cases it might have been over-zealous.'[243]

Although investigations into subversive individuals belonging to non-subversive organisations enabled MI5 to discover broader information about the activities of these groups, their investigations did not always reveal the full picture. In the case of the miners' strike, for example, evidence shows that they did not discover the information about the movements of pickets. Crucially, whatever investigations intelligence officials undertook, they emphasised that they did not perceive either strikers or protest movements to be, in themselves, subversive. The investigations of such groups meant that, on this point, the intelligence community clashed with the government. It is likely that throughout the twentieth century, the government of the day often wished the intelligence community to provide them with more information. In the 1970s and 1980s, however, there was a fundamental difference of opinion between government and intelligence agencies as to exactly what was and what was not subversive. Governments demanded an increasing amount of intelligence from intelligence officials and appear to have wanted information that was beyond the scope of the Security Service remit.

Strikers and protest groups strongly opposed the policies of the British government but do not seem to have posed a significant subversive threat to the British State. Intelligence officials recognised that politicians had difficulty in distinguishing between political and security threats. In 1977, John Jones, at the time MI5's DG, wrote in an internal memo that ministers and their senior officials had 'a natural tendency ... to equate subversion with activity which threatens a Government's policies or may threaten its very existence.'[244] Whilst communists in the 1920s and 1950s may have had the potential to threaten the British State, protesters and strikers in the 1970s and 1980s did not pose a security threat. Their threat was, instead, of a political nature.

CONCLUSION

Towards the end of the 1980s, the head of MI5's counter-subversion F-Branch remarked, 'we had always overestimated the threat [of communism] since Communists at no stage would have filled a football stadium.'[1] In the late 1980s, the CPGB was an insignificance, and the Soviet Union was in terminal decline. It appeared difficult, therefore, to justify the resources that the Security Service had spent on investigating communism. In 2026, with the benefit of hindsight, even more questions can be raised about why, for much of the twentieth century, Britain's intelligence agencies expended so much time and money in investigating both the CPGB and communist sympathisers. Communism only ever attracted support from a tiny proportion of the British public, yet the CPGB, its members, and other individuals who sympathised with communist ideology were scrutinised extremely closely for seven decades. If the CPGB was so small, why did intelligence officials monitor it?

The British intelligence community began to monitor communists and revolutionaries after the Bolshevik revolution because they were genuinely fearful that the ideology could spread in Britain and threaten British democracy.[2] The fears that arose in 1917 did not subside until the Soviet Union began to crumble in the late 1980s. It was only then that intelligence officials began to move away from routinely monitoring individuals who were believed to pose a subversive threat as a result of their links, real or imagined, to communism. In one way or another, it is the fear of communism which connects almost all the groups and individuals examined in this study. From the individuals involved in the General Strike of 1926, to atomic scientists in the 1950s, to CND campaigners in the 1980s, all were placed under surveillance because of a concern that they were or could be influenced by communist revolutionaries. Events during the short twentieth century introduced mass political surveillance in Britain and it is unquestionable that this was due to the need to combat the malign intentions of the Soviet Union. In late 1991 the Soviet Union collapsed. It was no coincidence that in 1992, MI5 stopped routinely monitoring political subversion.[3] Although communism may not have had any impact on the politics of the United Kingdom, its impact on Britain's security and intelligence agencies was profound.

From the Bolshevik revolution onwards, Russia or the Soviet Union sought to subvert and destabilise the British State. In 1918, Lenin's Bolsheviks had an unambiguous aim to spread revolution across Europe, including within Britain. Although, in the following decades, the ambitions of the Soviet leadership may have evolved as they realised that a worldwide revolution was not likely, they continued to try to undermine British democracy by infiltrating society and stealing State secrets. In 1971, the head of MI5, Martin Furnival Jones, made clear, 'there is virtually no information about this country or indeed about any country in the west which the Russian Intelligence Service [RIS] is not anxious to obtain.'[4] This was not unique to the 1970s; the RIS had held such ambitions since the Bolshevik era and continued to try to gain information until the Soviet Union's demise. It is understandable, therefore, that British security officials conducted extensive surveillance of a myriad of individuals, political groups and protest groups that they believed had links to communism and the Soviet Union. To do nothing to attempt to counter such a threat would have been a dereliction of duty.

The surveillance that took place may have been of individuals and groups who were advocating a political message, but it was not, in itself, politicised. Individuals who were attracted to communism were not placed under surveillance because the State disagreed

CONCLUSION

with their political beliefs; communism was never made illegal in Britain. Such people were instead closely scrutinised because the State had deep concerns that those political beliefs could lead such individuals to subvert British democracy. As Guy Liddell, MI5's then deputy Director General, wrote in February 1951, 'we were not studying the Communist Party primarily because we thought it was likely to create a revolution or resort to acts of violence in peace time: the basic reason was that the Party was a vehicle for espionage to Russia.'[5] Fundamentally, British intelligence officials prioritised the investigation of subversion related to communist ideology because communism was so indelibly linked with Britain's primary adversary for much of the short twentieth century—the Soviet Union. As the Cabinet Secretary, Sir Norman Brook, made clear in 1951, 'Communism is a world-wide force directed from the centre in the interests of Russian imperialism ... it is therefore impossible to consider the problem of Communism in this country as something detached from the Soviet threat.'[6]

A desire to politicise surveillance during the short twentieth century most often came from politicians and not intelligence officials. Ministers would often view any challenge to the government's authority as a threat to the nation rather than a mere political challenge to the government. This was particularly the case during industrial disputes; as the Security Service made clear during the 1970s, strikes 'may be damaging to the State, [but] cannot be described as subversive'.[7] Edward Heath and Margaret Thatcher both fervently believed the industrial disputes that took place during their respective premierships were inspired by subversives. They were not the only leaders who took such a view. Their immediate predecessors in Number 10, respectively Harold Wilson and James Callaghan, both pressurised the Security Service to investigate strikes. During the 1950s, MI5 even had to inform Anthony Eden that industrial unrest during his time in Downing Street 'was not a Communist Party inspired activity'.[8] It was undoubtedly the case that, as MI5 Director General John Jones stated in 1977, ministers tended 'to equate subversion with activity which threatens a Government's policies or may threaten its very existence.'[9]

Security officials may often have been more objective than ministers, but they were, themselves, over-suspicious of certain political opinions. The surveillance itself may not have been politicised, but those working in intelligence were frequently apprehensive about non-communist left-wing groups and individuals, viewing them as subversive when they were not. As the historian David Caute remarked, for the Security Service, '[on] a colour chart of political allegiances ... pale red tended to run like watercolour into deep red'. This was most apparent during the interwar years, when both the political and intelligence establishment failed to understand the motivations of strikers during the General Strike and were inherently suspicious of legitimate challenges to the status quo. They were particularly mistrustful of the Labour Party and the first Labour government of 1924. However, as they became more familiar with mainstream left-wing political views, most intelligence officials became less suspicious of the Left. Security officials worked well with Labour members of Churchill's War Cabinet and, after World War Two, began to see that the Labour Party was a useful ally in the battle against subversion from the far-left.

Fundamental misunderstandings about political ideologies not only led intelligence officials to investigate left-wingers who did not share the revolutionary aims of communists, but also meant that they only investigated particular types of communists. Too much time was spent investigating working-class rank-and-file CPGB members during the 1920s and 1930s, when communism was beginning to interest more professional, middle- and upper-class individuals. Security officials erroneously believed communism was an ideology that would attract only individuals in lower social classes who were poorly educated. Such attitudes enabled two Special Branch officers, Inspector Hubertus van Ginhoven and Sergeant Charles Jane, to go undetected for several years whilst they leaked secret information that was subsequently passed on to the Soviets. The failure to properly investigate individuals from higher social classes who held communist sympathies also meant that intelligence officials failed to discover the Soviet recruitment of students at universities in the 1930s, most notably the Cambridge spies, despite warnings that communist cells were forming at elite universities.

It would never have been possible to have identified all of the people who posed a significant subversive threat to Britain, as to do so would have required the country to become something of a police state, with the whole population investigated continuously. The very nature of a democracy meant that some individuals involved in espionage were able to slip through the net. Despite this, the mistakes during the interwar years were undoubtedly due to a blinkered, mistaken view of communism, communists, and the threat they posed. Misunderstandings about the subversive threat also resulted in politicians and officials being too slow to realise that there was another possible threat to democracy in the 1930s—that of fascism. Their all-encompassing fear of communism and belief in the necessity to do almost anything to combat it meant that fascism was not seen as capable of posing a subversive threat for most of the interwar period. It was primarily viewed as an anti-communist movement, and individual fascists were occasionally utilised, unofficially, to help the State counter communist activity. The British State was willing to turn a blind eye to fascists' worst excesses because they proved to be allies against communism. The State was not, however, pro-fascist. When fascists posed the primary subversive threat during the Second World War, communists were indirectly utilised by the State to help defeat fascism. Communist scientists, in particular, played a key role, most notably in atomic research. As the wartime Home Secretary, Sir John Anderson, stated when appointing the communist scientist J.D. Bernal as a governmental scientific adviser, 'I don't care if he's as red as the fires of hell. He's bright and he's committed to winning the war.'[10]

During the war, some security and intelligence officials remained concerned about communism; the most fervent anti-communists regarded the prioritisation of fascism over communism during the war as 'a dangerous interruption of the Service'.[11] Such views did not, however, dominate and investigations into communism took a back seat during wartime. Although lingering fears about the Soviet threat persisted throughout this period, the war led to a pause in Anglo-Soviet antagonism. This did not last, however, and by 1946 the Soviet Union had, once again, begun to be seen as Britain's greatest adversary. Intelligence officials started to place communists under closer scrutiny and, by the end of the 1940s, surveillance was again extensive. The surveillance that took place in the late 1940s and early 1950s was largely indiscriminate and involved widespread scrutiny of numerous individuals who were neither CPGB members nor engaged in subversive activity. It was, however, understandable. Decrypted telegrams began to reveal that that Soviets had managed to penetrate British society in the 1930s and 1940s; this information left politicians and security officials with no option other than to tighten security procedures. Unlike during the interwar years, the Soviet threat to Britain was palpable, particularly with the advent of nuclear weapons.

Over time, however, surveillance went beyond investigating people because of legitimate security concerns. It became irrational and was based on paranoia. The spy scandals of the 1950s, particularly those involving Guy Burgess, Donald Maclean, and Kim Philby, led some intelligence officials to develop grave concerns that numerous spies had infiltrated the British State and remained undiscovered. As the journalist Gordon Correra has written, 'a fire had been lit by Philby's betrayal ... it blazed with fierce intensity.'[12] A small number of intelligence officials developed a real fear that manifested itself in internal 'mole hunts' within MI5, and a revived suspicion about left-wing politics and politicians.

More widely, by the late 1960s, the surveillance of communists and communist sympathisers took place for no reason other than it had become the norm. By this stage, as the threat posed by communism was judged to have lessened, surveillance was often founded on feelings of suspicion rather than evidence. One generation of intelligence officials passed on ideas about the communist threat and the danger of the USSR to the next generation, who persisted with them. The threat remained sufficient for the next generation of officers to continue to undertake such activity unquestioningly. This only began to change in the late 1960s and early 1970s as new MI5 recruits, seeing that communism no longer posed as great a threat as it had previously, began to question the old orthodoxy. To them, routine monitoring of communists was both irrational and unnecessary.

Individuals who joined MI5 as new desk officers in the 1970s held this different perspective and saw little point in intensively scrutinising all aspects of the CPGB. They had not been exposed to the strongly anti-communist doctrine which had prevailed for the previous half-century within intelligence circles and had reservations as to why such surveillance continued to take place so automatically. Stella Rimington was one of those who began their intelligence career at this time, and later wrote in her memoirs about doing work that was 'pretty dull'—investigating regional branches of the CPGB—and described how she would 'while away the time reading ... novels under the desk'.[13] She was not the only person who held this opinion. One unnamed MI5 officer later stated, 'I found it hard to understand why we were spending so much time investigating the activities of [the CPGB], let alone worrying about attempting to identify someone who was presumed to have sympathies with Communism ... My contemporaries were of a similar opinion.'[14] The new intelligence officers may have privately questioned the necessity to continue to investigate communism so intensely but, as they were just beginning their careers, they did not 'challenge the assumptions of the [communist] threat.'[15] Miranda Ingram, an MI5 whistle-blower in the 1980s, said that counter-subversion could be seen as 'distasteful' as it involved 'monitoring one's fellow citizens'. She stated that such criticisms were not voiced, however, as 'in the prevailing right-wing atmosphere, an officer who dissents from the official line does not feel encouraged to voice his concerns. He feels that it will be futile or detrimental to his career.'[16]

Two individuals who, like Rimington, later led MI5— Stephen Lander and Eliza Manningham-Buller—both began their intelligence careers in the 1970s and also struggled to understand why the Security Service was focusing so intently on subversion. Speaking many years later, Lander described how he was 'unhappy' with counter-subversion, whilst Manningham-Buller thought it was 'something sordid ... slightly tacky.' She talked critically of the 1970s Security Service which, she said, was composed of many former colonial officers 'coming out of the sun worrying about the Communist Party in Woking ... There was a lot of drinking. One of the problems was the service was too isolated and too insulated. It was extraordinarily unhealthy.'[17]

Despite the private dissent of some new MI5 recruits, it was only in 1985, with the appointment of Sir Antony Duff as DG, that the Security Service became less 'isolated' and 'insulated'. Duff, a former diplomat who had chaired the JIC and also worked as Intelligence Co-Ordinator in the Cabinet Office, was able to bring to the Security Service something of an outsider's perspective. As he had not spent the whole of his working life in MI5, Duff was not conditioned to view communism as the single greatest threat to Britain or believe that counter-subversion was one of the Security Service's immediate priorities. It is not surprising, therefore, that during his time at MI5 he questioned the orthodoxies held by many intelligence officers—not only the continued investigation of communism but also the necessity for counter-subversion investigations themselves.[18]

Until Duff's appointment, MI5 undoubtedly spent too long investigating subversion in the 1970s and 1980s, when it no longer posed a significant threat. Organisations such as the AAM should not have been investigated merely because they had some communist members. It took a reformer such as Duff to finally put an end to the feverish communist-inspired surveillance that had been taking place ever since the first 'red scare' in the 1920s. Duff's apparent mission to 'run down' MI5's counter-subversion F-branch made it clear that, in previous years, surveillance operations had overstepped the mark; this also was acknowledged internally after the criticisms from the whistle-blower, Cathy Massiter.[19]

For much of the twentieth century, the British intelligence community was faced with two major difficulties. They needed to investigate a political ideology—communism that was committed to subverting British democracy but was not illegal. They also had to try to combat an adversary—the Soviet Union—which sought to undermine British society at every opportunity, despite the fact that the two nations were not at war. John Bruce Lockhart, who served as an MI6 officer between 1942 and 1965,

CONCLUSION

later reflected on this, writing, 'the democracies who find no difficulties in defining Intelligence objectives, methods, etc. in time of war, find themselves in a dilemma in a grey period of half-way between war and peace'.[20] Intelligence officials used surveillance to deal with this difficulty as it allowed them to gain information on individuals and organisations who might pose a threat in the future, without directly suppressing them in an anti-democratic way.

Such were the difficulties that it is, at the very least, possible to understand why certain groups and individuals were watched. Even those who may have been doing nothing wrong or illegal had the potential to raise suspicions and were, therefore, placed under investigation. The surveillance of CND, in particular, falls into this category. CND campaigners had the right to protest against nuclear weapons yet, viewed from the position of the security establishment, CND campaigns could have been to Moscow's advantage. Britain unilaterally renouncing nuclear weapons would undoubtedly have been beneficial to the Soviet Union. Security officials, therefore, would have understandably held concerns about groups advocating unilateralism. Their case was that it was necessary to investigate CND and anti-nuclear protesters to make sure that pro-Soviet factions were not driving the case for unilateralism. Sir Philip Knights, Chief Constable of West Midlands Police, later articulated this when he said, 'Unless you inquire, you don't find out. You can't just pick it out of thin air whether somebody is a subversive or not. You have to inquire.'[21]

Knights' argument and similar claims are credible and would be persuasive to some people. Intelligence and security officials were responsible for keeping Britain safe and, to be able to do so, they did what they thought was necessary. Security officials and politicians often seem to have adopted the view that it was better to play it safe, and that security was more important than liberty. However, in a liberal democracy is such an argument possible? Should people have so readily been investigated despite there being very little evidence to suggest they were doing something wrong?

Some of the surveillance that took place during Britain's short twentieth century was egregious, particularly to modern sensibilities, and went too far. As Stella Rimington later admitted, 'from the point of view of the twenty-first century, we could say that in some cases it might have been over-zealous.'[22] Such overzealous surveillance can partly be explained by the restrictions, or lack of restrictions, that were placed on the work of the security and intelligence services for much of the short twentieth century. Although MI5 had limits to the type of activities it could undertake—outlined in both the 1945 Findlater Stewart report and the 1952 Maxwell Fyfe Directive—they were not legally binding. The Security Service was not placed on a statutory footing, nor was it publicly avowed. Perhaps most importantly, subversion was not defined until 1972, meaning that MI5 could effectively decide what did and did not constitute subversion. For all intents and purposes, subversion could be whatever intelligence officials wanted it to be.[23]

It is important to note that although MI5's charter was a little vague and ill-defined, it did place a limitation on its work; the Security Service was able to reject government requests for surveillance in the 1970s and 1980s as going 'beyond its charter'. On the other hand, the police and Special Branch were far less restricted in their investigations; it seems that, at times, they did exactly what the government wanted them to do. This was particularly problematic as governments of all political colours tended to be overly suspicious of groups or individuals who challenged their authority, often believing them to be subversive even when they were not. Special Branch regularly watched those who the government believed to be a threat; as Merlyn Rees stated when Home Secretary in 1978, 'the Special Branch collects information on those whom I think cause problems to the State.'[24] This undoubtedly led to unjustifiable surveillance of individuals and groups who opposed the government but posed no subversive or security threat to the State.

Politicians were often even more security conscious than the intelligence and security agencies. They were likely to encourage excessive surveillance not only because they saw threats to their rule lurking in every corner, but also because they feared the consequences of security scandals. Fundamentally, they prioritised

CONCLUSION

security over all other considerations, including liberty. The academic Michael Ignatieff has argued, when talking more generally about this,

> the political system rewards overreaction because any politicians want to go to the country saying better safe than sorry. And so overreaction is rewarded rather than underreaction. No politician, regardless of party, would be able to survive ... the charge that he hadn't done enough to protect the country. That's why everybody's bound to overreact.[25]

Although Ignatieff was talking about security policies in the post-9/11 era, his comments apply equally to Britain during the short twentieth century. To maintain liberty, security is often sacrificed, and to maintain security, the liberty of individuals is sometimes reduced. Achieving a balance between the two has always been difficult, but it appears that sometimes security was prioritised ahead of an individual's liberty, and thus people were unreasonably placed under surveillance.

Benjamin Franklin once said, 'Those who would give up essential Liberty, to purchase a little temporary Safety, deserve neither Liberty nor Safety.'[26] Most people who believe in liberal democracy would find it hard to dispute these general principles. The surveillance that took place in twentieth-century Britain would be seen as encroaching on the liberty of individuals with legitimate, legal, political views. Yet would it have been right to allow all individuals committed to a legal political ideology—communism—to go about their business unchecked? Many communists were perfectly law-abiding people, but a small minority were committed to the revolutionary goals of communism and sought to undermine and potentially eliminate British democracy. However unlikely this end goal was, there was certainly a logic to scrutinising individuals who believed in it.

The German political philosopher Karl Loewenstein argued in the 1930s for the idea of a 'militant democracy' whereby it is necessary to use illiberal methods to defend democracy. 'The mechanism of democracy', he contended, 'is the Trojan horse by which the enemy enters the city'. He believed that if a democracy was not prepared to fight anti-democrats, it could potentially be encouraging its own destruction.[27] It may well have been that the threat posed to Britain during the period under examination did not reach the levels justifying the use of illiberal methods to defend democracy. Loewenstein's theory does, however, give cause for thought. It is possible to take the view that some of the surveillance which took place in twentieth-century Britain was excessive, illiberal activity, unwelcome in an advanced democracy whilst, simultaneously, understanding why it did take place. During the twentieth century, the Soviet Union undoubtedly posed a subversive threat to Britain. The Soviets wished to infiltrate British society and undermine it from within, and they did, at times, penetrate the highest levels of the British establishment. The CPGB may have been merely a tiny political party, but it was closely linked to the Soviet Union—receiving a subsidy from Moscow during the interwar years, and again between 1957 and 1979.[28] Moscow did not fund the CPGB for altruistic reasons.

Alongside surveillance, one of the key methods with which security officials sought to defend Britain against possible subversive threats was the use of vetting. Again, it could be viewed as illiberal, but vetting was a legitimate way to reduce the potential leakage of further British secrets to Moscow. Vetting created victims and led some individuals to be discriminated against because of their background or their political views. In effect, it resulted in some being viewed as 'guilty' unless they could prove their innocence. The measures did not entirely protect against espionage. In order to ensure a completely watertight security system, Harold Macmillan believed, it would be necessary to resort to totalitarian methods which were 'distasteful to our national sentiment and contrary to our long tradition'[29]. Despite this, improved security measures helped to reduce the subversive threat to Britain; the security scandals of the late 1950s and early 1960s, involving Klaus Fuchs, the Cambridge Five, George Blake, John Vassall, and the Portland Spies, were never replicated. Although several individuals slipped through the net and were subsequently convicted of passing secrets to the Soviets in the 1970s and 1980s, these cases were infrequent and less scandalous.[30] As Sir Dick White later said, 1951 (the year

CONCLUSION

positive vetting was first introduced) was 'the highpoint of Soviet espionage in Britain. They never had it so easy again. After that, it was downwards for them and upwards for us.'[31]

The extent of surveillance in Britain during the short twentieth century has only begun to become apparent over the last couple of decades. It is still not possible to fully appreciate how widespread it was. Due to both the destruction of files and the fact that not everything was documented, a definitive picture of the surveillance that did take place is unlikely to ever be seen. The particularly British culture of secrecy, which has long been woven into the very fabric of Whitehall, has also meant that it has been difficult to discover what exactly went on. This secrecy did, however, have the benefit of meaning that in Britain there was no witch-hunt of apparent subversives, and no martyrs were created. In large part, this was down to undoubted consensus in the British State and wider British society that McCarthyite actions would have been unpalatable; as was said at the time, the methods employed in the US were 'repugnant to British thinking'.[32] As the twentieth century progressed, much of British society continued blissfully unaware that a covert battle was being fought against domestic subversion. Politicians and officials were convinced that Britain was threatened by communist-inspired subversion, but they were unwilling to fight that fight in public. Harold Macmillan and others regularly argued that nothing good could come from the publicising of security scandals.

The culture of secrecy also arguably allowed the authorities to avoid scrutiny and perhaps even accountability. For a significant proportion of the twentieth century, Britain was a deferential society and thus the work of the government and its secret services were not regularly questioned. As the decades progressed, however, the public became less respectful of the State and showed a greater willingness to challenge authority. Indignation over surveillance in the 1970s and particularly in the 1980s showed that such activity, undertaken without any legal basis, would no longer be possible. The 1989 Security Service Act, which placed MI5 on a statutory footing, was introduced partly in response to a scandal about the surveillance of two members of the National Council of

Civil Liberties (NCCL), Harriet Harman and Patricia Hewitt.[33] As British society became less deferential, unlimited large scale political surveillance became less possible to justify.

Debates will continue about the legitimacy of the surveillance undertaken by MI5. Files were opened on hundreds of thousands of individuals, but some of those who were involved in espionage were often either not watched or not watched sufficiently closely. Others who were closely scrutinised even knew that they were under surveillance. Those individuals who were aware of surveillance often did not realise its extent; the CPGB was oblivious to how deeply MI5 had penetrated the organisation. It remains the case that many of those individuals on whom MI5 opened a file would never have noticed they were under some form of surveillance.

Viewing the files, it is impossible not to be struck by the sheer banality of much of the information collected on different people. MI5 scrutinised individuals for several decades yet had very little to show for it. The information they collected often provided minimal insight. Much of the surveillance that took place produced a great deal of irrelevant material, giving the impression that it was both excessive and unnecessary. Whilst it is possible to criticise the excessive surveillance, it should be acknowledged that cases were rarely ever clear cut.

The surveillance of Eric Hobsbawm is a good example of the difficulty faced by security officials. His file, which was compiled over a period of more than thirty years and ran to at least eight volumes, told the Security Service almost nothing useful. It is hard to see what they gained from watching him for such a long period. During the 1990s, however, Hobsbawm spoke about his communist beliefs during media interviews where he appeared to suggest that deaths of millions in the Soviet Union would have been justified if they had resulted in the formation of a 'communist utopia.'[34] Whilst he never blindly accepted communist dogma and was privately critical of the CPGB, his comments alluded to his deep commitment to the ideology. Hobsbawm was merely answering hypothetical questions. His answers, however, give cause for thought. If he truly believed what he said, would he have

CONCLUSION

been willing to encourage the destruction of British democracy if a 'communist utopia' had been realistic? Even more importantly, was he the only communist who held such strongly held convictions? If it was the case for one person, how many others would have taken such a view? It is, of course, impossible to say. It does, however, leave the impression that the Security Service was not entirely wrong to conduct surveillance of Hobsbawm and other committed communists. There were, at the very least, a small number of individuals who had a deep commitment to the ideology who would have gone a long way to achieve a 'communist utopia' in Britain.

Many CPGB members and communist sympathisers may not have been willing to betray British secrets to the Soviet Union but, it was impossible, as Whitehall officials articulated in the late 1940s, to 'separate the sheep from the goats.'[35] Security officials would have argued that it was necessary to monitor individuals who had some commitment to the ideology of communism in case Anglo-Soviet relations deteriorated in the future. The Security Service was dealing with 'known unknowns'—as a result of security scandals they knew some communists were untrustworthy but did not know which ones. Surveillance would, therefore, have been seen by those working in intelligence as something necessary to help to close the gaps in their knowledge. Writing in his in-house MI5 history, John Curry acknowledged that much of the information the Security Service collected on individuals was 'often dull' but argued that it was 'impossible to ignore [the CPGB's] potential importance as a factor making for disintegration in the life of this country.'[36] It may well have been the case that intelligence officials adopted a somewhat illiberal view—believing that they would be better off investigating one person too many rather than one person too few—but there were, at times, good reasons for such investigations. This may have resulted in unfair practices—many innocent individuals had their privacy invaded, be it in the form of phone taps and letter checks or simply by having their details collated by security officials—but most individuals were untroubled and able to continue their day-to-day lives.

The difficulty was always that MI5 could never be sure if a person was a threat until they had properly investigated them. Often this meant that they pursued leads that came to nothing. As the historian James Rusbridger has written, 'it is frequently said about advertising that half the money spent is wasted but no one knows which half. Much the same can be said about intelligence services.'[37] The mere fact that an individual had a file opened on them did not necessarily mean that they were to be heavily scrutinised or that they were under suspicion. At times, the Security Service just wanted to gain more knowledge. The information in the files of some people would include little more than a few newspaper cuttings and references to talks they had attended. Collecting information on innocent individuals may be viewed as a little distasteful but the purpose of surveillance was often, as one scholar has put it, 'passive observation—not active repression'.[38]

Depending on their perspective, some people will agree with the fact that surveillance took place, whilst others will argue it was wrong for a democratic State to collect information on so many citizens. One final question, however, remains—did the extensive surveillance of the wide variety of communists, communist sympathisers or other individuals help to protect British security during the twentieth century? Sir David Petrie, MI5 DG between 1941 and 1946 later explained, 'it is to the disadvantage of security work, by and large, that the results are apt to be mainly negative; that is to say, the better it is done the less there is to show for it.'[39] Very simply, as Christopher Andrew has argued, 'the success of a security service is better judged by things that do not happen (which are necessarily unquantifiable) than by things that do.'[40] Whilst it is impossible to say definitively whether the extensive surveillance that went on for much of the twentieth century helped to protect British security, vetting and surveillance are highly likely to have had a positive effect in helping to limit the opportunities of those individuals who sought to undermine British democracy.

Making a definitive judgement on the rights and wrongs of the surveillance is also difficult. It was necessary for a democratic society like Britain to protect individual liberty whilst also

CONCLUSION

protecting domestic security. At times the balance was weighted too far one way or the other. The very fact that so many people were watched can certainly seem unpalatable but, as the cases have shown, it was rarely straightforward. Judgements on the surveillance should not try to view it in terms of right or wrong but instead view it in a more nuanced manner. Some action was undoubtedly necessary to deal with the Soviet and communist threat. The fact that this often manifested itself in surveillance of individuals who held legal political views merely demonstrates that protecting the security of the State can be a somewhat grubby business, full of moral compromises.

Surveillance was, and remains, a necessary part of the protection of security in a democracy, and there is nothing wrong with political surveillance per se. It is a perfectly legitimate activity for State agencies to undertake if they believe that individuals or groups pose a threat to democratic norms. In Britain during the twentieth century, this was certainly true with surveillance in the cases of fascists and Irish republicans; it is entirely understandable why such movements were watched as they had the potential to pose, and did pose, significant security threats. There was also a legitimate reason to watch communists, despite the fact that the political ideology was never illegal. In the unlikely event that they had ever managed to gain power in Britain, both fascists and communists were committed to destroying democracy. Some individuals attracted to either ideology were unashamedly committed to pursuing such aims.

Concerns about surveillance only really arise when it becomes obvious that the secret State is investigating individuals with views and positions that do not bring them into conflict with democracy. As Sir David Omand, Director of GCHQ in the 1990s, has written, 'we ... give our intelligence officers a licence to operate by ethical standards different from those we would hope to see applied in everyday life, justified by the reduction in harm to the public they can achieve'.[41] It is, therefore, imperative that they do not take advantage of this licence; during the short twentieth century, they sometimes did. If intelligence officials of today could learn anything from the mistakes that were made during the short twentieth century, it is this—surveillance plays a key part in protecting both liberty and security in a democracy, but it should always be conducted in a legal and proportionate manner. Defending the realm should not be seen as choosing between liberty and security. Both are equally important. When considering surveillance and other somewhat illiberal methods used to protect domestic security, it would be wise to bear in mind the words of the philosopher Karl Popper. 'We must plan for freedom and not only for security', he wrote, 'if for no other reason than that only freedom can make security secure.'[42]

APPENDICES

APPENDIX 1 – Charter of the Security Service

The Security Service is part of the Defence Forces of the country. Its task is the Defence of the Realm as a whole, from external and internal dangers arising from attempts at espionage and sabotage, or from actions of persons and organisations whether directed from within or without the country, which may be judged to be subversive to the State.

You will take special care to see that the work of the Security Service is strictly limited to what is necessary for the purposes of this task.

It is essential that the Security Service should be kept absolutely free from any political bias or influence and nothing should be done that might lend colour to any suggestion that it is concerned with the interests of any particular section of the community, or with any other matter than the Defence of the Realm as a whole.

No enquiry is to be carried out on behalf of any Government Department unless you are satisfied that an important public interest bearing on the Defence of the Realm is at stake.

You and your staff will maintain the well-established convention whereby Ministers do not concern themselves with the detailed information which may be obtained by the Security Service in particular cases, but are furnished with such information only as may be necessary for the determination of any issue on which guidance is sought.

The Maxwell Fyfe Directive. Issued by the Home Secretary, Sir David Maxwell Fyfe, to the Director General of the Security Service, 24 September 1952. The directive served as the Security Service's charter until the 1989 Security Service Act.

APPENDIX 2 – Definition of subversion

Subversive activities are generally regarded as those which threaten the safety or wellbeing of the State, and which are intended to undermine or overthrow Parliamentary democracy by political, industrial or violent means. Militancy in the pursuit of trade union or other disputes with employers is obviously not necessarily subversive. We might define terrorism, for the purpose of this debate, as the use of violence for political ends. Not all subversive organisations are terrorist organisations. Terrorist groups generally have subversive aims, but not all the groups which have operated against British interests have the aim of subverting Parliamentary democracy in this country.

Lord Harris of Greenwich, Minister of State for Home Affairs, 26 February 1975

HL HANSARD 26 February 1975, Vol 357, col 947

APPENDIX 3 – Special Branch Guidelines

A Special Branch gathers information about threats to public order. Such information will enable the Branch to provide assessments of whether marches, meetings, demonstrations and pickets pose any threat to public order and help the chief officer to determine an appropriate level of policing.

A Special Branch assists the Security Service in carrying out its tasks of defending the realm against attempts at espionage and sabotage or from the actions of persons and organisations whether directed from within or without the country which may be judged to be subversive to the State. A large part of this effort is devoted to the study and investigation of terrorism, including the activities of international terrorists and terrorist organisations.

Home Office Guidelines on the work of a Special Branch, December 1984

Undercover Policing Inquiry, UCPI0000004538

https://www.ucpi.org.uk/wp-content/uploads/2023/01/UCPI0000035293.pdf

NOTES

INTRODUCTION

1. This work will use MI5 and Security Service interchangeably to refer to Britain's domestic intelligence agency. It will also use MI6 and SIS (Secret Intelligence Service) interchangeably to refer to Britain's foreign intelligence agency.
2. Rimington, *Open Secret*, p. 232. For more detail on the whole trip see, pp. 230–4.
3. During this book, the terms Russia and the Soviet Union will both be used. This is because the Soviet Union was not officially formed until 1922. This is a point that has also been acknowledged in Keeble, *Britain, The Soviet Union and Russia*, p. 371, footnote 1.
4. Rimington, *Open Secret*, pp. 239–40.
5. Hobsbawm, *The Age of Extremes*, p. 5. For the purposes of this work, the short twentieth century will run from 1917–1991, encompassing the life of the Soviet Union.
6. Porter, *Plots and Paranoia*, p. 142.
7. Kendall, *The Revolutionary Movement in Britain*, p. 189, pp. 381–2, footnote 1; Jeffery, *MI6*, p. 172.
8. The National Archives (hereafter TNA), CAB 23/14/45; Carlton, *Churchill and the Soviet Union*, pp. 5–6.
9. Olmstead, 'British and US Anticommunism', p. 90.
10. Walton, *Spies*, p. 44.
11. Keeble, *Britain, The Soviet Union and Russia*, pp. 49–51; Service, *Spies and Commissars*, particularly pp. 146–65.
12. Ferris, *Behind the Enigma*, p. 141.
    It is becoming increasingly common for historians to argue that the Cold War started after the Bolshevik Revolution. See, Walton, *Spies*, p. 8; Madeira, *Britannia and the Bear*, p. 1; Best, '"We are virtually at war with Russia"',

pp. 206–7; Carley, *Silent Conflict*, p. xiv; Goldstein, 'Britain and the Origins of the Cold War', pp. 11–14; Phillips, *Secret Twenties*, p. 4.
13. Oxford English Dictionary.
14. Best, '"We are virtually at war with Russia"', p. 210.
15. Ferris, *Behind the Enigma*, p. 143.
16. Mazower, 'Conclusion: The Policing of Politics in Historical Perspective', p. 244.
17. Subversion was only officially defined in 1972. See Appendices.
18. For a brief summary of the development of surveillance in Britain prior to the twentieth century see, Thomas, *Secret Wars*, pp. 76–8; Porter, *Plots and Paranoia*, pp. 129–35. For more on the development of a domestic 'Secret Service' in Britain from the late nineteenth century onwards see, TNA, KV 4/151, 'The Home Office Secret Service: Historical Note', 28 November 2021.
19. Andrew, *Secret World*, pp. 476–7; Walton, *Empire of Secrets*, pp. 3–5.
20. Solomon, *State Surveillance*, pp. 247–8, pp. 251-6; Quinlan, *Secret War*, p. 4; Wilson and Adams, *Special Branch*, pp. 55–66; Porter, *Plots and Paranoia*, pp. 131–2. The historian David Vincent identifies the 1911 National Insurance Act as an event which helped to normalise routine record keeping by the state on its citizens. By the time war broke out in 1914, the British state had, he argues, enthusiastically embraced the 'era of the card index'. See, Vincent, *Culture of Secrecy*, pp. 141–2.
21. Ferris, *Behind the Enigma*, p. 665.
22. TNA, CAB, 24/76/67.
23. Thomas, *Secret Wars*, pp. 80–1; Thurlow, *Secret State*, pp. 49–50; Andrew, *Secret Service*, pp. 229–33.
24. See, Andrew and Dilks, *The Missing Dimension*.
25. Andrew, *Secret World*, p. 731.
26. See, for example, Keeble, *Britain, The Soviet Union and Russia*; Carlton, *Churchill and the Soviet Union*; Folly, *Churchill, Whitehall and the Soviet Union*.
27. Andrew, *Secret World*, pp. 380–3; Cobain, *The History Thieves*, pp. 2–3; Vincent, *Culture of Secrecy*, pp. 1–3, p. 9; Porter, *Plots and Paranoia*, p. 78.
28. Ferris, *Behind the Enigma*, p. 665.
    These opinions did not, however, necessarily mean that individuals were not monitored during this period. Vlad Solomon has challenged conventional wisdom and outlines that a degree of surveillance did take place in the late nineteenth and early twentieth centuries. See, Solomon, *State Surveillance*, pp. 261–5.
29. Thompson, *The Making of the English Working Class*, p. 532.

1. COMMUNISM

   1. Reynolds, *The Long Shadow*, p. 46.
   2. Johnson, *Britain and the 1918–19 Influenza Pandemic*, p. 162.

3. Ibid., p. 175, p. 188, pp. 192–3; Spinney, *Pale Rider*, pp. 42–5, pp. 170–1, pp. 250–1.
4. Spinney, *Pale Rider*, p. 49.
5. Gerwarth, *The Vanquished*, pp. 96–8.
   One individual who referred to Bolshevism as a 'disease' was Baron Roman Rosen, the pre-Bolshevik Russian Ambassador to the United States. See, Rosen, 'The Russian Problem and Bolshevism', p. 240.
6. Madeira, *Britannia and the Bear*, p. 10; Phillips, *Secret Twenties*, p. 38.
7. Andrew, *Defence of the Realm*, p. 139.
8. Carley, *Silent Conflict*, p. 17; Andrew, *Defence of the Realm*, p. 139.
9. Gerwarth, *The Vanquished*, p. 129.
10. Ibid., pp. 154–6; Bennett, *Churchill's Man of Mystery*, p. 71.
11. TNA, CAB 24/67/79.
12. Udy, *Labour and the Gulag*, p. 50; Madeira, *Britannia and the Bear*, pp. 5, 11.
13. The 1918–22 cabinet was often divided between hardline anti-communists and more moderate characters. See, Maynard, 'Coalition and Conservative reactions to the Communist threat'.
14. Andrew, *Defence of the Realm*, p. 139; Porter, *Plots and Paranoia*, p. 143.
15. TNA, FO 608/11/17.
16. TNA, FO 608/27/7.
17. Madeira, "No Wishful Thinking Allowed", pp. 2–3. In 1918, members of the War Cabinet reportedly knew 'nothing' about key Bolsheviks—Lenin, Stalin and Trotsky—and did not even understand their 'outlandish ideas.' (Northedge and Wells, *Britain and Soviet Communism*, p. 27).
18. Jeffery, *MI6*, pp. 184–5.
19. Revolutionary feeling was particularly acute in 1919. See Webb, *1919: Year of Revolution*.
20. Andrew, *Defence of the Realm*, p. 106; Reynolds, *The Long Shadow*, pp. 59–61; Madeira, *Britannia and the Bear*, pp. 20–2, pp. 30–2; Porter, *Plots and Paranoia*, pp. 143–4; McLynn, *The Road Not Taken*, p. 365.
21. Morgan, *Conflict and Order*, pp. 80–2.
22. TNA, CAB 23/9/10; Morgan, *Conflict and Order*, pp. 75–6; Weinberger, *Keeping the Peace?* pp. 154–8; Andrew, *Secret Service*, pp. 233–4; Webb, *1919: Year of Revolution*, pp. 50–61.
23. Reynolds, *The Long Shadow*, pp. 60–1; Rosenberg, *1919*, p. 7; Hennessey and Thomas, *Spooks: 1909–39*, pp. 153–4.
24. See, McLynn, *The Road Not Taken*, pp. 363–66; Rosenberg, *1919*, p. 7.
25. Andrew, *Defence of the Realm*, p. 139.
26. Madeira, "No Wishful Thinking Allowed", p. 2.
27. See, Rosenberg, *1919*, p. 85; Ward, 'Intelligence Surveillance', p. 179; Webb, *1919: Year of Revolution*, pp. 163–4.
28. TNA, CAB 24/73/65. Long had previously expressed his fears about the

Bolshevik influence in Britain in a private letter to Basil Thomson. See, Andrew, *Defence of the Realm*, p. 107.
29. TNA, CAB, 24/76/67.
30. TNA, HO 144/1590/380368, Troup to Thomson, 17 April 1919; Wilson and Adams, *Special Branch*, pp. 97–101; Thurlow, *Secret State*, p. 50; Madeira, *Britannia and the Bear*, pp. 24–8.
31. Special Branch officers only covered the Metropolitan Police area, leaving local police forces to investigate in other areas of the country.
32. TNA, HO 144/7524, Troup to Chief Constables, 22 April 1919.
33. TNA, KV 4/151, Secret Service Committee Minutes, 7 February 1919.
34. See reports from May, June and July 1919. From TNA, CAB 24/79/54, Report 3, 14 May 1919 to TNA, CAB 24/83/16, Report 10, 3 July 1919. Weekly reports would often cover anywhere between fifteen and twenty different topics.
35. See, TNA, CAB 24/84/90; CAB 24/105/39; CAB 24/110/6; CAB 24/110/93.
36. Laybourn and Murphy, *Under the Red Flag*, pp. 42–5; Beckett, *Enemy Within*, pp. 11–16.
37. Laybourn and Murphy, *Under the Red Flag*, p. 47.
38. Thorpe, *The British Communist Party and Moscow*, pp. 65–6; Beckett, *Enemy Within*, p. 16; MacFarlane, *The British Communist Party and Moscow*, pp. 60–3. The CPGB was the first British political party to be funded by a foreign state. (Quinlan, *Secret War*, p. 16).
39. Laybourn and Murphy, *Under the Red Flag*, p. 47.
40. Beckett, *Enemy Within*, p. 22; Quinlan, *Secret War*, p. 23.
Some historians dispute the claim that the communists were merely Moscow's puppets. See, Thorpe, 'Comintern 'Control' of the Communist Party of Great Britain, 1920–1943', particularly pp. 637–52; Thorpe, *The British Communist Party and Moscow*, p. 84. For an example of how the CPGB did adhere to Moscow's line see, Callaghan and Phythian, 'State surveillance and Communist lives'.
41. TNA, CAB 24/111/30.
42. TNA, CAB 24/109/76; Jeffery, *MI6*, pp. 211–12.
43. TNA, CAB 24/111/88. Around £4.5 million as of writing. (see, Bank of England inflation calculator https://www.bankofengland.co.uk/monetary-policy/inflation/inflation-calculator).
44. TNA, CAB 24/110/72.
Questions have been raised about whether or not the CPGB stood for armed revolution. Initial Comintern instructions to CPs were that revolution would be unlikely to be possible without violence. In 1924, Stalin moderated this position, making clear 'a 'peaceful' path of development is quite possible for certain Capitalist countries', but still did not entirely reject the possibility of

the necessity of violence. (Beckett, *Enemy Within*, pp. 14–15; Curry, *Security Service*, pp. 82–3; Phillips, *Secret Twenties*, pp. 61–2).
45. TNA, CAB 24/112/37.
46. For more on Thomson's departure and the abolition of the Directorate see, Andrew, *Defence of the Realm*, pp. 117–19; Thurlow, *Secret State*, p. 51; Madeira, *Britannia and the Bear*, pp. 97–100; Porter, *Plots and Paranoia*, pp. 156–8.
47. Madeira, *Britannia and the Bear*, p. 100.
48. Childs, *Episodes and Reflections*, p. 209.
49. TNA, CAB 24/160/89.
50. Ewing and Gearty, *The Struggle for Civil Liberties*, pp. 112–15; Wilson and Adams, *Special Branch*, p. 110.
51. House of Commons Hansard Debate (hereafter HC Hansard Deb), 21 February 1924, vol 169 cc1980–82.
52. *Workers' Weekly*, 18 April 1924.
53. TNA, HO 144/7524, Special Branch Report, 'Communist Party Conference', 14 April 1924.
54. TNA, HO 144/7524, Childs to Anderson, 14 April 1924.
55. Twigge, Hampshire and Macklin, *British Intelligence Secrets*, pp. 36–7; Wilson and Adams, *Special Branch*, pp. 85–6. For further detail on the responsibilities of Special Branch see, TNA, FO 1093/68, Sir Russell Scott report, 12 October 1925; Wilson and Adams, *Special Branch*, pp. 107–13.
56. See, TNA, HO 144/22388.
57. Andrew, *Defence of the Realm*, p. 120, pp. 140–2.
58. Ibid., p. 122.
59. Ibid., pp. 142–3.
60. KV 4/126, JFC Carter to Chief Constables, 14 October 1931.
61. Wilson and Adams, *Special Branch*, p. 109.
62. Andrew, *Defence of the Realm*, p. 129.
63. Wilson and Adams, *Special Branch*, p. 70, pp. 112–13.
Its officers continued to report from ports, attend and report on political meetings and were, unlike members of MI5, permitted to make arrests.
64. Andrew, *Defence of the Realm*, pp. 95–7.
65. TNA, KV 2/4418, serial 2a.
66. TNA, KV 2/4418, serial 3a.
67. TNA, KV 2/4418, minute 4.
68. TNA, KV 2/4496, serial 1w.
69. TNA, KV 2/4496, minute 8.
70. Ambler, 'Martin Pollock', *The Guardian*, 17 February 2000. Accessed 27/10/25 at: https://www.theguardian.com/news/2000/feb/17/guardian obituaries.obituaries
71. TNA, KV 4/125, serial 1a.
Police officers continued to attend public meetings, providing MI5 with

information about overt communists or groups believed to be linked to the ideology.
72. Andrew, *Defence of the Realm*, pp. 134–5, pp. 334–5.
73. Beckett, *Enemy Within*, pp. 23–4; Davenport-Hines, *Enemies Within*, pp. 51–2; Adams and Wilson, *Special Branch*, p. 132.
74. TNA, CAB 24/92/71; TNA, KV 2/1905, serial 41a.
75. Malone initially joined the British Socialist Party in the summer of 1920, prior to the formation of the CPGB. See, TNA, CAB 24/108/92; Beckett, *Enemy Within*, p. 23.
76. TNA, CAB 24/114/68; Wilson and Adams, *Special Branch*, pp. 133–5.
77. The HOW system was introduced by Winston Churchill as Home Secretary in 1911. See, Andrew, *Secret World*, p. 480.
78. TNA, KV 2/1905, serial 8.
79. TNA, CAB 24/114/90; Wilson and Adams, *Special Branch*, pp. 136–9.
80. Malone was said to have abandoned communism after leaving prison and eventually gravitated towards the right of the Labour Party. After leaving Parliament, he became what one account has described as an 'international wheeler-dealer.' He died in 1965. (Udy, *Labour and the Gulag*, pp. 55–6; TNA, KV 2/1905, History Sheet, 'Malone C.J.L'E. 8 September 1931; Davenport-Hines, *Enemies Within*, p. 53).
81. Saklatvala lost his seat in the 1923 General Election but returned to Parliament in 1924 as a CPGB candidate.
82. TNA, KV 2/611, serial 50.
83. TNA, KV 2/614, serial 266.
84. See, TNA, KV 2/613, 'Duckworth Report 24.11.20' for an in-depth account of Saklatvala's activities between 1909 and 1920.
85. TNA, KV 2/611, serial 45, 'To Col. Carter', 29 May 1919; TNA, KV 2/613, serial 184, Hose to Kell, 29 Dec 1920.
86. TNA, KV 2/613, serial 189, 'The Case of Shapurji Dorabaji Saklatvala', 6.1.21.
87. TNA, KV 2/614, serial 376b; TNA, KV 2/614, serial 383b. For more on the IPI see, Andrew, *Defence of the Realm*, pp. 137–8; Walton, *Empire of Secrets*, pp. 16–18.
88. TNA, KV 2/614, serial 352a, serial 366a. Saklatvala later raised the matter in Parliament (HC Hansard Deb, 6 December 1927, vol. 211, cc1336–50).
89. TNA, KV 2/614, serial 387a, serial 413a.
90. TNA, HO 144/13544, 'Refusal of Passports to British Subjects Going Abroad', 29 May 1920.
91. TNA, HO 144/13544, 'Passports: Refusal of British Empire endorsement to Communists etc.', 14 August 1929, minute 17.8.29; TNA, HO 144/13544, 'Passports: Refusal of British Empire endorsements for Communists', 29 November 1929, 'MEMORANDUM'.
92. TNA, KV 2/612, serial 97, Kell to Wellinger, 16 September 1920.

93. TNA, KV 2/611, serial 15, Kell to Hose, 21 December 1918.
94. *HC Hansard Deb, 23 November 1922, vol 159 cc79–82*.
95. TNA, CAB 24/140/75, 21 December 1922.
96. TNA, HO 144/13544, 'Passports: Refusal of British Empire endorsement to Communists etc.', 14 August 1929, minute 17.8.29.
97. Beckett, *Enemy Within*, pp. 15–16, p. 61; TNA, KV 2/1753, minute 49. Gallacher had previously disagreed with many in the Party about communists standing for Parliament. He only changed his opinion after being persuaded by Lenin.
98. TNA, KV 2/1753, serial 126ax, serial 128b. At the time, there was no specific warrant on letters sent to Gallacher himself. Letters sent to him would often be opened as part of a warrant on any letters sent to the CPGB Headquarters. The General Post Office was, however, instructed to note whether Gallacher began to receive significantly more letters in the following couple of months. See, TNA, KV 2/1753, serial 132a, 133a, 134a.
99. TNA, KV 2/1753, minute 129.
100. TNA, KV 2/1753, serial 130a; TNA, KV 2/1753, serial 144a.
101. TNA, KV 2/1753, serial 143a.
102. For more information on the origins of interwar front organisations see, Rose, *Campaigns against Western Defence*, pp. 14–16, pp. 39–51.
103. SCR membership form in TNA, HO 45/25437, partially released after a FOI request.
104. TNA, KV 2/1576, serial 298a.
105. TNA, KV 2/1905, serial 35a.
106. For more on Rothstein see, Phillips, *Secret Twenties*, pp. 53–8.
107. TNA, KV 2/1576, serial 298a, serial 299a.
108. Lygo, 'Promoting Soviet Culture in Britain', pp. 576–8; TNA, KV 2/598, Home Office Warrant, Ivor Montagu, 26 June 1930.
109. As explained by Lygo, 'Promoting Soviet Culture in Britain', pp. 577–8.
110. TNA, MEPO 38/8, letter to P. Vickery, War Office, 24 January 1928.
111. TNA, KV 4/125, serial 1a.
112. One such report mentioned how some attendees 'were Jewish in appearance'. Indeed, in many of the intelligence files on Bolshevism during the interwar period there was often mention of Jews or Jewishness when discussing either communism, Bolsheviks or revolutionaries. Many of those in the intelligence community associated Jews with communism and their reporting revealed a significant degree of anti-Semitic feeling. See, TNA, MEPO 38/8, serial 15a, 'Film Show at the Cambridge Theatre'; Andrew, *Defence of the Realm*, p. 144.
113. Beckett, *Enemy Within*, p. 34, p. 59; Thurlow, *Secret State*, p. 112; Callaghan, *The Far Left*, p. 40.
114. Quinlan, *Secret War*, p. 32.
115. Thurlow, *Secret State*, p. 113, p. 132; Twigge, Hampshire and Macklin, *British Intelligence Secrets*, p. 34.

116. TNA, CAB 24/123/86.
117. Andrew, *Secret World*, pp. 578–9.
The government had passed the intercepted communications to the press for them to publish on the condition that they did not acknowledge the source. *The Times*, however, began its story with the line, 'the following messages have been intercepted by the British Government.' Bar-Joseph, *Intelligence Intervention in the Politics of Democratic States*, p. 269, footnote 23, pp. 291–4.
118. Wilson was one of the most fervent anti-communists within the British establishment. On one occasion he mused in his diary that, such was Lloyd George's accommodation of the Soviets, the Prime Minister himself may have been a traitor working with the Bolsheviks. Jeffery, *MI6*, p. 212; Carlton, *Churchill and the Soviet Union*, pp. 24–5; Aldrich and Cormac, *The Black Door*, pp. 37–8; Bar-Joseph, *Intelligence Intervention in the Politics of Democratic States*, pp. 265–7.
119. Andrew, *Secret World*, pp. 578–80.
120. The ARCOS raid caused uproar because the building in which its offices were contained was effectively Soviet diplomatic territory. Phillips, *Secret Twenties*, pp. 291–3; Andrew, *Defence of the Realm*, p. 153.
121. Phillips, *Secret Twenties*, pp. 270–82; Andrew, *Secret World*, p. 583.
122. Andrew, *Defence of the Realm*, pp. 155–6.
123. For an explanation on one-time pads see, Aldrich, *GCHQ*, pp. 18–19.
124. Andrew, *Secret World*, p. 584. The operational head of GC&CS, Alastair Denniston, accused the government of 'compromis[ing] our work beyond comprehension.' New staff at GC&CS in the years following were told of the incident 'as a warning of the depths of indiscretion to which politicians were capable of sinking.'
125. Andrew, 'Introduction', in, Curry, *Security Service*, pp. 1–3.
126. Curry, *Security Service*, p. 83. Curry defines 'conspiratorial methods' as including the use of 'codes, cyphers, secret inks, cover addresses, secret agents and the secret subsidising and secret direction by the Comintern of the national Communist Parties which are its sections in all or nearly all countries.'
127. Ibid., p. 84.
128. Ibid., p. 86.
129. TNA, T 162/1004, Murray to Scott, 25 March 1926. No action was immediately taken, with one Home Office official stating, 'if a Communist is eligible for election to Parliament, it is illogical to say one cannot serve in the Civil Service'. (TNA, T 162/1004, Scott to Murray, 3 May 1926).
130. TNA, CAB 24/186/19; TNA, CAB 23/55/5.
131. See, Andrew, *Defence of the Realm*, pp. 179–85.
132. TNA, T, 162/1004, Deputation of the Executive Council of the Amalgamated Engineering Union to the Admiralty, 11 October 1928.
133. TNA, AIR 2/15742, document 7b, 'Communists Employed under Government Departments', July 1932.

134. TNA, CAB 24/261/12; TNA, CAB 23/83/24.
135. See, TNA, CAB 24/97/46; TNA, KV 4/296, serial 176a, Kell to Sir Russell Scott, 31 October 1932, 'Communism and the CPGB'; Childs, *Episodes and Reflections*, pp. 209–10. Thomson even advocated intercepting copies of the *Daily Herald* before they could be sold, because they contained passages 'advocating revolution in very violent terms.' His idea was, however, rejected by the Cabinet. (TNA, CAB 23/25/2).
136. TNA, KV 4/295, Lord Stamfordham to Prime Minister, 5 August 1925. In 1921 the King had also 'written to the Home Secretary pointing out the grave danger of Communist propaganda and asking for an assurance that something is going to be done before the rising of Parliament.' (TNA, KV 4/295, serial 3c, Thomson to Horwood, 11 May 1921).
137. Childs, *Episodes and Reflections*, pp. 209–10. Childs believed that had it been up to William Joynson-Hicks, Home Secretary from 1924, and a man whom he saw as more anti-communist than himself, the Communist Party would have been swiftly banned.
138. Thurlow, *Secret State*, p. 112, p. 138.
139. Thurlow, "A very clever capitalist class", pp. 3–4.
140. Childs, *Episodes and Reflections*, p. 221.
141. Thurlow, 'The Security Service, The Communist Party of Great Britain and British Fascism', pp. 35–6. The great majority of the men working in intelligence, politics and the Civil Service came from similar social backgrounds, had been brought up with similar values, and often attended the same schools. They would have shared comparable views on communism, and who was likely to be a communist, and did not question the stereotypes. See, Madeira, *Britannia and the Bear*, pp. 17–18.
142. Andrew, *Defence of the Realm*, p. 153.
143. Ibid., p. 157.
144. Andrew, *Defence of the Realm*, pp. 157–8; Wilson and Adams, *Special Branch*, pp. 152–3; Callaghan and Phythian, 'State surveillance and Communist lives', p. 137.
145. Callaghan and Phythian, 'State surveillance and communist lives', p. 138.
146. See, Purvis and Hulbert, *When Reporters Cross the Line*, pp. 50–1; Andrew, *Defence of the Realm*, pp. 158–9; Davenport-Hines, *Enemies Within*, pp. 109–11.
147. See, TNA, KV 4/126.
148. Glading received numerous secret documents from contacts at the Woolwich Arsenal and photographed them before passing them on to his Soviet handlers. See, Andrew, *Defence of the Realm*, pp. 179–85.
149. Luff, 'Covert and Overt Operations', p. 749.
150. TNA, CAB 24/118/54; TNA, CAB 24/131/9; TNA, CAB 24/131/62.
151. TNA, CAB 24/131/9.
152. Madeira, *Britannia and the Bear*, p. 97.

153. Penrose and Freeman, *Conspiracy of Silence*, pp. 112–13; Beckett, *Enemy Within*, pp. 83–9; Quinlan, *Secret War*, pp. 88, 105–6.
154. Hemming, *M*, p. 313.
155. Andrew, *Secret Service*, p. 338.
156. Macintyre, *A Spy Among Friends*, p. 86.
157. Ibid., p. 141.
158. Lownie, *Stalin's Englishman*, p. 90.
159. Trevor-Roper, *The Philby Affair*, p. 69.
160. Madeira, *Britannia and the Bear*, p. 9.
161. Carlton, *Churchill and the Soviet Union*, p. 35. For more on Labour-Intelligence relations see, Kassimeris and Price, "Implacable Enemies'?'.
162. TNA, CAB 24/132/86.
163. Beers, *Your Britain*, p. 59.
164. Graubard, *British Labour and the Russian Revolution*, p. 258. The death of Lenin combined with the first Labour government 'nearly overwhelmed' the *Daily Herald*, which 'had to cover both at a time when a rail strike meant it was short of paper.' Bennett, *The Zinoviev Letter*, p. 29.
165. Phillips, *Secret Twenties*, pp. 167–8. George V had previously been known to make anti-Labour comments. After accepting his offer to form a new government, MacDonald expressed concern in his diary that the King 'is apprehensive.' However, despite such concerns, ministers and sovereign developed a warm and friendly working relationship. (Rose, *King George V*, pp. 328–33).
166. Pugh, *Speak for Britain!* p. 170; Bennett, *Churchill's Man of Mystery*, p. 80.
167. Phillips, *Secret Twenties*, pp. 166–7.
168. Bennett, *Churchill's Man of Mystery*, p. 79.
169. Kent, *Aftershocks*, p. 127; Pugh, *Speak for Britain!*, p. 172.
170. TNA, CAB 24/96/62, p. 18.
171. MacFarlane, *The British Communist Party*, pp. 277–9; Worley, *Labour inside the Gate*, p. 103; TNA, CAB 24/140/2.
172. Beckett, *Enemy Within*, pp. 22–3. The Party's manifesto for the 1922 General Election specifically sought to differentiate itself from communism. See, Graubard, *British Labour and the Russian Revolution*, p. 246.
173. Worley, *Labour inside the Gate*, pp. 103–4.
174. Jones, *The Russia Complex*, p. 4; Pugh, *Speak for Britain!*, pp. 132–3; Worley, *Labour inside the Gate*, pp. 104–5; White, 'British Labour in Soviet Russia', p. 634, pp. 638–40.
175. Thorpe, 'The Only Effective Bulwark', pp. 12–13.
176. Howell, *MacDonald's Party*, p. 226, pp. 382–3.
177. Reynolds, *The Long Shadow*, p. 61.
178. Pugh, *Speak for Britain!* p. 130.
179. Anderson, *Fascists, Communists and the National Government*, p. 32.
180. Andrew, *Secret Service*, p. 298.

181. TNA, HO 45/10741/263275, DPP to Under Secretary of State, 11 September 1914.
182. Andrew, *Defence of the Realm*, p. 146.
183. TNA, CAB 24/81/63; TNA, CAB 24/83/71.
184. Marquand, *Ramsay MacDonald*, p. 256.
185. TNA, CAB 24/87/37.
186. TNA, CAB 24/93/26.
187. 'The "Yard's" Secret Report on Ex-Premier', *John Blunt*, September 29, 1928, p. 6 (Cutting included in TNA, HO 144/20985).
188. Similar to the report in, TNA, CAB 24/80/68.
189. TNA, HO 144/20985, 1 October 1928, 4.10.28.
190. See, TNA, HO 45/10814/312987.
191. See, TNA, HO 144/1459/316786.
192. Jeffery, *MI6*, p. 215.
193. Andrew, *Secret Service*, p. 300; Porter, *Plots and Paranoia*, p. 159.
194. TNA, PRO 30/69/221, Gower to Childs, 30 January 1924; Childs to Gower, 2 February 1924.
195. Northedge and Wells, *Britain and Soviet Communism*, p. 38; Andrew, *Defence of the Realm*, pp. 146–7. Prior to becoming Prime Minister, MacDonald said that recognition of the Bolsheviks 'in no way meant that our Labour movement agreed with the Soviet government.' Whilst his government recognised the Bolsheviks, it declined to swap ambassadors with the Soviets.
196. Perkins, *A Very British Strike*, pp. 45–6; Davenport-Hines, *Enemies Within*, pp. 98–9; Udy, *Labour and the Gulag*, pp. 100–4.
197. Wish, 'Anglo-Soviet Relations', p. 400.
198. Marquand, *Ramsay MacDonald*, pp. 312–14; Perkins, *A Very British Strike*, pp. 39–40; Northedge and Wells, *Britain and Soviet Communism*, pp. 38–9; Rose, *King George V*, pp. 331–3.
199. Jeffery, *MI6*, p. 215; Andrew, *Defence of the Realm*, p. 147; Aldrich and Cormac, *The Black Door*, p. 47; Andrew, *Secret Service*, p. 300; Jones, *Whitehall Diary: Volume I*, p. 270, 1 February 1924, p. 274, 20 March 1924.
200. See, Andrew, *Secret World*, pp. 580–2.
201. See, for example, TNA PRO 30/69/220, Report No. 253, 1 May 1924.
202. Andrew, *Defence of the Realm*, p. 147.
203. Desmarais, 'Strikebreaking and the Labour Government of 1924', pp. 169–70; Marquand, *Ramsay MacDonald*, pp. 318–19; Morgan, *Conflict and Order*, p. 114.
204. Andrew, *Defence of the Realm*, pp. 147–8.
205. Phillips, *Secret Twenties*, pp. 182–6; Jeffery, *MI6*, p. 217.
206. Andrew, *Secret World*, p. 581.
207. Ibid., p. 582; Bennett, *The Zinoviev Letter*, p. 78.
208. Andrew, *Defence of the Realm*, p. 900, footnote 58; Pugh, *Speak for Britain!* p. 183; Madeira, *Britannia and the Bear*, p. 127.

209. Bennett, 'A most extraordinary and mysterious business', pp. 87–8, pp. 91–2.
210. Andrew, *Defence of the Realm*, p. 149–50. A similar point is made by Keith Jeffery in the authorised history of MI6. See, Jeffery, *MI6*, p. 216.
211. Bennett, 'A most extraordinary and mysterious business', pp. 45–6.
212. Andrew, *Defence of the Realm*, p. 150.
213. Wring, *The Politics of Marketing the Labour Party*, p. 20.
214. Ferris and Bar-Joseph, 'Getting Marlowe to Hold His Tongue', pp. 126–8.
215. Andrew, *Secret World*, p. 581.
216. Jeffery, *MI6*, p. 221.
217. Andrew, *Defence of the Realm*, pp. 158–9. MI5 believed that the decision not to prosecute the two Special Branch officers found to be providing intelligence to a Soviet espionage ring in 1928 was based on political reasons.
218. TNA, HO 532/10, PM's Secret Service Committee, 11 March 1927.
219. TNA, HO 144/20985, minute dated 27 September 1928.
220. TNA, CAB 24/97/46.
221. Davenport-Hines, *Enemies Within*, p. 56.
222. Morgan, *Conflict and Order*, pp. 117–18; Kent, *Aftershocks*, p. 121, pp. 129–34.
223. Rose, *King George V*, p. 340.
224. Renshaw, *The General Strike*, pp. 193–4; Perkins, *A Very British Strike*, pp. 145–56.
225. Andrew, *Secret Service*, pp. 321–2.
226. Jeffery and Hennessy, *States of Emergency*, p. 108.
227. Andrew, *Defence of the Realm*, p. 125.
228. TNA, KV 4/246, Appendix 1, Emergency Home Defence, 3. General Duties.
229. TNA, KV 4/246, P Report No. 6, 10 May 1926.
230. TNA, KV 4/246, P Report No. 7.
231. TNA, KV 4/246, P Report No. 1, 3 May 1926.
232. TNA, KV 4/246, P Report No. 2, 6 May 1926.
233. Perkins, *A Very British Strike*, pp. 263–4; McLynn, *The Road Not Taken*, p. 356, pp. 399–400; Taylor, 'Citrine's Unexpurgated Diaries' pp. 88–9.
234. Perkins, *A Very British Strike*, p. 112; Farman, *The General Strike*, pp. 192–3; Taylor, 'Citrine's Unexpurgated Diaries', p. 69, pp. 82–3.
235. Quinlan, *Secret War*, pp. 49–50.
236. Jeffery, *MI6*, p. 227.
237. Childs, *Episodes and Reflections*, p. 214.
238. Phillips, *Secret Twenties*, pp. 258–60; Quinlan, *Secret War*, pp. 52–3.
239. TNA, CAB 24/180/36.
240. Andrew, *Secret Service*, pp. 322–3.
241. See, Flory, 'The Arcos Raid'.
242. Supposedly a separate entity from the government, the OMS merged with the government strikebreaking organisation as soon as the strike began. (Renshaw, *The General Strike*, p. 131).
243. Perkins, *A Very British Strike*, pp. 70–2; Quinlan, *Secret War*, pp. 43–4.

244. Maguire, "The Fascists...are...to be depended upon.", p. 8.
245. TNA, CAB 23/51/1.
246. TNA, CAB 23/52/19.
247. Maguire, "The Fascists...are...to be depended upon.", pp. 7–8, p. 19.

2. FRIEND OR FOE?

1. TNA, HO 144/4775, Stamfordham to Boyd, 27 November 1923.
2. TNA, HO 144/4775, Boyd to Stamfordham, 26 November 1923.
3. TNA, HO 144/4775, Special Branch Report, British Fascisti, 14 December 1923. The report stated that the BF 'intend to stamp out the Crown on their Badge and Stationery'.
4. Linehan, *British Fascism*, p. 61; Cross, *The Fascists,* p. 58.
5. Griffiths, *Fellow Travellers*, p. 87.
6. Linehan, *British Fascism*, pp. 154–8; Hemming, *M*, pp. 24–5.
7. Thurlow, *Fascism in Britain*, p. 52. For details on the difficulty of getting a definitive figure for the BF membership see, Linehan, *British Fascism*, pp. 152–4.
8. TNA, MEPO 2/2040, minute 3, 4 April 1928; TNA, HO 144/4775 Special Branch Report, British Fascisti, 12 December 1923.
9. Copsey, *Anti-Fascism in Britain*, p. 3; Hemming, *M*, p. 25.
10. Copsey, *Anti-Fascism in Britain*, p. 3; Pugh, *Hurrah for the Blackshirts!* p. 51.
11. TNA, FO 371/11384/C9108, CJ Rowling, 18 August 1926.
12. TNA, HO 144/4775/451285/1, British Fascisti Movement 13 September 1923.
13. TNA, CAB 24/162/15; TNA, CAB 24/162/69; TNA, CAB 24/162/49.
14. TNA, KV 3/57, minute 5, V.G.W. Kell, 30 October 1923.
15. TNA, KV 3/57, Kell to Clarke, 8 January 1924.
16. TNA, KV 3/57, serial 35a, HOW on the British Fascists, 1 March 1924.
17. TNA, KV 3/57, serial 49a, 'Report No. 10'; serial 50a, 'BRITISH FASCISTS'.
18. TNA, KV 3/57, 'British Fascisti Movement' 14 September 1923.
19. TNA, KV 3/57, Report on "The British Fascists" 23 November 1924, p. 3.
20. TNA, KV 3/57, 'British Fascisti Movement' 14 September 1923.
21. TNA, KV 3/57, document 'E', 'CONFIDENTIAL, 5 November 1924.
22. TNA, KV 3/57, Report on "The British Fascists" 23 November 1924, p. 5.
23. Ibid., p. 4.
24. Ibid., p. 6.
25. Hemming, *M*, p. 47.
26. TNA, HO 144/4775, Raid on Communist Offices in Glasgow, 10 June 1925; Hemming, *M*, p. 47.
27. The National Fascisti broke away from the BF in 1924. Some information was collected on the organisation by the authorities, see, TNA, KV 3/121, but it is likely that it was too small to justify regular surveillance.

28. Copsey, *Anti-Fascism*, pp. 6–7; Perkins, *A Very British Strike*, p. 61; Benewick, *Political Surveillance*, p. 38.
29. Anderson, *Fascists, Communists and the National Government*, pp. 33–4; Mowat, *Britain Between the Wars*, pp. 296–7; Noel, *The Great Lock-Out*, p. 76.
30. HC Hansard Deb, 17 November 1925, vol 188 cc190–91.
31. Benewick, *Political Violence*, p. 38.
32. Wilson and Adams, *Special Branch*, p. 168; Hope, 'Fascism, the Security Service and the Curious Careers', p. 2.
33. TNA, CAB 24/97/46.
34. Benewick, *Political Violence*, p. 39; Hope, 'Fascism and the State in Britain', pp. 37–5; Hope, 'British Fascism and the State 1917–1927', p. 80; Hope, 'Surveillance or Collusion?', p. 658.
35. Andrew, *Defence of the Realm*, pp. 122–3.
36. Hemming, *M*, p. 50; Bennett, *Churchill's Man of Mystery*, pp. 71–2.
37. Andrew, *Defence of the Realm*, pp. 123–4.
38. Hemming, *M*, p. 28.
39. Ibid., p. 60.
40. Hope, 'Surveillance or Collusion?', p. 653.
41. Hemming, *M*, p. 40.
42. Ibid., pp. 50–1. For more detail on the Makgill-Morton relationship see, Jeffery, *MI6*, p. 215; Bennett, *Churchill's Man of Mystery*, pp. 72–9.
43. Hemming, *M*, p. 53; Andrew, *Defence of the Realm*, p. 125.
44. Hope, 'Surveillance or Collusion?', pp. 652–3.
45. Hemming, *M*, pp. 67–70.
46. Ibid., pp. 117–18.
47. Hemming, *M*, p. 47; Thurlow, 'Passive and Active Anti-Fascism', p. 165; Bean, 'Liverpool Shipping Employers', p. 22; Hope, 'Fascism, the Security Service and the Curious Careers', pp. 3–4.
48. Bean, 'Liverpool Shipping Employers', pp. 22–4.
49. Hope, 'Fascism, the Security Service and the Curious Careers', p. 3.
50. TNA, KV 2/997, serial 39a, 'McGUIRK HUGHES', 16 February 1926, A.W.G.T.
51. TNA, KV 2/997, 'James McGuirk HUGHES', December 1925.
52. Hope, 'Surveillance or Collusion?', p. 660.
53. Hollingsworth and Tremayne, *The Economic League*, pp. 1–2, pp. 5–7.
54. Jeffreys-Jones, *We Know All About You*, pp. 66–8.
55. See, Andrew, *Secret Service*, pp. 231–2; Jeffreys-Jones, *We Know All About You*, p. 67; Porter, *Plots and Paranoia*, p. 150.
56. Hope, 'Surveillance or Collusion', p. 662.
57. McIvor, 'A Crusade for Capitalism', pp. 634–5.
58. McIvor, 'Essay in Anti-Labour History', pp. 19–22.
59. Miller, 'Extraordinary Gentlemen', p. 127.

60. Hollingsworth and Tremayne, *The Economic League*, pp. 8–9; Hughes, *Spies at Work*, pp. 50–8.
61. Hemming, *M*, p. 8, p. 20.
62. TNA, KV 3/57, serial 45a, serial 46a; TNA, KV 3/57, EXTRACT Relating to: Enquiry by Mr FM Lowe regarding advisability of pensioners joining the British Fascisti, J Baker White to FM Lowe, 5 October 1923.
63. Hughes, *Spies at Work*, p. 125; Hope, 'Fascism and the State in Britain', p. 373; Linehan, *British Fascism*, pp. 45–9; Benewick, *Political Violence*, p. 41.
64. See, Hughes, *Spies at Work*, p. 124–5.
65. Hemming, *M*, p. 90.
66. See documents included in, TNA, HO 45/25475.
67. Taylor, *British Propaganda in the Twentieth Century*, p. 133, p. 148, footnote 90; Hollingsworth and Tremayne, *The Economic League*, pp. 8–10.
68. Hope, 'Fascism and the State in Britain', p. 371; Hope, 'Surveillance or Collusion?', pp. 668–70.
69. Brown, 'The Anti-Socialist Union', p. 255.
70. Farr, *The Development and Impact of Right-Wing Politics in Britain*, p. 56; Thomas, 'Confronting the Challenge of Socialism', p. 157.
71. TNA, KV 3/57, serial 51a, 'Major Phillips', 30 March 1925.
72. Pugh, *Hurrah for the Blackshirts!* p. 62; Woodbridge, 'Fraudulent Fascism', p. 496.
73. Thomas, 'Confronting the Challenge of Socialism', p. 141; Cross, *The Fascists*, pp. 58–9; Farr, *The Development and Impact of Right-Wing Politics in Britain*, p. 43; Pugh, *Hurrah for the Blackshirts!* p. 60.
74. Linehan, *British Fascism*, pp. 63–5; Benewick, *Political Violence*, p. 28; Thurlow, *Fascism in Britain*, pp. 51–2; Griffiths, *Fellow Travellers*, pp. 85–7; Cross, *The Fascists*, p. 58; Farr, *The Development and Impact of Right-Wing Politics in Britain*, p. 60; Dorril, *Blackshirt*, p. 196; Wilson and Adams, *Special Branch*, p. 171.
75. TNA, KV 4/331, minute 9.
76. Baker, 'The Extreme Right in the 1920s', p. 21; Thurlow, *Fascism in Britain*, p. 53; TNA, KV 3/57, serial 3a.
77. TNA, KV 3/59, serial 244a.
78. Linehan, *British Fascism*, p. 65.
79. Griffiths, *Fellow Travellers*, pp. 14–15.
80. Farr, *The Development and Impact of Right-Wing Politics in Britain*, p. 60.
81. Baker, 'The Extreme Right in the 1920s', p. 21.
82. TNA, HO 144/4775, Birmingham City Police, British Fascisti Meeting, 8 May 1925; Rafter, Birmingham Chief Constable to The Commissioner, Special Branch, 8 May 1925; Childs to the Home Secretary, 11 May 1925; Childs, *Episodes and Reflections*, p. 215.
83. Childs, *Episodes and Reflections*, p. 223.
84. Ibid., p. 216.

85. TNA, HO 144/4775, Raven to Scott, 30 October 1925; Scott to Anderson, 31 October 1925; Anderson to Scott, 3 November 1925.
86. TNA, KV 3/57, serial 58a. John Hope disputes that members of the forces were entirely prevented from being involved with the BF. See, Hope, 'Fascism and the State in Britain', pp. 367–8.
87. Jeffery, *MI6*, pp. 233–6. Sinclair said that 'the principal' [Knight] had not been involved in the BF for several years.
88. Stocker, 'Importing fascism' pp. 331–2; Hemming, *M*, pp. 58–9.
89. Stocker, 'Importing fascism', p. 345, footnote 49; Pugh, *Hurrah for the Blackshirts!*, pp. 110–15. The BF eventually disbanded in 1935.
90. Woodbridge, 'Fraudulent Fascism', pp. 496–8. Mosley would also routinely attack Baldwin's Conservative government as 'fascists.'
91. Farr, *The Development and Impact of Right-Wing Politics in Britain*, p. 82.
92. Cross, *The Fascists*, pp. 32–3.
93. Ibid., p. 68, pp. 72–3.
94. Curry, *Security Service*, p. 109.
95. Davenport-Hines, *EnemiesWithin*, p. 58.
96. Foley would be posthumously recognised for his work during the Second World War in helping Jews to escape from Nazi Germany by 'bending the rules' when issuing visas. He is said to have helped more than 10,000 people to flee. A statue of him in Mary Stevens Park, Stourbridge, was unveiled by Prince William in September 2018. For more see, Smith, *Foley: The Spy Who Saved 10,000 Jews*.
97. Brinson and Dove, *A matter of intelligence*, pp. 16–18; Andrew, *Defence of the Realm*, p. 189; Saunders, 'Stuck on the Flypaper', p. 3.
98. Andrew, *Defence of the Realm*, p. 190.
99. TNA, KV 4/111, 'The Liquidation of Communism, Left Wing Socialism & Pacifism in Germany' (Visit to Berlin 30 March 1933–9 April 1933), p. 17.
100. TNA, KV 4/140, serial 1x.
101. TNA, KV 3/58, serial 184a.
102. Ibid.
103. TNA, KV 3/58, serial 171a, pp. 2–3.
104. Ibid. pp. 14–15.
105. TNA, KV 4/331, serial 1z, p. 7.
106. Ibid., p. 9.
107. TNA, KV 3/58, serial 171a, p. 14.
108. TNA, HO 45/25384, Trenchard to Newsam, 21 July 1933.
109. Thurlow, 'The Failure of British Fascism', p. 70; Stevenson, 'Conservatism and the failure of fascism', p. 264.
110. Curry, *The Security Service*, p. 115.
111. Andrew, *Defence of the Realm*, p. 192; Grant, 'The Role of MI5 in the Internment of British Fascists', pp. 504–6.

112. TNA, HO 45/25384, document 114a; TNA, MEPO 2/10646, document 13a, document 15b, document 26a.
113. Cross, *The Fascists in Britain*, p. 79; TNA, MEPO 2/10646, document 45a, 19 December 1933.
114. Lewis, *Illusions of Grandeur*, pp. 160–3; Ewing and Gearty, *Struggle for Civil Liberties*, p. 329; Stevenson, 'The BUF, The Metropolitan Police and public order', p. 137.
115. The anti-fascist movement was often viewed by SB as a communist front. See, Lewis, *Illusions of Grandeur*, pp. 123–4; Thurlow, *Secret State*, p. 191.
116. Lewis, *Illusions of Grandeur*, p. 162.
117. Clark, *The National Council of Civil Liberties*, p. 84.
118. Lewis, *Illusions of Grandeur*, p. 115.
119. Lewis, *Illusions of Grandeur*, p. 121; Copsey, *Anti-Fascism*, p. 20.
120. Clark, *The National Council of Civil Liberties*, pp. 58–60; Dorril, *Blackshirt*, pp. 296–8; Lewis, *Illusions of Grandeur*, pp. 164–5; Ewing and Gearty, *The Struggle for Civil Liberties*, pp. 284–6.
121. TNA, MEPO 3/2490, document 1a.
122. TNA, MEPO 2/4319, minute 9.
123. TNA, MEPO 2/10977, document 27, 'Anti-Fascist Demonstration, Olympia', 9 June 1934; Ewing and Gearty, *The Struggle for Civil Liberties*, pp. 284–7; Morgan, *Conflict and Order*, pp. 260–1; Lewis, *Illusions of Grandeur*, p. 165.
124. Morgan, *Conflict and Order*, p. 260.
125. TNA, KV 3/58, serial 176a, pp. 6–7.
126. TNA, HO 45/25383, Anti-fascist Demonstrations, 593–597, 7 September 1934.
127. TNA, MEPO 2/10977, document 10a.
128. TNA, MEPO 2/10977, document 21a.
129. Lawrence, 'Fascist violence and the politics of public order', pp. 255–6; Hope, 'Blackshirts, Knuckle-Dusters and Lawyers', pp. 41–58.
130. TNA, MEPO 2/10978, document 15a, document 17a.
131. TNA, MEPO 2/10978, document 8g; TNA, MEPO/4319, document 13c.
132. See, for example, TNA, MEPO 2/10646, document 46a; TNA, HO 144/19845, Hunger Marchers—Contemplated Attacks on members of the BUF, 21 February 1934.
133. Newsinger, 'Blackshirts, Blueshirts and the Spanish Civil War', p. 835.
134. TNA, MEPO 2/10977, document 22a.
135. Trenchard was often wrongly seen as a friend of the fascists. See, Clark, *The National Council of Civil Liberties*, p. 71; Thurlow, *Secret State*, p. 188.
136. TNA, CAB 24/250/14, ANNEX.
137. TNA, CAB 24/249/31.
138. TNA, CAB 24/250/14.
139. TNA, MEPO 3/2490, document 11a.

140. Thurlow, *Secret State*, pp. 186–8; Thurlow, *Fascism in Britain*, p. 113; Pugh, *Hurrah for the Blackshirts!* p. 154.
141. Pugh, *Hurrah for the Blackshirts!* pp. 58–9.
142. Thurlow, *Secret State*, p. 181.
143. Cross, *The Fascists*, pp. 99–100; Dorril, *Blackshirt*, p. 289.
144. Pugh, *Hurrah for the Blackshirts!* p. 148; Dorril, *Blackshirt*, p. 289; Lewis, *Illusions of Grandeur*, p. 146.
145. Coleman, 'The Conservative Party and the Frustrations of the Extreme Right', p. 65.
146. Pugh, *Hurrah for the Blackshirts!* p. 149.
147. Benewick, *Political Violence*, p. 108; TNA, KV 3/58, serial 171a, p. 4.
148. There has been significant debate about the degree to which Olympia was responsible for Rothermere's removal of support for the BUF. Even after the formal withdrawal of support, Rothermere continued to meet Mosley socially. See, Lawrence, 'Fascist violence and the politics of public order' pp. 248–9; Pugh, *Hurrah for the Blackshirts!* pp. 168–9; Dorril, *Blackshirt*, pp. 307–8; Cross, *The Fascists*, pp. 116–17; Copsey, *Anti-Fascism*, pp. 20–1; Dack, 'It certainly isn't cricket!', p. 149.
149. TNA, KV 4/241, 'The British Union of Fascists', p. 5.
150. TNA, KV 3/58, serial 185a, p. 10–11.
151. TNA, KV 3/59, serial 195a, p. 5.
152. TNA, KV 3/59, serial 207, Report No. VI, p. 2.
153. See, TNA, HO 45/25384, Folder entitled 'British Union of Fascists, Report by MI5'. The authorities did not have definitive proof that the BUF was receiving money from foreign sources until 1940. (Thurlow, 'Passive and Active Anti-Fascism', p. 169).
154. Andrew, *Defence of the Realm*, p. 193.
155. Clark, *The National Council of Civil Liberties*, p. 107.
156. Andrew, *Defence of the Realm*, p. 194.
157. Cross, *The Fascists*, pp. 159–61; Thurlow, *Fascism in Britain*, pp. 109–11; Clark, *The National Council of Civil Liberties*, pp. 117–20; Dorril, *Blackshirt*, pp. 390–2; Copsey, *Anti-Fascism*, pp. 51–5.
158. Thurlow, *Fascism in Britain*, p. 111.
159. TNA, MEPO 3/2490, document 21a; TNA, CAB 24/264/36.
160. TNA, CAB 24/265/2.
161. Channing, *The Police and the Expansion of Public Order Law*, pp. 87–8; Clark, *The National Council for Civil Liberties*, pp. 122–5.
162. Pugh, *Hurrah for the Blackshirts!* p. 175; Ewing and Gearty, *The Struggle for Civil Liberties*, pp. 311–19; Channing, *The Police and the Expansion of Public Order Law in Britain*, pp. 85–9.
163. Dorril, *Blackshirt*, p. 408.
164. Thurlow, 'State Management of the British Union of Fascists', p. 35.

165. TNA, CAB 24/259/29; TNA, CAB 23/83/6; TNA, CAB 23/83/8; Thurlow, 'State Management of the British Union of Fascists', p. 34.
166. TNA, KV 3/59, serial 239a, p. 6.
167. Ibid., p. 9.
168. Andrew, *Defence of the Realm*, p. 194.
169. Curry, *Security Service*, p. 139; TNA, CAB 24/263/36.
170. Andrew, *Defence of the Realm*, p. 197; Curry, *Security Service*, p. 109.
171. Benewick, *Political Violence*, p. 94; TNA, KV 3/58, serial 171a, pp. 7–8.
172. Pugh, *Hurrah for the Blackshirts!* p. 146; TNA, MEPO 2/10646, document 75d.
173. See, TNA, KV 3/58, serial 176a, pp. 5–6; TNA, KV 3/58, serial 185a, pp. 4–6.
174. Pugh, *Hurrah for the Blackshirts!* p. 147.
175. TNA, KV 5/3, serial 1a.
176. TNA, KV 5/3, serial 69a. It also received money from companies such as Unilever Ltd and Dunlop Rubber.
177. Griffiths, *Fellow Travellers*, p. 184; Pugh, *Hurrah for the Blackshirts!* pp. 270–1.
178. TNA, KV 5/3, serial 69a. Temple, also known as William Ashley MP, was at one stage Chairman of the ASU. (Linehan, *British Fascism*, p. 46).
179. TNA, KV 5/3, serial 66a.
180. TNA, KV 5/3, serial 111a.
181. 'Exchange of Students with Germany', *The Times*, 17 March 1938.
182. TNA, KV 5/9, serial 171b.
183. Curry, *Security Service*, p. 123.
184. TNA, KV 5/8, serial 106a.
185. TNA, KV 5/8, serial 85a.
186. TNA, KV 5/8, serial 99a.
187. TNA, KV 5/7, serial 36a.
188. TNA, KV 5/87, serial 180k.
189. Ibid.
190. TNA, KV 2/3576, serial 12, serial 44a.
191. TNA, KV 5/3, serial 111a.
192. TNA, KV 5/2, serial 42x.
193. TNA, KV 5/2, reports on meeting seen in serial 11a; serial 93x; Hemming, *M*, p. 225.
194. TNA, HO 45/25390, Kell to Chief Constables, July 1939.
195. TNA, KV 5/2, serial 72a, letter to H.M.G. Jebb, 25 March 1939.
196. TNA, HO 144/21231, British Non-Sectarian Anti-Nazi Council.
197. TNA, HO 144/21231, Display of Anti-Nazi posters criticising Herr Hitler.
198. TNA, HO 144/21231, Display of Anti-Nazi posters criticising Herr Hitler, SB report, 21 Feb 1936.
199. TNA, HO 144/21231, Libellous attacks on prominent foreigners, Memorandum III, 'Press criticism upon prominent individuals in foreign countries'.

200. See, TNA, HO 144/21231, Folder 677509, 'German Minority Groups—co-ordination of outside Germany', letter to Newsam 4 March 1937.
201. Brinson and Dove, *A Matter of Intelligence*, pp. 115–25; Munzer, 'The Surveillance of Friends', pp. 137–8.
202. Brinson and Dove, *A Matter of Intelligence*, pp. 142–5; Munzer, 'The Surveillance of Friends', pp. 135–7.
203. See, TNA, HO 45/25518.
204. Dorril, *Blackshirt*, pp. 421–2.
205. Hope, 'Fascism, the Security Service and the Curious Careers', p. 4.
206. Ibid.
207. TNA, KV 2/994, minute 323.
208. TNA, KV 2/993, minute 259; TNA, KV 2/994, serial 400a.
209. TNA, KV 2/994, serial 422a.
210. TNA, HO 283/54, Advisory Committee to consider appeals against grades of Internment, John Charles Preen, 4 November 1941; TNA, HO 283/54, 'John Charles PREEN', 25 October 1941; Hope, 'Fascism, the Security Service and the Curious Careers', p. 4.
211. Hope, 'Fascism, the Security Service and the Curious Careers', p. 4.
212. Davenport-Hines, *Enemies Within*, p. 293, pp. 297–8.
213. Curry, *Security Service*, p. 148.
214. TNA, KV 4/140, serial 15a(2); Twigge, Hampshire and Macklin, *British Intelligence Secrets*, p. 45; Andrew, *Defence of the Realm*, p. 223–4.
215. TNA, CAB 65/7/28; Simpson, *In the Highest Degree Odious*, p. 113; Andrew, *Defence of the Realm*, pp. 226–7.
216. Goldman, 'Defence Regulation 18B', p. 134.
217. Twigge, Hampshire and Macklin, *British Intelligence Secrets*, p. 45.
218. Tate, *Hitler's British Traitors*, p. 311.
219. Others, including 'enemy aliens' were also interned. Aristocratic fascists, however, often were not. See, Cotter, 'Emergency Detention in Wartime', p. 258; Aldrich and Cormac, *The Black Door*, p. 99, pp. 106–7; Pugh, *Hurrah for the Blackshirts!* pp. 306–7; Beckett, *Fascist in the Family*, p. 267.
220. TNA, HO 45/23801, memo dated 28 May 1941.
221. TNA, HO 45/23801, 'Arthur DONALDSON—Lugton, Ayrshire'. For more on Scottish nationalism and Nazism see, Bowd, *Fascist Scotland*, particularly pp. 163–74.
222. Simpson, *In the Highest Degree Odious*, pp. 196–7; Thurlow, "A very clever capitalist class", pp. 9–12. The communist *Daily Worker* was banned, however.
223. TNA, KV 4/267, minute 119.
224. Grant, 'The Role of MI5 in the Internment of British Fascists', p. 501.
225. Simpson, *In the Highest Degree Odious*, p. 167; Dorril, *Blackshirt*, p. 519; Pugh, *Hurrah for the Blackshirts!* pp. 302–3; Thurlow, 'Passive and Active Anti-Fascism', p. 171.

226. Tate, *Hitler's British Traitors*, p. 353. For more on Roberts see, Hutton, *Agent Jack*.
227. Davenport-Hines, *EnemiesWithin*, p. 300.
228. Rothwell, *Britain and the Cold War*, pp. 114–23; Aldrich, *Hidden Hand*, pp. 43–63; Dorril, *MI6*, pp. 13–14; Folly, *Churchill,Whitehall and the Soviet Union*, p. 158; Greenwood, *Britain and the ColdWar*, pp. 11–12.
229. Aldrich, *Hidden Hand*, p. 43.
230. Rothwell, *Britain and the ColdWar*, pp. 119–20.
231. TNA, KV 4/331, serial 1a.
232. TNA, KV 4/331, minute 7, minute 21.
233. TNA, KV 4/331, minute 16.
234. Simpson, *In the Highest Degree Odious*, p. 408; Beckett, *Fascist in the Family*, p. 304.
235. TNA, KV 4/267, minute 176.
236. Rothwell, *Britain and the ColdWar*, p. 131; Folly, *Churchill,Whitehall and the Soviet Union*, pp. 143–4; Greenwood, *Britain and the ColdWar*, pp. 9–10; Dorril, *MI6*, p. 25; Aldrich, *Hidden Hand*, pp. 57–8.
237. Andrew, *Defence of the Realm*, p. 339.
238. Aldrich, 'Secret intelligence for a post-war world', p. 31.
239. Correra, *MI6*, p. 28; Aldrich and Cormac, *The Black Door*, pp. 137–8.
240. Bower, *The Perfect English Spy*, p. 78; Hennessey and Thomas, *Spooks: 1945-2009*, p. 55, p. 71.
241. Walton, 'British Intelligence and Threats to British National Security', p. 141; Andrew, *Defence of the Realm*, p. 350. As late as 1947 Britain's lack of knowledge on the Soviet Union was still being remarked upon. See, Dylan, *Defence Intelligence and the ColdWar*, p. 41.
242. Dorril, *MI6*, p. 18.

3. A 'RELIGIOUS DOGMA'

1. Macintyre, *A Spy Amongst Friends*, pp. 95–101; Andrew, *Defence of the Realm*, pp. 342–3; TNA, KV 4/466, 5 October 1945; Davenport-Hines, *Enemies Within*, pp. 371–2.
2. Kerbaj, *Secret History of the Five Eyes*, pp. 65–71; TNA, KV 4/466, 17 September 1945.
3. TNA, KV 4/466, 11 September 1945; Andrew, *Defence of the Realm*, pp. 340–1.
4. Davenport-Hines, *EnemiesWithin*, pp. 338–9.
5. Some observers have argued that Gouzenko's defection was the incident that started the Cold War. See, Davenport-Hines, *EnemiesWithin*, p. 331, pp. 338–9.
6. TNA, CAB 79/52/6, J.I.C.(46)70(O)(FINAL), 23 September 1946, 'The Spread of Communism throughout the world and the extent of its direction

from Moscow.', conclusion (j) and conclusion (l). For more detail on the JIC, its role and responsibilities see, Hennessy, *Secret State*, pp. 4–5; Walton, *Empire of Secrets*, p. xxvii.
7. TNA, CAB 130/20/GEN183, GEN 183/1, 'The Employment of Civil Servants, Etc. exposed to Communist Influence', 29 May 1947, paragraph 5; Hennessy, *Secret State*, pp. 88–90. The Working Party was set up to serve the Committee on Subversive Activities.
8. TNA, KV 4/253, serial 107a; TNA, KV 4/267, minute 119. In 1943 these suspicions were vindicated with the conviction of CPGB national organiser, Douglas Springhall, under the Official Secrets Act. Springhall had been in contact with a number of people who were engaged in secret work and obtained secret information from some, passing it to the Soviets. MI5 later concluded that the Communist Party abandoned much of its undercover work after Springhall's conviction. (TNA, KV 4/251, serial 39a).
9. TNA, KV 4/467, 28 June 1946, 2 July 1946.
10. Aldrich and Cormac, *The Black Door*, p. 141; Porter, *Plots and Paranoia*, p. 188.
11. TNA, CAB 301/31, Stewart Report, paragraph 1.
12. TNA, CAB 301/31, Stewart Report, paragraph 37; TNA, KV 4/467, 2 July 1946. MI5 justified keeping these files as Bennett's husband was an SOE officer and she had been said to have 'talked indiscreetly' about his job, whilst Martel had been in contact with General Fuller, a fascist.
13. TNA, CAB 301/31, Stewart Report, paragraph 42.
14. Ibid., conclusion (ii).
15. Lomas, '…the Defence of the Realm and Nothing Else', p. 809.
16. TNA, KV 4/267, minute 204.
17. TNA, CAB 130/16/GEN164, meeting, 6 January 1947; TNA, KV 4/469, 13 November 1947; TNA, KV 4/470, 27 January 1948.
18. TNA, KV 4/470, 24 March 1948. Several months later however, the Home Secretary turned down MI5 requests for a HOW to investigate the District Party Committees of the CPGB as he 'did not want any general prying into the affairs of the Communist Party'. (TNA, KV 4/470, 21 December 1948).
19. TNA, HO 45/25577, Sillitoe to Chief Constables, 29 October 1948.
20. TNA, KV 4/474, 24 November 1952; TNA, CAB 134/737, 4th Meeting, 20 October 1952.
21. See, TNA, KV 2/2033, serial 101a, serial 109a, serial 199a, serial 281a.
22. Winter, *Inside BOSS*, pp. 419–20.
23. See, TNA, KV 4/472, 8 September 1950; TNA, KV 4/162, serial 95b.
24. Aldrich, *GCHQ*, pp. 183–4; TNA, KV 4/162, serial 95b, p. 6; TNA, KV 4/473, 1 May 1951.
25. TNA, CAB 21/4014, 'With the compliments of Sir Percy Sillitoe', 6 April 1950.
26. Hemming, *M*, p. 318.
27. Andrew, *Defence of the Realm*, pp. 402–3.

28. Ibid., p. 400.
29. TNA, KV 4/471, 27 May 1949.
30. Sisman, *John Le Carré*, pp. 202–3; Hennessy, *Secret State*, p. 106.
31. Obituary, 'Julia Pirie', *The Telegraph*, 28 October 2008. Accessed 29/10/25 at: https://www.telegraph.co.uk/news/obituaries/3275532/Julia-Pirie.html
32. Ibid.; Andrew, *Defence of the Realm*, pp. 400–1; Hennessy, *Secret State*, p. 106; Wright, *Spycatcher*, pp. 40–1, pp. 54–6. The former MI5 officer Peter Wright stated that the Security Service had a cellar of 'literally thousands' of keys from various offices, hotels or private houses that had previously been entered during investigations.
33. Obituary, 'Julia Pirie', *The Telegraph*, 28 October 2008. Records copied during PARTY PIECE are contained in a number of PF's. See, TNA, KV 2/3983, serial 250a.
34. Obituary, 'Julia Pirie', *The Telegraph*, 28 October 2008; Wright, *Spycatcher*, pp. 56–8.
35. Wright, *Spycatcher*, p. 54.
36. Bower, *The Perfect English Spy*, p. 141.
37. Ibid., p. 145.
38. Andrew, *Defence of the Realm*, pp. 402–3.
39. TNA, KV 2/1832, serial 318abb.
40. TNA, KV 4/473, Minutes of DG meeting, 10 April 1951.
41. Andrew, *Defence of the Realm*, pp. 401–2.
42. Obituary, 'Julia Pirie', *The Telegraph*, 28 October 2008.
43. Beesley, *The Official History of Cabinet Secretaries*, p. 47.
44. Hennessy, *Secret State*, p. 23; Curry, *Security Service*, p. 357.
45. TNA, KV 4/267, 202y, p. 1.
46. TNA, CAB 134/53, Committee on Communism, 11th Meeting, 1 July 1949.
47. TNA, KV 4/245, serial 21a.
48. TNA, KV 4/245, serial 39a.
49. TNA, KV 4/245, serial 38y.
50. TNA, KV 2/4291, serial 51a. For information on who constituted a 'Category A' communist see, Andrew, *Defence of the Realm*, p. 405.
51. TNA, KV 2/4291, serial 50a.
52. TNA, KV 2/4292, serial 87a.
53. TNA, KV 2/4291, serial 81a; TNA, KV 2/4292, serial 86a.
54. TNA, KV 2/4292, serial 94a.
55. TNA, KV 2/4292, serial 97a. Although the British establishment was undoubtedly pleased to see the CPGB tearing itself apart over Khrushchev's speech and the crushing of the Hungarian uprising, it does not appear that any moves were made to take advantage of this. Both events did significant damage to the reputation of communism without the state having to intervene. See, Styles, 'British Domestic Security Policy', pp. 112–14.
56. TNA, KV 2/4293, serial 118a.

57. TNA, KV 2/4293, minute 120.
58. TNA, KV 2/4290, serial 19d; TNA, KV 2/3981, serial 126z.
59. TNA, KV 3/286, serial 599a, p. 3.
60. Hobsbawm, *Interesting Times*, p. 127; TNA, KV 2/3980, serial 2a, serial 3a.
61. Hobsbawm, *Interesting Times*, p. 155.
62. Kettle, 'MI5 cold-shoulders Hobsbawm request to see his file', *theguardian.com*, 2 March 2009. Accessed 24/10/25 at: https://www.theguardian.com/politics/2009/mar/02/eric-hobsbawm-mi5-civil-liberties
63. Hobsbawm, *Interesting Times*, pp. 155–6.
64. TNA, KV 2/3980, minute 61.
65. TNA, KV 2/3980, serial 92a.
66. TNA, KV 2/3980, minute 89; Evans, *Eric Hobsbawm*, pp. 262–8.
67. TNA, KV 2/3981, serial 152a.
68. TNA, KV 2/3981, serial 172a.
69. TNA, KV 2/3982, serial 195a.
70. TNA, KV 2/3983, serial 253a.
71. One interesting revelation from the files is that Hobsbawm had some contact with Alan Nunn May after the latter had been released from prison. MI5 do not appear to have investigated the relationship in much depth, and it was discovered through the surveillance of Nunn May, not Hobsbawm. See, TNA, KV 2/3982, serial 216b; TNA, KV 2/3983, serial 262z.
72. TNA, KV 2/3982, serial 204z; TNA, KV 2/3981, serial 183a.
73. TNA, KV 2/3982, serial 187a; serial 219a.
74. TNA, KV 2/3982, serial 218a.
75. TNA, KV 2/3983, serial 270g.
76. Hobsbawm, *Interesting Times*, pp. 216–17.
77. Evans, *Eric Hobsbawm*, pp. 589–92.
78. TNA, KV 4/267, 202y, p. 3.
79. TNA, CAB 79/52/6, J.I.C.(46)70(O)(FINAL), p. 8.
80. TNA, KV 2/2093, serial 85a; TNA, KV 2/3775, serial 51a, serial 52a.
81. CAB 130/37/GEN226, GEN 226/1, 'Security Measures against encroachments by Communists or Fascists in the United Kingdom', ANNEX, pp. 6–7.
82. TNA, CAB 134/53, Committee on Communism, 11th Meeting, 1 July 1949.
83. CAB 130/37/GEN226, GEN 226/1, ANNEX, p. 7.
84. TNA, CAB 130/17/GEN168, GEN 168/5 ANNEX IV, 'The Soviet Campaign Against This Country and Our Response to it', CFA Warner, 2 April 1946.
85. TNA, CAB 79/52/6, J.I.C.(46)70(O)(FINAL), 23 September 1946, Appendix B, p. 35.
86. TNA, KV 4/251, serial 66a.
87. TNA, CAB 130/20/GEN183, GEN183/1, paragraph 4.
88. TNA, CAB 79/52/6, J.I.C.(46)70(O)(FINAL), 23 September 1946, Appendix B, p. 34.

89. Deery, "The secret battalion", p. 9.
90. TNA, KV 4/251, serial 61a.
91. Hennessy, *Secret State*, p. 23, footnote 79, p. 423.
92. HC Hansard Deb, 15 March 1948, vol 448, cc1703–4.
93. The inclusion of fascists has been described as 'a piece of window-dressing'. See, Hennessy and Brownfield, 'Britain's Cold War Security Purge', p. 968.
94. See Chapter 1.
95. TNA, KV 4/251, serial 61a.
96. TNA, HO 45/25578, Civil Security Review. No. XXI, February 1950, pp. 28–30, p. 48; Beckett, *Enemy Within*, pp. 120–3. The CPGB resumed receiving subsidies from Moscow after the turmoil of 1956. (Beckett, *Enemy Within*, p. 147)
97. Styles, 'British Domestic Security Policy', p. 68; TNA, KV 4/472, 2 June 1950.
98. TNA, CAB 301/17, Paragraph 10.
99. Curry, *Security Service*, p. 357; TNA, KV 2/1811, serial 68a; Jones, *Science, Politics and the Cold War*, p. 13.
100. TNA, KV 4/251, serial 61a.
101. Gibbs, 'British and American Counter-Intelligence', pp. 130–1.
102. Moss, *Klaus Fuchs*, p. 110; Close, *Trinity*, pp. 174–5; Rossiter, *Spy Who Changed the World*, pp. 183–4.
103. TNA, KV 4/467, 10 July 1946.
104. TNA, KV 2/1658, serial 107a.
105. TNA, KV 2/1660, serial 196a.
106. TNA, KV 2/1246, serial 185a; TNA, KV 2/1248, serial 344a.
107. TNA, KV 2/2081, minute 60; TNA, KV 2/1251, serial 478b; Rossiter, *Spy Who Changed the World*, p. 301; Close, *Trinity*, pp. 244, 287, 411–12; TNA, KV 2/2080, serial 1a; TNA, KV 2/1247, serial 196a.
108. TNA, KV 2/2080, minute 8.
109. TNA, KV 2/2080, minute 13; serial 52a.
110. Goodman, *Spying on the Nuclear Bear*, p. 66.
111. Flowers, *Atomic Spice*, p. 136. Accessed 22/3/22 at: https://homepages.inf.ed.ac.uk/opb/atomicspice/atomicspice.pdf
112. Greenspan, *Atomic Spy*, pp. 278, 287.
113. Laucht, *Elemental Germans*, p. 112.
114. Greenspan, *Atomic Spy*, p. 278. Kearton had himself been investigated in 1949. See, Rossiter, *Spy Who Changed the World*, pp. 280–1; Greenspan, *Atomic Spy*, pp. 201–2, 235–6.
115. TNA, CAB 130/20/GEN183, 5th Meeting, 5 April 1950; Hennessy, *Secret State*, pp. 95–6; Andrew, *Defence of the Realm*, p. 387.
116. Gibbs, 'British and American Counter-Intelligence', pp. 291–2.
117. Andrew, *Defence of the Realm*, p. 386.
118. Gibbs, 'British and American Counter-Intelligence', pp. 291–2.

119. Goodman, 'Who Is Trying to Keep What Secret from Whom', pp. 136, 142–3.
120. Hennessy and Brownfield, 'Britain's Cold War Security Purge', pp. 969–70.
121. Hennessy, *Secret State*, p. 98; TNA, CAB 130/20/GEN183, GEN 183/8, Committee on Positive Vetting Report, 27 October 1950; TNA, CAB 130/20/GEN183, 6th Meeting, 13 November 1950.
122. Andrew, *Defence of the Realm*, p. 391; TNA, CAB 21/4526, Chief of Staffs Committee, Positive Vetting Procedure – Note by the War Office, 1 December 1953, ANNEX.
123. Hennessy, *Secret State*, p. 102; Hollingsworth and Norton-Taylor, *Blacklist*, p. 29; Beesley, *The Official History of Cabinet Secretaries*, p. 174.
124. TNA, KV 4/472, 27 October 1950.
125. See, Kassimeris and Price, "What did you do to them Klaus?", pp. 266–9.
126. 'Atom Sensation No.2: Harwell ban on another scientist', *Daily Express*, 28 August 1953.
127. HC Hansard Deb, 1 Dec 1964, vol 703, c230. These individuals were never publicly named.
128. TNA, CAB 301/17, Paragraph 10. Whitehall officials also discussed the susceptibility of scientists to communism later in 1951. See, TNA, CAB 134/737, 3rd Meeting, 10 July 1951.
129. TNA, CAB 21/4035, Security Conference of Privy Councillors, Report of the Conference, 24 January 1956, Paragraph 31.
130. TNA, KV 2/2579, minute 139.
131. See, 'The Lessons of the Fuchs Case', in, Lee, *Sir Rudolf Peierls: Selected Private and Scientific Correspondence*, pp. 221–2, document 500.
132. TNA, PREM 11/536, Hollis to Colville, 16 February 1953; Colville to Hollis, 24 February 1953.
133. Hennessy, *Having it so Good*, pp. 174–5.
134. TNA, CAB 128/16/27; TNA, CAB 21/4013, folio 85, 'Communist employees of contractors engaged on secret work'.
135. HC Hansard Deb, 8 March 1954, vol 524, c1735. The individual was dismissed after he could not be found alternative work.
136. Andrew, *Defence of the Realm*, p. 937, footnote 15.
137. HC Hansard Deb, 20 May 1949, vol 465.
138. *The Times*, 26 April 1949, p. 2; *The Times*, 30 April 1949, p. 5; *The Times*, 5 May 1949, p. 2. In May 1949, the ban was extended to include fascists.
139. HC Hansard Deb, 03 May 1949, vol 464, c842; HC Hansard Deb, 20 May 1949, vol 465, cc841–56.
140. Hennessy, *Secret State*, p. 103.
141. TNA, CAB 21/4524, 'Positive Vetting Procedure: Revision of the Security Questionnaire', Report by the Personnel Security Committee, 14 March 1957; TNA, CAB 21/4012, memo from Winnifrith, 29 March 1957.
142. Davenport-Hines, *Enemies Within*, pp. 475–8; Andrew, *Defence of the Realm*, pp. 492–3; Kerr, *British Traitors*, pp. 245–54.

143. Andrew, *Defence of the Realm*, p. 399.
144. For more detail on the vetting procedure see, Hollingsworth and Norton-Taylor, *Blacklist*, pp. 99–100; Mills, *The BBC*, pp. 47–55; Andrew, *Defence of the Realm*, pp. 396–7.
145. TNA, CAB 134/53, 9th Meeting, 27 June 1949; TNA, CAB 134/737, 3rd Meeting, 10 July 1951; 4th Meeting, 17 July 1951.
146. TNA, CAB 134/737, 5th Meeting, 2 October 1951.
147. A teacher at a public school was dismissed because he was a communist. See, Munro, 'George Rudé—Communist Activist and Inactivist', p. 148, p. 154.
148. Hobsbawm, *Interesting Times*, p. 174.
149. Ibid., p. 182.
150. Parsons, 'British 'McCarthyism'', pp. 233–5.
151. TNA, HO 325/173, 'Security Service Enquiries in Schools about Pupils', September 1960.
152. TNA, CAB 21/4011, 'Employment of Fascists and Communists in the Civil Service', Memorandum by the Prime Minister, 17 February 1948. By 1957, security officials sought to persuade university teacher unions that lecturers at universities should reveal information about former students to vetting officers. See, TNA, CAB 21/4015, S.(P.S.)(57)5, 'Requests for Information about field inquiries', 25 January 1957.
153. TNA, HO 325/173, memo by GC Cunningham, 24 October 1960.
154. Potter, 'British 'McCarthyism'', p. 144; Jeffreys-Jones, *We Know all about You*, pp. 111–12.
155. Schlaepfer, 'Signals Intelligence and British Counter-subversion', p. 95.
156. See, for example, TNA, CAB 21/4011, extract from minutes of the Personnel Security Committee, 1st Meeting, 6 January 1955; extract from minutes of the Official Committee on Security, 3rd Meeting, 13 July 1956; S.(P.S.)(56)13, Personnel Security Committee, 'Positive Vetting Procedure', Note by the Treasury, 18 July 1956.
157. Parsons, 'British 'McCarthyism'', p. 125. Hyde was a member of the CPGB until 1948 when he left the party and became an outspoken critic of communism.
158. Andrew, *Defence of the Realm*, p. 393; Hennessy, *Secret State*, p. 102. Finding completely accurate details for the numbers of people who were purged is difficult. See, Andrew, *Defence of the Realm*, p. 939, footnote 82.
159. Andrew, *Defence of the Realm*, p. 393.
160. See, Mahoney, 'Constitutionalism, the Rule of Law, and the Cold War', p. 128; Shaw, *British Cinema and the Cold War*, pp. 177–8.
161. TNA, KV 2/3106, serial 35a.
162. TNA, KV 2/1306, serial 11a. He avoided a direct relationship with communism in Britain but displayed 'strong Left-Wing sympathies.' TNA, KV 2/1306, serial 28a.
163. TNA, KV 2/1306, serial 32a.

164. Devlin, *Sam Wanamaker*, p. 66.
165. TNA, KV 2/1306, serial 45a.
166. TNA, CAB 130/20/GEN183, GEN 183/8, Committee on Positive Vetting Report, 27 October 1950; Beesley, *The Official History of Cabinet Secretaries*, p. 51.
167. HC Hansard Deb, 01 November 1950, vol 480, cc195–7; TNA, CAB 134/2, 1st Meeting, 6 February 1951.
168. Hennessy and Brownfield, 'Britain's Cold War Security Purge', pp. 969–70; Rossi, 'The British Reaction to McCarthyism', pp. 12–13. Attlee's successor as Labour leader, Hugh Gaitskell, also criticised McCarthyism. See, Black, 'The Bitterest Enemies of Communism', p. 41.
169. Hennessy, *Having it so Good*, pp. 171–2. Hennessy says that the passage was likely to be, 'Parliamentary institutions, with their free speech and respect for the rights of minorities, and the inspiration of a broad tolerance in thought of its expression—all this we conceive to be a precious part of our way of life and outlook.'
170. TNA, KV 2/3875, serial 24a.
171. TNA, KV 2/3875, serial 30a, serial 31a.
172. TNA, KV 2/3875, serial 36a.
173. TNA, KV 2/3700, minute 18.
174. TNA, KV 2/2093, serial 96a, minute 97.
175. HC Hansard Deb, 27 October 1947, vol 443, cc503–4.
176. See, for example, HC Hansard Deb, 13 March 1950, vol 472 c744.
177. Glees, *The Secrets of the Service*, p. 4.
178. TNA, PREM 11/995, Memo to Prime Minister from P. G. Oates, 15 July 1952.
179. HC Hansard Deb, 25 February 1952, vol 496, c703.
180. TNA, KV 4/469, 24 October 1947.
181. HL Hansard Deb, 29 March 1950, vol 166, cc607–31.
182. Potter, 'British McCarthyism', pp. 145–7.
183. Defty, *Britain, America and Anti-Communist Propaganda*, p. 229.
184. TNA, FO 371/81635, Hoyer-Millar to Wright, 4 April 1950.
185. TNA, CAB 21/4742, Official Committee on Security, 'Review of Purge Cases', Draft Report by the Personnel Security Committee, 20 December 1957; 'Review of Purge Cases', Note by the Security Service, 4 February 1958. No defined procedure to review purge cases was formulated and each case was taken on its own merits.
186. See Chapter 1; TNA, KV 2/1016, serial 1101a.
187. TNA, KV 2/1016, serial 1073a.
188. TNA, CAB 301/399, Strang Report, pp. 12–13; Lashmar and Oliver, *Britain's Secret Propaganda War*, p. 27. The IRD was funded in part by the secret vote, and its existence was deliberately kept secret. The IRD did not wish for its material

to be produced verbatim. See, Defty, *Britain, America and Anti-Communist Propaganda*, p. 76; Schwartz, *Political Warfare against the Kremlin*, pp. 50–4, 64.
189. See, TNA, CAB 134/1342, A.C.(H)(57)1st Meeting, 29 August 1957.
190. Wilford, 'The Information Research Department', p. 360.
191. Aldrich, *Hidden Hand*, pp. 457–8; Schwartz, *Political Warfare Against the Kremlin*, pp. 64–5; TNA, CAB 301/399, Strang Report, p. 27. Foreign countries also received IRD material directly. See, TNA, CAB 301/399, Strang Report, p. 63.
192. Purvis and Hulbert, *When Reporters Cross the Line*, pp. 55–7.
193. TNA, KV 2/1017, serial 1105a, serial 1110a.
194. Purvis and Hulbert, *When Reporters Cross the Line*, pp. 41–2.
195. KV 2/4393, serial 1z; KV 2/4396, serial 231a, paragraph 8.
196. TNA, KV 4/473, 20 July 1951.
197. Ibid.
198. TNA, KV 4/473, 21 July 1951.
199. TNA, KV 4/473, 24 July 1951. Liddell wrote that the Security Service 'only submitted this case to the D. of P. P.' so that in the event of adverse publicity and questions in Parliament 'we should be in a position to say that FLOYD's [prosecution] had been considered.'
200. Hulbert, 'David Floyd: The Traitor who was forgiven and forgotten', *The Sunday Times*, 25 February 2018.
201. Lashmar and Oliver, *Britain's Secret Propaganda War*, p. 121; TNA, FCO 168/932, 'Mr. DAVID FLOYD', R.M. Russell, 30 January 1963.
202. TNA, FCO 168/932, 'Mr. DAVID FLOYD', R.M. Russell, 5 February 1963; TNA, FCO 168/7067, list of IRD contacts in the UK in press, radio and television.
203. Davenport-Hines, *Enemies Within*, p. 349.
204. See, Barnes, *Dead Doubles*.
205. See, Andrew, *Defence of the Realm*, pp. 484–93; Kuper, *Happy Traitor*.
206. Bower, *The Perfect English Spy*, pp. 267–8; Kuper, *Happy Traitor*, pp. 93–7.
207. Macintyre, *A Spy Among Friends*, pp. 241–3.
208. Ibid., pp. 255–72.
209. Macintyre, *A Spy Among Friends*, pp. 260–1, pp. 270–2; Norton-Taylor, *The State of Secrecy*, p. 194; Carter, *Anthony Blunt*, p. 445.
210. Penrose and Freeman, *Conspiracy of Silence*, pp. 434–40; Bower, *The Perfect English Spy*, pp. 324–5; Smith, *The Last Cambridge Spy*, pp. 202–5. Blunt was finally publicly exposed in 1979 and Cairncross was publicly named in 1990. (Davenport-Hines, *Enemies Within*, p. 526; Andrew, *Defence of the Realm*, p. 707)
211. Carter, *Anthony Blunt*, pp. 448–9; Davenport-Hines, *Enemies Within*, pp. 513–4.
212. Kuper, *Happy Traitor*, pp. 124–6; Macintyre, *A Spy Among Friends*, pp. 242–3. Blake was not a man of the British establishment, having been born and brought up abroad. Class would not, however, be a reasonable explanation for

Cairncross as, unlike the others, he was lower-middle class and had not been schooled for high society. See, Smith, *The Last Cambridge Spy*, pp. 25, 62–9.
213. Bower, *The Perfect English Spy*, p. 95.
214. Ibid., p. 295; Carter, *Anthony Blunt*, pp. 446–8.
215. For more on VENONA see, Andrew, *Defence of the Realm*, pp. 366–79; Kerbaj, *Secret History of the Five Eyes*, pp. 47–53, 82–92.
216. Close, *Trinity*, pp. 228–9; TNA, KV 2/1249, serial 376c.
217. See, Close, *Trinity*, pp. 333–4, 341–2; Davenport-Hines, *Enemies Within*, pp. 69–70; Barnes, *Dead Doubles*, pp. 135–6; Kuper, *Happy Traitor*, pp. 95–6.
218. Horne, *Macmillan 1957-1986: Volume II*, p. 461.
219. Beesley, *The Official History of Cabinet Secretaries*, p. 173. The phrase was later endorsed by one of Macmillan's successors as Prime Minister, Harold Wilson. See, Andrew, *Defence of the Realm*, p. 954, footnote 4.
220. Horne, *Macmillan 1957-1986: Volume II*, p. 457.
221. Davenport-Hines, *Enemies Within*, p. 495.
222. Pearce, *Spymaster*, p. 257.
223. Caute, *Red List*, pp. 11–12; Andrew, *Defence of the Realm*, pp. 49–50.
224. Aaronovitch, *Party Animals*, pp. 258–66; Beckett, *Enemy Within*, p. 138; Barnett, *Britain's Cold War*, pp. 118–21.
225. TNA, CAB 21/4035, Security Conference of Privy Councillors, Report of the Conference, 24 January 1956, paragraph 5.
226. TNA, CAB 21/4011, 'Employment of Fascists and Communists in the Civil Service', 2 March 1948.

4. SUBVERSION AND THE LABOUR PARTY

1. Howard and West, *The Making of The Prime Minister*, pp. 238–9.
2. Andrew, *Defence of the Realm*, pp. 415–6. In 1954, prior to Attlee's retirement as Labour leader, MI5 picked up a conversation in the CPGB's headquarters in which leading figures of the CP spoke of how they favoured Wilson as Attlee's successor.
3. Wilson did report these visits to the Foreign Office. See, PREM 11/1604.
4. Andrew, *Defence of the Realm*, pp. 416–17.
5. Andrew and Mitrokhin, *The Mitrokhin Archive*, pp. 527–9.
6. Andrew, *Defence of the Realm*, p. 417.
7. Ibid., p. 944, footnote 119.
8. Andrew and Mitrokhin, *The Mitrokhin Archive*, pp. 528–9.
9. Dorril and Ramsay, *Smear!* pp. 41–3, 113–15; Aldrich and Cormac, *The Black Door*, p. 276; Wright, *Spycatcher*, p. 364.
10. Aldrich and Cormac, *The Black Door*, pp. 138–9.
11. Lomas, *Intelligence, Security and the Attlee Governments*, pp. 42–5.
12. Jeffery, *MI6*, pp. 352–3; Lomas, *Intelligence, Security and the Attlee Governments*, p. 37.

13. Hennessy and Jeffery, *States of Emergency*, pp. 149–50; Bew, *Citizen Clem*, p. 356.
14. Toye, 'Winston Churchill's "Crazy Broadcast"', p. 655.
15. For the reactions to the speech see, Bew, *Citizen Clem*, pp. 332–6; Toye, 'Winston Churchill's "Crazy Broadcast"', pp. 665–7; Tinline, *The Death of Consensus*, pp. 120–3.
16. See, Bew, *Citizen Clem*, p. 348.
17. Lomas, *Intelligence, Security and the Attlee Governments*, pp. 61–2.
18. Dorril, *MI6*, p. 35.
19. Lomas, *Intelligence, Security and the Attlee Governments*, p. 55; Aldrich, *GCHQ*, p. 66.
20. Lomas, *Intelligence, Security and the Attlee Governments*, p. 55.
21. TNA, KV 2/511, serial 7a references Wilkinson's PF as PF 42136.; TNA, KV 2/668, serial 24a mentions Aneurin Bevan's PF as PF 41747.
22. TNA, KV 2/668, minute 41.
23. TNA, KV 2/787, serial 131a.
24. TNA, KV 2/787, minute 134, minute 135.
25. TNA, KV 2/787, serial 133a, minute 136.
26. TNA, KV 2/787, serial 131a.
27. See, Young, 'Cold War Insecurities and the Curious Case of John Strachey'.
28. TNA, KV 4/472, 11 Oct 1950.
29. Porter, *Plots and Paranoia*, pp. 191–2; TNA, KV 4/471, 1 January 1949. Liddell did, however, find it highly amusing that several American officials thought that the Labour government was a 'communist' one. (TNA, KV 4/471, 15 July 1949).
30. Lomas, *Intelligence Security and the Attlee Governments*, p. 186; Shaw, *British Cinema and the Cold War*, p. 35.
31. Adonis, *Ernest Bevin*, p. 45, p. 68, pp. 122–3.
32. Vincent, *Culture of Secrecy*, p. 199; Hennessy, *Never Again*, p. 245; Aldrich, *Hidden Hand*, pp. 130–1; Defty, *Britain, America and Anti-Communist Propaganda*, p. 34.
33. TNA, CAB 301/399, Strang Report, pp. 12–13.
34. TNA, CAB 134/53, 19th Meeting, 16 November 1949; TNA, CAB 134/737, 2nd Meeting, 22 June 1951; TNA, CAB 134/2, 1st Meeting, 6 February 1951.
35. Bew, *Citizen Clem*, p. 369, pp. 376–9; Hennessy, *Secret State*, pp. 50–1; Adonis, *Ernest Bevin*, pp. 263–4. Attlee did not trust all of his cabinet with information on the atomic bomb. See, Hennessy, *The Prime Minister*, p. 166.
36. Adonis, *Ernest Bevin*, pp. 290–2; Bew, *Citizen Clem*, pp. 461–4.
37. Macintyre, *A Spy Amongst Friends*, pp. 92–3.
38. Lomas, *Intelligence, Security and the Attlee Governments*, p. 189; Andrew, *Defence of the Realm*, p. 321.
39. Hennessey and Thomas, *Spooks: 1945-2009*, pp. 54–5.
40. TNA, KV 4/196, 29 May 1945.

41. TNA, KV 4/468, 19 November 1946.
42. Andrew, *Defence of the Realm*, p. 322.
43. Ibid., p. 847. This taking place in practice can be seen in a memo sent to Margaret Thatcher shortly after she became Prime Minister in 1979. See, TNA, PREM 19/2845, John Hunt to Prime Minister, 4 May 1979.
44. TNA, KV 4/468, 19 November 1946.
45. Andrew, *Defence of the Realm*, p. 411.
46. Dodds and Swingler were Labour MPs. Pritt had been elected as a Labour MP in 1935 but, after being expelled from the Party in 1940, he then sat as an 'Independent Labour' member.
47. TNA, KV 2/3812, serial 333a.
48. TNA, KV 2/3812, serial 309a; TNA, KV 4/468, 19 November 1946.
49. TNA, KV 2/3812, serial 311a.
50. TNA, KV 2/3812, serial 317b, serial 320a, serial 325a, serial 329a.
51. TNA, KV 2/3813, minute 349.
52. TNA, KV 2/3813, serial 359a, minute 360. A Security Liaison Officer was an MI5 officer stationed in Empire and Commonwealth countries. (Walton, *Empire of Secrets*, p. xxviii).
53. See Chapter 2.
54. TNA, KV 2/996, serial 695a.
55. TNA, KV 2/996, minute 689.
56. TNA, KV 2/996, minute 693.
57. TNA, KV 2/996, serial 700a.
58. TNA, KV 2/996, minute 725.
59. TNA, KV 2/996, minute 726.
60. TNA, KV 2/996, serial 728a.
61. TNA, KV 2/996, serial 731b, serial 753a.
62. TNA, KV 2/996, minute 759.
63. Bower, *The Perfect English Spy*, p. 89; Defty, Bochel and Kirkpatrick, 'Tapping the Telephones', p. 680, footnote 23.
64. See, LHASC, LP/GS/LS.
65. Andrew, *Defence of the Realm*, p. 411.
66. Hopkins, 'Herbert Morrison, the Cold War and Anglo-American Relations', p. 23; Schneer, *Labour's Conscience*, p. 110.
67. Lomas, *Intelligence, Security and the Attlee Governments*, p. 201.
68. Ibid., pp. 101–2.
69. Schneer, *Labour's Conscience*, p. 115.
70. Ibid., pp. 112–18; Weiler, *British Labour and the Cold War*, pp. 214–15; Andrew, *Defence of the Realm*, pp. 411–12.
71. Mikardo, *Back-Bencher*, p. 131.
72. LHASC, LP/GS/LS/3i.
73. LHASC, LP/GS/LS/14.
74. LHASC, LP/GS/LS/16.

75. TNA, FCO 168/2724, Labour Party Annual Conference 1967, minute JE Tyrer, 22 September 1967.
76. TNA, FCO 168/426, note JET Egg, 26 October 1961; TNA, FCO 168/1190, Labour Party Conference December 1964.
77. TNA, FCO 168/520, J.E.T. Egg, 29 January 1962; 'North Islington Constituency Labour Party', 31 January 1962.
78. TNA, FCO 168/426, Labour Party Contacts Receiving IRD Material Regularly or in Personal Contact.
79. TNA, FCO 168/1184, Note, JE Tyrer, 30 June 1964.
80. TNA, FCO 168/1183, Home Regional Meeting, 111th Meeting, 18 June 1964.
81. Dorril and Ramsay, *Smear!* p. 24; Shaw, *Discipline and discord*, pp. 119–21.
82. Mikardo, *Back-Bencher*, pp. 130–1; Dorril and Ramsay, *Smear!* p. 24.
83. Andrew, *Defence of the Realm*, pp. 412–13.
84. For all the names on the list see, Andrew, *Defence of the Realm*, pp. 414, 942, footnote 88.
85. Andrew, *Defence of the Realm*, p. 413.
86. Ibid., p. 943, footnote 90, p. 415.
87. Hennessy, *Winds of Change*, p. 475.
88. Andrew, *Defence of the Realm*, pp. 526–7.
89. HC Hansard Deb, 17 November 1966, vol 736, cc634–41; Defty, Bochel and Kirkpatrick, 'Tapping the Telephones', p. 676.
90. For more on the Wilson Doctrine see, Strickland, Dawson and Godec, *The Wilson Doctrine*.
91. HC Hansard Deb, 17 November 1966, vol 736, c639. Its limits were explained in 2014 by then Home Secretary Theresa May. See, HC Hansard Deb, 15 July 2014, vol 584, c713.
92. Defty, Bochel and Kirkpatrick, 'Tapping the Telephones', p. 676.
93. Aldrich, *GCHQ*, p. 227; Aldrich and Cormac, *The Black Door*, pp. 261–2; Andrew, *Defence of the Realm*, pp. 522–3; Benn, *Out of the Wilderness*, p. 182, 10 November 1964. Somewhat ironically, given his forceful commitment to security, Wigg had originally been included on the list compiled by Morgan Phillips in the 1940s on Labour MPs viewed as 'Lost Sheep'.
94. Andrew, *Defence of the Realm*, pp. 532–3.
95. Ibid., p. 528. For the reports MI5 provided to Wilson on the strike see, TNA, CAB 301/233.
96. HC Hansard Deb, 20 June 1966, vol. 730, cc42–3.
97. Hennessy and Jeffery, *States of Emergency*, p. 229.
98. TNA, CAB 301/234, note of meeting between the Prime Minister and the Leader of the Opposition, 21 June 1966; Andrew, *Defence of the Realm*, p. 530.
99. For a detailed account of the strike see, Thorpe, 'The 'Juggernaut Method''.
100. Aldrich and Cormac, *The Black Door*, p. 278.
101. Andrew, *Defence of the Realm*, pp. 534–5.

102. Ibid., pp. 524–5; Benn, *Out of the Wilderness*, pp. 328–9, 29 September 1965; HL Hansard Deb, 19 May 1981, vol. 420, cc857–60.
103. Andrew, *Defence of the Realm*, p. 412.
104. Ramsay and Dorril, *Smear!* pp. 157–8.
105. Lilleker, *Against the Cold War*, p. 6.
106. Norton-Taylor, *The State of Secrecy*, p. 181.
107. Ramsay and Dorril, *Smear!* pp. 118–20.
108. Ibid., pp. 158–9.
109. Wright, *Spycatcher*, p. 364.
110. TNA, KV 2/4393, serial 1z, serial 17c.
111. Dorril and Ramsay, *Smear!* pp. 103–4, pp. 154–5; Wright, *Spycatcher*, p. 264.
112. Davenport-Hines, *Enemies Within*, pp. 518–19; TNA, KV 2/4394, serial 177a; Andrew, *Defence of the Realm*, pp. 538–41; TNA, KV 2/4394, serial 178a.
113. TNA, KV 2/4394, serial 188a.
114. TNA, KV 2/4394, minute 190, minute 192, minute 193, minute 197, minute 201, serial 202a; TNA, KV 2/4394, serial 204a; TNA, KV 2/4394, serial 206a.
115. TNA, KV 2/4395, serial 218a; KV 2/4396, serial 231a; serial 234a; KV 2/4397, serial 259a; serial 261a.
116. TNA, KV 2/4395, serial 218a, paragraph 102; KV 2/4396, serial 234a, paragraph 83.
117. TNA, KV 2/4397, serial 261a, paragraph 4.
118. TNA, KV 2/4397, serial 281a.
119. TNA, KV 2/4397, serial 285a. Peter Wright wrongly claimed in his memoir *Spycatcher* (p.266) that Floud committed suicide the day after the final interview.
120. Dorril and Ramsay, *Smear!* p. 197.
121. Lilleker, *Against the Cold War*, pp. 7–8.
122. Anderson and Davey, *Moscow Gold*, pp. 115–16, footnote 148; Lilleker, *Against the Cold War*, p. 123, p. 238.
123. Lilleker, *Against the Cold War*, pp. 5–6, pp. 10–11; Anderson and Davey, *Moscow Gold,* p. 120. For an example of this see, Macintyre, *The Spy and the Traitor*, pp. 117–22.
124. It should be noted that Frolik was not seen as entirely reliable. See, TNA, PREM 16/1848, memo by John Hunt 3 June 1975.
125. Andrew, *Defence of the Realm*, p. 413.
126. TNA, BA 19/110, 'Information on which the prosecution of William James Owen was based', 28 May 1970; 'Release of Classified Information to the Estimates Committee', 13 July 1970.
127. Andrew, *Defence of the Realm*, p. 542.
128. TNA, BA 19/110, 'Information on which the prosecution of William James Owen was based', 28 May 1970.
129. Andrew, *Defence of the Realm*, p. 413, p. 543. The prosecution's star witness

was Josef Frolik. However, since he had not actually seen any of the classified documents passed over by Owen, the Judge dismissed such allegations as 'hearsay'.
130. Andrew and Mitrokhin, *The Mitrokhin Archive*, p. 526.
131. Ibid., pp. 522–5.
132. Davenport-Hines, *Enemies Within*, pp. 484–6; Andrew and Mitrokhin, *The Mitrokhin Archive*, pp. 524–5.
133. Andrew and Mitrokhin, *The Mitrokhin Archive*, p. 526.
134. Andrew, *Defence of the Realm*, p. 414.
135. Hemming, *M*, pp. 109–10, p. 230; Davenport-Hines, *Enemies Within*, pp. 215, 323.
136. Hemming, *M*, pp. 321–3.
137. West, *Historical Dictionary of British Intelligence*, pp. 184–5.
138. Andrew, *Defence of the Realm*, p. 541.
139. HC Hansard Deb, 17 December 1974, vol. 883, cc1353–4.
140. Andrew, *Defence of the Realm*, p. 707.
141. TNA, PREM 19/360, Armstrong to Prime Minister, 7 July 1980.
142. TNA, PREM 19/360, Armstrong to Prime Minister, 11 September 1980; Memo to PM 1 Oct 1980; Memo to PM 3 Oct 1980.
143. TNA, PREM 19/360, Mr John Stonehouse, 6 October 1980.
144. TNA, PREM 16/1848, Mr John Stonehouse, 21 June 1978.
145. Andrew, *Defence of the Realm*, pp. 707–8.
146. Corera, 'Tory MP Raymond Mawby sold information to Czech spies', BBC News, 28 June 2012. Accessed 22/4/20 at: www.bbc.co.uk/news/uk-18617168
147. Keeble, *Britain, the Soviet Union and Russia*, pp. 270–5.
148. Ibid., p. 272.
149. Andrew, *Defence of the Realm*, pp. 503–21; Correra, *MI6*, pp. 192–218.
150. Morgan, 'Conspiracy and Contemporary History', pp. 167–8.
151. Beckett, *When the Lights Went Out*, pp. 177–82, 376–80; Morgan, 'Conspiracy and Contemporary History', pp. 167–71; Tinline, *Death of Consensus*, pp. 184–9, pp. 216–18; Sandbrook, *Seasons in the Sun*, pp. 124–49, particularly pp. 132–5, pp. 145–7.
152. Lashmar and Oliver, *Britain's Secret Propaganda War*, pp. 166–7; Andrew, *Defence of the Realm*, pp. 627–32. In March 1974, at about the time Wilson returned to office, the MI5 DG, Michael Hanley, sought to further conceal the existence of the file held on him by the Security Service.
153. Aldrich and Cormac, *The Black Door*, p. 315; Beckett, *When the Lights Went Out*, pp. 166–9.
154. Porter, *Plots and Paranoia*, pp. 210–11; Andrew, *Defence of the Realm*, pp. 635–8; Sandbrook, *Seasons in the Sun*, pp. 66–8; Aldrich and Cormac, *The Black Door*, pp. 324–5.
155. Sandbrook, *Seasons in the Sun*, p. 67.

156. The microphones were temporarily removed after Macmillan left office, but appear to have been quickly re-established, remaining until 1977.
157. Aldrich and Cormac, *The Black Door*, p. 230, pp. 236–9; Sandbrook, *Seasons in the Sun*, pp. 74–5. This information was initially blocked from being made public when MI5's authorised history was published. Christopher Andrew wrote in the introduction to *The Defence of the Realm* that there had been 'one significant excision' which he believed was 'hard to justify'. (Andrew, *Defence of the Realm*, p. xxi).
158. Aldrich and Cormac, *The Black Door*, p. 277.
159. Sandbrook, *Seasons in the Sun*, pp. 135–41; Morgan, 'Conspiracy and Contemporary History', pp. 169–71; Aldrich and Cormac, *The Black Door*, pp. 325–7.
160. Wright, *Spycatcher*, pp. 368–72.
161. Andrew, *Defence of the Realm*, p. 642.
162. Aldrich and Cormac, *The Black Door*, p. 323.
163. Morgan, 'Conspiracy and Contemporary History', p. 172.
164. Correra, *MI6*, p. 214; Pearce, *Spymaster*, p. 342.
165. Morgan, 'Conspiracy and Contemporary History', pp. 166–7; Andrew, *Defence of the Realm*, pp. 642–3.
166. Lilleker, *Against the Cold War*, pp. 176–7.
167. TNA, CAB 301/489, 'The Threat of Subversion to the UK', Security Service, April 1976, pp. 1–2.
168. Thurlow, *Secret State*, pp. 322–4. For information about the way MI5 perceived Trotskyism before the 1970s see, Kassimeris and Price, 'A new and disturbing form of subversion', pp. 358–62.
169. Crick, *Militant*, pp. 103–7; Thomas-Symonds, 'A Reinterpretation of Michael Foot's Handling', pp. 31–2; Gould, *Witchfinder General*, p. 216.
170. Andrew, *Defence of the Realm*, pp. 660–1.
171. TNA, CAB 301/489, 'The Threat of Subversion to the UK', Security Service, April 1976, p. 7.
172. Crick, *Militant*, pp. 17–19.
173. Callaghan, *The Far Left*, p. 197; Crick, *Militant*, pp. 76–85.
174. TNA, CAB 301/489, 'The Threat of Subversion to the UK', Security Service, April 1976, p. 7; Massey, 'The Militant Tendency', p. 240; Andrew, *Defence of the Realm*, p. 660.
175. Crick, *Militant*, p. 127.
176. Andrew, *Defence of the Realm*, p. 661.
177. Ibid., p. 663.
178. Ibid., p. 661.
179. TNA, CAB 301/485, SPL(85)8(Revised) The Threat of Subversion in the Civil Service, ANNEX B, The Threat from Subversion: 1985, paragraph 9.
180. Evans and Lewis, *Undercover*, pp. 146–8.

181. TNA, CAB 301/485, Note for Record, Militant Tendency, RP Hatfield, 16 January 1985.
182. TNA, CAB 301/485, SPL(85)8(Revised) ANNEX B, The Threat from Subversion: 1985, paragraph 9; Sandbrook, *Seasons in the Sun*, p. 307.
183. *True Spies*, BBC Two, Episode 2 'Something better change', 3 November 2002.
184. Crick, *Militant*, pp. 197–9; TNA, CAB 301/485, SPL(85)8(Revised) ANNEX B, The Threat from Subversion: 1985, paragraph 10.
185. Rosenbaum, 'The monitoring of MPs', *BBC News*, 21 October 2008. Accessed 12/12/20 at: www.bbc.co.uk/blogs/opensecrets/2008/10/the_monitoring_of_mps.html
186. *True Spies*, BBC Two, 'Something better change'.
187. Crick, *Militant*, p. 274, Appendix 4 pp. 333–7.
188. Andrew, *Defence of the Realm*, p. 681; Crick, *Militant*, p. 274.
189. Crick, *Militant*, p. 282, pp. 312–17.
190. 'Dave Nellist: The Coventry MP who gave away half his pay', *BBC News*, 13 July 2013. Accessed 12/12/20 at: www.bbc.co.uk/news/uk-england-coventry-warwickshire-23289962
191. Crick, *Militant*, pp. 316–17.
192. Massey, 'The Militant Tendency', p. 247; Massey, 'The Labour Party's inquiry into Liverpool District Labour Party', p. 301.
193. Massey, 'The Militant Tendency', pp. 247–50, p. 252; Crick, *Militant*, pp. 277–8, pp. 312–14.
194. Crick actually identifies 1982–3 as the time in which Militant was at the peak of its influence within the Labour Party nationally, although its membership further increased, and it continued to have control in Liverpool for a number of years. Crick, *Militant*, pp. 275–6.
195. Crick, *Militant*, p. 276; Massey, 'The Militant Tendency', pp. 248–9.
196. TNA, CAB 301/486, SPL(87)1, 28 January 1987, paragraphs 12–13.
197. Ibid., paragraph 14.
198. For debates about vetting Trotskyists prior to the 1980s see, TNA, T 216/971, I. de L. Radice, 15 November 1961; note for Sir Lawrence Helsby, 14 November 1963; Hennessy, *Secret State*, p. 103.
199. TNA, PREM 19/1377, Robert Armstrong to Prime Minister, 15 October 1984.
200. TNA, CAB 301/485, Note for Record, Industrial Relations, RP Hatfield, 10 January 1985.
201. Timmins, 'Benefits strike ends, but pensioners must wait for cash', *The Times*, 18 December 1984, p. 2.
202. TNA, CAB 301/485, Stowe to Armstrong, 23 November 1984; TNA, CAB 301/485, Note for Record, Industrial Relations, RP Hatfield, 10 January 1985.
203. TNA, CAB 301/485, Stowe to Armstrong, 23 November 1984.

204. TNA, CAB 301/485, Note for Record, Militant Tendency, RP Hatfield, 16 January 1985.
205. TNA, CAB 301/485, SPL(85)8(Revised) The Threat of Subversion in the Civil Service, paragraphs 10–12, paragraph 15.
206. Ibid., ANNEX B, The Threat from Subversion: 1985, Appendix II 'Govt Departments—holders of subversive records on 31 December 1984'.
207. Ibid., ANNEX B, The Threat from Subversion: 1985, paragraph 18.
208. TNA, CAB 301/485, 'SUBVERSION IN PUBLIC LIFE', Speaking Notes for Sir Robert Armstrong; TNA, CAB 301/485, SPL(85)8(Revised) The Threat of Subversion in the Civil Service, paragraph 19; TNA, CAB 301/485, Note for Record, Industrial Relations, RP Hatfield, 10 January 1985.
209. TNA, CAB 301/485, SPL(85)8(Revised) The Threat of Subversion in the Civil Service, paragraph 25, Recommendations; TNA, CAB 301/485, Robert Armstrong to Prime Minister, 6 December 1985.
210. TNA, CAB 301/485, NL Wicks to Armstrong, 9 December 1985.
211. Maguire, 'Counter-Subversion in Early Cold War Britain', pp. 646–8; Lashmar and Oliver, *Britain's Secret Propaganda War*, pp. 108–9.
212. TNA, CAB 301/509, AC(H)(WG)(67)2, 'The Subversive Threat to the United Kingdom—March 1967', Security Service, 22 March 1967; TNA, CAB 301/509, AC(H)(WG)(67)5(Revise), 'Subversion in the United Kingdom—Autumn 1967', Security Service, October 1967; TNA, CAB 301/509, AC(H)(WG)(67)6(Revised), 'Subversion in the United Kingdom', Paper by the Security Service, October 1967; TNA, CAB 301/509, AC(H)(WG)(68)1, 'Subversion in the United Kingdom—Spring 1968', Security Service, 10 May 1968; Callaghan, *The Far Left*, pp. 119–21.
213. TNA, CAB 301/495, SH(69)2, 'Subversion in the United Kingdom', Note by the Security Service, January 1969.

5. ENEMIES OF THE STATE OR ENEMIES OF THE GOVERNMENT?

1. Hennessy, *The Prime Minister*, p. 332.
2. Jack Jones later wrote that Heath 'made real efforts 'to establish a spirit of camaraderie with trade union leaders' and 'revealed a human face of Toryism, at least to the union leaders who met him frequently.' (Jones, *Union Man*, pp. 259–62). The number of working days lost as a result of industrial action in 1970 was the most since 1926. (Turner, *Crisis? What Crisis?* p. 11).
3. Andrew, *Defence of the Realm*, pp. 588–9.
4. Ibid., pp. 589–90.
5. TNA, CAB 301/490/1, 'Industrial Action: The Role of the Security Service', 27 January 1971, pp. 3–4.
6. Ibid., pp. 2–4.
7. TNA, CAB 301/509, AC(H)(WG)(67)2, 'The Subversive Threat to the

United Kingdom', 22 March 1967; TNA, CAB 301/509, AC(H)(WG)(67)6(Revised), 'Subversion in the United Kingdom', October 1967.
8. TNA, CAB 134/1346, AC(H)(61)9, 'Communism in the United Kingdom and Countermeasures', June 1961.
9. TNA, CAB 301/490/1, 'Subversion in Industry and the Mass Media, 1965-1971', 10 June 1971, p. 3.
10. TNA, PREM 15/170, 'Note for record', RTA, 17.xi.70; Andrew, *Defence of the Realm*, pp. 588–9. Whilst they were permitted by the Home Secretary to tap Jones' phone, MI5 had also wanted to install a listening device in his flat.
11. Andrew, *Defence of the Realm*, p. 589.
12. TNA, CAB 301/490/1, 'Subversion in Industry and the Mass Media, 1965-1971', 10 June 1971, p. 3.
13. Andrew, *Defence of the Realm*, p. 589; Macintyre, *The Spy and the Traitor*, pp. 115–16. See, Lilleker, *Against the Cold War*, pp. 5–11.
14. Andrew, *Defence of the Realm*, p. 589.
15. Vincent, *Culture of Secrecy*, p. 251.
16. Hughes, 'Giving the Russians a Bloody Nose', pp. 236–40; Keeble, *Britain and the Soviet Union*, pp. 279–80; Correra, *MI6*, pp. 241–2; Aldrich, *GCHQ*, pp. 283–4; Kerbaj, *Secret History of the Five Eyes*, pp. 146–8.
17. Bower, *The Perfect English Spy*, p. 364.
18. Aldrich and Cormac, *The Black Door*, pp. 300–1.
19. TNA, CAB 301/490/1, 'Subversion in Industry and the Mass Media, 1965-1971', 10 June 1971, pp. 1–2. MI5 believed the trade union movement was important to the CPGB because of 'the political influence which it could exercise on the Labour Party through the trade unions' collective voting strength at Labour Party Conferences and their substantial contribution to its funds.' The CPGB sought to 'exploit any positions of strength it can acquire in the trade unions as an indirect means of influencing Labour Party policy.'
20. Sandbrook, *State of Emergency*, pp. 118–29; Phillips, 'The 1972 Miners' Strike', pp. 192–5; Hennessy and Jeffery, *States of Emergency*, pp. 234–5.
21. TNA, CAB 301/490/1, Armstrong to Trend, 21 February 1972.
22. TNA, CAB 301/490/1, Hanley to Trend, 24 February 1972. This is not to say that the unions had no political thoughts. Shortly before the strike began, the general secretary of the NUM Laurence Daly said, 'I believe it is possible to create a broad unity in the trade union movement that will smash Conservative economic policy and help to pave the way for the defeat of the Tory government and return a Labour government.' (Turner, *Crisis? What Crisis?*, pp. 14–15).
23. Andrew, *Defence of the Realm*, pp. 592–3.
24. *True Spies*, BBC Two, Episode 1 'Subversive My Arse', 27 October 2002.
25. TNA, CAB 301/490/1, 'Subversion in the UK—1972', Paper by the Security Service, 16 March 1972.
26. Wright, *Spycatcher*, p. 359.

27. CAB 301/491, R.T. Armstrong to Sir William Armstrong, 17 November 1972; Burke Trend to Sir William Armstrong, 24 November 1972; 'Industrial Intelligence', Burke Trend, 20 December 1972. Reference is given to the pressure placed on the Security Service by ministers in an MI5 memo from December 1972. See, UCPI0000031256, 'Relations with M.P.S.B. about Industrial Subversion', 7 December 1972. Accessed 17/5/23 at: https://www.ucpi.org.uk/publications/security-service-note-for-policy-file-entitled-relations-with-m-p-s-b-about-industrial-subversion/
28. TNA, CAB 301/491, SPL(72)1(Final) 'Impact of Subversive Groups on Trade Union Activity', p. 2.
Most of the cabinet believed strikes were because of a 'subversive conspiracy.' Ministers did not, however, make their case so strongly in public. Andrew, *Defence of the Realm*, pp. 595–6; HC Hansard Deb, 5 December 1972, vol 847 cc1092–93.
29. TNA, CAB 301/491, SPL(72)1(Final) 'Impact of Subversive Groups on Trade Union Activity' p. 6.
30. For more detail on the strike see, Clutterbuck, *Britain in Agony*, pp. 77–88.
31. Smith and Chamberlain, *Blacklisted*, pp. 56–9; TNA, CAB 301/491, SPL(72)1(Final) Appendix III 'Communist Involvement in Major Disputes 1972'. Communist involvement in the Building Workers' Charter is readily acknowledged in, Smith and Chamberlain, *Blacklisted*, p. 53.
32. *True Spies*, BBC Two, 'Subversive My Arse'.
33. Turner, *Crisis? What Crisis?*, p. 77
34. *True Spies*, BBC Two, 'Subversive My Arse'.
35. Smith and Chamberlain, *Blacklisted*, pp. 58–9. During a House of Commons debate on the case in January 2014, Labour MP, David Anderson, went as far as to state that not only was there no violence, but that 'the police actually congratulated the leaders of the pickets on the disciplined way in which they conducted their activities'. (HC Hansard Deb, 23 January 2014, vol 574 c484).
36. See, HC Hansard Deb, 23 January 2014, vol 574 cc479–83; Smith and Chamberlain, *Blacklisted*, p. 60; HC Hansard Deb, 9 December 2015, vol 603 c377WH.
37. HC Hansard Deb, 9 December 2015, vol 603 cc379–80WH.
38. 'Building pickets' leader jailed for three years', *The Times*, 20 December 1973, p. 3.
39. 'Flying pickets in building strike lose their appeals', *The Times*, 30 October 1974, p. 5.
40. *Red Under the Bed* was followed by a studio discussion which, although not broadcast in every ITV region, aired in the region covering Shrewsbury. In 2017, Tomlinson alleged that the presenter of the discussion, Richard Whiteley, later famous for presenting *Countdown*, was 'a member of the intelligence

services.' Such a claim is, however, completely unproven. ('Richard Whiteley was a spy, claims Ricky Tomlinson', *The Telegraph*, 2 March 2017).
41. TNA, PREM 15/2011, 'RED UNDER THE BED', TC Barker, 21 November 1973.
42. TNA, PREM 15/2011, RT Armstrong, 21 January 1974.
43. 'Shrewsbury 24: Court of Appeal clears picketers' convictions', *BBC News*, 23 March 2021, Accessed 23/2/22 at: https://www.bbc.co.uk/news/uk-england-shropshire-56494701; Evans and Syal, 'Shrewsbury 24: court of appeal overturns 1970s picketing convictions', *The Guardian*, 23 March 2021, Accessed 23/2/22 at: https://www.theguardian.com/law/2021/mar/23/shrewsbury-24-court-of-appeal-overturns-1970s-picketing-convictions
44. Sandbrook, *State of Emergency*, p. 577.
45. Andrew, *Defence of the Realm*, pp. 598–9. The author of the memorandum sent to Heath 'had a lead role in drafting Harold Wilson's celebrated denunciation of the seamen's leaders in 1966.'
46. Beckett, *When the Lights Went Out*, pp. 146–8; Sandbrook, *State of Emergency*, p. 583, p. 612. Opinion polling had shown that a majority of the public disapproved of the miners' actions and believed that the government should not give in to their demands.
47. TNA, CAB 301/489, 'The Threat of Subversion to the UK', Paper by the Security Service, April 1976.
48. Whilst the Callaghan government was dominated by industrial disputes in its latter years—1978 and 1979—Callaghan's first year in office, 1976, represented the year with the fewest industrial disputes in the twentieth century up to that point. (Andrew, *Defence of the Realm*, p. 656).
49. TNA, PREM 16/1491, Note of a meeting at Chequers on 26 June 1977.
50. TNA, PREM 16/1491, Grunwick Dispute, 5 July 1977; Andrew, *Defence of the Realm*, pp. 664–5.
51. Andrew, *Defence of the Realm*, pp. 664–7.
52. Beckett, *When the Lights Went Out*, pp. 45–9; Sandbrook, *Seasons in the Sun*, pp. 663–4, pp. 760–1.
53. 'Red Robbo: The man behind 523 car factory strikes', *BBC News*, 4 November 2017. Accessed 19/5/20 at: https://www.bbc.co.uk/news/uk-england-birmingham-41834559
54. *True Spies*, BBC Two, Episode 2 'Something better change', 3 November 2002.
55. Andrew, *Defence of the Realm*, p. 672.
56. *True Spies*, BBC Two, 'Something better change'; Sandbrook, *Who Dares Wins*, p. 315.
57. Obituary, Derek Robinson, *The Times*, 1 November 2017. Accessed 03/11/25 at: https://www.thetimes.com/article/derek-robinson-obituary-65r8pvz8f
58. Andrew, *Defence of the Realm*, p. 672.
59. Ibid., pp. 671–2.
60. Seldon and Meakin, *The Cabinet Office*, p. 208.

61. UCPI0000035314, 'PREM 19-2843—Letter from Sir John Hunt to the Prime Minister attaching a Security Service paper on 'The Threat of Subversion in the UK'. Accessed 12/5/23 at: https://www.ucpi.org.uk/publications/prem-19-2843-letter-from-sir-john-hunt-to-the-prime-minister-attaching-a-security-service-paper-on-the-threat-of-subversion-in-the-uk/
62. Andrew, *Defence of the Realm*, pp. 670–1. Thatcher's own concern about subversives and the influence of communism was long standing and could be traced back to at least the early 1950s. See, Sandbrook, *Who Dares Wins*, p. 179.
63. By the time it began, both sides had anticipated a 'showdown' for many years. See, Vinen, *Thatcher's Britain*, pp. 155–9; Beckett and Hencke, *Marching to the Fault Line*, pp. 37–46; Vinen, 'A War of Position?'.
64. Vinen, *Thatcher's Britain*, pp. 163–4; Milne, *The Enemy Within*, p. 19; Beckett and Hencke, *Marching to the Fault Line*, pp. 47–53.
65. Thatcher MSS, document 13358, Text of Walker speech in Oxford, 30 May 1984 Accessed 1/6/20 at: https://www.margaretthatcher.org/document/133358
66. Steber, 'Fundamentals at stake', pp. 62–4, pp. 68–9; Milne, *Enemy Within*, pp. 26–7.
67. TNA, PREM 19/1331, John Redwood to Prime Minister, 13 July 1984.
68. 'Attack on enemy within', *The Times*, 20 July 1984. The 'enemy within' was referenced in comparison to the 'enemy without'—General Galtieri, the Argentine leader defeated in the Falklands War. See, Turner, *Rejoice! Rejoice!* pp. 178–9.
69. 'The Speech that never was—Thatcher papers for 1984 open to the public', Accessed 12/5/23 at: https://www.cam.ac.uk/research/news/the-speech-that-never-was-thatcher-papers-for-1984-open-to-the-public; Travis, 'Thatcher was to call Labour and miners "enemy within" in abandoned speech', *The Guardian*, 3 October 2014, Accessed 12/5/23 at: https://www.theguardian.com/politics/2014/oct/03/thatcher-labour-miners-enemy-within-brighton-bomb
70. Andrew, *Defence of the Realm*, pp. 676–7.
71. TNA, PREM 19/1334, '10 Downing Street' AT [Turnbull] to FERB [Butler], 15 October 1984.
72. TNA, HO 325/624, MJA Partridge to Caffarey, 23 July 1984.
73. TNA, HO 325/624, Leon Brittan to Thatcher, 3 August 1984.
74. The National Reporting Centre coordinated the local police forces into a national response.
75. TNA, HO 325/624, 'Intelligence Related to the Miners' Dispute', RA Harrington, F4 Division, 16 July 1984.
76. TNA, HO 325/624, Leon Brittan to Thatcher, 3 August 1984.
77. Beckett and Hencke, *March to the Fault Line*, pp. 84–5; Turner, *Rejoice! Rejoice!*

pp. 180–3. See also, Coulter, Miller, Walker, *A State of Siege*, particularly pp. 26–45.

78. 'Queen 'appalled' by police charge on miners during Battle of Orgreave', *The Times*, 22 August 2023.
79. Johnson, '"Battle of Orgreave": Police "had been relishing" clashes', *BBC News*, 10 October 2016. Accessed 7/6/23 at: https://www.bbc.co.uk/news/uk-37609965
80. In 2012, the BBC discovered numerous police statements from Orgreave were identical. Johnson, 'Orgreave: The battle that's not over', *BBC News*, 10 October 2016. Accessed 7/6/23 at: https://www.bbc.co.uk/news/uk-37562740; 'Miners' strike policing: Labour calls for Orgreave enquiry', *BBC News*, 22 October 2012. Accessed 7/6/23 at: https://www.bbc.co.uk/news/uk-england-19982118
81. Vinen, *Thatcher's Britain*, p. 176.
82. Milne, *Enemy Within*, pp. 358–9.
83. TNA, HO 504/34, 'Reviews after the NUM dispute', Sir Brian Cubbon, 16 November 1984.
84. TNA, HO 504/34, 'AFTER THE NUM DISPUTE', HMCIC. Questions about the role of Special Branch were not restricted to the strike. In 1980, David Heaton, a civil servant at the Home Office, raised the question, "how can the work of police officers (which all members of Special Branches are) in investigating subversion, as currently defined, be justified given that the definition covers some activities which are not, as such, unlawful?" See, Mitting, *Undercover Policing Inquiry Tranche 1 Interim Report*, June 2023, pp. 93–4. Accessed 22/8/23 at: https://www.gov.uk/government/publications/undercover-policing-inquiry-tranche-1-interim-report
85. 'Brittan defends Special Branch right to spy on strikers', *The Times*, 29 January 1985, p. 5.
86. HC Hansard Deb, 2 March 1978, vol 945, cc649–50.
87. Milne, *Enemy Within*, p. 385. See also, Coulter, Miller, Walker, *A State of Siege*, pp. 46–7.
88. Andrew, *Defence of the Realm*, p. 677.
89. TNA, HO 325/624, 'Intelligence Related to the Miners' Dispute', RA Harrington, F4 Division, 16 July 1984.
90. TNA, HO 325/624, Caffarey to Partridge, 25 July 1984.
91. Rimington, *Open Secret*, p. 163.
92. Ibid., p. 165.
93. TNA, HO 325/624, MJA Partridge to Caffarey, 23 July 1984. See also, TNA, PREM 19/1579, document 24a, Robert Armstrong to Prime Minister, 1 February 1985.
94. Beckett and Hencke, *Marching to the Fault Line*, p. 155; Milne, *Enemy Within*, p. 349–51; McSmith, *No Such Thing As Society*, pp. 164–5. The original fine

had come about after the High Court had ruled that the NUM had broken its constitution by holding a strike without having a national ballot.

95. TNA, FCO 28/6513, 'Soviet Money for British Miners', MJF Duncan, Soviet and East European Research Department, 21 November 1984.
96. Andrew, *Defence of the Realm*, pp. 679–80; Macintyre, *The Spy and the Traitor*, p. 188.
97. Macintyre, *The Spy and the Traitor*, pp. 199–200; Andrew, *Defence of the Realm*, p. 680; Beckett and Hencke, *Marching to the Fault Line*, p. 184.
98. *True Spies*, BBC Two, 'Something better change'.
99. Vinen, *Thatcher's Britain*, p. 159.
100. TNA, PREM 19/1579, document 24a, Robert Armstrong to Prime Minister, 1 February 1985.
101. Ibid. Fears that information of the meetings with Larkins would not remain private were proven to be unfounded.
102. As well as investigating Soviet funding, the Security Service also investigated allegations that Libya provided the NUM with funds. See, Andrew, *Defence of the Realm*, pp. 677–9; Milne, *Enemy Within*, pp. 166–89, 415; Beckett and Hencke, *Marching to a Fault Line*, pp. 159–65, 270.
103. Andrew, *Defence of the Realm*, p. 677.
104. Steber, 'Fundamentals at stake', p. 61, p. 68; Beckett and Hencke, *Marching to the Fault Line*, pp. 24–5, 119–20; Vinen 'A War of Position?' pp. 138–9; Milne, *Enemy Within*, pp. 15–18; Phillips, 'The 1972 Miners' Strike', pp. 194–5.
105. TNA, CAB 301/491, SPL(72)5(FINAL), 'The National Union of Mineworkers', 15 January 1973, APPENDIX p. 29.
106. Andrew, *Defence of the Realm*, p. 598, p. 676.
107. Joannou, "Fill a bag and feed a family", pp. 180–1.
108. Andrew, *Defence of the Realm*, p. 676.
109. Ibid., p. 979, footnote 45.
110. Rimington, *Open Secret*, p. 163; Andrew, *Defence of the Realm*, p. 677; *True Spies*, BBC Two, 'Something better change'. For information on Scargill not holding a strike ballot see, McSmith, *No Such Thing As Society*, pp. 155–6, Turner, *Rejoice! Rejoice!* pp. 179–80.
111. *True Spies*, BBC Two, 'Something better change'.
112. 'Pit leaders seek backing for big pay increases', *The Times*, 5 July 1983; MacGregor, *The Enemies Within*, p. 11.
113. Andrew, *Defence of the Realm*, p. 677.
114. TNA, HO 325/624, MJA Partridge to Caffarey, 23 July 1984.
115. TNA, HO 325/624, Leon Brittan to Thatcher, 3 August 1984.
116. *True Spies*, BBC Two, 'Something better change'.
117. TNA, HO 325/624, 'Intelligence Related to the Miners' Dispute', RA Harrington, F4 Division, 19 July 1984.
118. TNA, HO 325/624, Leon Brittan to Thatcher, 3 August 1984.
119. See, Ewing and Gearty, *Freedom Under Thatcher*, pp. 52–4.

120. Sandbrook, *Seasons in the Sun*, p. 328.
121. Lashmar and Oliver, *Britain's Secret Propaganda War*, pp. 150–1.
122. One arm of the state—the IRD—was involved in the referendum and covertly 'propagate[d] the reasons for voting yes'. See, Mayhew, *A War of Words*, p. 46; Lashmar and Oliver, *Britain's Secret Propaganda War*, pp. 145–51.
123. Rose, *Campaigns against Western Defence*, pp. 130–2.
124. TNA, HO 325/149, Special Branch Report – 'Aldermaston March Committee', 8 April 1958.
125. Wilson and Adams, *Special Branch*, pp. 250–1.
126. Hewison, *In Anger*, pp. 164–6; Rose, *Campaigns against Western Defence*, pp. 133; Grant, *After the Bomb*, p. 131; Hennessy, *Secret State*, p. 113.
127. TNA, CAB 134/1345, AC(H)(60)15, 'The Communist Party of Great Britain and its attitude towards unilateral nuclear disarmament', 14 October 1960. The CPGB, like Moscow, believed in multilateral disarmament.
128. TNA, CAB 134/2489, S(PS)(62)14, 'The Security Significance of membership of the Campaign for Nuclear Disarmament and the Committee of 100', 10 May 1962.
129. TNA, KV 2/3775, serial 65a, 'Ext. from C.C. Cardiff', 11.6.59; TNA, CAB 134/1345, AC(H)(60) 2nd meeting, 24 October 1960.
130. TNA, CAB 134/2489, S(PS)(62)14.
131. Wilson and Adams, *Special Branch*, pp. 248–51; Hennessy, *Secret State*, pp. 116–17; TNA, CAB 134/2489, S(PS)(62)14, 'The Security Significance of membership of the Campaign for Nuclear Disarmament and the Committee of 100', 10 May 1962.
132. TNA, CAB 134/2490, S(PS)(63)7, 'Spies for Peace', 9 May 1963.
133. TNA, CAB 134/2498, S.C.(63)7, 'Spies for Peace', 14 October 1963.
134. Ibid.
135. TNA, FCO 168/2804, 'Information Research Department's (IRD) Responsibilities on the Home Front', 6 March 1968.
136. TNA, CAB 134/2498, S.C.(63)7, 'Spies for Peace', 14 October 1963.
137. For discussion on when the decline began see, Hennessy, *Winds of Change*, pp. 295, 297–8, 302; Grant, *After the Bomb*, pp. 131–4.
138. Rose, *Campaigns against Western Defence*, pp. 135–6; Sandbrook, *Never Had It So Good*, p. 273.
139. Wilson and Adams, *Special Branch*, p. 250; Phythian, 'CND's Cold War', pp. 142–9; Rose, *Campaigns against Western Defence*, pp. 137–9.
140. TNA, CAB 134/3143, PSC(71)4, 'Security Significance of Membership of the Campaign of Nuclear Disarmament', 19 March 1971. Communists did have sufficient involvement in CND in the 1970s to fill the posts of vice-chairman, national organiser and press officer. (See, Rose, *Campaigns against Western Defence*, p. 139) By the mid-1970s, eight of fifteen members of the CND national executive were CPGB members. (Andrew, *Defence of the Realm*, p. 673)

141. McSmith, *No Such Thing As Society*, pp. 51–2 Rose, *Campaigns Against Western Defence*, pp. 141–4; Phythian, 'CND's Cold War', pp. 150–1; Ewing and Gearty, *Freedom Under Thatcher*, pp. 95–6.
142. Andrew, *Defence of the Realm*, p. 673.
143. Sandbrook, *Who Dares Wins*, pp. 399–400.
144. Rose, *Campaigns Against Western Defence*, pp. 140–1.
145. Andrew, *Defence of the Realm*, pp. 674–5.
146. TNA, CAB 134/4645, PSC(82)9, The security significance of Membership of or support for the Campaign for Nuclear Disarmament, Note by the Security Service.
147. See, HC Hansard Deb, 10 December 1984, vol 69 c737; HC Hansard Deb, 12 March 1985, vol 75 c156.
148. Andrew, *Defence of the Realm*, p. 676.
149. TNA, HO 325/569, JG Pilling, Home Office, to Box 500, 15 November 1983.
150. TNA, HO 325/569, PM Imbert, Chief Constable Thames Valley Police to JG Pilling, Home Office, 5 December 1983.
151. TNA, DEFE 24/2877, 'Threat Posed by CND', Major PW Snell, 3 June 1982.
152. TNA, DEFE 24/2877, 'CND Activity', Lt Col MEA Berryman, 1 July 1982.
153. TNA, DEFE 24/2877, 'Threat Posed by CND', Major PW Snell, 3 June 1982.
154. TNA, DEFE 24/2877, Loose Minute, 'CND ACTIVITY', RTR Jackson, 27 July 1982. Jackson noted 'I hate to think what [investigative journalist] Duncan Campbell could do with it.'
155. TNA HO 325/566, MoD Security Sub Committee – Counter Extremists, 6 July 1983; TNA, HO 325/620, MoD Security Sub Committee – Counter Extremists, 1 May 1985.
156. Gill, *Policing Politics*, p. 225; Aldrich, *GCHQ*, p. 368; Ewing and Gearty, *Freedom Under Thatcher*, p. 61.
157. Andrew, *Defence of the Realm*, p. 676.
158. 'Strategic Tory attack on the nuclear disarmers', *The Guardian*, 14 February 1983, p. 3. The same report states that the Coalition had informal links and meetings with Peter Blaker MP, Minister of State for Defence.
159. 'The Curse of the President's men', *The Guardian*, 8 October 1983. For a Coalition report on CND that was sent to the MoD see, TNA, FCO 66/1731, 'CND Annual Conference, Sheffield, November 1982', Coalition for Peace through Security, January 1983.
160. *The Guardian*, 22 February 1985.
161. Aldrich and Cormac, *The Black Door*, p. 357.
162. 'Peace link denied by Cameron', *The Times*, 2 February 1983; 'Churchill denies smearing CND', *The Times*, 30 April 1983. The Churchill 'campaign' is also referred to in, Thatcher MSS, document 122590, Lord Beloff memo, 14 December 1982. Accessed 22/8/23 at: https://www.margaretthatcher.org/document/122590

163. Thatcher MSS, document 122776, Conservative Party: Shipley minute to Parkinson, 7 June 1982. Accessed 3/3/21 at: https://www.margaretthatcher.org/document/122776
164. Thatcher MSS, document 122590, Lord Beloff memo, 14 December 1982. Accessed 22/8/23 at: https://www.margaretthatcher.org/document/122590
165. Rimington, *Open Secret*, p. 163.
166. Andrew, *Defence of the Realm*, p. 673.
167. HL Hansard Deb, 17 December 1986, vol 483 c176.
168. 'Phone-tap girl tells how MI5 broke rules', *The Observer*, 24 February 1985.
169. Andrew, *Defence of the Realm*, p. 675; 'Phone-tap girl tells how MI5 broke rules', *The Observer*, 24 February 1985.
170. Andrew, *Defence of the Realm*, p. 758.
171. 'Phone-tap girl tells how MI5 broke rules', *The Observer*, 24 February 1985.
172. Ewing and Gearty, *Freedom under Thatcher*, p. 62.
173. Andrew, *Defence of the Realm*, pp. 675–6.
174. Ibid., pp. 673–4.
175. *True Spies*, BBC Two, Episode 3 'It Could Happen to You', 10 November 2002.
176. Andrew, *Defence of the Realm*, p. 681, p. 979, footnote 67.
177. Urban, *UK Eyes Alpha*, pp. 48–9; Andrew, *Defence of the Realm*, p. 560.
178. McSmith, *No Such Thing As Society*, p. 51; Sandbrook, *Who Dares Wins*, pp. 384–408.
179. *True Spies*, BBC Two, 'It Could Happen to You'; HC Hansard Deb, 21 December 1983, vol 51 cc 540–6.
180. HC Hansard Deb, 21 December 1983, vol 51 cc 540–6.
181. Ibid., c542.
182. *True Spies*, BBC Two, 'It Could Happen to You'.
183. Sandbrook, *White Heat*, pp. 535–6; Wilson and Adams, *Special Branch*, pp. 251–5; Thomas, 'Protests Against the Vietnam War', pp. 342–3.
184. *True Spies*, BBC Two, 'Subversive My Arse'.
185. Evans and Lewis, *Undercover*, pp. 14–16.
186. Ellison and Morgan, *Review of Possible Miscarriages of Justice*, pp. 13–14; Taylor, 'Investigation into links between the Special Demonstration Squad and Home Office', p. 13.
187. Most notably through the work of Rob Evans and Paul Lewis in *The Guardian* and later in their book *Undercover: The True Story of Britain's Secret Police*.
188. See, www.ucpi.org.uk
189. Evans, 'Undercover police spied on more than 1,000 political groups in UK', *The Guardian*, 27 July 2017. Accessed 17/1/20 at: https://www.theguardian.com/uk-news/2017/jul/27/undercover-police-spied-on-more-than-1000-political-groups-in-uk For a list of the groups, see, https://www.theguardian.com/uk-news/ng-interactive/2018/oct/15/uk-political-groups-spied-on-undercover-police-list Accessed 17/1/20.

190. Mitting, *Undercover Policing Inquiry Tranche 1*, p. 95. Accessed 22/8/23 at: https://www.gov.uk/government/publications/undercover-policing-inquiry-tranche-1-interim-report Mitting wrote, 'In the era of the Cold War and the "Troubles", the infiltration of groups which in fact threatened the safety or well-being of the state (or in the 1952 formulation, gave rise to an internal danger to it) could have been justified. In the period covered by Tranche 1 [1968–1982], only three groups penetrated by the SDS satisfied either of these criteria—(Provisional) Sinn Fein and two [classified] groups identified in the closed interim report. The great majority of deployments by the SDS in this period did not satisfy either criterion.'
191. Evans and Lewis, *Undercover*, pp. 18–19.
192. TNA, MEPO 2/11477/2, document 17b, 21 November 1969.
193. Mitting, *Undercover Policing Inquiry Tranche 1*, p. 24. Accessed 22/8/23 at: https://www.gov.uk/government/publications/undercover-policing-inquiry-tranche-1-interim-report
194. TNA, HO 325/125, document 6a, 'Springbok Tour, Conference of Chief Constables, General Considerations', November 1969.
195. MPS-0736296, document 8a, SB report, STST, 5 May 1970. Accessed 22/6/21 at: https://www.ucpi.org.uk/publications/special-branch-report-noting-that-a-branch-of-the-stst-is-to-be-set-up-at-the-north-west-polytechnic/
196. TNA, MEPO 2/11477/1, document 2, K. Oxford to J. Lawlor, 16 January 1970; MEPO 2/11477/2, document 16a, 'Twickenham Rugby Football Ground London Counties v Springboks', 23 November 1969.
197. TNA, MEPO 31/30, document 25a, 'South African Cricket Tour', 23 March 1970.
198. MPS-0736190, Special Branch report covering a conference of Stop the Seventy Tour, 7 March 1970. Accessed 12/4/23 at: https://www.ucpi.org.uk/publications/special-branch-report-covering-a-conference-of-stop-the-seventy-tour/; UCPI0000008660, Special Branch report authored by HN135 covering the first National Conference of Stop the Seventy Tour, 9 March 1970. Accessed 12/4/23 at: https://www.ucpi.org.uk/publications/special-branch-report-authored-by-hn135-covering-the-first-national-conference-of-stop-the-seventy-tour/
199. Listed under attendees as 'Dave Gower' on p. 5.
200. TNA, MEPO 31/30, Special Branch Report, 'South Africa Cricket Tour', 4 June 1970. The Hains moved to Britain from South Africa in 1966.
201. Winter, *Inside BOSS*, p. 417.
202. See, for example, TNA, KV 2/4045, serial 172a.
203. TNA, HO 325/117, document 3a, 'Anti-Apartheid Movement', 31 January 1970.
204. TNA, FCO 45/732, folio 3, 'Anti-Apartheid Movement (AAM)', KR Crook, IRD, 17 February 1970.

205. *The Times*, 14 March 1970, p. 3; Bunyan, *The History and Practice of the Political Police*, p. 233; Hollingsworth and Norton-Taylor, *Blacklist*, p. 206.
206. For greater detail about the post-war EL see, Hollingsworth and Norton-Taylor, *Blacklist*, pp. 149–54, 164–73.
207. Andrew, *Defence of the Realm*, p. 672.
208. Hollingsworth and Tremayne, *The Economic League*, pp. 37–8; Hollingsworth and Norton-Taylor, *Blacklist*, pp. 164–5.
209. Rosenbaum, 'Tracking the Anti-Apartheid Groups', BBC News, 27 September 2005. Accessed 27/1/25 at: http://news.bbc.co.uk/1/hi/uk_politics/4285964.stm; Evans, 'Documents show how Special Branch infiltrated Anti-Apartheid Movement', *The Guardian*, 27 September 2005. Accessed 27/1/25 at: https://www.theguardian.com/politics/2005/sep/27/uk.freedomofinformation; Apartheid Document 2. Accessed 27/1/25 at: https://www.theguardian.com/politics/foi/images/0,9069,1581236,00.html
210. Hain, 'Why were Special Branch watching me even when I was an MP?', *The Guardian*, 25 March 2015. Accessed 11/2/20 at: https://www.theguardian.com/commentisfree/2015/mar/25/special-branch-watching-me-mp-democracy
211. TNA, FCO 45/732, folio 1, William Wilson, 12 February 1970; folio 3, 'Anti-Apartheid Movement (AAM)', KR Crook, IRD, 17 February 1970.
212. Bunce and Field, *Darcus Howe*, p. 118, footnote 1.
213. TNA, HO 325/143, letter to DHJ Hillary, Home Office, 31 December 1971.
214. Bunyan, *The History and Practice of the Political Police*, pp. 146–7.
215. Bunce and Field, *Darcus Howe*, pp. 93, 97–104.
216. Ibid., pp. 108–18.
217. TNA, HO 325/143, 'Black Power Demonstration', 9 August 1970.
218. TNA, HO 325/143, '"Black Power" in the United Kingdom', 11 August 1970, p. 8.
219. Bunce and Field, *Darcus Howe*, pp. 131–4.
220. Ibid., p. 113.
221. TNA, HO 325/143, DHJ Hillary letter dated 19 Jan 1972; letter to DHJ Hillary, Home Office, 25 January 1972.
222. See, 'Half-Yearly reports for the period…', included in TNA, CAB 134/3840.
223. TNA, CAB 301/489, 'The Threat of Subversion to the UK', April 1976, p. 14.
224. TNA, CAB 134/2491, S(O)(PS)(63)6, 'Employment of Coloured Staffs by Security Departments', 4 December 1963.
225. TNA, CAB 134/2491, S(O)(PS)(63)1st Meeting, 13 December 1963.
226. TNA, CAB 134/2467, S(O)(64)1st Meeting, 19 February 1964.
227. TNA, CAB 134/2467, S(O)(64)3, 'Employment of Coloured Staffs by Defence Departments', 20 January 1964.
228. TNA, CAB 134/2467, S(O)(64)12, 'Employment of Coloured Staffs by Defence Departments', 9 June 1964.

229. TNA, CAB 134/2498, S(64)5, 'Employment of Coloured Staffs by Defence Departments', 30 June 1964.
230. TNA, CAB 134/2498, S(64)2nd Meeting, 7 July 1964.
231. TNA, CAB 134/3270, SM(O)(PS)67 2nd Meeting, 19 April 1967.
232. TNA, CAB 134/3253 SM(67)3, 'Employment on Classified Work of Staff and Service personnel not of United Kingdom Origin', 29 September 1967, paragraph 7. This was later publicised by Norman Lever in a written answer to a parliamentary question. (HC Hansard Deb, 28 June 1968, vol 767 c148w).
233. TNA, CAB 134/3256, SM(O)67, 2nd Meeting, 24 May 1967; Lomas, "Crocodiles in the Corridors", p. 162.
234. TNA, CAB 134/3271, SM(O)(PS)(68)4, 'Race Relations Bill: Security Implications', 13 March 1968; TNA, CAB 134/3271, SM(O)(PS)(68) 2nd Meeting, 18 March 1968; TNA, CAB 134/3253, SM(67)3, Report by the Chairman of the Official Committee on Security, 29 September 1967; TNA, CAB 134/3270 SM(O)(PS)(67) 3rd meeting, 17 July 1967.
235. TNA, CAB 134/3271, SM(O)(PS)(68)4, 'Race Relations Bill: Security Implications', 13 March 1968; Lomas, "Crocodiles in the Corridors", pp. 167–8.
236. TNA, CAB 134/3143, PSC(72)5, Security Precautions in Connection with persons not of United Kingdom origin or who have Alien connections, 7 August 1972, ANNEX A, paragraph 10; Lomas, "Crocodiles in the Corridors", p. 168.
237. For much more detail on the vetting process with regards to black people and foreign nationals see, Lomas, "Crocodiles in the Corridors".
238. TNA, CAB 134/3270, SM(O)(PS)(67)7, 'Candidates for Appointment to the Civil Service: Assignment of Coloured Candidates to Security Departments', 10 July 1967; Lomas, "Crocodiles in the Corridors", p. 161.
239. Ferris, *Behind the Enigma*, p. 411.
240. Ibid., pp. 454–7. In the late 1940s, intelligence officials discussed compiling a list of Jews who had 'past access to secret and confidential' information. See, KV 2/3211, minute 114, Lt. Col. M.C.S. Phipps, 20 July 1949. For more information about MI5 attitudes towards Jews see, Andrew, *Defence of the Realm*, pp. 363–4.
241. Smith, *New Cloak, Old Dagger*, p. 68.
242. Rimington, *Open Secret*, pp. 161–2.
243. *True Spies*, BBC Two, 'Subversive My Arse'.
244. Andrew, *Defence of the Realm*, pp. 659, 854.

CONCLUSION

1. Andrew, *Defence of the Realm*, p. 853.
2. It is true that, immediately after the First World War, it was opportune for British intelligence officials to warn of a growing threat posed by Bolshevism.

Threatened with budget cuts following the 1918 Armistice, they may have helped to safeguard their own future by providing numerous reports on the grave threat posed by communism and the Soviet Union to Britain. Most intelligence officials did, though, genuinely believe in the threat.
3. Andrew, *Defence of the Realm*, p. 780.
4. Vincent, *Culture of Secrecy*, p. 251.
5. TNA, KV 4/473, 16 February 1951.
6. TNA, CAB 21/5003, Ministerial Committee on Communism, 5 February 1951.
7. TNA, CAB 301/490/1, 'Industrial Action: The Role of the Security Service', 27 January 1971, pp. 3–4.
8. Hennessy, *The Prime Minister*, p. 211.
9. Andrew, *Defence of the Realm*, pp. 659, 854.
10. Penrose and Freeman, *Conspiracy of Silence*, p. 140. Similar comments were made by other officials including Dick White. See, Penrose and Freeman, *Conspiracy of Silence*, p. 265; Carter, *Anthony Blunt*, pp. 258–9.
11. Walton, *Empire of Secrets*, pp. 67–8; Bower, *The Perfect English Spy*, p. 66; Dorril, *MI6*, p. 18.
12. Correra, *MI6*, p. 215.
13. Rimington, *Open Secret*, p. 95.
14. Andrew, *Defence of the Realm*, pp. 667–8.
15. Ibid.
16. Smith, *New Cloak, Old Dagger*, pp. 66–7.
17. Norton-Taylor, *The State of Secrecy*, p. 178; Norton-Taylor, 'The Secret Servants' *The Guardian*, 11 July 2009. Accessed 5/7/23 at: https://www.theguardian.com/uk/2009/jul/11/mi5-interviews-uk-security-terrorism
18. Smith, *New Cloak, Old Dagger*, pp. 67–9; Andrew, *Defence of the Realm*, p. 675, pp. 680–1. Duff was not the only 'outsider' appointed as MI5 DG during the twentieth century—Sir Howard Smith had also previously been a diplomat—but he was the only one who sought to reform the organisation.
19. Andrew, *Defence of the Realm*, pp. 560, 680–2.
20. Lockhart, 'Intelligence: A British View', p. 37.
21. *True Spies*, BBC Two, 'It Could Happen to You'.
22. *True Spies*, BBC Two, 'Subversive My Arse'.
23. See Appendices; Gill, *Policing Politics*, pp. 119–21. For discussions about defining subversion see, TNA, CAB 301/491, Lord Rothschild to Prime Minister, 14 December 1972. For a good summary of the process of defining subversion and subsequent clarifications see, UCPI, Witness Statement, First Witness Statement of Security Service Witness Z, 21 March 2021, pp. 2–5. Accessed 14/7/23 at: https://www.ucpi.org.uk/publications/first-witness-statement-of-security-service-witness-z/
24. HC Hansard Deb, 2 March 1978, vol 945, cc649–50.
25. Interview: Michael Ignatieff Discusses His Book "The Lesser Evil: Political

Ethics in an Age of Terror", *Talk of the Nation*, 7 June 2004. Accessed 12/7/23 at: https://legacy.npr.org/programs/totn/transcripts/2004/jun/040607.ignatieff.html. Originally quoted in, Bonino and Kaoullas, 'Preventing Political Violence in Britain', p. 827.

26. Library of Congress, *Respectfully Quoted: A Dictionary of Quotations* (New York: Dover Publications Inc., 2010) p. 201; Jay A (ed.), *Oxford Dictionary of Political Quotations, 4th Edition* (Oxford: Oxford University Press, 2012) p. 114.
27. Loewenstein, 'Militant Democracy', pp. 423–4. Loewenstein was writing about fascism during the 1930s but the points he makes are equally applicable to revolutionary communism. His arguments are credible even outside of the particular horror of the 1930s.
28. Beckett, *Enemy Within*, p. 147.
29. Horne, *Macmillan 1957–1986: Volume II*, p. 457.
30. Most notably the cases of Michael Bettaney and Geoffrey Prime.
31. Bower, *The Perfect English Spy*, p. 364.
32. TNA, CAB 130/20/GEN183, GEN 183/8, Committee on Positive Vetting Report, 27 October 1950; Beesley, *The Official History of Cabinet Secretaries*, p. 51.
33. Andrew, *Defence of the Realm*, pp. 766–7.
34. Evans, *Eric Hobsbawm*, pp. 589–92.
35. TNA, CAB 130/20, 'The Employment of Civil Servants, etc. exposed to Communist influence', Working Party of the Cabinet Committee on Subversive Activities, 1 May 1947.
36. Curry, *Security Service*, p. 86.
37. Phillips, *Secret Twenties*, p. 77.
38. Styles, 'British Domestic Security Policy', pp. 199–200.
39. Pearce, *Spymaster*, p. 71. Another former head of a British intelligence agency, Sir David Omand, Director of GCHQ between 1996 and 1997, has also attended to this theme. 'Intelligence agencies prefer to keep quiet about successes so that they can repeat them', he said, 'but failures can become very public'; Omand, *How Spies Think*, p. 6.
40. Andrew, *Defence of the Realm*, p. 841.
41. Omand, *How Spies Think*, pp. 4–5.
42. Hennessy, *Secret State*, p. 415.

BIBLIOGRAPHY

Primary Sources

The National Archives (TNA)

AIR 2 – Air Ministry and Ministry of Defence: Registered Files
BA 19 – Treasury, and Civil Service Department: Management (Personnel) Division: Personnel Management (MP and PM Series) Files
CAB 21 – Cabinet Office and predecessors: Registered Files (1916 to 1965)
CAB 23 – War Cabinet and Cabinet: Minutes
CAB 24 – War Cabinet and Cabinet: Memoranda
CAB 65 – War Cabinet and Cabinet: Minutes
CAB 79 – War Cabinet and Cabinet: Chiefs of Staff Committee: Minutes
CAB 128 – Cabinet: Minutes
CAB 130 – Cabinet: Miscellaneous Committees: Minutes and Papers
CAB 134 – Cabinet: Miscellaneous Committees: Minutes and Papers (General Series)
CAB 301 – Cabinet Office: Cabinet Secretary's Miscellaneous Papers
DEFE 24 – Ministry of Defence: Defence Secretariat Branches and their Predecessors: Registered Files
FCO 28 – Foreign Office and Foreign and Commonwealth Office: Northern Department and East European and Soviet Department (and succeeding departments): Registered Files
FCO 45 – Commonwealth Office and Foreign and Commonwealth Office: Southern African Department and predecessors: Registered Files

BIBLIOGRAPHY

FCO 168 – Foreign Office and Foreign and Commonwealth Office: Information Research Department; Registered Files
FO 371 – Foreign Office: Political Departments: General Correspondence from 1906-1966
HO 45 – Home Office: Registered Papers
HO 144 – Home Office: Registered Papers, Supplementary
HO 283 – Home Office: Defence Regulation 18B, Advisory Committee Papers
HO 325 – Home Office: Queen's Peace (QPE Symbol Series) Files
HO 504 – Home Office: Inspectorate of Constabularies (IC Symbol Series) Files
HO 532 – Home Office: Security Planning
KV 2 – The Security Service: Personal (PF Series) Files
KV 3 – The Security Service: Subject (SF series) Files
KV 4 – The Security Service: Policy (Pol F Series) Files
KV 5 – The Security Service: Organisation (OF series) Files
MEPO 2 – Metropolitan Police: Office of the Commissioner: Correspondence and Papers
MEPO 3 – Metropolitan Police: Office of the Commissioner: Correspondence and Papers, Special Series
MEPO 31 – Metropolitan Police: Registered Files, Police Organisation and Administration
MEPO 38 – Metropolitan Police: Special Branch: Registered Files
PREM 11 – Prime Minister's Office: Correspondence and Papers, 1951-1964
PREM 15 – Prime Minister's Office: Correspondence and Papers, 1970-1974
PREM 16 – Prime Minister's Office: Correspondence and Papers, 1974-1979
PREM 19 – Records of the Prime Minister's Office: Correspondence and Papers, 1979-1997
PRO 30 – James Ramsay MacDonald and predecessors and successors: Papers
T 162 – Treasury: Establishments Department: Registered Files

Labour History Archive & Study Centre, People's History Museum, Manchester (LHASC)

Labour Party Archive, General Secretary's Papers, LP/GS

BIBLIOGRAPHY

Margaret Thatcher Foundation Archive (Thatcher MSS)

Document 122590, Lord Beloff memo ("The anti-CND campaign"), 14 December 1982

Document 122776, Conservative Party: Shipley minute to Parkinson (observations on previous day's CND demonstration), 7 June 1982

Document 13358, Text of Walker speech in Oxford, 30 May 1984

Newspapers, websites and periodicals

BBC News, bbc.co.uk
Daily Express
London Review of Books
The Guardian
The Independent
The Telegraph
The Times
Workers' Weekly

Official Reports and Briefing Papers

Ellison M and Morgan A, *Review of Possible Miscarriages of Justice: Impact of Undisclosed Undercover Police Activity on the Safety of Convictions, Report to the Attorney General*, HC 291 (July 2015)

Mitting J, *Undercover Policing Inquiry Tranche 1 Interim Report* (June 2023)

Strickland P, Dawson J and Godec S, *The Wilson Doctrine* (House of Commons Library Briefing Paper No 4258) (12 June 2017)

Taylor S, 'Investigation into links between the Special Demonstration Squad and Home Office' (Home Office, June 2015)

Secondary Sources

Books, book chapters and journal articles

Aaronovitch D, *Party Animals: My Family and Other Communists* (London: Vintage, 2017)

Adonis A, *Ernest Bevin: Labour's Churchill* (London: Biteback Publishing, 2021)

Aldrich RJ, 'Secret intelligence for a post-war world: reshaping the British intelligence community, 1944–51', in, Aldrich RJ (ed.), *British Intelligence, Strategy and the Cold War, 1945–51* (London: Routledge, 1992) pp. 15–49

—, *The Hidden Hand: Britain, America, and Cold War Secret Intelligence* (Woodstock; New York: The Overlook Press, 2002)

—, *GCHQ: The Uncensored Story of Britain's Most Secret Intelligence Agency* (London: Harper Press, 2011)

Aldrich RJ and Cormac R, *The Black Door: Spies, Secret Intelligence and British Prime Ministers* (London: William Collins, 2017)

Anderson GD, *Fascists, Communists and the National Government: Civil Liberties in Great Britain, 1931–1937* (Columbia; London: University of Missouri Press, 1983)

Anderson P and Davey K, *Moscow Gold? The Soviet Union and the British left* (Ipswich: Aaaargh! Press, 2017)

Andrew C, *Her Majesty's Secret Service: The Making of the British Intelligence Community* (New York: Viking, 1986)

—, *The Defence of the Realm: The Authorised History of MI5* (London: Penguin, 2010)

— *The Secret World: A History of Intelligence* (London: Penguin, 2018)

Andrew C and Dilks D, *The Missing Dimension: Governments and Intelligence Communities in the Twentieth Century* (London: Macmillan, 1984)

Andrew C and Mitrokhin V, *The Mitrokhin Archive: The KGB in Europe and the West* (London: Allen Lane, 1999)

Baker D, 'The Extreme Right in the 1920s: Fascism in a Cold Climate, or 'Conservatism with Knobs on'?', in, Mike Cronin (ed.), *The Failure of British Fascism: The Far Right and the Fight for Political Recognition* (Basingstoke: Macmillan, 1996) pp. 12–28

Bar-Joseph U, *Intelligence Intervention in the Politics of Democratic States: The United States, Israel, and Britain* (Pennsylvania: The Pennsylvania State University Press, 1995)

Barnes T, *Dead Doubles: The extraordinary worldwide hunt for one of the Cold War's most notorious spy rings* (London: Weidenfeld and Nicolson, 2021)

Barnett N, *Britain's Cold War: Culture, Modernity and the Soviet Threat* (London: I.B. Tauris, 2020)

Bean R, 'Liverpool Shipping Employers and the Anti-Communist Activities of J. M. Hughes, 1920–25', Bulletin of Society for the Study of Labour History, No. 34 (1977) pp. 22–6

Beckett A, *When the Lights Went Out: What Really Happened to Britain in the Seventies* (London: Faber and Faber, 2010)

Beckett F, *Enemy Within: The Rise and Fall of the British Communist Party* (London: Merlin Press, 1995)

—, *Fascist in the Family: The Tragedy of John Beckett MP* (Oxon: Routledge, 2017)
Beckett F and Hencke D, *Marching to the Fault Line: The Miners' Strike and the Battle for Industrial Britain* (London: Constable, 2009)
Beers L, *Your Britain: Media and the Making of the Labour Party* (Cambridge, MA.; London: Harvard University Press, 2010)
Beesley I, *The Official History of the Cabinet Secretaries* (London: Routledge, 2017)
Benn T, *Against the Tide: Diaries 1973–76* (London: Hutchinson, 1989)
—, *Out of the Wilderness: Diaries 1963–67* (London: Arrow Books, 1991)
Benewick R, *Political Violence and Public Order: A Study of British Fascism* (London: Allen Lane, 1969)
Bennett G, *'A most extraordinary and mysterious business': The Zinoviev Letter of 1924* (London: Library and Records Department, Foreign & Commonwealth Office, 1999)
—, *Churchill's Man of Mystery: Desmond Morton and the World of Intelligence* (Oxon: Routledge, 2007)
—, *The Zinoviev Letter: The Conspiracy that Never Dies* (Oxford: Oxford University Press, 2020)
Best A, "We are virtually at war with Russia': Britain and the Cold War in East Asia, 1923–40', *Cold War History*, Vol. 12, No. 2 (May 2012) pp. 205–225
Bew J, *Citizen Clem: A Biography of Attlee* (London: Riverrun, 2017)
Black L, "The Bitterest Enemies of Communism': Labour Revisionists, Atlanticism, and the Cold War', *Contemporary British History*, Vol. 15, No. 4 (Autumn 2001) pp. 26–62
Bonino S and Kaoullas LG, 'Preventing Political Violence in Britain: An Evaluation of over Forty Years of Undercover Policing of Political Groups Involved in Protest', *Studies in Conflict and Terrorism*, Vol. 38, Issue 10 (2015) pp. 814–40
Bowd G, *Fascist Scotland: Caledonia and the Far Right* (Edinburgh: Birlinn Limited, 2013)
Bower T, *The Perfect English Spy: Sir Dick White and the Secret War* (London: Mandarin, 1996)
Brinson C and Dove R, *A matter of intelligence: MI5 and the surveillance of Anti-Nazi refugees, 1933–1950* (Manchester: Manchester University Press, 2014)
Brown KD, 'The Anti-Socialist Union, 1908–49', in, Kenneth D. Brown, *Essays in Anti-Labour History: Responses to the Rise of Labour in Britain* (Basingstoke; London: Macmillan, 1974) pp. 234–61

BIBLIOGRAPHY

Bunce R and Field P, *Darcus Howe: A Political Biography* (London: Bloomsbury, 2015)

Bunyan T, *The History and Practice of the Political Police in Britain* (London: Julian Friedmann Publishers, 1976)

Callaghan J, *The Far Left in British Politics* (Oxford: Basil Blackwell, 1987)

Callaghan J and Phythian M, 'State Surveillance of the CPGB Leadership: 1920s–1950s', *Labour History Review*, Vol. 69, No. 1 (April 2004) pp. 19–33

—, 'State surveillance and communist lives: Rose Cohen and the Early British Communist Milieu', *Journal of Intelligence History*, Vol. 12, Issue 2 (2013) pp. 134–55

Carley MJ, *Silent Conflict: A Hidden History of Early Soviet-Western Relations* (Plymouth: Rowmann & Littlefield, 2017)

Carlton D, *Churchill and the Soviet Union* (Manchester: Manchester University Press, 2000)

Carter M, *Anthony Blunt: His Lives* (London: Macmillan, 2001)

Caute D, *Red List: MI5 and British Intellectuals in the Twentieth Century* (London: Verso, 2022)

Channing I, *The Police and the Expansion of Public Order Law in Britain, 1829–2014* (Abingdon: Routledge, 2015)

Childs W, *Episodes and Reflections* (London: Cassell & Company Ltd, 1930)

Clark J, *The National Council of Civil Liberties and the Policing of Interwar Politics* (Manchester: Manchester University Press, 2012)

Close F, *Trinity: The Treachery and Pursuit of the Most Dangerous Spy in History* (London: Penguin, 2020)

Clutterbuck R, *Britain in Agony: The Growth of Political Violence* (Harmondsworth: Penguin Books, 1980)

Cobain I, *The History Thieves: Secrets, Lies and the Shaping of a Modern Nation* (London: Portobello Books, 2017)

Coleman B, 'The Conservative Party and the Frustrations of the Extreme Right', in, Thorpe A (ed.), *The Failure of Political Extremism in Inter-War Britain* (Exeter: Department of History and Archaeology, University of Exeter, 1989) pp. 49–66

Copsey N, *Anti-Fascism in Britain (Second Edition)* (Oxon: Routledge, 2017)

Correra G, *MI6: Life and Death in the British Secret Service* (London: Weidenfeld and Nicolson, 2012)

Cotter CP, 'Emergency Detention in Wartime: The British Experience', *Stanford Law Review*, Vol. 6, No. 2 (March 1954) pp. 238–86

BIBLIOGRAPHY

Coulter J, Miller S and Walker M, *A State of Siege, Politics and Policing of the Coalfields: Miners' Strike 1984* (London: Canary Press, 1984)

Cross C, *The Fascists in Britain* (London: Barrie and Rockliff, 1961)

Crick M, *Militant* (London: Biteback Publishing, 2016)

Curry JC, *The Security Service 1908–1945: The Official History* (Kew: Public Record Office, 1999)

Dack J, 'It certainly isn't cricket!' – Media Responses to Mosley and the BUF', in, Nigel Copsey and Andrzej Olechnowicz (eds.) *Varieties of Anti-Fascism: Britain in the Inter-War Period* (Basingstoke: Palgrave Macmillan, 2010) pp. 140–61

Davenport-Hines R, *Enemies Within: Communists, the Cambridge Spies and the Making of Modern Britain* (London: William Collins, 2018)

Deery P, "The secret battalion': Communism in Britain during the Cold War', *Contemporary British History*, Vol.13, Issue 4 (1999) pp. 1–28

Defty A, *Britain, America and Anti-Communist Propaganda 1945–53: The Information Research Department* (Abingdon: Routledge, 2004)

Defty A, Bochel H and Kirkpatrick J, 'Tapping the Telephones of Members of Parliament: The 'Wilson Doctrine' and Parliamentary Privilege', *Intelligence and National Security*, Vol. 29, No. 5 (2014) pp. 675–97

Desmarais RH, 'Strikebreaking and the Labour Government of 1924', *Journal of Contemporary History*, Vol. 8, No. 4 (Oct 1973) pp. 165–75

Devlin D, *Sam Wanamaker: A Global Performer* (London: Oberon Books, 2019)

Dorril S, *MI6: Fifty Years of Special Operations* (London: Fourth Estate, 2000)

—, *Blackshirt: Sir Oswald Mosley and British Fascism* (London: Penguin, 2007)

Dorril S and Ramsay R, *Smear! Wilson and the Secret State* (London: Fourth Estate, 1991)

Dylan H, *Defence Intelligence and the Cold War: Britain's Joint Intelligence Bureau 1945–1964* (Oxford: Oxford University Press, 2014)

Evans RJ, *Eric Hobsbawm: A Life in History* (London: Little Brown, 2019)

Evans R and Lewis P, *Undercover: The True Story of Britain's Secret Police* (London: Guardian Books, 2014)

Ewing KD and Gearty CA, *Freedom Under Thatcher: Civil Liberties in Modern Britain* (Oxford: Clarendon Press, 1990)

—, *The Struggle for Civil Liberties: Political Freedom and the Rule of Law in Britain 1914–1945* (Oxford: Oxford University Press, 2000)

Ewing KD, Mahoney J and Moretta A, *MI5, The Rule of Law and the Cold War* (Oxford: Oxford University Press, 2020)

Farman C, *The General Strike* (St Albans: Granada Publishing, 1974)

Farr BS, *The Development and Impact of Right-Wing Politics in Britain, 1903–1932* (London; New York: Garland Publishing, 1987)

Ferris J, *Behind the Enigma: The Authorised History of GCHQ, Britain's Secret Cyber-Intelligence Agency* (London: Bloomsbury, 2020)

Ferris J and Bar-Joseph U, 'Getting Marlowe to Hold His Tongue: The Conservative Party, the Intelligence Services and the Zinoviev Letter', *Intelligence and National Security*, Vol. 8, No. 4 (October 1993) pp. 100–37

Flory H, 'The Arcos Raid and the Rupture of Anglo-Soviet Relations, 1927', *Journal of Contemporary History*, Vol. 12, No. 4 (October 1977) pp. 707–23

Folly MH, *Churchill, Whitehall and the Soviet Union, 1940–45* (Basingstoke: Macmillan, 2000)

Gerwarth R, *The Vanquished: Why the First World War Failed to End, 1917–1923* (London: Penguin, 2017)

Gill P, *Policing Politics: Security Intelligence and the Liberal Democratic State* (London: Frank Cass, 1994)

Glees A, *The Secrets of the Service: British Intelligence and Communist Subversion 1939–51* (London: Jonathan Cape, 1987)

Goldman AL, 'Defence Regulation 18B: Emergency Internment of Aliens and Political Dissenters in Great Britain during World War II', *Journal of British Studies*, Vol. 12, No. 2 (May 1973) pp. 120–36

Goldstein E, 'Britain and the Origins of the Cold War', in, Hopkins MF, Kandiah MD and Staerck G, *Cold War Britain, 1945–1964* (Basingstoke: Palgrave Macmillan, 2003) pp. 7–14

Goodman MS, 'Who Is Trying to Keep What Secret from Whom and Why? MI5- FBI Relations and the Klaus Fuchs Case', *Journal of Cold War Studies*, Vol. 7 Issue 3 (Summer 2005) pp. 124–46

—, *Spying on the Nuclear Bear: Anglo-American Intelligence and the Nuclear Bomb* (Stanford: Stanford University Press, 2007)

Gould J, *The Witchfinder General: A Political Odyssey* (London: Biteback Publishing, 2016)

Grant J, 'The Role of MI5 in the Internment of British Fascists during the Second World War', *Intelligence and National Security*, Vol. 24, No. 4 (August 2009) pp. 499–528

Grant M, *After the Bomb: Civil Defence and Nuclear War in Britain, 1945–68* (Basingstoke: Palgrave Macmillan, 2010)

BIBLIOGRAPHY

Graubard SR, *British Labour and the Russian Revolution, 1917–1924* (London: Oxford University Press, 1956)

Greenspan NT, *Atomic Spy:The Dark Lives of Klaus Fuchs* (NewYork:Viking, 2020)

Greenwood S, *Britain and the ColdWar, 1945–51* (Basingstoke: Macmillan, 2000)

Griffiths R, *Fellow Travellers of the Right: British Enthusiasts for Nazi Germany, 1933–9* (London: Constable, 1980)

Hemming H, *M: Maxwell Knight, MI5's Greatest Spymaster* (London: Arrow Books, 2018)

Hennessey T and Thomas C, *Spooks:The Unofficial History of MI5 From M to Miss X, 1909–39* (Stroud: Amberley, 2010)

Hennessey T and Thomas C, *Spooks:The Unofficial History of MI5 From the First Atom Spy to 7/7, 1945–2009* (Stroud: Amberley, 2011)

Hennessy P, *The Prime Minister: The Office and its Holders since 1945* (London: Penguin, 2001)

—, *Never Again: Britain 1945–1951* (London: Penguin, 2006)

—, *Having it so Good: Britain in the Fifties* (London: Penguin, 2007)

—, *The Secret State: Preparing for theWorst 1945–2010* (London: Penguin, 2010)

—, *Winds of Change: Britain in the Early Sixties*, (Penguin Books, 2020)

Hennessy P and Brownfield G, 'Britain's Cold War Security Purge: The Origins of Positive Vetting', *The Historical Journal,* Vol. 25, Issue 4 (1982) pp. 965–73

Hewison R, *In Anger: Culture in the ColdWar 1945–60* (London:Weidenfeld and Nicolson, 1981)

Hobsbawm E, *The Age of Extremes:The Short Twentieth Century, 1914–1991* (London: Abacus, 1995)

—, *Interesting Times: A Twentieth-Century Life* (London: Abacus, 2003)

Hollingsworth M and Norton-Taylor R, *Blacklist:The Inside Story of Political Vetting* (London:The Hogarth Press, 1988)

Hollingsworth M and Tremayne C, *The Economic League: The Silent McCarthyism* (London: National Council for Civil Liberties, 1989)

Hope J, 'Fascism, the Security Service and the Curious Careers of Maxwell Knight and James McGuirk Hughes', *Lobster*, No. 22 (1991) pp. 1–5

—, 'British Fascism and the State 1917–1927: a re-examination of the documentary evidence', *Labour History Review*, Vol. 57, No.3 (1992) pp. 77–83

—, 'Fascism and the State in Britain: The Case of the British Fascist',

Australian Journal of Politics and History, Vol. 39, Issue 3 (December 1993) pp. 367–80

—, 'Surveillance or Collusion? Maxwell Knight, MI5 and the British Fascisti', *Intelligence and National Security*, Vol. 9, No. 4 (October 1994) pp. 651–75

—, 'Blackshirts, Knuckle-Dusters and Lawyers: Documentary Essay on the Mosley versus Marchbanks Papers', *Labour History Review*, Vol. 65, No. 1 (2000) pp. 41–58

Hopkins MF, 'Herbert Morrison, the Cold War and Anglo-American Relations, 1945–1951', in Hopkins MF, Kandiah MD and Staerck G, *Cold War Britain, 1945–1964* (Basingstoke: Palgrave Macmillan, 2003) pp. 17–29

Horne A, *Macmillan 1957–1986:Volume II of the Official Biography* (London: Macmillan, 1989)

Howard A and West R, *The Making of The Prime Minister* (London: Jonathan Cape, 1965)

Howell D, *MacDonald's Party: Labour Identities and Crisis, 1922–1931* (Oxford: Oxford University Press, 2002)

Hughes G, "Giving the Russians a Bloody Nose': Operation *Foot* and Soviet Espionage in the United Kingdom, 1964–71, *Cold War History*, Vol. 6, No. 2 (May 2006) pp. 229–49

Hughes M, *Spies at Work* (Wroclaw: Amazon Fulfilment, 2012)

Hutton R, *Agent Jack: The True Story of MI5's Secret Nazi Hunter* (London: Weidenfeld & Nicolson, 2019)

Jeffery K, *MI6: The History of the Secret Intelligence Service* (London: Bloomsbury, 2011)

Jeffery K and Hennessy P, *States of Emergency: British Governments and Strikebreaking since 1919* (London: Routledge & Keegan Paul, 1983)

Jeffreys-Jones R, *We Know All About You: The Story of Surveillance in Britain and America* (Oxford: Oxford University Press, 2017)

Joannou M, "Fill a bag and feed a family': the miners' strike and its supporters', in, Davis J and McWilliam R, *Labour and the Left in the 1980s* (Manchester: Manchester University Press, 2018) pp. 172–91

Johnson N, *Britain and the 1918–19 Influenza Pandemic: A dark epilogue* (London: Routledge, 2006)

Jones B, *The Russia Complex: The British Labour Party and the Soviet Union* (Manchester: Manchester University Press, 1977)

Jones G, *Science, Politics and the Cold War* (London: Routledge, 1988)

Jones J, *Union Man*, (London: Collins, 1986)

Jones T, *Whitehall Diary:Volume I, 1916–1925* (London: Oxford University Press, 1969)

Kassimeris G and Price O, "A new and disturbing form of subversion': Militant Tendency, MI5 and the threat of Trotskyism in Britain, 1937–1987', *Contemporary British History*, Vol. 36, Issue 3 (2022) pp. 355–79

—, "What did you do to them Klaus?': The Klaus Fuchs Atomic Espionage Case and its Impact on the Scientific Community in early Cold War Britain', *Twentieth Century British History*, Vol. 34, Issue 2, (2023) pp. 246–74

—, "Implacable Enemies'? The Labour Party and the intelligence community in 1920s Britain', *Contemporary British History*, Vol. 38, Issue 2 (2024) pp. 183–218

Keeble C, *Britain, The Soviet Union and Russia* (Basingstoke: Macmillan, 2000)

Kendall W, *The Revolutionary Movement in Britain 1900–1921* (London: Weidenfeld and Nicolson, 1969)

Kent SK, *Aftershocks: Politics and Trauma in Britain, 1918–1931* (Basingstoke: Palgrave Macmillan, 2009)

Kerbaj R, *The Secret History of the Five Eyes: The Untold Story of the International Spy Network* (London: Blink, 2022)

Kerr G, *British Traitors: Betrayal and Treachery in the Twentieth Century* (Harpenden: Oldcastle Books, 2022)

Kuper S, *The Happy Traitor, Spies, Lies and Exile in Russia: The Extraordinary Story of George Blake* (London: Profile Books, 2021)

Lashmar P and Oliver J, *Britain's Secret Propaganda War* (Stroud: Sutton Publishing, 1998)

Laucht C, *Elemental Germans: Klaus Fuchs, Rudolf Peierls and the Making of British Nuclear Culture 1939–59* (Basingstoke: Palgrave Macmillan, 2012)

Lawrence J, 'Fascist violence and the politics of public order in inter-war Britain: the Olympia debate revisited', *Historical Research*, Vol. 76, No 192 (May 2003) pp. 238–67

Laybourn K and Murphy D, *Under the Red Flag: A History of Communism in Britain, 1849–1991* (Stroud: Sutton, 1991)

Lee S (ed.), *Sir Rudolf Peierls: Selected Private and Scientific Correspondence, Vol. 2* (London: World Scientific Publishing, 2009)

Lewis DS, *Illusions of Grandeur: Mosley, Fascism and British Society, 1931–81* (Manchester: Manchester University Press, 1987)

Lilleker D, *Against the Cold War: The History and Political Traditions of Pro-*

Sovietism in the British Labour Party 1945–89 (London: I.B. Tauris, 2004)

Linehan G, *British Fascism 1918–39: Parties, Ideology and Culture* (Manchester: Manchester University Press, 2000)

Lockhart JB, 'Intelligence: A British View', in Robertson KG (Ed.), *British and American Approaches to Intelligence* (Basingstoke: Macmillan, 1987) pp. 37–51

Lomas DWB, "…the Defence of the Realm and Nothing Else': Sir Findlater Stewart, Labour Ministers and the Security Service', *Intelligence and National Security*, Vol. 30, No.6 (2015) pp. 793–816

—, *Intelligence, Security and the Attlee Governments: An uneasy relationship?* (Manchester: Manchester University Press, 2017)

—, "Crocodiles in the Corridors": Security Vetting, Race and Whitehall, 1945–1968', *The Journal of Imperial and Commonwealth History*, Volume 49, Issue 1 (2021) pp. 148–77

Loewenstein K, 'Militant Democracy and Fundamental Rights, I', *The American Political Science Review*, Vol. 31, No. 3 (June 1937) pp. 417–32

Lownie A, *Stalin's Englishman: The Lives of Guy Burgess* (London: Hodder, 2016)

Luff J, 'Covert and Overt Operations: Interwar Political Policing in the United States and the United Kingdom', *American Historical Review*, Vol. 122, Issue 3 (June 2017) pp. 727–57

Lygo E, 'Promoting Soviet Culture in Britain: The history of the Society for Cultural Relations between the peoples of the British Commonwealth and the USSR, 1924–1945', *The Modern Language Review*, Vol. 108, No. 2 (April 2013) pp. 571–96

MacFarlane LJ, *The British Communist Party and Moscow: Its origin and development until 1929* (London: MacGibbon and Kee, 1966)

Macintyre B, *A Spy Among Friends: Philby and the Great Betrayal* (London: Bloomsbury, 2015)

—, *The Spy and the Traitor: The Greatest Espionage Story of the Cold War* (London: Penguin, 2019)

Madeira V, "No Wishful Thinking Allowed': Secret Service Committee and Intelligence Reform in Great Britain, 1919–23', *Intelligence and National Security*, Vol. 18, No. 1 (Spring 2003) pp. 1–20

—, *Britannia and the Bear: The Anglo-Russian Intelligence Wars 1917–1929* (Woodbridge: The Boydell Press, 2016)

Maguire RC, "The Fascists…are…to be depended upon.' The British Government, Fascists and Strike-breaking during 1925 and 1926', in, Copsey N and Renton D (eds.), *British Fascism, the Labour Movement and the State* (Basingstoke: Palgrave Macmillan, 2005) pp. 6–26

Maguire TJ, 'Counter-Subversion in Early Cold War Britain: The Official Committee on Communism (Home), the Information Research Department, and 'State-Private Networks'', *Intelligence and National Security*, Vol. 30, No. 5 (2015) pp. 637–66

Mahoney J, 'Civil Liberties in Britain During the Cold War: The Role of Central Government', *The American Journal of Legal History*, Vol. 33, Issue 1 (Jan 1989) pp. 53–100

Mahoney J, 'Constitutionalism, the Rule of Law, and the Cold War', in, Campbell T, Ewing KD and Tomkins A (eds.), *The Legal Protection of Human Rights: Sceptical Essays* (Oxford: Oxford University Press, 2011)

Marquand D, *Ramsay MacDonald* (London: Jonathan Cape, 1977)

Massey C, 'The Labour Party's inquiry into Liverpool District Labour Party and Expulsion of Nine Members of the Militant Tendency, 1985–1986', *Contemporary British History*, Vol. 34, No. 2 (2020) pp. 299–324

Massey C, 'The Militant Tendency and Entryism in the Labour Party', in, Smith E and Worley M (eds.), *Waiting for Revolution: The British Far Left from 1956* (Manchester: Manchester University Press, 2017) pp. 238–57

Mayhew C, *A War of Words: A Cold War Witness* (London; New York: I.B. Tauris, 1998)

Mazower M, 'Conclusion: The Policing of Politics in Historical Perspective', in, Mazower M (ed.), *The Policing of Politics in the Twentieth Century* (Oxford: Berghahn Books, 1997) pp. 241–56

McIvor A, 'Essay in Anti-Labour History: Political black listing and anti-socialist activity between the wars', *Society for the study of Labour History Bulletin*, Vol. 53, Part 1 (Spring 1988) pp. 18–26

—, "A Crusade for Capitalism': The Economic League, 1919–39', *Journal of Contemporary History*, Vol. 23, No. 4 (Oct 1988) pp. 631–55

McLynn F, *The Road Not Taken: How Britain Narrowly Missed a Revolution* (London: The Bodley Head, 2012)

McSmith A, *No Such Thing As Society: A History of Britain in the 1980s* (London: Constable, 2011)

Mikardo I, *Back-Bencher* (London: Weidenfeld & Nicolson, 1988)

Miller CW, 'Extraordinary Gentlemen: the Economic League,

business networks, and organised labour in war planning and rearmament', *Scottish Labour History*, 52 (2017) pp. 120–51

Mills T, *The BBC: Myth of a Public Service* (London: Verso, 2016)

Milne S, *The Enemy Within: The Secret War Against the Miners* (London: Pan Books, 1995)

Morgan J, *Conflict and Order: The Police and Labour Disputes in England and Wales, 1900–1939* (Oxford: Clarendon Press, 1987)

—, 'Conspiracy and Contemporary History: Revisiting MI5 and the Wilson Plot[s]', *Journal of Intelligence History*, Vol 13, No. 2 (2014) pp. 161–75

Moss N, *Klaus Fuchs: The Man Who Stole the Atom Bomb* (London: Sharpe Books, 2018)

Mowat CL, *Britain Between the Wars: 1918–1940* (London: Methuen & Co, 1955)

Munro D, 'George Rudé – Communist Activist and Inactivist', *Working USA: The Journal of Labor and Society*, Vol. 19, Issue 2 (June 2016) pp. 147–62

Münzner D, 'The surveillance of friends: MI5 and friendly aliens during the Second World War', *Journal of Intelligence History*, Vol. 13, Issue 2 (2014) pp. 131–43

Newsinger J, 'Blackshirts, Blueshirts and the Spanish Civil War', *The Historical Journal*, Vol. 44, No. 3 (Sept 2001) pp. 825–44

Noel G, *The Great Lock-Out of 1926* (London: Constable, 1976)

Northedge FS and Wells A, *Britain and Soviet Communism: The Impact of a Revolution* (Basingstoke: Macmillan, 1982)

Norton-Taylor R, *The State of Secrecy: Spies and the media in Britain* (London: IB Tauris, 2020)

Olmstead K, 'British and US Anticommunism Between the World Wars', *Journal of Contemporary History*, Vol. 53, No. 1 (2018) pp. 89–108

Omand D, *How Spies Think: Ten Lessons in Intelligence* (London: Viking, 2020)

Parsons S, 'British 'McCarthyism' and the Intellectuals', in, Fryth J, *Labour's Promised Land? Culture and Society in Labour Britain 1945–51* (London: Lawrence & Wishart, 1995) pp. 224–45

Pearce M, *Spymaster: The Life of Britain's Most Decorated Cold War Spy and Head of MI6, Sir Maurice Oldfield* (London: Corgi Books, 2017)

Penrose B and Freeman S, *Conspiracy of Silence: The Secret Life of Anthony Blunt* (London: Grafton Books, 1987)

Perkins A, *A Very British Strike* (London: Macmillan, 2006)

Phillips J, 'The 1972 Miners' Strike: Popular Agency and Industrial

Politics in Britain', *Contemporary British History*, Vol. 20, No. 2 (June 2006) pp. 187–207

Phillips T, *The Secret Twenties: British Intelligence, The Russians and The Jazz Age* (London: Granta Books, 2017)

Phythian M, 'CND's Cold War', *Contemporary British History*, Vol. 15, No. 3 (Autumn 2001) pp. 133–56

Porter B, *Plots and Paranoia: A History of Political Espionage in Britain 1790–1988* (London: Unwin Hyman, 1989)

Potter K, 'British McCarthyism', in, Jeffreys-Jones R and Lownie A (eds.), *North American Spies: New Revisionist Essays* (Edinburgh: Edinburgh University Press, 1991) pp. 143–57

Pugh M, *'Hurrah for the Blackshirts!': Fascists and Fascism in Britain between the Wars* (London: Jonathan Cape, 2005)

—, *Speak for Britain! A New History of the Labour Party* (London, Vintage Books, 2011)

Purvis S and Hulbert J, *When Reporters Cross the Line: The Heroes, The Villains, The Hackers and the Spies* (London: Biteback Publishing, 2013)

Pye N, 'Militant's Laboratory: Liverpool City Council's Struggle with the Thatcher Government', in, J. Davis and R. Rohan Mcwilliam (eds.), *Labour and the Left in the 1980s* (Manchester: Manchester University Press, 2018) pp. 151–71

Quinlan K, *The Secret War Between the Wars* (Woodbridge: The Boydell Press, 2014)

Renshaw P, *The General Strike* (London: Eyre Methuen, 1975)

Reynolds D, *The Long Shadow: The Great War and the Twentieth Century* (London: Simon & Schuster, 2014)

Rimington S, *Open Secret: The Autobiography of the Former Director-General of MI5* (London: Arrow Books, 2002)

Rose C, *Campaigns against Western Defence: NATO's adversaries and critics* (Basingstoke: Macmillan, 1986)

Rose K, *King George V* (London: Weidenfeld and Nicolson, 1983)

Rosen R, 'The Russian Problem and Bolshevism', *The North American Review*, Vol. 210, No. 765 (August 1919) pp. 235–43

Rosenberg C, *1919: Britain on the Brink of Revolution* (London: Bookmarks, 1987)

Rossi JP, 'The British Reaction to McCarthyism, 1950–54', *Mid-America*, Vol. 70, No. 1 (1988) pp. 5–18

Rossiter M, *The Spy Who Changed the World* (London: Headline, 2015)

Rothwell V, *Britain and the Cold War 1941–47* (London: Jonathan Cape, 1982)

Sandbrook D, *Never Had It So Good: A History of Britain from Suez to the Beatles* (London: Abacus, 2006)

—, *White Heat: A History of Britain in the Swinging Sixties* (London: Abacus, 2007)

—, *State of Emergency, The Way We Were: Britain, 1970–1974* (London: Penguin, 2011)

—, *Seasons in the Sun: The Battle for Britain, 1974–1979* (London: Penguin, 2013)

—, *Who Dares Wins: Britain 1979–1982* (London: Penguin, 2020)

Saunders FS, 'Stuck on the Flypaper', London Review of Books, Vol. 37 No. 7 (April 2015)

Schlaepfer C, 'Signals Intelligence and British Counter-subversion in the Early Cold War', *Intelligence and National Security*, Vol. 29, Issue 1 (2014) pp. 82–98

Schneer J, *Labour's Conscience: The Labour Left 1945–51* (Boston: Unwin Hyman, 1988)

Schwartz LH, *Political Warfare against the Kremlin: US and British Propaganda Policy at the Beginning of the Cold War* (Basingstoke: Palgrave Macmillan, 2009)

Seldon A and Meakin J, *The Cabinet Office, 1916–2016* (London: Biteback, 2016)

Service R, *Spies and Commissars: Bolshevik Russia and the West* (Basingstoke; Oxford: Macmillan, 2011)

Shaw E, *Discipline and discord in the Labour Party: The politics and managerial control in the Labour Party, 1951–87* (Manchester: Manchester University Press, 1988)

Shaw T, *British Cinema and the Cold War: The State, Propaganda and Consensus* (London: I.B. Tauris, 2006)

Simpson AWB, *In the Highest Degree Odious: Detention Without Trial in Wartime Britain* (Oxford: Clarendon Press, 1992)

Sisman A, *John Le Carré: The Biography* (London: Bloomsbury, 2015)

Smith C, *The Last Cambridge Spy: John Cairncross, Bletchley Park Mole and Soviet Agent* (Cheltenham: The History Press, 2022)

Smith D and Chamberlain P, *Blacklisted: The secret war between big business and union activists* (Oxford: New Internationalist Publications Ltd, 2015)

Smith J, *British Writers and MI5 Surveillance 1930–1960* (Cambridge: Cambridge University Press, 2013)

Smith M, *New Cloak, Old Dagger: How Britain's Spies Came in from the Cold* (London: Victor Gollancz, 1996)
— *Foley: The Spy Who Saved 10,000 Jews* (London: Hodder & Stoughton, 1999)
Solomon V, *State Surveillance, Political Policing and Counter-Terrorism in Britain, 1880–1914* (Woodbridge: The Boydell Press, 2021)
Spinney L, *Pale Rider: The Spanish Flu of 1918 and How it Changed the World* (London: Vintage, 2017)
Steber M, 'Fundamentals at stake: the Conservatives, industrial relations and the historical framing of the miners' strike in 1984/85', *Contemporary British History*, Vol. 32, No. 1 (2018) pp. 60–77
Stevenson J, 'Conservatism and the failure of fascism in interwar Britain' in, Blinkhorn M (ed.), *Fascists and Conservatives: The Radical Right and the Establishment in Twentieth-Century Europe* (London: Unwin Hyman, 1990) pp. 264–82
Stevenson J, 'The BUF, The Metropolitan Police and public order', in, Lunn K and Thurlow R (eds.), *British Fascism: Essays on the radical right in inter-war Britain* (London: Croom Helm, 1980) pp. 135–49
Stocker P, 'Importing fascism: reappraising the British fascisti, 1923–1926', *Contemporary British History*, Vol. 30, No. 3 (2016) pp. 326–48
Tate T, *Hitler's British Traitors: The Secret History of Spies, Saboteurs and Fifth Columnists* (London: Icon Books, 2018)
Taylor PM, *British Propaganda in the Twentieth Century: Selling Democracy* (Edinburgh: University Press, 1999)
Taylor R, 'Citrine's Unexpurgated Diaries, 1925–26: "The Mining Crisis and the National Strike"', *Historical Studies in International Relations*, Issue 20 (September 2005) pp. 67–102
Thomas G, *Secret Wars: One Hundred Years of British Intelligence Inside MI5 and MI6* (New York: St Martin's Griffin, 2010)
Thomas N, 'Protests Against the Vietnam War in 1960s Britain: The Relationship between Protesters and the Press', *Contemporary British History*, Vol. 22, No. 3 (September 2008) pp. 335–54
Thomas-Symonds N, 'A Reinterpretation of Michael Foot's Handling of the Militant Tendency', *Contemporary British History*, Vol. 19, No. 1 (Spring 2005) pp. 27–51
Thompson EP, *The Making of the English Working Class* (London: Penguin, 1980)
Thorpe A, 'Comintern 'Control' of the Communist Party of Great

Britain, 1920–1943', *The English Historical Review*, Vol. 113, No.452 (June 1998) pp. 637–62

—, *The British Communist Party and Moscow, 1920–43* (Manchester: Manchester University Press, 2000)

—, 'The membership of the Communist Party of Great Britain, 1920–1945', *The Historical Journal*, Volume 43, Issue 3 (September 2000) pp. 777–800

Thorpe A, "The Only Effective Bulwark Against Reaction and Revolution': Labour and the Frustration of the Extreme Left', in, Thorpe A (ed.), *The Failure of Political Extremism in Inter-War Britain* (Exeter: Department of History and Archaeology, University of Exeter, 1989) pp. 11–28

Thorpe K, 'The 'Juggernaut Method': The 1966 State of Emergency and the Wilson Government's Response to the Seamen's Strike', *Twentieth Century British History*, Vol. 12, Issue 4 (January 2001) pp. 461–85

Thurlow R, *Fascism in Britain: A History, 1918–1985* (Oxford: Basil Blackwell, 1987)

—, *The Secret State: British Internal Security in the Twentieth Century* (Oxford: Blackwell, 1995)

—, "A Very Clever Capitalist Class'. British Communism and State Surveillance', *Intelligence and National Security*, Vol. 12, No. 2 (April 1997) pp. 1–21

Thurlow R, 'Passive and Active Anti-Fascism: The State and National Security, 1923–45', in, Copsey N and Olechnowicz A (eds.) *Varieties of Anti-Fascism: Britain in the Inter-War Period* (Basingstoke: Palgrave Macmillan, 2010) pp. 162–80

Thurlow R, 'State Management of the British Union of Fascists in the 1930s', in, Cronin M (ed.), *The Failure of British Fascism: The Far Right and the Fight for Political Recognition* (Basingstoke: Macmillan, 1996)

Thurlow R, 'The Failure of British Fascism' in, Thorpe A (ed.), *The Failure of Political Extremism in Inter-War Britain* (Exeter: Department of History and Archaeology, University of Exeter, 1989) pp. 67–84

Thurlow R, 'The Security Service, The Communist Party of Great Britain and British Fascism, 1932–51', in, Copsey N and Renton D (eds.), *British Fascism, the Labour Movement and the State* (Basingstoke: Palgrave Macmillan, 2005) pp. 27–45

Tinline P, *The Death of Consensus: 100 Years of British Political Nightmares* (London: Hurst, 2022)

Toye R, 'Winston Churchill's "Crazy Broadcast": Party, Nation and the 1945 Gestapo Speech', *The Journal of British Studies*, Vol. 49, Issue 3 (July 2010) pp. 655–80

Trevor-Roper H, *The Philby Affair: Espionage, Treason, and Secret Services* (London: William Kimber, 1968)

Turner AW, *Crisis? What Crisis? Britain in the 1970s* (London: Aurum, 2013)

—, *Rejoice! Rejoice! Britain in the 1980s* (London: Aurum, 2013)

Twigge S, Hampshire E and Macklin G, *British Intelligence Secrets, Spies and Sources* (Kew: National Archives, 2009)

Udy G, *Labour and the Gulag: Russia and the Seduction of the British Left* (London: Biteback, 2017)

Urban M, *UK Eyes Alpha: The Inside Story of British Intelligence* (London: Faber and Faber, 1997)

Vincent D, *The Culture of Secrecy: Britain, 1832–1998* (Oxford: Oxford University Press, 1998)

Vinen R, *Thatcher's Britain: The Politics and Social Upheaval of the Thatcher Era* (London: Simon & Schuster, 2009)

—, 'A War of Position? The Thatcher Government's Preparation for the 1984 Miners' Strike', *English Historical Review*, Vol. 134, No. 566 (February 2019) pp. 121–50

Walton C, *Empire of Secrets: British Intelligence, The Cold War and the Twilight of Empire* (London: William Collins, 2014)

—, *Spies: The Epic Intelligence War Between East and West* (London: Abacus Books, 2023)

Ward SR, 'Intelligence Surveillance of British Ex-Servicemen, 1918–1920', *The Historical Journal*, Vol. 16, Issue 1 (1973) pp. 179–88

Webb S, *1919: Britain's Year of Revolution* (Barnsley: Pen & Sword, 2016)

Weiler P, *British Labour and the Cold War* (Stanford: Stanford University Press, 1988)

Weinberger B, 'Police perceptions of labour in the inter-war period: the case of the unemployed and miners on strike', in, Snyder F and Hay D (eds.), *Labour, Law and Crime: An historical perspective* (London; New York: Tavistock Publications, 1987) pp. 150–79

—, *Keeping the Peace? Policing Strikes in Britain, 1906–1926* (Oxford: Berg, 1991)

West N, *Historical Dictionary of British Intelligence* (2nd ed.) (Plymouth: Rowman & Littlefield, 2014)

White S, 'British Labour in Soviet Russia, 1920', *The English Historical Review*, Vol. 109, No. 432 (June 1994) pp. 621–40

BIBLIOGRAPHY

Wilford H, 'The Information Research Department: Britain's secret Cold War weapon revealed', *Review of International Studies*, Vol. 24, Issue 3 (July 1998) pp. 353–69

Wilson R and Adams I, *Special Branch, A History: 1883–2006* (London: Biteback Publishing, 2015)

Winter G, *Inside BOSS: South Africa's Secret Police* (London: Penguin, 1981)

Wish H, 'Anglo-Soviet Relations during Labour's First Ministry (1924)', *The Slavonic and East European Review*, Vol. 17, No. 50 (January 1939) pp. 389–403

Woodbridge S, 'Fraudulent Fascism: The Attitude of Early British Fascists towards Mosley and the New Party', *Contemporary British History*, Vol. 23, No. 4 (Dec 2009) pp. 493–507

Worley M, *Labour inside the Gate: A History of the Labour Party between the Wars* (London: IB Tauris, 2005)

Wright P, *Spycatcher* (Richmond, Victoria: Heinemann Australia, 1987)

Wring D, *The Politics of Marketing the Labour Party* (Basingstoke: Palgrave Macmillan, 2005)

Young K, 'Cold War Insecurities and the Curious Case of John Strachey', *Intelligence and National Security*, Vol. 29, No. 6 (2014) pp. 901–25

Unpublished works

Flowers M, *Atomic Spice: A Partial Autobiography*, (Unpublished, 2009)

Gibbs TS, 'British and American Counter-Intelligence and Atom Spies, 1941–1950', PhD Thesis, University of Cambridge, 2007

Maynard LA, 'Coalition and Conservative reactions to the Communist threat to Britain 1917–1927', PhD Thesis, Queen Mary University of London, 2020

Styles W, 'British Domestic Security Policy and Communist Subversion: 1945–1964', PhD Thesis, University of Cambridge, 2016

Thomas I, 'Confronting the Challenge of Socialism: the British Empire Union and the National Citizens' Union 1917–1927', MA Thesis, University of Wolverhampton, August 2010

Walton C, 'British Intelligence and Threats to British National Security after the Second World War', Unpublished PhD Thesis, University of Cambridge, 2006

INDEX

Adams, Ian, 184
Aldermaston march, 183–4
Allen, Phillip, 142, 168
All-Russian Co-operative Society (ARCOS) raid, 25, 45, 142, 236n
Amis, Kingsley, 150
Anderson, John, 15, 61, 81, 211
Andrew, Christopher, 12, 25, 32, 39–40, 43, 54, 128, 141, 147, 177, 190, 222
Anglo-German Academic Bureau, 76
Anglo-German Fellowship (AGF), 76
Anglo-Soviet relations 1–4, 13–14, 34, 87, 89–91, 178–9, 185–6, 211–12
   and the Bolshevik Revolution, 2–4, 9–12
   détente, 149–50
   Operation FOOT, 165–6
   severing of diplomatic relations (1927), 23–5
   and WWII, 1–2, 81, 83–5
Anti-Apartheid Movement (AAM), 6, 183, 196–8
anti-fascists, 17, 67–70, 73, 245n
anti-Nazis, refugees, 78–80

anti-nuclear campaigners, 6, 183–90, 192–3, 215
Armstrong, Robert, 157–8, 170, 179, 180
Army Intelligence Corps, 187
Asquith, Herbert, 33–4
Atomic Energy Research Establishment (AERE), Harwell, 104–5, 107, 115
Attlee, Clement, 91, 101–2, 106, 114–5, 126, 129–34, 136–8, 143, 159, 259n
Auslands Organisation, 75

Baden-Powell, Robert, 77
Bakatin, Vadim V., 1
Baker White, John, 57–8
Baldwin, Stanley, 28, 33–4, 39, 41, 43, 71
Ball, Joseph, 40–1, 59
Barker, Sara, 139
Beloff, Lord Max, 189
Bennett, Eileen, 92, 250n
Benvenuto, Ludimila, 143
Bernal, J. D., 98, 211
Bevan, Aneurin, 130, 259n
Bevin, Ernest, 132, 133, 137
Bing, Geoffrey, 134–5

INDEX

Birkenhead, Lord (FE Smith), 33
Blake, George, 121–2, 218, 257n
Blunt, Anthony, 6, 30, 122, 257n
Bolshevik Revolution (1917), 1–3
    repercussions in Britain, 4–5, 207, 208
Bolshevism, 2, 4
    disease, 4, 10, 231n
    global spread of, 9–12
    virus/a plague, 9
Bottomley, Horatio, 36–7
Bowden, Herbert, 138
Boy Scouts' Association, 77
Brearley, Mike, 195
British Black Power Movement, 199–200
British Fascisti (BF), 49–53, 61–2
    anti-communism, 58–9
    'Bloody Fools', 50
    and British Union of Fascists (BUF), 59–60
    and Conservative Party, 51, 58–61
    decline 61–2
    and Economic League (EL), 56–7
    and General Strike, 45–6, 52
    ideology, 46, 59–60
    and the intelligence community, 53-4
    'K', 52
    and Maxwell Knight, 54–6
    opposition to socialism, 51–3
    and Scotland Yard, 52
    State suspicion of 60–2
    State tolerance of, 45–6, 50–1, 52–3, 85–6
British Gazette (newspaper), 43
British Leyland (BL), 172
British Union of Fascists (BUF), 62–3, 65
    anti-Communism, 80–1
    and BF, 59–60, 62, 85–6
    clashes with anti-Fascists 66–70
    and Mussolini, 72–3
    Olympia meeting (1934), 67–8
    surveillance of, 64–5, 66–7, 86
    wartime detention of members, 81–3
Brittan, Leon, 175, 177, 182
Brook, Norman, 107–8, 209
Brooke, Field Marshal Sir Alan, 83
Browning, Freddie, 41
Burgess, Guy, 30, 32, 147–8
    impact of espionage, 110, 112, 121, 125, 212
Burn, Colonel Sir Charles, 50
Byford, Sir Lawrence, 176

Cable Street, 73–4
Cairncross, John, 30, 122, 257n
Callaghan, James, 142, 153, 171–2, 209
Cambridge Five, 6, 30–2, 122, 144, 210–11, 218
Campaign for Nuclear Disarmament (CND), 183–92
    first wave (1957–64), 183–5
    revival in 1980s, 185–89
Campbell, John Ross, 38, 41
Carr, Robert, 169
Caute, David, 210
Childs, Wyndham, 15, 28–9, 33, 37–8, 44–5, 60–1
Churchill, Winston, 2, 10, 24, 33, 109, 116
    and the Labour Party, 34, 129–30
    and McCarthyism, 114–5
    and Nazi Germany, 75, 81
    and the Soviet Union, 24, 33, 83, 84–5
    Winston Churchill MP (grandson), 189

INDEX

Citrine, Walter, 44
Clarke, William, 130
Clynes, JR, 35
Coalition for Peace Through Security (CPS), 188, 274n
Collard, John, 103
Comintern, 10, 13–4, 19, 34, 39, 64, 232n, 236n
Cominform, 103
Committee of 100, 184–5
Communist Party of Great Britain (CPGB)
   and apartheid, 195, 196–7
   and espionage. 27, 29, 30, 31, 103, 124, 144,-5, 210, 11, 237n, 250n
   formation, 13
   Historians' Group, 97
   influence on strikes, 39, 44–5, 141, 164–5, 168–9, 170–1, 172–3, 180–1
   and the Labour Party, 34–5, 133–7, 140
   membership, 18, 23, 66, 92–3, 94, 95, 100–3, 124, 221
   and nuclear disarmament, 183–5, 190–2, 273n
   possible banning of, 28, 71, 114, 116
   relationship with Moscow, 13–14, 95–7, 132, 218, 232n, 251n, 253n
   and revolution, 26, 232n
   surveillance of, 15–18, 23–4, 25–6, 28–9, 55–7, 82, 91–5, 102–3, 134, 147–8, 191, 197, 207, 212–14, 220–1, 250n
   Yorkshire District Committee, 96
communist sympathisers, 18, 27–31, 78, 91, 100–4, 113–4, 125, 207, 210–12, 221–2

Correra, Gordon, 212
Cox, John, 191–2
Cripps, Stafford, 130–1
Cubbon, Sir Brian, 176
Curry, John, 26, 63, 76, 81, 221
Curtis-Bennett, Sir Henry, 52
Curzon, Lord, 10, 24–5
Czech Refugee Trust Fund, 79

Daily Herald (newspaper), 14, 24, 29, 53, 118, 237n, 238n
Daily Mail (newspaper), 34, 39, 71, 73, 166
Daily Worker (newspaper), 105, 113, 248n
Dalton, Hugh, 129
Defence of the Realm Act, 37
Defence Secretariat 19 (DS19), 188
Directorate of Intelligence, 5, 12–13, 15, 16, 233n
Domvile, Barry, 77
Donaldson, Arthur, 82
Downing Street, 127, 151
Duff, Sir Antony, 152, 192, 214
Dundas, Ian Hope, 67

Eastern Growers Marketing Association, 110
Economic League (EL), 56–8, 61, 197–8
Eden, Anthony, 117, 209
Edwardes, Michael, 172
Edwards, Bob, 140–1
Elliott, Nicholas, 133
Ennals, David, 196
Ennals, Martin, 196
European Economic Community (EEC) Referendum (1975), 182–3
Ewer, William Norman, 29–30, 118–19

Ferris, John, 3, 203

INDEX

Fletcher, Ray, 145, 146
Floud, Bernard, 144–5, 262n
Flowers, Brian, 105
Floyd, David, 119–21, 257n
Foley, Frank, 63, 244n
Foster, George Carey, 32
Francis-Hawkins, Neil, 78
Franklin, Benjamin, 217
'front' organisations, 21–3, 75–6, 79–80
Fuchs, Klaus, 6, 104–5, 122, 218
    repercussions of espionage, 105–9
Furnival Jones, Martin, 141, 142, 143, 145, 164, 202, 208

Gaitskell, Hugh, 139, 140, 256n
Gallacher, Willie, 21, 31, 235n
Game, Sir Philip, 73
George V (King), 28, 33, 38, 43, 49, 238n
Gilligan, Arthur E. R., 50
Gilmour, John, 70–1
Glading, Percy, 27, 30, 237n
Goebbels, Joseph, 66
Golitsyn, Anatoly, 128
Gollan, John, 94–5
Gorbachev, Mikhail, 178–9
Gordon Walker, Patrick, 139–40, 143, 146, 147
Gordievsky, Oleg, 146, 165, 178, 186
Gormley, Joe, 167
Gouzenko, Igor, 89–90, 249n
    Canadian Royal Commission that followed, 91
Gower, David, 196, 276n
Grant, Ted, 154
Greene, Graham, 120
Greenham Common Peace Camp, 191–2
Greig, Commander Louis, 75

Haigh, Madeline, 193
Hain, Peter, 196, 198
Haldane, J. B. S., 95
Hall, Admiral Sir William 'Blinker', 2, 32–3, 41, 56–7, 59
Hankey, Maurice, 38
Hanley, Michael, 153, 166–8, 263n
Hannon, Patrick, 50
Harman, Harriet, 220
Hatton, Derek, 155, 156
Heath, Edward, 163, 169–70, 209, 266n
    and Operation FOOT 165–6
    relationship with MI5, 163–4, 166–8, 170–1
Hemming, Henry, 55
Henderson, Arthur, 35, 39
Hewitt, Patricia, 220
Hill, Christopher, 97
Hitlerjugend, 76–7
Hobsbawm, Eric, 1, 95–100, 111–12, 220–1, 252n
Hodges, Frank, 14
Hollis, Roger, 101, 140, 150
Holt-Wilson, Eric, 43, 74
Home Office Warrant (HOW), 19, 39, 51, 66, 93, 98, 140–1, 142, 165, 180, 192, 234n, 250n
Horne, Alistair, 123
Howard, Sir Michael, 5
Howe, Geoffrey, 186
Hughes, James McGuirk, 56, 81
Hungarian uprising (1956), 96, 99, 124, 251n
Hunt, John, 152
Hurd, Douglas, 193
Hyde, Douglas, 113, 255n

Ignatieff, Michael, 217
Incitement to Mutiny Act, 38, 53
Indian Political Intelligence Office (IPI), 20, 234n

INDEX

Industrial Intelligence Bureau (IIB), 54–7
Information Research Department (IRD), 117–20, 132, 138–9, 159, 170, 256n, 257n, 273n
Ingram, Miranda, 213
Interdepartmental Group on Subversion in Public Life (SPL), 156–8
Isaacs, George, 110

Jane, Charles, 29–30, 210
January Club, 75–6
John Blunt (magazine), 36, 41
John Lewis Partnership, 110
Johnson, Hewlett, 116
Joint Intelligence Committee (JIC), 90–1, 250n
Jones, Jack, 163, 165, 266n, 267n
Jones, John, 205–6, 209
Jones, Thomas, 38
Jowitt, Viscount William, 117
Joyce, William, 59
Joynson-Hicks, William, 34, 43, 45–6, 237n

Kaufman, Gerald, 190
Kearton, Frank, 105, 253n
Kell, Sir Vernon, 16, 28, 50–1, 54, 55, 64, 72, 74, 76–7, 78, 123
Kemp, Peter, 17
Kent, Monsignor Bruce, 190
Kerr, Ann, 183
Keynes, John Maynard, 22
KGB, 1, 110, 119, 121, 127–8, 141, 143, 145, 147, 165, 166, 179, 186, 190
Khrushchev, Nikita, 96, 99, 124, 251n
Knight, Maxwell, 31, 57, 58, 78, 118, 147–8
and the BF 54–6, 59, 61–2, 78, 118, 147, 244n
Knights, Sir Philip, 192, 193, 215

Labour Party,
1924 government, 33–4, 37–9
and communism 33–5, 38, 132–3, 136–7
and the CPGB, 34–5, 140, 267n
and crypto-communists, 134, 136–8, 139–40, 142–9, 159, 260n, 261n
and the intelligence services, 33–4, 38–9, 39–41, 128, 129–32, 133–4, 139–40, 151–2, 159–60, 210, 238n
and the IRD, 132, 138–9
National Executive Committee (NEC), 137–8, 147, 153, 160
Trotskyists and, 153–7, 160–1, 265n
and the Zinoviev letter, 39–41, 151–2
Lander, Stephen, 198, 213
Lansbury, George, 15, 79
Lansing, Robert, 10
Lenin, Vladimir, 3, 10, 20, 33, 34, 208, 231n, 235n, 238n
Lessing, Doris, 100
Lever, Norman, 203, 278n
Liddell, Guy, 63–4, 92, 104, 116, 119, 132, 133–4, 209, 257n, 259n
Lintorn-Orman, Rotha, 49–50
Lloyd George, David, 9, 10–11, 24, 28, 236n
Lockhart, John Bruce, 214–5
Lockhart, Robert Bruce, 3
Loewenstein, Karl, 217–8, 280n
Long, Walter, 10–11, 12, 24, 231n

INDEX

MacColl, Ewan, 100
MacDermot, Niall, 143–4
MacDonald, James Ramsay, 28, 34, 35, 44, 238n, 239n
   relationship with intelligence community, 37–8, 128
   surveillance of, 35–7, 41
   and Zinoviev letter, 39
Maclean, Donald, 30, 110, 112, 119, 121, 125, 212
Macmillan, Harold, 121, 123, 151, 218, 219
Makgill, Donald, 75
Makgill, George, 54–8, 242n
   British Empire Union (BEU), 56
Malone, Cecil L'Estrange, 18–19, 234n
Manhattan Project, 104
Manningham-Buller, Eliza, 213–14
Mark, Sir Robert, 169
Marquand, David, 36
Marshall-Cornwall, James, 63
Martin, Arthur, 150
Martin, Kingsley, 100
Massiter, Cathy, 190–1, 204, 214
Maudling, Reginald, 164
Mawby, Ray, 149
Maxwell Fyfe Directive, 216
Mayhew, Christopher, 118
Mazower, Mark, 4
McCarthyism, 112–20, 219
McGahey, Mick, 167, 171, 180
McMahon Act (USA, 1946), 106
Middlesex Education Authority, 111
Mikardo, Ian, 139
Militant or Militant Tendency (MT), 154–7
   and the Civil Service, 157–9
Millar, Frederick Hoyer, 117
Ministry of Defence (MoD), 187–8, 200

Mitchell, Graham, 84, 112, 127, 140, 150
Mitrokhin, Vasili, 128
Molotov, Vyacheslav, 132
   Molotov-Ribbentrop Pact, 82
Morrison, Herbert, 74, 125, 129, 137
Morton, Desmond, 40, 55, 242n
Mosley, Oswald, 62, 65, 66, 71, 73–4, 81–2, 244n, 246n
Muggeridge, Malcolm, 120
Munro, Robert, 11

National Council of Civil Liberties (NCCL), 219–20
National Fascisti, 53, 241n
National Unemployed Workers' Movement (NUWM), 22
National Union of Mineworkers (NUM), 166–7, 267n, 271n, 272n
   and communism, 170–1
   surveillance of, 177–82
Nazi Germany, 2, 244n
   Fifth Column, 81–3
   Oswald Mosley and, 66
   propaganda and influence in Britain, 76–9
   threat posed by, 63–4, 81
Nellist, Dave, 155–6
Newbold, Walton, 18, 20–1
Norman John Worthington. *see* Wilson, Harold
Nunn May, Alan, 90, 91, 101–3, 120, 252n

Official Secrets Act, 80, 90, 135, 147, 250n
Oldfield, Maurice, 123, 152
Omand, David, 223, 280n
Oppenheimer, J. Robert, 115
Organisation for the Maintenance of Supplies (OMS), 45–6, 61, 240n

INDEX

Owen, Will, 146–7, 262n

Peierls, Rudolf, 104
Petrie, David, 84, 222
Philby, Kim, 32, 89, 121–2, 212
Phillips, Morgan, 137–8, 145, 159
'phoney-war', 86
Pilling, Joe, 187
Pirie, Julia, 93–5
Poliakoff, Joseph, 109
Pollitt, Harry, 14, 52, 102
Pollock, Martin, 17–18
Popper, Karl, 224
Priestley, J. B., 100
Public Order Act (1936), 74, 86

Queen Elizabeth II, 115, 122, 127, 175

Race Relations Act (1968), 202–3
Ramelson, Bert, 96
Rawlinson, Peter, 169
Redgrave, Michael, 100
Red Under the Bed (TV programme), 170, 268n
Redwood, John, 174
Reed, Ronnie, 108
Rees, Merlyn, 153–4, 177, 216
Reilly, Sidney ('ace of spies'), 2
Revolutionary Socialist League (RSL), 154
Reynolds, Gerry, 138
Ribbentrop, Joachim von, 76, 77
  Molotov-Ribbentrop Pact, 82
Rimington, Stella, 1, 178, 179, 190, 205, 213, 216
Roberts, Eric, 83
Robertson, James, 104
Robinson, Derek, 172–3
Robinson, Tony, 169
Rothermere, Lord, 39–40, 71–2, 246n

Rothschild, Victor, 84
Rothstein, Andrew, 22, 235n
Royal Aircraft Establishment (RAE), Farnborough, 80, 135
Ruddock, Joan, 190
Russian Civil War, 3
Russian Intelligence Service (RIS), 143, 165, 208
Russian Trade Delegation, 14, 24–5, 109

Saklatvala, Shapurji, 19–20, 234n
Sandys, Duncan, 109
Scanlon, Hugh, 142, 165
Scargill, Arthur, 171, 176, 178, 180–2, 272n
Scottish nationalism, 17, 82, 248n
Secret Service Bureau (1909), 4
Secret Service Committee, 12, 41
Shaw, George Bernard, 53
Shawcross, Hartley, 90
Shinwell, Manny, 130
Shipley, Peter, 189
Shortt, Edward, 11
Sillitoe, Sir Percy, 91–2, 133
Simon, John, 73–4
Simpkins, Anthony, 164
Sinclair, Admiral Sir Hugh, 24–5, 44–5, 61, 244
Skardon, Jim, 119, 136
Skinner, Erna, 104
Skinner, Herbert, 104–5
Smith, Sir Howard, 173, 279n
Smithers, Sir Waldron, 116
Snell, P. W., 187
Snowden, Phillip, 35, 37
Society for Cultural Relations with the Soviet Union (SCR), 22–3
Spanish Civil War, 163
Spanish influenza, 9
Special Demonstration Squad (SDS), 194, 276n

INDEX

Special Operations Executive (SOE), 129
Spedding, David, 184
Spiller, Roger, 191
Stalin, Joseph, 3, 84, 96, 99, 124, 132, 231n, 232n
Stamfordham, Lord, 28, 33, 49, 237n
StB, (Czech Intelligence Service), 145–9
Stewart, Findlater, 92, 216
Stonehouse, John, 148–9
Stop The Seventy Tour (STST), 194–6
Stowe, Kenneth, 157–8
Strachey, John, 130–1
strikes
    British Leyland strike (1979), 172–3
    Department of Health and Social Security strike (1984), 157–8
    General Strike (1926), 41–6, 52, 57, 173, 210
    Grunwick (1976), 171
    miners' strike (1972), 166–8
    miners' strike (1974), 170–1
    miners' strike (1984–5), 173–82
    National Building Strike (1972), 168–70
    National Union of Seamen strike (1966), 142, 261n
    police strikes (1918–19), 11
    Winter of Discontent (1978–9), 171–2
Stross, Barnett, 145–6
Supply and Transport Committee, 39
Swingler, Stephen, 134, 143, 260n

Taaffe, Peter, 154
Thatcher, Margaret, 149, 158–9, 193
    attitude to communism, 186, 209, 270n
    and CND, 186, 188–9
    'enemy within', 174
    and the miners' strike, 173–4, 176, 178, 181, 209
    relationship with MI5, 173, 174, 178, 186, 188, 260n
Thistlethwaite, Dick, 135
Thomas, Jimmy, 35, 44
Thompson, E. P., 7–8, 95–7, 99
Thomson, Basil, 10, 13, 14–5, 24, 25, 28, 30–1, 34, 36–7, 42, 54, 57, 233n, 237n
    Anglo-Soviet trade, 14
    communist cells, 30
Tomlinson, Ricky, 169–70, 268n
Trenchard, Lord, 66, 70–1, 245n
Trend, Burke, 168
Trevelyan, Charles Philips, 37
Trevor-Roper, Hugh, 32
Trotsky, Leon, 154, 231n
Trotskyism, 131, 139, 153–61, 160, 173, 177, 182, 191, 264n, 265n
Tyrrell, William, 3–4, 41

Undercover Policing Inquiry (UCPI), 194
Underhill, Reg, 153

van Ginhoven, Hubertus, 29–30, 210
Vansittart, Lord, 116–17
Van Witchhunt, Lord, 116–7
Vassall, John, 110–11, 121, 123
Veltheim, Erkki, 19
Vernon, Wilfrid, 80–1, 135–6
Vetting, 27–8, 30, 102, 105, 106–12, 113, 117–8, 125–6, 158–9, 184–5, 200–2, 218–9, 222, 253n, 255n, 256n, 265n, 278n
Volkov, Konstantin, 89

INDEX

Wanamaker, Sam, 113–14
Warner, Christopher, 101
Weiss, Ernst David, 135
White, Dick, 85, 121, 122, 133, 135–6, 166, 218–19, 279n
Widgery, Lord, 169
Wigg, George, 141, 261n
Wilkinson, Ellen, 130, 259n
Wilson, Carroll, 106
Wilson, Harold, 127, 146–7, 258n
   files held on, 127–8, 263n
   relationship with intelligence community, 140–1, 141–2, 143–4, 148, 159–60, 209, 261n
   Plot, 149–53
Wilson, Henry, 2, 24, 236n
Wilson, Ray, 184
Wilson, Woodrow, 9–10
Wilson Doctrine, 141, 261n
Wolff, Henry Drummond, 71
Woolf, Virginia, 22
Woolfstein, Alfred Abraham, 78–9
Workers' Weekly (newspaper), 15
Wright, Peter, 94, 145, 150, 151–2, 167, 251n, 262n
Wynn, Arthur, 119

Young Communist League (YCL), 31, 93, 180, 191

Zilliacus, Konni, 137–9
Zinoviev, Grigori, 12
Zinoviev letter, 39–41, 152